MANAGING INTERNATIONAL TRADE RISK

CONTEMPORARY COMMERCIAL LAW

Maritime Law in China
Emerging Issues and Future Developments
Edited by Johanna Hjalmarsson and Jenny Jingbo Zhang

Illegality in Marine Insurance Law
Feng Wang

Insurance Law Implications of Delay in Maritime Transport
Ayşegül Buğra

Online Arbitration
Faye Fangfei Wang

Double Insurance and Contribution
Nisha Mohamed

The Law and Autonomous Vehicles
Matthew Channon, Lucy McCormick and Kyriaki Noussia

FIDIC Yellow Book
A Commentary
Ben Beaumont

The Contract of Carriage
Multimodal Transport and Unimodal Regulation
Paula Bäckdén

FIDIC Red Book
A Commentary
Ben Beaumont

Blockchain Technology and the Law
Opportunities and Risks
Muharem Kianieff

Third Party Protection in Shipping
Carlo Corcione

Multi-sided Music Platforms and the Law
Copyright, Law and Policy in Africa
Chijioke Ifeoma Okorie

Reinsurance and the Law of Aggregation
Event, Occurrence, Catastrophe, Cause
Oliver D. William

Comparative Analysis of Interim Measures
Interim Remedies (England and Wales) v Preservation Measures (China)
Vivek Jain, Thomas Macey-Dare QC and Shengnan Jia

Knock-for-Knock Indemnities and the Law
Contractual Limitation and Delictual Liability
Edited by Kristoffer Svendsen, Endre Stavang and Greg Gordon

Managing International Trade Risk
Customs, Revenue and VAT Compliance
Mark Rowbotham

For more information about this series, please visit: www.routledge.com/Contemporary-Commercial-Law/book-series/CCL

MANAGING INTERNATIONAL TRADE RISK

CUSTOMS, REVENUE AND VAT COMPLIANCE

MARK ROWBOTHAM

informa law
from Routledge

First published 2025
by Informa Law from Routledge
4 Park Square, Milton Park, Abingdon, Oxon OX14 4RN

and by Informa Law from Routledge
605 Third Avenue, New York, NY 10158

Informa Law from Routledge is an imprint of the Taylor & Francis Group, an informa business

British Library Cataloguing-in-Publication Data
A catalogue record for this book is available from the British Library

Library of Congress Cataloging-in-Publication Data
Names: Rowbotham, J. Mark, author.
Title: Managing international trade risk: customs, revenue and VAT compliance/Mark Rowbotham.
Description: Abingdon, Oxon; New York, NY: Routledge, 2025. |
Series: Contemporary Commercial Law |
Includes bibliographical references and index.
Identifiers: LCCN 2022043864 | ISBN 9781032376653 (hardback) |
ISBN 9781032376721 (paperback) | ISBN 9781003341345 (ebook)
Subjects: LCSH: Customs administration–Law and legislation. |
Tariff–Law and legislation.
Classification: LCC K4620.R69 2025 | DDC 343.05/6–dc23/eng/20230403
LC record available at https://lccn.loc.gov/2022043864

ISBN: 978-1-032-37665-3 (hbk)
ISBN: 978-1-032-37672-1 (pbk)
ISBN: 978-1-003-34134-5 (ebk)

DOI: 10.4324/9781003341345

Typeset in Times New Roman
by Deanta Global Publishing Services, Chennai, India

CONTENTS

TABLE OF LEGISLATION

United Kingdom

United States

PREFACE

The Challenge of Indirect Tax

Companies which are engaged in international trade face a labyrinth of complex import, export and border security regulations, regardless of where in the world they are based. These regulations must be carefully addressed and navigated to maintain compliance and pursue the benefits of cost-saving opportunities, as well as guaranteeing a low-risk status as far as government Customs Authorities are concerned.

An importer or exporter can address risks while managing operational and resource efficiencies by developing a series of standardised trade processes and automating trade compliance. Furthermore, process standardisation and automation can provide a stronger foundation to achieve potential benefits from special trade programmes available worldwide. However, this may not be so easy, when:

- The ever-growing complexity of each country's import and export rules, trade preference agreements, and audit initiatives make import and export compliance increasingly burdensome;
- The global focus on national border security issues and trade security programmes requires greater awareness of compliance obligations and planning opportunities.

Indirect taxes have grown to be a major source of revenue for governments and as such, indirect tax policies, legislation and compliance are all under increased scrutiny by governments and tax officials. A possible reason for this is the shifting balance from direct tax to indirect tax with much more emphasis on VAT.

From a risk management perspective, VAT is important as it can become a huge expense if it is not correctly accounted for. Even minor errors can have a significant cumulative effect where the volume of transactions is significant. In addition, incorrect treatment of Customs and Excise Duties can significantly impact on the bottom line and severely interrupt the production and logistical process in case of flaws in the processes and compliance.

Indirect Tax Management and Due Diligence

Every time goods cross a border, they are potentially subject to a host of indirect taxes and indirect tax compliance obligations, including:

- Export licensing;
- VAT/GST/HST* reporting and documentation (to support an export exemption);
- Customs and Excise Duty reporting and compliance documentation (duty suspension regimes, etc.);
- Customs reporting and documentation;
- Customs Duties on importation;
- Excise Duties on importation;
- VAT/GST and other sales taxes on importation;
- VAT/GST reporting and documentation (to support input tax recovery);
- Export compliance obligations.

* **Goods and Services Tax** – In Canada this is linked to Harmonised Sales Tax (HST) in some eastern provinces, which is a combination of Federal Goods and Services (General Sales) Tax and Provincial Sales Tax (PST). The HST system operates in the provinces of Ontario, New Brunswick, Prince Edward Island and Nova Scotia. In terms of collection, all such tax is collected by Revenue Canada as a single amount and is then split into GST and PST, and the PST is given to each province participating in the HST scheme. In all other Canadian provinces, PST is completely separate from GST and differs between provinces.

Tax Due Diligence

Tax is 1 of the most important components that determine the overall profitability of a company. It is so important that it has its own place in the company's financial report in the name of items such as net profit before tax, net profit after tax, deferred tax, etc. Therefore, it goes without saying that the tax aspect cannot be overlooked in the due diligence during mergers and acquisitions.

What is Tax Due Diligence?

Tax due diligence is a thorough investigation of different types of taxes that affect the target company. For example, in the case of direct tax, when an acquirer is considering a merger or an acquisition, it is important for them to recognise any significant tax exposure to the target company. The word "significant" is very important here. A target company making a net profit of US$100,000 will not be much affected by a potential future tax liability of US$500. However, if the tax liability is said to be US$10,000, then this exposure will definitely affect the buyer's decision. Thus, tax due diligence considers the liabilities that will crucially affect the profitability of the target company.

Types of Tax Due Diligence

There are 2 types of tax due diligence – seller's side and buyer's side.

The target company conducts a **seller's side** due diligence to recognise and remedy any major tax exposure before inviting prospective buyers.

A **buyer's side** due diligence is when the buyer wants to recognise the target company's tax exposure before making the buying decision.

Both are extremely helpful to different parties in mergers or acquisitions. In this article, we will discuss the buyer's side due diligence.

Tax Due Diligence – Areas of Investigation

A tax due diligence exercise is usually conducted after preliminary analysis. After the buyer likes the idea of acquiring a target company based on its business model, financial stability, sustainability, presence in the market, management, and culture, it starts digging to find tax exposures.

So what does an acquirer look for during tax due diligence? There are 5 common areas:

Tax Compliance

The very basic and starting drill for tax due diligence is to confirm that the target company is adhering to all government tax compliance. This may include a review of all applicable types of taxes such as – corporation tax, sales/value-added tax, excise tax, customs duties, employee tax and other specific taxes applicable to the target company.

The acquirer intends to understand the potential liabilities of the target, be it past, present, or future. The liability may be definite or contingent, recorded or maybe unrecorded in the target's books of accounts. Such holistic understanding will bring into light the compliance risk during a mergers and acquisitions deal and will direct towards appropriate precautions that must be taken against these risks. Furthermore, the target company's exposure to tax liabilities will help the buyer determine a purchase price.

Tax Liabilities/Assets

Identifying tax liabilities is the most time-consuming and detail-oriented task. This is because the buyer has to analyse all the past financial information of the target company. Furthermore, the buyer must also study the tax liabilities of the target company's subsidiaries, sister concerns, or any other related company. The tax liabilities of these companies will increase the target company's tax exposure. Once the acquirer has identified the liabilities, it is time to quantify them. After that, this amount of tax liability will be used to make a buying decision or set a fair acquisition price.

Transfer Pricing

Investopedia's definition of transfer pricing states – "Transfer Price is the price at which divisions of a company transact with each other, such as the trade of supplies or labour between departments".

In the context of tax due diligence, transfer pricing has many risks.

In most transactions, the exchange of goods/services is between sister concerns under the same parent company. Furthermore, these companies are under different jurisdictions and are operating under different tax laws. This carries a risk of over-calculating taxes, double counting, or not charging taxes where applicable. In order to avoid tax liabilities arising out of these transactions, the acquirer must look into the target company's transfer pricing agreements, and it must also analyse all such past transactions.

From this discussion, it can be concluded that the benefits of tax due diligence can far exceed its cost. In terms of revenue risk, especially concerning national revenue authorities, tax due diligence is vital to any commercial activity, in terms of both direct and indirect tax. For the purposes of this text, indirect tax is the main area of concern, especially where taxes such as VAT, GST and Sales Tax prevail.

A tax due diligence exercise can easily identify potential risk exposures arising out of overstated losses, underreported tax liabilities, non-filing exposures, failure to charge taxes, payroll errors and other tax miscalculations. Suppose these risks go undetected during the due diligence process. In that case, it will create a negative impact on cash flow, profitability, and reputation of the acquirer at some point of time in the future. Furthermore, if there are irreversible tax exposure risks, then it is in the best interest of the acquirer to walk away from the deal, no matter how tempting it may be.

Period of Tax due diligence is determined basis the period up to which assessment/audit/adjudication may be conducted by the tax authority. The period, however would be extended for any open assessment, enquiries, tax dispute, etc.

The main areas to be addressed are:

- Careful and methodological investigation of financial and tax records;
- Highlighting ambiguities in compliances of tax legislations;
- Examining appropriateness of the tax positions taken by the target;
- Identify potential exposures due to aggressive/inaccurate tax positions;
- The reviewer must have in-depth knowledge and practical exposure of indirect tax compliance process.

It is critical to examine:

- All ledger accounts related to indirect taxes;
- Contingent liabilities reported in financial data;
- Unutilised incentive scrips received under different schemes of FTP;
- Year wise tax refunds reported in tax returns;
- Admissibility and quantification of VAT refund filed or yet to be filed;
- Input tax credits appearing in the financial records vis-a-vis reports in returns/Audit reports;
- Unclaimed backward area incentives – admissibility to the buyer/ new entity;
- Amendments required in different registrations vis-a-vis GST/VAT/ Sales Tax;
- Identification of lapses in tax compliances, if any, and quantification of tax exposure;
- Analysis of tax positions taken by the target and assessing their impact going forward;
- Analysis of risk profile of ongoing litigations of the target company;
- Identifying underreported tax liabilities and ascertaining provisions requirements;
- Validating representation made by the seller at the time of pre-deal negotiation;
- Ascertaining representations, warranties and indemnities to be sought and adjustments to be made in the enterprise value on account of findings during tax due diligence.

Indirect Tax Risks

Even as the world is shrinking, businesses and their growth strategies are becoming more complicated. A schematic drawing of the functions of a typical multinational today might look like a Rube Goldberg contraption, i.e. a complex of moving parts that must connect 1 to another for tax, regulatory and reporting purposes.

And unlike the more contained structure for handling income-based taxes, responsibilities and key drivers for indirect taxes may be spread throughout the enterprise, residing not just in the tax department but in any of such diverse departments as finance, information technology, supply chain management and logistics, human resources, and beyond.

Added is the growing trend toward Shared Service Centres (SSCs) that are responsible for operational processes including accounts payable and accounts receivable as well as other outsourced functions for tax, finance and treasury. Tax determination and reporting for the entire operation may be governed by 1 or more enterprise resource planning systems, which in turn may be integrated to varying degrees, with or without the benefit of sophisticated technology tools.

All these factors make for a changing and increasingly sophisticated business environment that requires a different approach to business indirect tax advice.

VAT is a tax on consumption. It is collected in stages by the businesses (or intermediaries) and is fully borne by the final purchaser. As a consequence, VAT is a transactional tax with the potential to impact all transactions with suppliers and customers.

Measuring risks is often based on the balance between output VAT (Sales) and input VAT (Purchases) and not on the total amount of VAT/GST throughput (also called VAT "under management").

The findings listed above are not surprising as often the question is asked what risk management even has to do with VAT/GST. The reasoning behind this question is that VAT/GST is typically cost neutral for most businesses: "a cash in and cash out" scenario. However, every indirect tax function knows that deductible input VAT and liable output VAT have to be managed separately to avoid substantial VAT assessments, penalties and interest payments.

It is a risky business to monitor only the balance between output VAT and input VAT. Neutrality can only be achieved – better is the word "earned" – if certain formal and material requirements are met.

It starts with the people in the organisation becoming aware of the amounts that are at stake and the risks of something going wrong. Various surveys show unanimously that there is a concern over amounts of €5 billion concerning indirect tax.

Benchmark studies repeatedly create the same picture: too little control, too few KPIs and when a mistake is made in the control, it usually concerns large amounts of money.

Tax authorities, due to technological innovations, have become increasingly better in executing their tax audit. The probability that the tax authorities will issue additional assessments and penalties in the near future because errors in indirect tax are detected, increases by the day. Tax authorities collect and analyse already indirect tax data (e.g. SAF-T (Standard Audit File – Taxation) for VAT).

The focus is not only about timely and accurate VAT reporting but as well whether on high-risk areas an effective tax control framework is in place. Tax risk management methods are assessed.

A tax trend is that companies due to regulations will have to become transparent about their attitude to tax risk, its appetite and its approach to its relationship with tax authorities. It will cover the governance framework describing the way a business takes decisions on taxation including information on the systems and controls in place to manage tax risk.

It is therefore essential that documentation exists of the (automated) tax control framework and a logbook – risk register – is kept of all identified inconsistencies. The internal tax function should always have insight into the areas for attention through this logbook. This allows tax managers to set the right priorities and take measures timely.

Failures in VAT-critical systems and processes can result in overpayments of VAT that represent a real cost to the business, or in under-declarations that entail the threat of penalties and reputational risk.

The correctness of VAT reporting is checked only afterwards by the tax authorities. Non-compliance could result in that over many years an assessment can be levied (this depends on country's assessment period: for example the Netherlands is 5 years) including interest and increased with penalties.

The penalties for incorrect invoicing can be a percentage of the turnover, so amounts can quickly become material – up to 27% VAT in Europe on the turnover plus penalties.

Take for example the risk when incorrectly the zero VAT rate is applied. The supplier is responsible for ensuring that all the conditions for applying the zero VAT rate are met. If not, the tax authorities will seek to recover tax due from this supplier via a levy of a tax assessment.

If the applicable VAT rate is 25%, the tax assessment will be 25/125 of the consideration charged. This assessment has to be increased with interest and penalties to determine the total tax burden.

Something as basic as a billing error leading to invoices issued in the wrong name could not only delay revenue receipt but also result in non-recoverable VAT. The penalties for incorrect invoicing can be a percentage of the turnover, so amounts can quickly become material – up to 25% VAT in Northern Europe, specifically Scandinavia, including Norway (Hungary 27%) on the turnover plus penalties.

As written before, it is risky business to monitor only the balance between output VAT and input VAT. Neutrality can only be achieved – better is the word earned – if certain formal and material requirements are met.

- An oil and gas company had to pay US$2 million in VAT instead of getting the refund they expected in the same amount;
- A mining company was assessed US$500 million in taxes and penalties because they lacked the proper documentation;
- A consumer products company missed out on a US$20 million VAT refund;
- A Fortune 100 company saw its officials put in jail because of personal liability.

A single operational failure in the systems and processes that manage the flow of indirect taxes through the supply chain can have significant consequences in terms of additional assessments, penalties, blocked VAT refunds and delayed payments from customers.

But it must be asked whether these taxes and tax planning opportunities get the attention they need, especially in light of increasingly complicated and globalised business models.

There is 1 common denominator that is too often missing from the strategic or planning elements of a financial transformation – indirect tax. And although these tax considerations may not be among the issues that drive a financial transformation decision, tax can certainly give rise to some significant and costly challenges. That is particularly true of value-added tax (VAT), which hits a number of disparate points within the enterprise as diverse as finance, procurement, IT or HR.

Root Cause Examples

- A process failure (either within or outside of the accounting system) to apply the correct VAT liability to a transaction (either not charging VAT when it should be charged, or charging VAT when it should not be);
- A failure to identify a requirement to register for VAT within a jurisdiction (establishment is often unnecessary in creating an obligation – a mere sale of goods can be sufficient to create an obligation to register for VAT);
- A failure to evidence the non-application of VAT to a transaction, e.g. lack of export documentation, etc.;
- A failure to account for VAT on inter-company transactions;
- A failure to reconcile VAT turnover to Accounts Receivable (AR);
- A rejection of a VAT credit through Accounts Payable (AP) because of invalid documentation, e.g. the purchase invoice to support the credit was missing or defective;

- A failure to claim credit for VAT charged at importation;
- A failure to self-assess VAT on the receipt of services from a non-resident or on transfers of goods from 1 EU Member State to another.

The tax function should be able to understanding business activities/objectives including R&D and get aligned with other functions like legal, HR and IT.

The tax objective is to mitigate risk and identifying opportunities to support company's supply chain. Failures in VAT-critical systems and processes can result in overpayments of VAT that represent a real cost to the business, or in under-declarations that entail the threat of penalties and reputational risk.

Risk Identification and Mitigation

Keep a logbook – risk register – of all identified inconsistencies. The internal tax function should always have insight into the areas for attention through this logbook.

The risk register should contain the following labels:

- Number;
- Name of the risk;
- Risk definition;
- Cause for the risk to occur;
- Risk category; and
- The risk owner.

This all allows tax managers to set the right priorities and take measures timely.

Managing risk is about making decisions at all levels of an organisation, to limit the effect and likelihood of threats happening and to increase the effect and likelihood of opportunities. It is about taking the right amount of the right risk.

- Review the categories of VAT risk the company is facing as well as the likelihood of occurrence, its potential impact and mitigation measures;
- Review the company's risk appetite and risk tolerance and the way in which risks is measured.

Risk Definitions

Risk	*Definition*
Reputational Risk	Exposures associated with the wider impact on the company that arises from a company's actions or errors and have become public knowledge.
Strategic Risks	Strategic risks can impact the achievement of strategic objectives of the tax department, such as governance, tax planning, mergers and acquisitions, and financial transformation outsourcing. Is the level of tax risk at an acceptable level? Has the tax function been involved during the design and implementation? Is what is agreed upon properly documented, correctly implemented and in time.
Compliance Risks	Compliance risks impact the compliance of the company with regulatory and legal requirements and the resolution of government inquiries. Compliance risks occur due to incorrect numbers in the system, for example, because of lack of data, misinterpretation of the law, or miscommunication or misinterpretation leading to wrong conclusions or actions.
Operational Risks	Operational risks are both internal and external risks impacting the operations of the tax department, e.g. tax activities embedded in business operations, the underlying systems and tools, access to data, and knowledge. Examples of operational risks from not having embedded proper tax procedures in the business processes include the hold-up of goods at the border due to failure to properly handle customs duties, missing VAT registrations are missing or failing to update an ERP system's setup of processes and controls when VAT law or the supply chain has changed.
Financial Risks	Financial risks are any risks that impact the financial reporting processes of the tax department, e.g. accounting and reporting, SOX 404 and other regulatory regimes. Financial risks include, for example, not disclosing adequate or timely tax information resulting in regulatory scrutiny, not correctly estimating contingency reserves for uncertain tax positions, and not being able to support the calculation of deferred taxes and related valuation allowances reported in the financial statements. For a transactional tax like VAT, the financial risks are almost identical to the compliance risk as VAT returns are based on financial accounting data. An example of additional financial risk is the scenario where the applied VAT rate is 0%, and there is no sufficient evidence for the correctness of applying 0% VAT, which could result in VAT assessments for the VAT liability. These VAT assessment amounts are not automatically recorded in the financial statements automatically.

A Case Study

The following is an example of the premise that what can go wrong, will. It highlights the potential failures incurred owing to the relocation of an international company, and in this case, it highlights what happens when a company relocates from the EU into a non-EU country.

A multinational company based in France with a Shared Service Centre decided to centralise and transfer these functions to Switzerland. Not only did the company neglect to document the processes and thoroughly analyse the VAT impact, but they also lost staff that were familiar with the functions. As a result, the company lost access to the historical data relating to the preparation of VAT returns and had employees that were unfamiliar with the methods for preparing the returns or making manual adjustments.

At the time the VAT audit was announced, major panic ensued and the SSC staff had to work around the clock to obtain more insight into the original processes and collect information for reconstructing the VAT returns.

The company was at risk for the full amount of the VAT and for penalties of up to 100% of the VAT owed. In short, the potential benefits of the SSC migration were largely overshadowed by the additional time and money that had to be spent on this emergency response and the disruption to orderly operations.

The golden rule, if there is 1, is that such companies must never destroy historical tax data, especially where relocation is involved, as there is a statutory need to retain historical tax records for a given period of time, generally 5 years, but this can in some cases increase, depending upon the country concerned and its national revenue authority.

As multinational companies (MNCs) move increasingly to the shared service model to meet their varied objectives, the responsibility for indirect taxes migrates with them, especially in the case of VAT and goods and service tax. Also, complexity in managing these taxes increases exponentially when cross-border activities are involved, especially in today's VAT environment, where all too often controls are external, processes are manual and procedures are not documented.

A European Union study conducted in 2013 stated that at the time the bloc's member nations were probably losing almost €200 billion (US$267 billion) annually in value-added tax revenues due to tax evasion and a lack of enforcement.

The EU Tax Commissioner at the time, Algirdas Semeta, said that the amount of revenues slipping through the governments' nets is "unacceptable, particularly given the impact such sums could have in bolstering public finances".

The study for the European Commission, the bloc's executive arm, found member states lost an estimated €193 billion (US$258 billion) in VAT revenues in 2011, or 1.5% of the EU's economic output.

Actively combatting VAT fraud is a priority for the European Commission and local governments. New measures are being taken, such as the introduction of individual liability for not remitting VAT if the buyer knew or should have known that he was buying from a fraud. To prevent such a condition of liability, the ability to demonstrate that sufficient control measures have been taken is essential.

GLOSSARY OF TERMS AND ABBREVIATIONS

ADD	Anti-Dumping Duties
AEO	Authorised Economic Operator
ATO	Australian Taxation Office
AWRS	Alcohol Wholesaler Registration Scheme
B/L	Bill of Lading
C-TPAT	Customs & Trade Partnership Against Terrorism (US)
CAP	EU Common Agriculture Policy
CIF	Cost Insurance Freight
CN Code	Commodity Code
CPEI	Customs Procedures with Economic Impact
CRMF	Customs Risk Management Framework
DAP	Delivered At Place
DDP	Delivered Duty Paid
DMAIC	**D**efine **M**easure **A**nalyse **I**mplement **C**ontrol (Six Sigma)
DPU	Delivered At Place Unloaded
EAD	Export Accompanying Document
ECJU	Export Control Joint Unit
ECO	Export Controls Organisation
ENS	Entry Declaration System (Cargo pre-Clearance)
EORI	Economic Operator Registration Identifier
EU	European Union
EXS	Exit Declaration System (Cargo pre-Clearance)
EXW	Ex Works
FCA	Free Carrier
FOB	Free on Board
GB	Great Britain (excluding Northern Ireland)
HMRC	His Majesty's Revenue and Customs
IMDG	International Movement of Dangerous Goods Convention
INCOTERMS 2020	The **In**ternational **Co**mmercial **Terms** of Delivery 2020 Version
INTRASTAT	**Intra**-EU **Stat**istical Reporting (Intra-EU Cross-Border Movements of Goods)

ISO	International Standards Organisation
IPR (IP)	Inward Processing Relief
JCCC	Joint Customs Council Committee
MRN	Movement Reference Number
MSS	Management Support System (HMRC)
NCTS	New Community Transit System
OGEL	Open General Export Licence
OGL	Open General Licence
OIEL	Open Individual Export Licence
PDCA	**P**lan **D**o **C**heck **A**ct (The Deming Cycle)
PVA	Postponed VAT Accounting
Raw risk	The level of risk prior to a risk analysis and mitigating actions
Residual risk	The level of risk following a risk analysis and resulting mitigating actions
RKC	Revised Kyoto Convention
SAF-T	Standard Audit File - Taxation
SAFE Framework	Security and Accountability in the Freight Sector
SBC	Systems-Based Control
SCRM	Supply Chain Risk Management
SIEL	Standard Individual Export Licence
SOLAS	Safety of Lives At Sea Convention
SOPs	Standard Operating Procedures
SPIRE	UK Export Licence Online Application System
TSS	Trader Support System (Trade with Northern Ireland)
UCC	Union Customs Code
UK	United Kingdom (including Northern Ireland)
UNECE	United Nations Economic Commission for Europe
US CBP	US Customs and Border Protection Agency
VAT	Value-Added Tax
WCO	World Customs Organisation

INTRODUCTION

Risk

Risk is the potential of losing something of value. Values (such as physical health, social status, emotional well-being or financial wealth) can be gained or lost when taking risk resulting from a given action, activity and/or inaction, foreseen or unforeseen. For example, reading this book could seriously affect your wealth, positively or negatively. Risk can also be defined as the intentional interaction with uncertainty. Uncertainty is a potential, unpredictable, unmeasurable and uncontrollable outcome, whereas risk is a consequence of action taken in spite of uncertainty. Risk could therefore include reading this text – it may highlight areas of vulnerability within international business which require addressing immediately. It could even suggest ways of reducing risk in international trading practices and dealing with Customs controls.

There are many formal methods used to "measure" or quantify risk, and these depend upon the nature of the risk and the organisation involved. They also depend upon the complexity of the risk and how many factors influence it.

In many cases, the probability of a negative event is estimated using the frequency of past similar events and is thus based on precedent. However, probabilities for rare failures may be difficult to estimate. This makes risk assessment difficult in hazardous industries, such as nuclear energy, where the frequency of failures is rare, while the harmful consequences of failure are severe. Conversely, car breakdowns may be frequent, but their consequences are not generally severe.

Statistical methods may also require the use of a cost function, which in turn may require the calculation of the cost of loss of a human life. This is a difficult problem. One approach is to ask what people are willing to pay to insure against accidents, but as the answers depend very strongly on the circumstances, it is not clear that this approach is effective.

Risk is often measured as the expected value of an undesirable outcome. This combines the probabilities of various possible events and some assessment of the corresponding harm into a single value. The simplest case is

DOI: 10.4324/9781003341345-1

a binary possibility of *accident* or *no accident*. The associated formula for calculating risk is then:

R = (probability of the accident or adverse event occurring) × (expected loss in the case of the accident or adverse event)

For example, if performing activity *X* has a probability of 0.01 of suffering accident type *A*, with a loss of 1,000, then the total risk is a loss of 10, the product of 0.01 and 1000. By expanding this, if the same entity performs activity *Y* with a probability of 0.05 of suffering more serious accident type *B*, with a loss of 10,000, then the total risk is a loss of 500, i.e. the product of 0.05 and 10,000. The evident choice would be to perform activity A, where the total risk is significantly lower.

Situations are sometimes more complex than the simple binary possibility case. In a situation with several possible accidents, the total risk is the sum of the risks for each different accident, provided that the outcomes are comparable:

R = Σ(all events) (probability of the adverse event occurring) × (expected loss in case of the adverse event)

For example, if performing activity *X* has a probability of 0.01 of encountering an adverse event *A*, with a financial loss of 1,000, and a probability of 0.000001 of encountering an adverse event of type *B*, with a financial loss of 2,000,000, then the total loss expectancy is 12, which is equal to a loss of 10 from accident type *A* and 2 from accident type *B*. However, despite the difference in values of the loss between *A* and *B*, this does not mean that 1 adverse event is preferable over the other, as in the phrase: "Better the devil you know …"; it infers that 1 event is likely to impose less of an impact than the other and is thus less harmful. However, in reality, both adverse events should be avoided as much as possible.

From this, it can be deduced that risk pervades all aspects of business and associated activities, including taxation and international trade. The purpose of this text is to define more closely the elements of risk in international trade, and in particular Customs procedures and controls associated with international trade. In recent years, new global initiatives have been implemented to mitigate many risk factors in Customs controls, but although these have occurred at the government level, there is still much to be done to ensure overall compliance from international business itself. This text seeks to address many of these issues and provide a detailed approach to mitigating risk in international trade and Customs compliance.

Risk can work 2 ways. It affects government revenue collection and protection, but it also affects business viability and management. Government policy implements taxes, and the revenue department has the task of revenue collection and protection. The risk is that the revenue is compromised in some way, i.e. that government revenue targets are not achieved for whatever reason, either due to non-compliance on the part of traders or because of fraud. Fraud is deliberate, whereas non-compliance may occur for a variety of reasons. Either way, the revenue department needs to take steps to recover the outstanding debts and therefore must engage in a tax risk strategy implemented and maintained by a specialist team within the department dedicated to tax risk management.

Similarly, companies need to assess risk within their own functions, and indeed 1 of the present policies of government revenue departments is to ensure that companies engage in this. Indeed, non-compliant companies are likely to be registered by the government revenue department on a high-risk assurance list until they take acceptable steps to manage their tax affairs efficiently. There is, therefore, a great responsibility on the part of the company to manage its tax affairs diligently and ensure that its tax risk is kept to a minimum. In areas of Customs compliance, the government's Customs department will ensure that the company's Customs risk is minimal before considering granting any form of Customs facility such as Inward Processing Relief or Customs Warehousing. Notwithstanding this, Customs require any company applying for a facility that results in either an actual or potential Customs debt to obtain a financial guarantee that would cover such debts.

Risk in terms of Customs and Tax management is a very serious and prevalent matter and requires a significant degree of management if it is not to become a major problem for both traders and tax departments alike. It is perhaps unfortunate that it has never been taken seriously in terms of analysis and management, and in an age of increasing levels of tax compliance, risk management has become an equally serious and prevalent issue. Although risk is studied in many quasi-academic courses, its applications mean that there is a greater need to study the subject as a pivotal area in both commercial and taxation management. Risk reduction leads to not only better and more efficient management but also leads to greater degrees of trust in terms of the relationship between corporate entities and government fiscal functions. Indeed, the more that a company engages in corporate and risk management, the more likely it is that government fiscal departments will grant it more access to specific tax relief facilities, enabling it to save more money and run its affairs more cost-effectively, especially where the global supply chain is involved. The Authorised Economic Operator (AEO) facility is part of this, and the facility allows companies that have been AEO-approved by the government revenue department to gain large economic and fiscal benefits as a result.

CHAPTER 1

Risk Management

Risk management is the identification, assessment and prioritisation of risks, as defined in ISO 31000 as *the effect of uncertainty on objectives*) followed by coordinated and economical application of resources to minimise, monitor, and control the probability and/or impact of unfortunate events or to maximise the realisation of opportunities. Risk management's objective is to assure uncertainty does not deflect the endeavour from the business goals.

Risks can come from various sources: e.g. uncertainty in financial markets, threats from project failures (at any phase in design, development, production or sustainment life-cycles), legal liabilities, fiscal liabilities, namely unplanned duties and taxes, credit risk, accidents, natural causes and disasters, as well as deliberate attacks from an adversary, or events of uncertain or unpredictable root cause. There are 2 types of events, namely **negative** and **positive**. Negative events can be classified as risks, as they can be deemed to incur a loss of some kind, while positive events are classified as opportunities, as they can lead to some form of gain. Crossing a busy road, whether by pelican crossing or at an uncontrolled point, can be seen as a risk, since there is a possibility, however remote, that we may be knocked down by a speeding car; while if there is an overbridge or underpass, this is seen as an opportunity, in that it avoids the road itself and its traffic, and enables us to reach the other side of the road safely and possibly quicker too (chickens take note!). Similarly, if we travel anywhere outside our own country or we send goods to another part of the world, we automatically incur risks concerning flight reliability or health issues (don't drink the local water!), or, in the case of the movement of goods, the goods could be damaged or even lost in transit. For this reason, we can lower the risk by taking out an insurance policy, which covers us in the event of an adverse occurrence and thus indemnifies us.

Methods, definitions and goals vary widely according to whether the risk management method is in the context of project management, security, engineering, industrial processes, financial portfolios, actuarial assessments or public health and safety. They also vary widely in terms of the level of adversity, the likelihood or probability of the adverse event occurring and the probable impact in terms of the quantification of loss. In this respect, the higher

DOI: 10.4324/9781003341345-2

the level of likelihood or impact, the greater the need for risk mitigation, i.e. concrete action to lower the risk wherever possible.

Risk sources are more often identified and located not only in infrastructural or technological assets and tangible variables, but also in human factor variables, mental states and decision-making. The interaction between human factors and tangible aspects of risk highlights the need to focus closely on human factors as 1 of the main drivers for risk management, a "change driver" that comes first of all from the need to know how humans perform in challenging environments and in the face of risks.

Strategies to manage threats (uncertainties with negative consequences) typically include transferring the threat to another party, avoiding the threat, reducing the negative effect or probability of the threat, or even accepting some or all of the potential or actual consequences of a particular threat, and the opposites for opportunities (uncertain future states with benefits).

Certain aspects of many of the risk management standards have come under criticism for having no measurable improvement on risk, whereas the confidence in estimates and decisions seems to increase. For example, it has been shown that 1 in 6 IT projects experiences cost overruns of 200% on average, and schedule overruns of 70%.

In general, risk management methods consist of the following elements, performed, more or less, in the following order:

1. Identify and characterise threats;
2. Assess the vulnerability of critical assets to specific threats;
3. Determine the risk (i.e. the expected likelihood and consequences of specific types of attacks on specific assets);
4. Identify ways to reduce those risks;
5. Prioritise risk reduction measures based on a strategy.

Risk management concentrates on the identification and control of events that have the potential to cause significant problems. These events can be subdivided into Likelihood and Impact, with a combination of both resulting in the perceived or actual level of risk as determined by a Risk Index or Matrix. In Customs trade terms, this means the identification of imports that represent the greatest risk of non-compliance so that the Customs Organisation can focus its resources in those areas. The key to risk management is to systematically isolate and treat risk identified throughout the trade compliance process.

Risk Analysis and Risk Assessment

Risk analysis is the assessment of the risks and vulnerabilities that could negatively impact the confidentiality, integrity and availability of the electronic protected information held by a covered entity, and the likelihood of occurrence. The risk analysis may include taking inventory of all systems and applications that are used to access and house data and classifying them by level of risk. A thorough and accurate risk analysis would consider all relevant losses that would be expected if the security measures were not in place, including loss or damage of data, corrupted data systems and anticipated ramifications of such losses or damage.

Risk management is the actual implementation of security measures to sufficiently reduce an organisation's risk of losing or compromising its electronic protected information and to meet the general security standards.

At a high level, Risk analysis is a subset of **Risk assessment**. Risk management implements measures to mitigate and control risk.

Risk assessment determines the risks associated with given threats on an asset, given identified vulnerabilities with given existing safeguards. Typically the output is the Annual Loss Expectation.

Risk analysis determines the risk associated with given threats on an asset, considering how the vulnerabilities change as a function of different safeguards being considered. Typically the output is the determination of:

a) Safeguards with positive Return On Investment (ROI);
b) Deflecting (some of) the risks with an insurance policy;
c) No safeguard at all (ignoring the risks); or
d) A combination of a) and b).

Risk analysis dwells with the side of understanding the impact that a risk may have into a group of assets/company/state/personal welfare and the probability of it to happen, that is to materialise in a negative/positive outcome to the subject who manages, holds or owns the assets. It involves certainty building risk scenarios (with optimistic and pessimistic scenarios) and basically answering the questions: "What is the likelihood of this risk to happen?" and "What is at stake if it materialises (pessimistic scenarios), and what is the opportunity I can seize if the materialisation of risk brings positive outcomes?"

Risk assessment is a higher-level component of the discipline of Risk Management and it includes primarily the task of:

- Compiling a list of risks that the company/asset/person may be exposed to in the first place (which dwells into using the bottom-up, top-down or other methodologies to come up with a set of meaningful risks the subject is exposed to (regardless of impact and probability));
- It includes risk analysis (which was explained above);
- It includes the exercise of aligning the outcome of the risk analysis to the regulatory environment and risk appetite which the company/

person/state has. It is essentially answering the question "Now that I know how much I can lose/win and the likelihood of it, what is going to be my risk appetite towards it (i.e. how much am I willing to lose/win), and what is my tolerance level to that?" Once you have that answer, you can also prioritise the risks.

The risk appetite (i.e. acceptance of the exposure to risk) comprises what are referred to as risk options, otherwise known as the "4 T's". These are:

- **Tolerate** (We accept the risk as it is and do nothing);
- **Treat** (We need to rectify certain higher-risk areas and reduce the risk to As Low As Reasonably Possible – ALARP);
- **Transfer** (We accept that we cannot control the risk ourselves, so we pass it to more specialist agencies, e.g. Logistics providers, insurance providers);
- **Terminate** (We terminate the activity that was generating the high risk in the first instance).

The risk ratings for these options is:

Tolerate (Low Risk);
Treat (Medium);
Transfer (Medium to High);
Terminate (High).

The final stage of risk assessment is to look at the control framework which one has already embedded to mitigate the risk (or take advantage of the risk), which may answer the question "how to further respond/invest in order to mitigate the risk to an acceptable level?", and may give you insights into the strategy to achieve that. The embedded controls certainly include the relevant 1st line, 2nd line and 3rd line controls (if applicable), i.e. the controls required at each stage of the risk assessment.

It means that it is necessary to examine and assess the residual risk levels once the existing control framework is embedded, and to try to understand (through the information provided by monitoring tools/processes) if that level of residual risk is still within the risk appetite parameters set by the management, or if further action plans are required to further mitigate those risks. The risk assessment allows the creation of the risk profile of the company.

The other components of risk management (risk response, monitoring and reporting), are part of a continuous improvement cycle that feeds back into the risk assessment exercise in order to understand if the risk profile of the company or organisation has indeed changed (as risks normally do).

Risk analysis is therefore 1 of the tasks required to perform in order to carry out a full risk assessment.

Risk Assessment and Contingency Planning

Every business needs a risk management plan, whether it is as simple as purchasing liability insurance or so complex as to require full-time risk managers to execute it. Risk assessment and contingency planning is the process of determining the risks a business faces and what it must do if those risks are realised. While it may not be possible to plan for every possible emergency, most businesses can identify those they are most likely to face and those that will cost them the most if they come to pass.

Risk Forecasting

The first step in risk assessment is determining the quantity and level of risks that a business faces. Identify the threats that a business faces whether they are human, operational, financial, environmental/weather-related, political, procedural, technical or project-based. Measure each of these threats based on how likely they are to occur and how much damage they could do to the business. There are several techniques for identifying risks including group brainstorming, interviews, surveys, root-cause analysis, review of past accident reports, SWOT (Strengths, Weaknesses, Opportunities and Threats) analysis and diagramming.

Composite Risk Index (CRI)

The standard formula for risk assessment is that risk equals the probability of an event multiplied by the cost of the event. Each identified risk can be rated on a scale of 1 to 5, with 1 being the least likely to occur and causing the least damage and 5 being the most likely to occur and causing the most damage. All risks can then be sorted into low, medium or high depending on the rating.

The formula can also be re-written in terms of a composite risk index, as follows:

$$\text{Composite Risk Index} = \text{Impact of risk event} \times \text{Probability of occurrence}$$

The impact of the risk event is commonly assessed on a scale of 1 to 5, where 1 and 5 represent the minimum and maximum possible impact of an occurrence of a risk (usually in terms of financial losses). However, the 1 to 5 scale can be arbitrary and need not be on a linear scale.

The probability of occurrence is likewise commonly assessed on a scale from 1 to 5, where 1 represents a very low probability of the risk event actually occurring, while 5 represents a very high probability of occurrence. This axis may be expressed in either mathematical terms (event occurs once a year, once in 10 years, once in 100 years, etc.) or may be expressed in "plain English" (event has occurred here very often; event has been known to occur here; event has been known to occur in the industry, etc.). Again, the 1 to 5 scale can be arbitrary or non-linear depending on decisions by subject-matter experts.

The Composite Risk Index thus can take values ranging (typically) from 1 through 25, and this range is usually arbitrarily divided into 3 sub-ranges. The overall risk assessment is then Low, Medium or High, depending on the sub-range containing the calculated value of the Composite Risk Index. For instance, the 3 sub-ranges could be defined as 1 to 8, 9 to 16 and 17 to 25.

Note that the probability of risk occurrence is difficult to estimate, since the past data on frequencies are not readily available, as mentioned above. After all, probability does not imply certainty.

Likewise, the impact of the risk is not easy to estimate since it is often difficult to estimate the potential loss in the event of risk occurrence.

Further, both the above factors can change in magnitude depending on the adequacy of risk avoidance and prevention measures taken and due to changes in the external business environment. Hence it is absolutely necessary to periodically re-assess risks and intensify/relax mitigation measures, or as necessary. Changes in procedures, technology, schedules, budgets, market conditions, political environment or other factors typically require re-assessment of risks.

The CRI is therefore generally composed of 3 sub-divisions, namely:

- Low;
- Medium;
- High.

The CRI is quantified by 5 graduations for both Likelihood and Impact, gauged as follows:

LIKELIHOOD

1. Unlikely;
2. Possible;
3. Probable;
4. Likely;
5. Very Likely.

IMPACT

1. Minimal;
2. Low;
3. Medium;
4. Major;
5. Severe/Critical.

Thus, when each graduation for Likelihood is multiplied by each graduation for Impact, the result is the numbers 1–25, with 1 being the lowest, and 25 being the highest. The numbers are then divided into 3 main sections as follows:

1–8 (Low);
9–16 (Medium);
17–25 (High).

These numbers can then be inserted in a 5 × 5 Risk Mapping Matrix, with Likelihood measured on the vertical scale, and Impact measured on the horizontal scale, with 1 in the bottom left-hand box, and 25 in the top right-hand box.

5 × 5 Risk Matrix

The 5 × 5 method can be used where data is available or a good degree of judgement can be applied to estimates of the frequency and consequences of each hazardous event in the form of a simplified matrix. This risk ranking approach allows for a normal level of accuracy and consistency in the risk estimates that can be obtained.

Note: The size of the matrix and the factor difference in frequency and consequence rankings can be altered to give the best ranges to suit a particular organisation's operation.

This solution works for any factor difference (2, 5, 10, 100, etc.) providing both the frequency and consequence ranking estimates are separated by the same factor.

IMPACT					
LIKELIHOOD ↓	*MINIMAL (1)*	*LOW (2)*	*MODERATE (3)*	*HIGH (4)*	*CRITICAL (5)*
VERY LIKELY (5)	5	10	15	20	25
REGULAR (4)	4	8	12	16	20
FREQUENT (3)	3	6	9	12	15
INFREQUENT (2)	2	4	6	8	10
VERY UNLIKELY (1)	1	2	3	4	5

LEVELS

1–8: LOW (ALARP)
9–16: MEDIUM
17–25: HIGH

Note how the coloured risk levels move diagonally from bottom left to top right, showing the various levels of risk.

The 7 × 7 Risk Matrix expands these graduations, thus providing a more detailed and complex matrix.

7 x 7 Risk Matrix

IMPACT							
LIKELIHOOD ↓	*MINIMAL (1)*	*VERY LOW (2)*	*LOW (3)*	*MODERATE (4)*	*SIGNIFICANT (5)*	*HIGH (6)*	*CRITICAL (7)*
VERY LIKELY (7)	7	14	21	28	35	42	49
REGULAR (6)	6	12	18	24	30	36	42
FREQUENT (5)	5	10	15	20	25	30	35
OCCASIONAL (4)	4	8	12	16	20	24	28
INFREQUENT (3)	3	6	9	12	15	18	21
RARE (2)	2	4	6	8	10	12	14
VERY UNLIKELY (1)	1	2	3	4	5	6	7

In a 7 × 7 Composite Risk Index (CRI) and Risk Matrix, there are more levels of analysis given the complexity of the operation, as well as more opportunities to more precisely define the risk levels.

COMPOSITE RISK INDEX COLOUR CODES AND LEVELS:

1–7: MINIMAL (ALARP) – NO ACTION REQUIRED
8–14: VERY LOW – NO IMMEDIATE ACTION, BUT SOME OCCASIONAL MONITORING
15–21: LOW – SOME MONITORING REQUIRED
22–28: MODERATE – FREQUENT MONITORING REQUIRED
29–35: SIGNIFICANT – MONITORING AND LONG-TERM ACTION
36–42: HIGH – SHORT-TERM RECTIFICATION REQUIRED
43–49: VERY HIGH/CRITICAL (UNACCEPTABLE) – IMMEDIATE RADICAL ACTION REQUIRED

In **low** areas, the level of risk is such that it costs more to monitor the activities of a target than to gain any specific benefits, therefore no action should be required.

In **moderate/significant** areas, risk is higher, and monitoring is required on a more frequent basis, with remedial action to be taken in areas marked “Significant”. Such action should be based on both present and historical evidence, in order to ascertain the true level of risk, especially where this may be marginal between Medium and High level.

In **high** areas, risk is much higher, and requires immediate remedial action to recover and protect the revenue, as well as place the target organisations on a High-Risk Assurance List.

Application to Revenue Protection

According to Standard 6.3 of the Revised Kyoto Convention (RKC) and the corresponding Guidelines, risk management from a Customs perspective is defined as the systematic application of management procedures and practices which provide the Customs Authority with the necessary information to address movements or consignments that present a risk.

Risk management concentrates on identifying and controlling events that have the potential to cause significant problems. In Customs trade terms, that means identifying imports that represent the greatest risk of non-compliance so that we can focus our resources in those areas. The key to risk management is to systematically isolate and treat risk identified throughout the trade compliance process.

Risk management does not create any new work, but rather combines existing programmes to maximise resources. Risk management requires clear responsibility and accountability for each programme or action. Some of the programmes that are currently being used to manage risk include compliance measurement, compliance assessment, selectivity and account management. Risk management also shows field personnel how their work affects the work of the authority.

In the US, this is carried out in a 4-stage process.

1. Collect Data and Information:

Proper risk management requires a structured approach to collecting data.

2. Analyse and Assess Risk:

Analyse the data and determine the likelihood of non-compliance.

3. Prescribe Action:

Once the potential risk has been identified and analysed, it is time to design the appropriate action and dedicate the necessary resources.

4. Track and Report:

Once the appropriate action is designed, ownership for the action must be assigned and its results tracked and fed back into the risk management process.

This process is cyclical, and in many ways relates to the Six Sigma DMAIC process, which is analysed elsewhere in this text.

With regard to revenue protection, the 7 × 7 Risk Matrix provides an opportunity to more closely define the various levels of risk concerning not only the protection of the revenue but also the extent to which revenue collection procedures may be compromised by anomalies and weaknesses in compliance and operational procedures.

For low risk levels, there is little advantage in addressing these issues on a regular basis, as this would consume significant levels of resources in return for little if any positive results. Low risk can often be associated with minor errors or oversight on the part of the organisation concerned.

Medium risk suggests that more needs to be done to monitor organisations in this level on a long-term basis in order to assess the threat to the revenue. Although benefits may be gained concerning revenue collection and protection, these may be considered more long-term rather than short-term, and may therefore be given a lower priority than those in the high-risk level.

However, higher levels of risk suggest deliberate fraud or gross incompetence on the part of the organisations concerned, with the consequence that more needs to be done to address these issues on a more concentrated basis and examine all revenue protection procedures so as to guarantee compliance and due diligence. These levels of risk require much greater levels of monitoring and review on a regular continuous basis by the Customs Authority, in order to maintain tight control over the company's import and export activities.

The following diagram of the Australian Taxation Office (ATO) Risk Matrix puts the matrix into perspective in terms of addressing the various issues of risk concerning traders, and the appropriate actions to be taken in each case with regard to monitoring and review of specific traders.

CONTINUOUS MONITORING	**CONTINUOUS REVIEW**	**Proactive**
PERIODIC MONITORING	**PERIODIC REVIEW**	**Reactive**

Risk Option Evaluation

Once identified, a business can decide what it will do with the risk it faces. The 4 basic approaches to risk are risk avoidance, risk reduction, risk sharing or transfer, and risk retention. Risk avoidance involves not doing the project or task that will bring the business into contact with the risk. Risk reduction means putting procedures into place that will make the risk less likely to occur or mitigate the effects if it does occur. Risk sharing or transfer typically involves buying insurance to cover losses or outsourcing the task so that someone else bears the burden of risk. Risk retention is the process of accepting the possibility of loss and budgeting to cover the risk.

Risk mitigation measures are usually formulated according to 1 or more of the following major risk options, which are:

1. Design a new business process with adequate built-in risk control and containment measures from the start;
2. Periodically re-assess risks that are accepted in ongoing processes as a normal feature of business operations and modify mitigation measures;
3. Transfer risks to an external agency (e.g. an insurance company);
4. Avoid risks altogether (e.g. by closing down a particular high-risk business area).

As defined previously, the risk options can also be expressed as;

- Tolerate;
- Treat;
- Transfer;
- Terminate.

Once the risks have been identified and assessed, all techniques to manage the risk fall into 1 or more of these 4 major categories, which amount to the above but in reverse order:

- Avoidance (eliminate, withdraw from or not become involved);
- Reduction (optimise – mitigate);
- Sharing (transfer – outsource or insure);
- Retention (accept and budget).

From the above, a risk management plan should be implemented which takes into account all the risk options.

It is important to select appropriate controls or counter-measures to measure each risk, as risk mitigation needs to be approved by the appropriate level of management. For instance, a risk concerning the image of the organisation should have top management decision behind it, whereas IT management would have the authority to decide on computer virus risks. Customs risk would possibly fall between logistics, accounts or import/export. Depending upon where these functions lie, e.g. sales, purchasing.

The risk management plan should propose applicable, practical and effective security controls for managing each of the risks. For example, an observed high risk of computer viruses could be mitigated by acquiring and implementing antivirus software. Similarly, an observed high risk of Customs compliance, e.g. Tariff Commodity Codes, would be mitigated by an extensive review of all Commodity Codes used and an application for

Binding Tariff Rulings from Customs. Consequently, a good risk management plan should contain a schedule for control implementation and responsible persons for those actions.

According to ISO/IEC 27001, as well as ISO 31000, the stage immediately after completion of the risk assessment phase consists of preparing an appropriate risk treatment plan, which should document the decisions about how each of the identified risks should be handled. Risk mitigation often infers the selection of security controls, which should be documented in a Statement of Applicability, which identifies which particular control objectives and controls from the standard have been selected, and why they have been selected. Risk mitigation should also detail the exact and precise actions taken to mitigate the specific risk, so that any future review can establish the extent to which the mitigation achieved a significant reduction in the risk concerned.

Contingency Plan Creation

If a business decides to mitigate or accept the risk concerned or identified, it will benefit from having a contingency plan in place to deal with the situation should it occur. In generic terms, this can range from a fire evacuation plan to appointing an emergency coordinator to help with evacuations or media contacts. In international trade, this can include budgeting for unpredicted events such as damage or loss to cargoes, or additional reserves in case of additional tax or duty liability. Where Import Duty liability is very low, it is often the case that such risk can be accepted and built into costs, as long as the customer is prepared to accept these costs as part of the overall Supply Chain. Global reductions in Import Duty, as well as trade preferences leading to elimination in import tariffs by way of Free Trade Agreements, often mean that there is little point in going down the route of Import Duty Reliefs, as the cost of implementing the duty relief mechanism can be higher than accepting the Import Duty liability itself. The plan may also specifically include insurance policies to cover these events, however unlikely they may be. Risk managers can create detailed plans to deal with the most likely situations the organisation will face or those that will do the most harm. They must then communicate these plans to all necessary personnel in the workplace and possibly schedule specific courses of action, provide training or purchase equipment.

Plan Evaluation

Businesses need to review their plans frequently, usually on an annual basis, to ensure that they are up to date, and that any risk areas are constantly monitored. They should also evaluate their plans after an emergency or an adverse event occurs, such as an unexpected bill from Customs, to ensure that the plan worked the way it was supposed to and to make any needed adjustments.

Strategic Contingency Planning

The development of strategies for how a business will use its money, materials and people to accomplish its goals and objectives is part of starting up and running a business. Within the strategic planning process, a contingency plan serves as a backup in cases where a business veers off course as a result of from 1 or more unintended outcomes. Strategic contingency planning attempts to lessen the effects of less than favourable circumstances and keep a business afloat during difficult periods.

Strategic Planning

Strategic planning plays a significant role in how a business intends to run its operations and market its products, services or brand. Strategies for future growth also require planning in accordance with a company's objectives and goals. Part of the strategic planning process involves comparing the different directions a company can move in and determining which one will best suit the company's purpose. In order to do this, managers may develop "what-if" scenarios that incorporate particular objectives and examine the possible effects of each scenario within the company's strategic plan. These scenarios can include a change in Tariff Commodity Codes, the introduction of new Customs processes (as in the Union Customs Code), new Free Trade Agreements or changes in overseas suppliers.

Contingency Planning

In the process of developing a company's overall strategic plan, business managers may develop alternative strategies as a means to accommodate unexpected conditions or events, such as economic recessions, unexpected Customs assessments, or catastrophic events, or indeed anything which can affect an International Supply Chain risk management plan. Contingency planning involves having alternative strategies in place as a way of preparing for the unexpected. These types of plans may also be categorised as disaster recovery plans or business continuity plans, depending on the overall purpose of the plan. The primary purpose for a contingency plan provides a strategy for minimising the effects of unexpected circumstances. By doing so, business managers increase the likelihood that a business' main operations will continue with minimal losses or damages.

Developing Scenarios

While strategic contingency planning cannot actually predict future events and outcomes, developing possible scenarios can provide plans of action that apply within different circumstances. Business managers develop scenarios that address known challenges confronting a business, such as economic recessions, changes within a particular industry or political influences that impact a company's financial obligations or marketing channels. In effect, a strategic contingency plan provides a map for any possible future unknowns while strategic planning charts the overall course and direction a business will take.

Timing

Developing 2 or more strategic contingency plans provides actionable steps to follow within different circumstances. However, knowing when to enact 1 plan or another requires additional consideration and planning, as it depends upon the circumstances as to which plan is more expedient. In order to incorporate timing factors into a contingency plan, business managers must identify specific circumstance or conditions that would warrant the need to put an alternate plan in place. For example, a 30% decline in product sales could serve as an indicator that a particular contingency plan is needed. As contingency plans are based on anticipated challenges or conditions, managers can identify timing factors during the course of developing each alternative plan.

Audit Risk

Audit risk (also referred to as **residual risk**) refers to the risk that an auditor may issue an unqualified report or incorrect opinion due to the auditor's failure to detect material misstatement either due to error or fraud. This risk is composed of inherent risk (IR), control risk (CR) and detection risk (DR), and can be calculated thus:

$$AR = IR \times CR \times DR$$

Where AR is *audit risk*, IR is *inherent risk*, CR is *control risk* and DR is *detection risk*.

IR refers to the risk involved in the nature of business or transaction. Example, transactions involving exchange of cash may have higher IR than transactions involving settlement by checks.

CR refers to the risk that a misstatement could occur but may not be detected and corrected or prevented by entity's internal control mechanism. Example, control risk assessment may be higher in an entity where separation of duties is not well defined.

DR is the probability that the audit procedures may fail to detect existence of a material error or fraud. While CR depends on the strength or weakness of the internal control procedures, DR is either due to sampling error or human factors.

Examples of inappropriate audit opinions include the following:

- Issuing an unqualified audit report where a qualification is reasonably justified;
- Issuing a qualified audit opinion where no qualification is necessary;
- Failing to emphasise a significant matter in the audit report;
- Providing an opinion on financial statements where no such opinion may be reasonably given due to a significant limitation of scope in the performance of the audit.

From the above, audit risk = inherent risk × control risk × detection risk

Audit risk may be considered as the product of the various risks which may be encountered in the performance of the audit. In order to keep the overall audit risk of engagements below acceptable limit, the auditor must assess the level of risk pertaining to each component of audit risk.

Explanation of the 3 elements of audit risk is as follows.

Inherent Risk

Inherent risk is the risk of a material misstatement in the financial statements arising due to error or omission as a result of factors other than the failure of controls (factors that may cause a misstatement due to absence or lapse of controls are considered separately in the assessment of control risk).

Inherent risk is generally considered to be higher where a high degree of judgement and estimation is involved or where transactions of the entity are highly complex.

For example, the inherent risk in the audit of a newly formed financial institution which has a significant trade and exposure in complex derivative instruments may be considered to be significantly higher as compared to the audit of a well-established manufacturing concern operating in a relatively stable competitive environment.

Control Risk

Control risk is the risk of a material misstatement in financial or fiscal statements arising due to absence or failure in the operation of relevant controls of the organisation.

It is therefore the probability that a material misstatement exists in an assertion because that misstatement was not either prevented from entering the organisation's financial information, or it was not detected and corrected by the internal control system of that organisation. In the context of Customs controls, this means that incorrect information was included in a Customs Declaration but was not detected at the time of submission of the declaration.

It is the responsibility of the management and those charged with governance to implement the internal control system and maintain it appropriately, which includes managing control risk.

Organisations must have adequate internal controls in place to prevent and detect instances of fraud and error. Control risk is considered to be high where the audit entity does not have adequate internal controls to prevent and detect instances of fraud and error in the financial statements.

Assessment of control risk may be higher, for example, in case of a small sized entity in which segregation of duties is not well defined and the financial statements are prepared by individuals who do not have the necessary technical knowledge of accounting and finance.

There can be many reasons for control risk to arise and why it cannot be eliminated absolutely. However, some of them are as follows:

- Cost-benefit constraints;
- Circumvention of controls;
- Inappropriate design of controls;
- Inappropriate application of controls;
- Lack of control environment and accountability;
- Novel situations;
- Outdated controls.

Using the principles of raw/inherent risk and residual risk, the identification of the above issues should lead to the reduction in the level of risk and hence the corresponding reduction in control risk accordingly.

Detection Risk

Detection risk is the risk that the auditors fail to detect a material misstatement in the financial statements.

An auditor must apply audit procedures to detect material misstatements in the financial statements whether due to fraud or error. Misapplication or omission of critical audit procedures may result in a material misstatement remaining undetected by the auditor. Some detection risk is always present due to the inherent limitations of the audit such as the use of sampling for the selection of transactions.

Detection risk can be reduced by auditors by increasing the number of sampled transactions for detailed testing.

The audit risk model is used by the auditors to manage the overall risk of an audit engagement. Auditors proceed by examining the inherent and control risks pertaining to an audit engagement while gaining an understanding of the entity and its environment. Detection risk forms the residual risk after taking into consideration the inherent and control risks pertaining to the audit engagement and the overall audit risk that the auditor is willing to accept. Where the auditor's assessment of inherent and control risk is high, the detection risk is set at a lower level to keep the audit risk at an acceptable level. Lower detection risk may be achieved by increasing the sample size for audit testing. Conversely, where the auditor believes the inherent and control risks of an engagement to be low, detection risk is allowed to be set at a relatively higher level.

The terms attitude, appetite and tolerance are often used similarly to describe the attitude of an organisation or individual towards risk taking. Risk averse, risk neutral and risk seeking are examples of the terms that may be used to describe a risk attitude. Risk tolerance looks at acceptable/unacceptable deviations from what is expected. Risk appetite looks at how much risk one is willing to accept. There can still be deviations that are within a risk appetite. For example, recent research finds that insured individuals are significantly likely to divest from risky asset holdings in response to a decline in health, controlling for variables such as income, age and out-of-pocket medical expenses.

Raw Risk, Residual Risk and Inherent Risk

Raw risk is the prevalent risk before anything is done to mitigate or manage it, i.e. before controls are put in place.

Residual risk is the risk that remains after all appropriate controls or mitigation actions have been implemented.

Therefore, residual risk is the risk remaining after measures have been implemented to mitigate the original raw risk and therefore reduce it.

Inherent risk, in a financial or fiscal audit, measures the auditor's assessment of the likelihood that there are material misstatements due to error or fraud in segment before considering the effectiveness of internal control. If the auditor concludes that a high likelihood exist, the auditor will conclude that inherent risk is high.

The risk posed by an error or omission in a financial statement due to a factor other than a failure of control. In a financial audit, inherent risk is most likely to occur when transactions are complex, or in situations that require a high degree of judgement in regards to financial estimates. This type of risk represents a worst-case scenario because all controls have failed.

Inherent risk is 1 of the risks auditors must look for when reviewing financial statements, along with control risk and detection risk. When conducting an audit, the auditor will try to gain an understanding of the nature of the business while examining control risks and inherent risks. If inherent and control risks are considered to be high, an auditor can set the detection risk to a lower level to keep the overall audit risk at a reasonable level.

Companies operating in highly regulated sectors, such as the financial sector, are more likely to have higher inherent risk, especially if the company does not have an audit department or has an audit department without an oversight committee with a financial background. The ultimate risk posed to the company also depends on the financial exposure created by the inherent risk if the process for accounting for the exposure fails.

Complex financial transactions, such as those undertaken in the years leading up to the financial crisis of 2007–2008, can be difficult for even the cleverest financial professionals to understand. Asset-backed securities, such as collateralised debt obligations (CDOs), became difficult to account for as tranches of varying qualities were repackaged again and again. This complexity may make it difficult for an auditor to make the correct opinion, which in turn can lead investors to consider a company to be more (or less) financially stable than it actually is.

There are 4 basic ways of dealing with risk: reduce it, avoid it, accept it or transfer it. Since residual risk is unknown, many organisations choose to either accept residual risk or transfer it, for example, by purchasing insurance to transfer the risk to an insurance company.

When addressing residual risk, organisations should:

- Identify relevant governance, risk and compliance (GRC) requirements;
- Determine the organisation's control framework's strengths and weaknesses;
- Acknowledge existing risks;
- Define the organisation's risk appetite;
- Identify available options for offsetting unacceptable residual risks.

Governance, risk and compliance is a combined area of focus within an organisation that developed because of interdependencies between the 3 components. GRC software products, available from a number of vendors, typically facilitate compliance with legal requirements, such as those specified in Customs legislation at a national or supranational level, such as the European Union.

The residual risk is therefore the risk or danger of an action or an event, a method or a (technical) process that, although being abreast with science, still conceives these dangers, even if all theoretically possible safety measures would be applied (scientifically conceivable measures).

The formula to calculate residual risk is (inherent risk) × (control risk) where inherent risk is (threats × vulnerability).

Therefore, we have the following summary definitions:

> **Inherent risk:** The risk that an activity would pose if ***no controls*** or other mitigating factors were in place (the gross risk or risk before controls)
>
> **Residual risk:** The risk that remains *after controls* are taken into account (the net risk or risk after controls).

This leads to a more accurate definition of inherent risk:

1. The risk that a process poses to the business before controls are taken into account;
2. The risk that a process poses to the business based on the financial exposure if the process fails and the presence of threats that could exploit a vulnerability in that process.

In the first definition, there is the temptation to treat all processes as having a high inherent risk. For example, there is always the risk that a financial record will be inaccurate before controls are put in place. Hence, the first definition is not very helpful in setting priorities.

The second definition provides better guidance by first determining the impact to the business if the financial record were to be inaccurate. Are we talking about a US$1 or US$1 million line item? Second, you also need to determine the potential for a mistake to be made in preparing the financial record or that someone will intentionally misrepresent the amount. Once these assessments are made the accountant can then better determine which financial records deserve close attention (i.e. have a higher inherent risk).

The Risk Register

A **risk register** is a risk management tool commonly used in risk management and compliance. It acts as a central repository for all risks identified by the organisation and, for each risk, includes information such as source, nature, treatment option, existing counter-measures, recommended counter-measures and so on.

In general, an ideal way of addressing essential risk issues is to arrange them on a tabular chart. This provides brief details of the areas subject to risk, the levels of risk defined as raw risk (L, M, H), the remedial actions defined as risk mitigation, and the resulting residual risk (L, M, H).

A typical example for an international trade process could be:

RAW RISK				*RESIDUAL RISK*			
DETAIL	*L*	*M*	*H*	*REMEDIAL ACTION*	*L*	*M*	*H*
Import Documents		X		Checking on Receipt	X		
Export Documents		X		Advance Planning and Issue	X		
Customs Declarations			X	Accurate Information Checks	X		
Compliance			X	Internal Documented Procedures	X		
Staff Knowledge			X	Training Courses	X		

The purpose of the risk register is to highlight the main issues at stake, and its advantage is that it can be continuously monitored and reviewed on a regular basis, in order to maintain adequate controls over the process concerned.

Typically, a more complex risk register contains:

- A description of the risk;
- The impact should this event actually occur;
- The probability of its occurrence;
- Risk Score (the multiplication of Probability and Impact);
- A summary of the planned response should the event occur;
- A summary of the mitigation (the actions taken in advance to reduce the probability and/or impact of the event).

The risks are often ranked by Risk Score so as to highlight the highest priority risks to all involved.

Risk Register for Project "Customs Training Course"

In a "**qualitative**" risk register, descriptive terms are used: for example, a risk might have a "High" impact and a "Medium" probability.

In a "**quantitative**" risk register, the descriptions are enumerated: for example, a risk might have a "US$1 million" impact and a "50%" probability.

Contingent response – the actions to be taken should the risk event actually occur.

Contingency – the budget allocated to the contingent response.

Trigger – an event that itself results in the risk event occurring (for example, the risk event might be "flooding" and "heavy rainfall" the trigger).

Although risk registers are commonly used tools not only in projects and programmes but also in companies, research has found that they can lead

Risk Category	*Risk Name*	*Risk Number*	*Probability (1–3)*	*Impact (1–3)*	*Risk Score*	*Mitigation*	*Contingency*	*Risk Score after Mitigation*	*Action By*	*Action When*
Delegates	The delegates find the course boring	1.1.	2	2	4	Introduce more interactive topics and activities	Find a "YouTube" example; Introduce Case Studies	2	Trainer	within 2hrs
Delegates	Heated Arguments	1.2.	1	3	3	Calm the proceedings down, suggest break in session	Coffee Break	1	Trainer	Now
Nature	Room too Hot	2.1.	2	2	4	Open Windows	Switch on Air-Conditioning	0	Everyone	10 mins
Nature	Fire	2.2.	1	3	3	Start the course with instructions on what to do in the event of fire	Implement the appropriate response plan	1	Everyone	As per plan
Food	Inadequate Catering	3.1.	1	2	2	Complain to Hotel Management	Order more food	1	Hotel	30 mins
Timing	Course overruns	3.2.	1	3	3	Time Management	Cut down on Comments, Q&A	1	Trainer	After

to dysfunctions. For instance, Toyota's risk register listed reputation risks caused by car malfunctions, but the company failed to take action. Risk registers often lead to ritualistic decision-making, an illusion of control and the fallacy of misplaced concreteness, e.g. mistaking the map for the territory. However, if used with common sense, risk registers are a useful tool to stimulate cross-functional debate and cooperation, and provide a basis for in-depth analysis and resolution of common problems.

ISO 31000 – Risk Management

Risks affecting organisations can have consequences in terms of economic performance and professional reputation, as well as environmental, safety and societal outcomes. Therefore, managing risk effectively helps organisations perform well in an environment full of uncertainty.

ISO 31000 is a family of standards relating to risk management codified by the International Organisation for Standardisation (ISO). The specific purpose of ISO 31000:2009 is to provide principles and generic guidelines on risk management. ISO 31000 seeks to provide a universally recognised paradigm for practitioners and companies employing risk management processes to replace the myriad of existing standards, methodologies and paradigms that differed between industries, subject matters and regions.

Currently, the ISO 31000 family includes:

- ISO 31000:2009 – Principles and Guidelines on Implementation;
- ISO/IEC 31010:2009 – Risk Management – Risk Assessment Techniques;
- ISO Guide 73:2009 – Risk Management – Vocabulary.

ISO also designed its ISO 21500 Guidance on Project Management standard to align with ISO 31000:2009.

ISO 31000 was published as a standard on 13 November 2009, and provides a standard on the implementation of risk management. A revised and harmonised ISO/IEC Guide 73 was published at the same time. The purpose of ISO 31000:2009 is to be applicable and adaptable for "any public, private or community enterprise, association, group or individual". Accordingly, the general scope of ISO 31000 – as a family of risk management standards – is not developed for a particular industry group, management system, or subject-matter field in mind, rather to provide best practice structure and guidance to all operations concerned with risk management.

ISO 31000:2009

ISO 31000:2009 provides generic guidelines for the design, implementation and maintenance of risk management processes throughout an organisation. This approach to formalising risk management practices will facilitate broader adoption by companies who require an enterprise risk management (ERM) standard that accommodates multiple "silo-centric" management systems.

The scope of this approach to risk management is to enable all strategic, management and operational tasks of an organisation throughout projects, functions, and processes to be aligned to a common set of risk management objectives.

Accordingly, ISO 31000:2009 is intended for a broad stakeholder group including:

- Executive level stakeholders;
- Appointment holders in the enterprise risk management group;
- Risk analysts and management officers;
- Line managers and project managers;
- Compliance and internal auditors;
- Independent practitioners.

One of the key paradigm shifts proposed in ISO 31000 is a controversial change in how risk is conceptualised. Under the ISO 31000:2009 and a consequential major revision of the terminology in ISO Guide 73, the definition of "risk" is no longer "chance or probability of loss", but "the effect of uncertainty on objectives" ... thus causing the word "risk" to refer to positive possibilities as well as negative ones.

ISO 31000:2009 has been developed on the basis of an existing standard on risk management.

The intent of ISO 31000 is to be applied within existing management systems to formalise and improve risk management processes, as opposed to wholesale substitution of legacy management practices. Subsequently, when implementing ISO 31000, attention is to be given to integrating existing risk management processes into the new paradigm addressed in the standard.

The focus of many ISO 31000 "harmonisation" programmes has centred on:

- Transferring accountability gaps in enterprise risk management;
- Aligning objectives of the governance frameworks with ISO 31000;
- Embedding management system reporting mechanisms;
- Creating uniform risk criteria and evaluation metrics.

Most implications for adopting the new standard concern the re-engineering of existing management practices to conform with the documentation, communication and operation of the new risk management operating paradigm, as opposed to the wholesale re-orientation of management practice throughout an organisation. Accordingly, most senior position holders in an enterprise risk management organisation will need to be aware of and be able to understand the implication for adopting the standard and be able to develop effective strategies for implementing the standard across Supply Chains and commercial operations.

Certain aspects of top management accountability, strategic policy implementation and effective governance frameworks will require more consideration by organisations that have previously used risk management methodologies which have since become redundant.

In some domains that concern risk management, in particular security and corporate social responsibility, which may operate using relatively unsophisticated risk management processes, more material change will be required, particularly regarding a clearly articulated risk management policy, formalising risk ownership processes, structuring framework processes and adopting continuous improvement programmes.

ISO 31000:2009 gives a list on how to deal with risk:

1. Avoiding the risk by deciding not to start or continue with the activity that gives rise to the risk;
2. Accepting or increasing the risk in order to pursue an opportunity;
3. Removing the risk source;
4. Changing the likelihood;
5. Changing the consequences;
6. Sharing the risk with another party or parties (including contracts and risk financing);
7. Retaining the risk by informed decision.

ISO 31000:2009, Risk Management – Principles and Guidelines, provides principles, framework and a process for managing risk. It can be used by any organisation regardless of its size, activity or sector. Using ISO 31000 can help organisations increase the likelihood of achieving objectives, improve the identification of opportunities and threats and effectively allocate and use resources for risk treatment.

However, ISO 31000 cannot be used for certification purposes, but does provide guidance for internal or external audit programmes. Organisations using it can compare their risk management practices with an internationally recognised benchmark, providing sound principles for effective management and corporate governance.

ISO/IEC 31010:2009, Risk Management – Risk Assessment Techniques, focuses on risk assessment. Risk assessment helps decision-makers understand the risks that could affect the achievement of objectives as well as the adequacy of the controls already in place. ISO/IEC 31010:2009 focuses on risk assessment concepts, processes and the selection of risk assessment techniques.

CHAPTER 2

The International Commercial Terms of Delivery (INCOTERMS)

The term "INCOTERMS" refers to the rights, responsibilities and risks of sellers and buyers associated with the international movement of cargoes, and which party, either seller or buyer, bears those risks and responsibilities. In short, it covers the issue of "who pays the ferryman". The term INCOTERM is an acronym, meaning the International Commercial Terms of Delivery. There are 11 terms in all, although some are abbreviated to a simplified form depending upon the nature of how the consignment is to be arranged. Over the past several decades, several INCOTERMS have been changed depending upon their relevance, although those which have been removed, such as "*Franco Domicile*" are still understood by many who have worked in the international trade field for some years. The most recent review of the INCOTERMS was made in 2019, and the INCOTERMS were significantly reviewed and amended accordingly, resulting in INCOTERMS 2020.

The 11 terms are arranged as follows:

- EXW (Ex Works);
- FCA (Free Carrier);
- FAS (Free Alongside Ship);
- FOB (Free on Board);
- C&F/CFR (Cost and Freight);
- CPT (Carriage Paid To …);
- CIF (Cost Insurance Freight);
- CIP (Carriage and Insurance Paid …);
- DAP (Delivered At [Named] Place);
- DPU (Delivered at Place Unloaded – replaces DAT (Delivered At Terminal));
- DDP (Delivered Duty Paid).

The 2 abbreviated terms are:

- Freight Collect;
- Freight Prepaid.

DOI: 10.4324/9781003341345-3

One of the above INCOTERMS is generally not used for Sea Freight, namely DDP, and this is omitted for the purpose of this text. Certain other terms, such as FCA, CPT, CIP, DAP and DPU, can also be used for Air Freight, as they cover a multi-modal form of transportation. One term, EXW, is not seen as an International Term of Delivery, as it simply allows for the collection of the goods from the seller's premises by the buyer, regardless of where the buyer is located, and, according to the latest INCOTERMS book, should only be used for price quotations and not as a physical INCOTERM for shipment purposes. The main terms, however, for Sea Freight alone are:

- FAS;
- FOB;
- C&F/CFR;
- CIF.

The terms used for multimodal shipments are:

- EXW;
- FCA;
- CPT;
- CIP;
- DAP;
- DPU;
- DDP.

EXW (Ex Works)

The only responsibility of the seller is to make the consignment ready for shipment at their premises (the "Factory Gate") and to notify the buyer that the consignment is ready for collection. It is the responsibility of the buyer to arrange and pay for all transport for the consignment to the ultimate destination and the buyer's premises, as well as to shoulder all risks associated with the transport of that consignment. The buyer arranges all documentation for the shipment, as well as all export and import Customs clearance in the case where the consignment passes through Customs controls en route to its final destination. The seller bears no risks or responsibilities connected with the shipment, other than making the consignment ready for collection by the buyer's representative, although in reality they are deemed to be the Exporter of Record by their national Customs Authority, and thus require some form of proof of shipment, such as a Certificate of Shipment provided by the freight forwarder of the carrier, and a copy of the appropriate Customs Export Declaration at the point of export for Customs purposes. It is also the express duty of the seller to inform the buyer of the exact nature of the cargo in order to ensure that the correct shipping documentation is raised, especially where the cargo is of a hazardous or dangerous nature. Under the new INCOTERMS 2010, EXW should only be quoted as a price quotation, and should not be used for the purposes of shipment of the consignment.

Ex Works means that the seller fulfils his obligation to deliver when he has made the goods available at his premises (i.e. works, factory, warehouse, etc.) to the buyer. In particular, he is not responsible for loading the goods on the vehicle provided by the buyer or for clearing the goods for export, unless otherwise agreed. The buyer bears all costs and risks involved in taking the goods from the seller's premises to the desired destination. This term thus represents the minimum obligation for the seller.

This term should not be used when the buyer cannot carry out directly or indirectly the export formalities, especially when they are not VAT-registered in the country of export.

For export purposes as required by the Customs Authority in the country of export, the exporter must ensure that the correct instructions are issued to the clearing agent for the purposes of export clearance and the submission of the Export Declaration to the Customs Authority. This would not happen under the term Ex Works, as the exporter is not responsible for the Export Declaration. The minimum term to be used would be **FCA (Free Carrier),** where the exporter has the task and responsibility of loading the vehicle of export and sanctioning the raising of the Export Customs Declaration, thus issuing correct clearance instructions to the clearing agent for the Export Declaration. Similarly, the term Ex Works should *not* be used for trade with the EU, as the exporter *must* obtain full evidence of export shipment, namely the copy of the CMR Consignment Note, as well as a stamped and signed copy (Copy 3) of the receipted CMR Notes by the customer as proof that the consignment has arrived at its destination. This allows VAT zero-rating to be applied by the exporter for shipments to the EU. For international exports, the condition would be that the exporter also receives a copy of the full Customs Export Declaration. In cases where the exporter does not receive any proof of export from the buyer or their agent, the exporter is required under Customs and VAT law to charge the buyer the VAT as if the consignment were subject to a domestic delivery. Indeed, EXW is not deemed to be an international term of delivery and should only be used for price quotation purposes.

The INCOTERMS 2020 book, published by the International Chamber of Commerce (ICC), states for Ex Works that it is suitable for domestic trade, while the term FCA is more appropriate for international trade, which is somewhat diplomatic. This is because the term FCA enables the exporter to raise the Customs Export Declaration in accordance with compliance requirements set out by the national Customs Authority.

The difference between EXW and FCA is that under EXW, the exporter has no legal right to insist on the export being done in their name or to obtain evidence of export from the freight company, which effectively means that the goods may simply go to a destination in the exporter's country and are therefore chargeable for VAT. With FCA, the exporter is legally responsible to "free the goods for export" so, even though the freight company may be paid by the exporter's customer, they act on the exporter's behalf to prepare the Export Declaration, and they must send the C88/eAD declaration and transport document to the exporter as proof of declaration and dispatch, in this case from the UK.

In both cases, if the exporter cannot provide adequate evidence of export, they must treat it as a domestic supply and charge VAT to the customer.

In brief, EXW is *not* an international term; it is a domestic freight collect term and should not be used internationally other than for price quotations.

FCA (Free Carrier)

The term FCA has 2 distinct meanings, and these are explained as follows.

First, whereas under the EXW term, the seller simply notifies the buyer that the consignment is ready for shipment and does not even bear responsibility for loading the vehicle at the point of dispatch, under the FCA term the seller has the responsibility of loading the vehicle and obtaining a dispatch document, as well as a Customs Export Declaration.

Second, where consolidation is involved and the consignment is to be grouped or consolidated with several other loads at a central point of loading, the seller is responsible for the carriage of the consignment to that point and ensuring that it is loaded aboard the container, although in general, the buyer pays for and arranges the actual loading of the container by the consolidating agent. The consolidating agent arranges both the consolidation, or Master Bill of Lading for the container, plus the individual House Bills of Lading for each consignment loaded aboard the container. The buyer arranges the consolidation and the full international journey of the container or their consignment within that container right up to their premises, assuming that there will be a deconsolidation or breakbulk operation conducted at a point close to their premises. Under the new INCOTERMS 2020, FCA has been extended to include the transfer of risk and responsibility from the seller to the buyer at the quayside of the port of departure, thus substituting FAS (Free Alongside Ship).

FAS (Free Alongside Ship)

This term is very much of a maritime nature and concerns the passing of risk and responsibility from the seller to the buyer at the quayside where the consignment is to be loaded aboard the vessel. The buyer takes complete control from there on and therefore has responsibility for loading the consignment off the quayside and on board the vessel, thus also accepting liability for all port handling and loading charges. In this respect, FAS is also usable in conjunction with the "net form" of voyage charter of a vessel, where the charterer takes charge of all loading activities and responsibilities for the cargo when loading the vessel. FAS, however, is not normally used with container shipments, as the arrangement to load the container will have taken place at some point inland from the port of loading.

FOB (Free on Board)

The term "Free on Board" has a variety of applications, although its actual meaning is fairly simple. It has been amended in the INCOTERMS 2010 to state that the responsibility for the carriage of the consignment transfers from seller to buyer the moment the container or cargo is properly loaded *and secured* onboard the vessel, either on deck or in the ship's hold. Although it does apply to container transport, it has always applied to more general cargo, given the means by which the cargo is lifted from the quayside and lowered into the hold of the vessel, and to this extent, it has now become more definitive in its meaning. There is a legal implication to the term under the conditions of an FOB Contract. The term is used with the "gross form" of voyage charter, where the shipper relies on the owner of the vessel to ensure that the cargo is correctly loaded aboard the vessel. In the same way, the shipper is reliant upon the port authority to ensure that the cargo is correctly lifted from the quayside and onto the vessel. Should the consignment fall from the crane, 2 possibilities arise:

1) The cargo lands on the quayside and is damaged. The seller is responsible for the damage and must either replace the consignment or reimburse the buyer;
2) The cargo falls from the crane and lands on the vessel, damaging the vessel as well as being damaged itself. The seller is responsible for all damage, including that to the vessel, and must pay the appropriate amount of money as well as incur costs for a replacement consignment, given that the consignment had not been properly loaded or secured aboard the vessel.

Under the terms of a strict FOB contract, the buyer can reject a consignment at the point of loading if they feel that the contract has not been properly fulfilled, in operational or documentary terms. This is partly because at the time of loading, a Bill of Lading has not yet been issued and thus the buyer is not fully responsible for the shipment until the vessel has been properly loaded with the consignment. Once this has been undertaken, the buyer becomes responsible for the issuing of the Bills of Lading and thus the contract of carriage with the carrier. The seller, however, is responsible for Customs clearance and the raising of the Customs Export Declaration, which will in any case be lodged with and acknowledged by the Customs Authority prior to the consignment being loaded at port.

The other use of the FOB term is in generating export statistics. The FOB term signifies an export in terms of its value, and thus contributes to the overall data compiled by the government in support of its yearly trade balance.

C&F/CFR (Cost and Freight)

Whereas the FOB term refers to the passage of risk and responsibility for the cargo consignment from seller to buyer at the time of loading, C&F/CFR implies that the seller arranges the shipment up to the point of unloading at a named overseas port. The seller arranges the international shipment by sea and pays for the freight, as well as the cost of port handling charges at the port of loading. However, the risk and responsibility for the consignment passes from seller to buyer when the consignment is being loaded over the ship's rail on board the vessel. The buyer is responsible for insuring the consignment, as well as the carriage of the consignment from the point of loading. The seller also arranges for the issuing of all Bills of Lading, and their transfer to the buyer, as well as all Customs clearance at the point of export.

CPT (Carriage Paid To ...)

Every INCOTERM is accompanied by a named place or port. In maritime terms, the term CPT refers to the carriage of the consignment to an inland destination, usually by multimodal or intermodal transport. In this respect, the term operates in the reverse of the term FCA and implies that the consignment will be consolidated at an inland point along with other consignments into a container, transported to the port, loaded aboard a vessel, shipped to an overseas port, then unloaded and transported to an inland destination, where it will be deconsolidated at the named inland destination. The Seller arranges this total shipment and passes all responsibility and risk for it, other than the insurance of the consignment, to the buyer at the point of loading as with the Term CFR. The shipping documents raised for the consignment can be either through Bills of Lading, Container Bills of Lading or Combined Transport Bills of Lading, detailing, where appropriate, all means of transport up to the point of deconsolidation and unloading from the container, and clearance through Customs.

CIF (Cost Insurance Freight)

The term CIF is 1 of the most common terms used in the process of international trade. Like C&F, it implies that the seller arranges the international carriage of the consignment to a named port of destination but passes the risk and responsibility for the carriage of the consignment at the point of secure loading aboard the vessel, literally at the time the consignment is secured either on deck or in the ship's hold. As with the C&F term, while the seller is responsible for the loading of the vessel at the port of dispatch, the buyer is responsible for the unloading of the vessel at the port of destination. However, the main difference between C&F and CIF lies in the application of insurance. With C&F (CFR), the buyer is responsible for the arrangement of insurance of the cargo. With CIF, the seller arranges the insurance for the cargo and transfers the insurance policy to the buyer at the point of secure loading of the cargo either on the deck of the vessel or in the ship's hold, in the same manner as the transfer of risk from seller to buyer in an FOB contract, and equally under CFR terms.

The buyer then assumes responsibility for the insurance of the cargo the moment it has been securely loaded aboard the vessel. However, although the buyer may have the right to claim indemnity for the cargo in the event of loss or damage while the cargo is in the charge of the carrier, they cannot actually claim the cargo at the point of arrival until they have received a copy of the Bill of Lading, assuming that the Bill of Lading is of the negotiable form. However, should the cargo be lost or damaged in transit, the buyer has the legal right to claim compensation for the loss or damage from the carrier, as stated in the Hague-Visby and Hamburg Rules. Under the INCOTERMS 2020, the insurance requirements are based on the Institute of Cargo Insurers Clauses level C (Minimum Risks), as the unloading of the cargo from the vessel occurs at the arrival of the vessel at the port of destination. The insurance policy becomes the responsibility of the Buyer when the cargo is securely loaded aboard the vessel.

Under a CIF Contract, the buyer must have paid for the consignment in order to receive the Bills of Lading from their bank. The Bills are sent to the buyer's bank by the exporter under the payment terms "Cash Against Documents", and a Bill of Exchange is sent along with the Invoice to the buyer. The buyer is obliged to pay or make suitable credit term arrangements with the seller through the buyer's bank in order to facilitate the transfer of the Bills of Lading by the bank to the buyer. Once this transaction has been achieved, the buyer may present the Bills of Lading to the shipping agent for the transfer of the consignment. The Shipping Agent, or the Shipping Line, will only release the consignment to the buyer once the buyer has presented the agent with the Bill of Lading. In this respect, the carrier is responsible for the carriage of the consignment up to the point where the consignment is released and handed over to the buyer or the buyer's representative in the form of the import freight agent or Customs Clearance Broker. Owing to the terms of payment involved in this form of contract, the ownership or title of the consignment can pass from seller to buyer while the consignment is being carried on the high seas. The carrier must be notified of this arrangement, as they will only release the consignment at the point of arrival at the port of destination to the legal owner of the consignment. Under the terms of a charter party, the charterer of the vessel may also be the owner of the cargo, in which case the charterer must also be the holder of the Bills of Lading. Where ownership of the consignment passes from the charterer to the buyer under a CIF contract, this point of transfer must be notified to all parties concerned with the transaction, especially where responsibility for unloading the vessel is concerned.

It is also important to note that the term CIF is used for the purposes of Import Declarations to the Customs Authority at the point of import. For seafreight purposes, Import Duty is calculated based on the purchase cost of the goods, international freight costs and cargo insurance, i.e. cost, insurance and freight, and this is referred to as the Import Landed Cost.

CIP (Carriage and Insurance Paid ...)

The term CIP operates in a similar manner to the term CIF, except that the contract of carriage is less strict under CIP conditions. CIP is an intermodal term, implying that the responsibility and risk associated with the carriage of the consignment passes from seller to buyer at the point of loading of the consignment. Unlike CPT, the seller arranges the insurance of the consignment and passes the insurance policy to the buyer prior to the arrival of the consignment at its destination. As with the term CPT, through Bills of Lading may be issued, as these refer to the entire intermodal or multimodal journey, inclusive of all modes of transport up to its destination. In general, the CIP term is used predominantly with container transport, on the grounds that the container will be transported from the port of arrival to an inland destination for unloading and deconsolidating.

For insurance purposes, the term CIP means that insurance must be arranged on the basis of Institute of Cargo Insurers Clauses level A (All Risks). This is because the seller arranges the unloading of the vessel at the port of arrival and the transfer of the cargo to a designated inland clearance premises nominated by the buyer.

DAP (Delivered At [Named] Place)

The term DAP (Delivered At [Named] Place) is a new term in the INCOTERMS 2010, and, although a multimodal term, can be used for seafreight purposes. It means that the seller bears the risk and responsibility for the consignment up to the buyer's premises, and pays all freight costs and insurance up to that point, although insurance is not directly quoted in the term. The buyer is responsible for the unloading of the means of transport at his premises and also is responsible for the clearance of the consignment through Customs and the payment of all Import Duties and Taxes.

DPU (Delivered At [Named] Place Unloaded)

Under the term DPU (Delivered At Place Unloaded), a new term in the INCOTERMS 2010 replacing DAT, the responsibility and risk for the consignment passes from seller to buyer at the time the consignment has arrived at the designated terminal, be it quayside, depot, warehouse or other place of receipt other than the buyer's premises, and has been unloaded from the arriving means of transport. It therefore means that the risk and responsibility pass to the buyer once the consignment has been transferred into a warehouse either adjacent to the quay or close by, such as in a Free Zone, a Remote Transit Shed or an Inland Depot or Warehouse. In this respect, the term DPU can be used alongside CPT or CIP and is the exact opposite of the term FCA.

DDP (Delivered Duty Paid)

The term DDP means that the exporter is responsible for not only delivering the consignment to the buyer's premises, but is also responsible for the payment of Import Duties and Taxes, i.e. Sales Tax or VAT. Its other meaning is the delivery of the consignment to the buyer's premises under Free Circulation conditions, i.e. that no Import Duty is payable because the consignment is in free circulation within the EU Single Market trading bloc. However, under this term, the exporter must be able to declare the consignment to the Customs Authorities in the country of the importer, which means that they must have a declarant's reference number, implying that they must be registered with the Tax and Customs Authorities in the country of import.

Many importers and exporters often choose DDP for their shipments because traditionally it is what they have always used. Until something goes wrong, most businesses are unaware of the negative consequences that can stem from using the term DDP. The following issues are just a few examples of how a DDP shipment can create problems.

For Exporters

1. VAT (Value-Added Tax)

DDP assigns the seller/exporter the responsibility of paying the VAT (although this can be changed with the consent of buyer and seller). Value-Added Tax can be expensive, sometimes 15–25% of the value of the goods plus Import Duty. Ironically, in many cases and depending on what they do with the goods, the buyer may be eligible for a VAT refund, as VAT refunds accrue to the buyer by way of the buyer's VAT return filed with their local revenue authority. This means that, at best, the exporter has to absorb the VAT, or at worst, absorb the VAT while their customer obtains a VAT refund.

2. *Storage and Demurrage*

Under DDP, the seller must absorb the costs associated with Customs clearance. This includes any storage or demurrage charges incurred due to delays by Customs authorities, other government agencies, delivery drivers, and air/ocean carriers. Since these are unanticipated costs, they can quickly eat into the exporter's profits or completely negate them.

3. *Foreign Customs Compliance*

The exporter or seller is responsible for clearing the goods through foreign Customs. This includes complying with the foreign country's import regulations and recordkeeping requirements. The question must therefore be asked as to whether the exporter knows anything about import regulations in Brazil or Germany, or even the national import tariff of that country for the purposes of tariff classification using commodity codes that they do not understand or have not researched. It must equally be asked if the exporter would want to be held accountable with foreign Customs authorities if something goes wrong, especially if they are not registered with the tax authorities in question. If not, then it is advisable to avoid using DDP.

4. *Legal Issues*

DDP puts the exporter's business at greater legal risk if foreign bribery occurs. All it takes is 1 small bribe offered while trying to clear goods through foreign Customs (or any other agency abroad) and the exporter could be facing severe legal consequences from the overseas Department of Justice and the foreign country's government and legal system.

If the exporter's company is found violating the Foreign Corrupt Practices Act, they can expect a very expensive and public investigation courtesy of the Department of Justice, especially in the US, where anti-bribery legislation is very stringent. In addition to dealing with the DOJ back home, the exporter, especially in the US, can certainly expect the foreign government to capitalise on the opportunity to legally prosecute them for breaking the law in their country. Bribery is almost universally illegal.

For Importers

1. Penalties and Fines

When goods are shipped DDP, the seller's forwarder arranges the transport. This arrangement has the unfortunate consequence of bypassing any controls that the importer's forwarder/broker has in place to prevent the importer's Import Security File (especially in the US) and even Import Declarations from being late or incorrect. Without these controls in place, your company is exposed to some stiff penalties — in the case of the US, this can be US$5,000 per violation and up to US$10,000 per shipment. In essence, DDP requires the importer to be responsible for timely and accurate declaration filing but allows them zero control over the movement of the freight, which in itself can be quite costly if arranged by the seller. Other issues such as US Customs Bond Fees prevail, as does the whole issue of the registered Importer of Record, for which legislation is contained in national Customs legislation. In the UK, this is covered by the 1979 Customs and Excise Management Act (CEMA), and in the US by Title 19 US Code 1484. Customs legislation in most countries requires the Importer of Record to be the declarant for all imported goods that they purchase, which therefore means that the importer must be tax-registered with the revenue authority of their country. This is partly to enable the importer to reclaim Import VAT/GST on the imported consignment, but also for compliance purposes, as they will be frequently monitored for import compliance by their local Tax and Customs Authorities. If an exporter takes responsibility for the liability and payment of Import Duties and local VAT/GST, by nature of Customs legislation in the country of import, they must be tax-registered with the revenue authorities in that country.

2. Supply Chain Visibility

Since the seller and their forwarder control the inbound transportation on a DDP shipment, you, the buyer/importer, will have limited visibility and reporting, if any. Good luck trying to get any information from your seller's forwarder. They are beholden to their client, the seller, not you, the buyer.

3. Double Dip Pricing and Mark Ups

While the liability on a DDP shipment is technically upon the seller, it is frequently and erroneously passed on to the buyer/importer. This results in "double dip" pricing, where the seller has lifted their price to cover clearance costs but never pays the duty and clearance fees.

DDP also makes it easier for the seller to mark up the freight invoice. For these types of transactions, the buyer's clearance and delivery costs are included in the cost of the goods. These costs are typically marked up, in some cases very significantly. There have been documented cases of sellers marking up freight bills from US$3,000 to US$7,000. Once again, the buyer loses out.

4. Customs Examinations

When DDP is handled properly, the seller's agent in the country of import arranges clearance with the seller as the importer of record. While this removes most of the import liability from the buyer, it creates another problem: an increased likelihood of a Customs examination. In the case of the US, the Customs and Border Protection agency assigns a higher risk score to inbound shipments with foreign importers. The higher the shipment's risk score, the more likely Customs is to select the shipment for an examination. It happens quite often, and it is the buyer who inevitably loses out.

5. Delivery Delays

Even if the buyer is fortunate enough to do business with a seller that includes clearance and delivery at cost, they still have no guarantee that the seller has obtained the best price for the level of service required. To keep their costs down, many sellers will choose the lowest cost services for transportation and clearance. Cheaper transport and clearance for the seller usually translate to delivery delays for the buyer.

Freight Collect and Freight Prepaid

In the present-day era of integrated container transport from seller to buyer, the use of INCOTERMS has become a somewhat convoluted affair. There is no need for the use of some of the traditional INCOTERMS, as the responsibility and risk for the consignment do not always pass from seller to buyer at these points. The container is loaded inland and is unloaded at an inland destination away from the port. Although the terms FCA and CIP exist for this kind of operation, there are 2 terms that are more commonly and widely used for this purpose. They are "Freight Collect" and "Freight Prepaid".

Freight Collect is the term used where the buyer pays for the freight and arranges the shipment from the point of loading the container to the point of unloading.

Freight Prepaid is the term used where the seller pays for the freight and arranges the shipment from the point of loading the container to the point of unloading and passes the cost on to the buyer. Insurance may be arranged by either party.

Either term must be stated on the Bills of Lading, as it must be made completely clear which party is arranging and paying for the shipment under the terms of the Bill of Lading. It then becomes clear which party has contracted with the carrier for the carriage of the consignment.

In terms of risk level, the terms EXW to FOB are low risk with regard to logistics as far as the exporter is concerned (although EXW is high risk in terms of Customs and VAT compliance). CFR/CIF/CPT/CIP are medium risk, given the international element of these terms, while DAP/DAT/DDU are high risk. DDP in particular is high risk to the exporter, as the exporter is required to pay import duties and local sales tax on behalf of the importer, which in reality is actively discouraged by the World Customs Organisation (WCO), given that under Customs law, the importer is required to act as declarant for the purposes of Import Duty and national Sales Tax.

The converse is true for the Importer, with the following risk applications:

EXW/FCA/FAS/FOB – High Risk;
CFR/CIF/CPT/CIP – Medium Risk;
DAP/DAT/DDP – Low Risk.

However, the importer must still rely on the information contained in all commercial documents to ensure that the correct details are used on the Import Declaration for the purpose of calculating Import Duty and Sales Tax.

CHAPTER 3

Risk Management in International Trade

Every organisation faces some form of risk and must balance its attitude towards risk and reward. This is particularly so in the field of international trade, where risks can be increased owing to the international nature of business, and how commercial activities are made significantly more uncertain owing to the international nature of commerce, be it credit and finance, transport and logistics, or Customs controls. The key question is: "What is the acceptable risk?" This level of risk depends upon the type of company, its size, its market share, its vulnerability or its viability. High-risk ventures may collapse, yet they can also deliver the biggest reward. Conversely, fewer, safer and more conservative risks within an organisation may mean modest returns but long-term survival.

Where investors are concerned, they are looking for the following:

- Profitable Operations;
- Sound Background;
- Significant Return on Investment;
- Low-Risk Strategy;
- Guaranteed Returns;
- Long-term Commitment;
- Stability;
- Steady Performance;
- Optimistic Vision.

Present-day international trade risks can include:

- Supplier Reliability;
- Customer Reliability;
- Contractual Issues;
- Consignment Security;
- Cargo Security;
- Insurance;

DOI: 10.4324/9781003341345-4

- Financial Security;
- Payment Risk;
- Market Uncertainty;
- Currency Exchange;
- Freight Rate Uncertainty;
- Piracy;
- Safety and Security of Transport;
- Potential Loss;
- Damage to Cargo;
- Pilferage;
- Fraud;
- Delay;
- *Force Majeure*;
- Customs Issues;
- Trade Controls;
- Tax Issues.

Also, the degree of risk must be considered.

- Low;
- Medium;
- High.

Market uncertainty can include:

- Country of destination/dispatch;
- Political risk;
- Economic/commercial Risk;
- Currency exchange;
- Supply of and demand for products;
- Competition;
- Transparency of contract;
- Taxation and duties;
- Contract viability;
- Freight rates;
- Currency risk.

Key issues of risk management in international trade:

- Supply and demand;
- Best practice – focus on a risk management system in a trading company;

- Risk – exposure and uncertainty;
- Understanding risk appetite and how it shapes management strategy;
- Quantitative and qualitative elements in risk management evaluation and strategy;
- Strategic risks;
- Risks to products, people and systems;
- Corporate risks;
- On multiple levels and layers;
- Take account of the "big picture" and overall scenario;
- Influence of external factors;
- Take account of day-to-day operations.

Although there is no "official list" of the risks affecting the international trade sector, the most likely risk elements include:

- Strategic;
- Market;
- Credit;
- Financial;
- Operational;
- Legal;
- Organisational;
- Sovereign.

In terms of strategy, long-term performance is more difficult to assess, as the present global financial and economic uncertainties have led to caution in the shipping business. Although certain ambitious decisions have been taken in the recent past to introduce larger, more efficient vessels in several shipping sectors, including the container and Ro-Ro sectors, this means that more goods can be carried globally in a single vessel, the risks of delay, damage and overall compromise to the cargo are greater. This was borne out by the grounding of the Evergreen mega-vessel *Ever Given* in the Suez Canal in 2021, and the consequent implications for the ship itself, its cargo, and other vessels following it. The increase in container rates has significantly compromised the cost-effectiveness of international trade concerning shipping costs and the guarantee of shipping goods to the recipient markets in the required time, thus also compromising the International Supply Chain. There is still no guarantee that the introduction of mega-vessels of 20,000 TEU (Twenty-Foot Equivalent Unit) container size will be economically viable in the long term, given their size, capacity and their access to many of the world's ports.

Market risk is dependent upon the state of the international markets, in terms of products and commodities. Markets are generally driven by a combination of supply and demand, as well as elasticity based on prices and the imposition of unit taxes such as Import Duties. Market risk can also be influenced by the PESTEL factors, namely:

- **P**olitical;
- **E**conomic;
- **S**ocial;
- **T**echnological;
- **E**nvironmental;
- **L**egal.

All these factors have a part to play in determining the degree to which market entrants will succeed or fail. Much of the success of a marketing strategy depends upon the level of research conducted by a company prior to entering that market. Success or failure is largely determined by the level of research conducted by companies into the potential entry of a product into the market, and what actions must be taken to make the product concerned suitable for the market for which it is destined.

Credit risk concerns the ability of the seller to be paid based on customer credit. Credit research is required where a potential customer wishes to buy a product from a supplier, as the supplier must ensure that they have undertaken sufficient due diligence to ensure that there is little or no risk concerning the ability of the potential customer to pay for the goods. In such cases, credit finance and insurance can be arranged, but it is a costly exercise, as the provider of such credit facilities needs to be sure that the credit is based on a firm guarantee of payment. Factoring companies have become a major element of such credit finance, but in some cases, such as Greensill, such activities have become much less certain and have led to the failure of the financing company. Credit risk is generally linked with financial risk, i.e. the risk that the financial liquidity of either seller or buyer may at some point be severely compromised, owing to loans, debts or financial loss.

Operational risk concerns the ability to supply goods according to the demands of the customer. In many cases, the potential customer requires such quantities that would compromise the operational efficiency or productivity of the supplier concerned. In such cases, it might be difficult for the supplier to meet the demands of the customer in terms of capacity to produce. Indeed, the availability of the product may be limited owing to the sheer demands placed on such suppliers because of market demands. Such factors are the main elements of procurement strategy on the part of the buyer, namely:

- Price;
- Quantity required;

- Quality;
- Capacity;
- Availability.

Legal risk concerns the nature of the contract of sale and the degree to which either party is able to commit to the contract and abide by it. The laws of the Sale of Goods are very specific and generally encompass specific issues, including the Implied Terms and Specific Performance. In English law, as part of the 1979 Sale of Goods Act, these are:

- Section 12 – Title over the Goods;
- Section 13 – Description;
- Section 14 – Quality and Fitness;
- Section 15 – Sale by Sample.

Where there is a breach of contract, i.e. a breach of condition, the injured party is entitled to compensation, mostly by financial means such as monetary compensation. A breach of warranty is considered to be less significant and may be remedied by specific performance on the part of the seller.

Most national laws take these terms into account, although the structure of the pertinent national laws may differ from 1 country to another.

Organisational risk concerns the management of both the organisation as a trading entity and its ability to trade with other companies. Some of this ability is governed by the Viable Systems Model (VSM) of the cybernetician Stafford Beer, who defined 5 elements, namely:

- Departmental activity and communication;
- Inter-departmental activity and communication;
- Company organisation (including monitoring and auditing);
- Externalities;
- Overall company mission and policy.

Within these 5 factors, challenges and adversities can conspire to destabilise this structure, but overall, a successful organisation is 1 that can co-ordinate and control these activities to the point of maximum operational efficiency.

There are essentially 3 specific categories concerning the chances and consequences of risk occurring in international trade, and these identify the essential processes of risk management:

- Risk identification – Identifying the threats to the organisation and its day-to-day operations;

- Risk measurement and evaluation – Categorising risks within the company's overall hierarchy of threats, ranging from absolute to relative;
- Risk management actions – Strategic and operational changes to contain risks within acceptable bounds.

Risk management in trade concerns the concepts behind international trade risk and strategies that trading companies can evaluate. It assesses, in turn each of the major risk sectors faced in shipping and concludes with thoughts on potential best practice.

One logical starting point in any aspect of risk management is to model and evaluate the "do nothing strategy", also considered as the "Null Hypothesis". There will be instances when this is an acceptable approach and might even be the best approach. The "doing something" strategy effectively creates a process of strategic and operational changes, plus risk transfer, that leads to risk being brought within the acceptable risk parameters, being measurable, and being controllable.

It can also can explain the ways in which proactive risk management can lead to strategic changes that bring profound additional benefits for businesses.

Effective risk management solutions should encompass:

Practical changes in the operation of the vessel and the company with relation to the particular threats identified;

Evaluation of the financial impact of changes and consideration of appropriate risk transfer through insurance;

"What if ...?" scenarios should be enacted and contingency plans drawn up by risk managers.

Current globalisation trends in the global economy and trade, as well as integration processes, have significantly aggravated and exacerbated competition and have consequently complicated the nature of the foreign economic interactions of companies from different countries, especially where the level of economic development in such countries differs from country to country. At the same time, the ambiguity and lack of transparency in the development of these processes are expressed by the increased degree of probability of the influence of numerous uncertainty factors in international markets, generating a set of specific foreign trade risks and financial losses exacerbated by currency fluctuation and credit risk to which most foreign and domestic companies engaged in foreign economic activity are exposed.

Despite the fact that most of the risks of international trade are formed in a competitive market environment, they are also due to other reasons. In particular, issues pertaining to the economic and political instability in the development of individual countries and military conflicts in various international regions, coupled with global terrorism and security risks, expand the boundaries of risk factors and at the same time increase the scale of the monetary and financial losses of foreign companies operating there. The global financial and economic crises, exacerbating the instability of the situation and position of companies in international markets, have a significant impact on the modern environment of global trade risks. Along with this, the subjects of foreign economic activity, providing the most profitable direction of international integration, are objectively associated with in-country production, business and management risks that complement the systemic risks of international trade.

The realisation of the interests of the subjects of contractual legal relations implies the possibility of obtaining not only a positive result in the form of achieving the desired good, usually profit, but also the possibility of unprofitable consequences such as financial loss. This is especially pronounced in the sphere of international commodity exchange, which is characterised by the greatest degree of uncertainty, the complexity of trade relations, invariance, multifactor and dynamism, where commodity prices fluctuate on a daily basis.

Modern economic relations cannot exist chaotically, i.e. outside the framework of legal regulation. To this extent, the importance of developing the category of "risk", i.e. contract risk, is emphasised, and looking through the prism allows the individual to effectively manage activities in the product market in conditions of scenario uncertainty. It also makes it possible to evaluate from a new angle the legal structures and legal means available from the point of view of their economic feasibility. Foreign trade risk is only included in the system of contractual risks when it is potentially managed by a foreign trade contract. This goal is achieved by influencing not only the risk factor but also minimising it by numerous contractual and financial means.

Risk is often characterised by an attitude or approach toward potential events and consequences, or a combination of them, and risk is described as a combination of the consequences of an event … and its associated probability. For example, let us suppose that a major company relies on the supply of a specific commodity. Without warning, supplies of that commodity are cut off owing to a major environmental catastrophe. The impact of this adversity relates not only to the collapse in the supply of this commodity but also to the sudden increase in global prices of the commodity concerned. Therefore, the elements of risk are also the probability and sources of risk. Thus, risk can be described as a combination of the following elements:

- Event – incident or accident;
- Consequences;
- Probability of occurrence;
- Source of risk – risk element.

In other words, to identify the risk, it is necessary to consider the event that may happen (the level of uncertainty is characterised by the probability of occurrence) due to the presence of sources of risk, and also to predict its possible consequences. These consequences, in turn, will affect personal and organisational goals.

The classification of risk analysis methods is associated with the stages of the risk assessment process:

- Risk identification;
- Risk analysis – analysis of the consequences;
- Risk analysis – a qualitative, mixed or quantitative assessment of the probabilistic characteristics of the risk, i.e. the level of probability of the occurrence of the risk concerned;
- Risk analysis – assessment of the effectiveness of existing controls;
- Risk analysis – a quantitative assessment of the level of risk;
- Comparative risk assessment.

For each stage of the risk assessment process, the applicability of the risk assessment method is determined on a scale; i.e. it is strictly applicable, applicable and not applicable. If it is not applicable, the process should not be performed. Where it is strictly applicable, strict methods of analysis must be performed in order to assess and manage the risk accordingly. For example, transport risk analysis infers that all methods of transport must be considered, along with their costs and suitability. No company is going to use sea freight if the movement of the cargo is time-sensitive. However, if the cost or quantity factors are significant elements in the transport of goods, then sea freight becomes a more viable option. The international supply is subject to market and economic elasticity, and under such conditions cost and time factors are significant elements of this approach.

It is therefore prudent to consider the method for risks of international trade contracts, namely the bow-tie analysis.

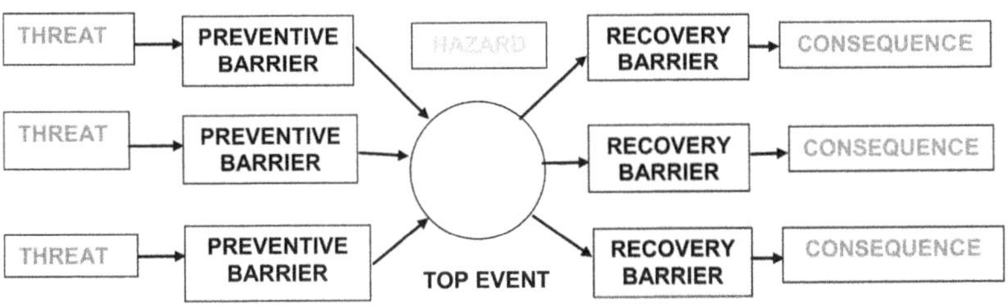

A typical bow-tie analysis.

Bow-tie analysis is a schematic way of describing and analysing the path of a dangerous event from cause to effect. This method combines the investigation of the causes of an event using a fault tree and the analysis of consequences using an event tree. However, the focus of the bow-tie method is focused on the barriers between causes and dangerous events and dangerous events and results. Bow-tie diagrams can be built on the basis of identified faults and event trees, but more often they are made directly in the process of brainstorming.

A bow-tie analysis is used to study risk based on a demonstration of a range of possible causes and consequences. The method should be used in situations where it is difficult to conduct a full analysis of the fault tree or when the study is more focused on creating barriers or controls for each failure path.

Bow-tie analysis is a schematic way of describing and analysing the path of a dangerous event from cause to effect. This method combines the investigation of the causes of an event using a fault tree and the analysis of consequences using an event tree. However, the focus of the bow-tie method is focused on the barriers between causes and dangerous events and dangerous events and results. Bow-tie diagrams can be built on the basis of identified faults and event trees, but more often they are made directly in the process of brainstorming.

The method can be useful in situations where there are well-established independent paths leading to failure.

Bow-tie analysis is often much easier to understand than an event tree or fault tree analysis, and therefore it can be useful for exchanging information using less complex methods.

The input to the method is information on the causes and consequences of hazardous events, risks, barriers and controls that can prevent, mitigate or stimulate them.

A bow-tie analysis should be constructed in accordance with the following procedure:

a) Identify the hazardous event selected for study and display it as the central node of the bow-tie;
b) Listing the causes of an event by examining the sources of risk (or danger);
c) Identification of a hazard development mechanism prior to a critical incident;
d) Drawing a line separating the cause from the event allows the creator to form the left side of the butterfly. Additionally, factors that can lead to the escalation of dangerous activity and its consequences can be identified and included in the diagram;
e) Drawing or defining vertical barriers across the line corresponding to obstacles to prevent undesirable effects. If factors are identified that

can trigger an escalation of a hazardous event, then additional restrictions can be presented to avoid such an escalation. This approach can be used for positive consequences when the barriers reflect the controls that stimulate the appearance and development of the event;

f) Identification on the right side of the butterfly of the various consequences of dangerous activity and drawing of lines connecting the central event with each possible result;
g) Image of barriers as barriers to the aftermath. This approach can be used for positive consequences when the boundaries reflect the means of control that ensure the appearance of favourable results;
h) Display under the bow-tie diagram the auxiliary controls related to restrictions (such as training and checks), and connect them to the appropriate authorities.

In the bow-tie diagram, some types of quantitative assessments can be applied, for example, in a situation where the paths are independent and the probability of specific consequences or results is known. Such a quantitative assessment is necessary to ensure management effectiveness. However, it must be noted that in many situations, the paths and barriers are interdependent, and the controls can be associated with the chosen evaluation method. Therefore, the management effectiveness is uncertain.

The output of the method is a simple diagram showing the main paths of hazardous events and the barriers established to prevent or mitigate unwanted consequences and/or enhance and accelerate the expected effects.

The benefits of the bow-tie analysis method are as follows:

- The process provides a clear, simple and precise graphical representation of the problem;
- The method is focused on controls aimed at preventing and/or reducing the consequences of dangerous or harmful events and assessing their effectiveness;
- The technique can be applied with regard to beneficial effects;
- The application of the method does not require the involvement of highly qualified experts.

The disadvantages of the method are as follows:

- The method does not allow the display of the totality of causes that arise simultaneously and result in consequences;
- The method can present complex situations in an overly simplified form, especially when applying any form of quantitative assessment.

In order to understand how these elements are interconnected, the example can be further used of a company that decides to involve a contractor operating in another country with significantly lower operating costs in providing customer support services. The main risk will be that regular customers may not like the quality of services, and they may terminate the contract.

If an enterprise involves another company with a completely different business culture in rendering customer support services, or if there are flaws in the contract that limit the influence of the company on the quality of the services provided, these 2 elements, either individually or in combination with other factors, may lead to adverse events, i.e. the loss of a regular customer, which can be seen as having a high impact.

Both of these factors also have a substantial effect on the likelihood of an event occurring. For example, with an insufficient assessment of the contract, the probability of customer dissatisfaction with the quality of services is much higher. Similarly, if an enterprise or organisation engages a company from a country with which it is familiar, the likelihood of an adverse outcome will be lower than in a situation where both sources of risk are present. In this case, risk is governed by prior knowledge, with the risk level commensurate with the level of prior knowledge about the target country in question. For example, when trading with the EU, it is more likely that a customer located in the UK knows more about trading with suppliers located in the Republic of Ireland or the Netherlands than they do about suppliers located in Bulgaria or Romania.

In this case, even if both sources of risk are present, there is no certainty that the event will occur. If something is already known – if we are confident that customers will be disappointed – then this is not a risk, it is a fact. If an event occurs, its consequences will be the loss of a regular customer (direct costs) or damage to the reputation of the company.

Consequently, the enterprise may decide to implement a risk management strategy to minimise the effect of uncertainty on the organisation's goals and objectives.

The use of risk management tools will allow the decision-maker to:

1) Avoid opportunity costs;
2) Avoid direct costs;
3) Take precautionary measures commensurate with the risks.

A company may consider several alternative strategies:

- Employ a contractor (accept risk);
- Employ a sub-contractor (transfer risk);
- Attract a contractor while maintaining control over business processes (mitigate risk);

- Provide the service themselves (avoid the risks associated with attracting contractors).

It should be noted that in the case of the employment of contractors or subcontractors, specific terms and conditions will apply to such contracts, as such contracts are often subject to employment law, which, for international purposes, may be more complex and bureaucratic depending upon the nature of the contract, thus inducing greater risk depending upon the risk options applicable.

Risk management, as already stated, is a prerequisite to achieve organisational goals and objectives. This, in turn, requires the systematic implementation of processes, including legal implications, to reduce or avoid potential or actual risks wherever possible.

CHAPTER 4

Introduction to Financial Ratios

Much of international trade and, for that matter, Customs and VAT scrutiny, concerns the company's financial stability. In terms of international trade, this affects and is affected by issues such as borrowing and cashflow, as well as credit terms and the ability of the company to operate in cases of longer-term credit such as 90 or 120 days' credit. This can be exacerbated by currency exchange risks or, at worst, customer default, and even adversities such as the recent COVID-19 pandemic.

HMRC, like any national Revenue Authority, also takes an interest in company liquidity, as any company applying for a Duty or VAT Relief must be able to show by way of its balance sheet and profit and loss account that it is capable of paying Duty (Customs or Excise) and VAT on default in cases of non-compliance, often by way of default payments against its Deferment Account. It also may need to supply a financial guarantee to support this, and it may be the case that a guarantee is especially required where the company's financial liquidity status does not satisfy HMRC requirements. For this reason, HMRC requires the company concerned to be able to pay any outstanding Customs or Excise actual or potential debt immediately where anomalies or non-compliances have occurred in the company's transactions, be they import, export or excise.

To this extent, HMRC, or any other national Revenue Authority, will examine the company's accounts over a period of 3 years to ascertain the company's financial status. This will enable the Revenue Authority to determine the financial risk of the company in terms of its ability to pay any outstanding debts to the Revenue Authority as required. Assuming that the risk is low, the company is more than likely to be approved for any particular activity, be it Excise Bonded Warehousing, Customs Warehousing or Inward Processing Relief (IP). High financial risk makes such approvals much less likely.

The other side of this policy is that the examination of financial ratios enables the trader to determine the following:

- Working capital;
- Financial liquidity.

DOI: 10.4324/9781003341345-5

This is especially important when determining the potential liability if a potential Customs debt becomes an actual debt and becomes liable for payment. If there is no working capital in the company, then the likelihood of payment of that debt is minimal. However, if the company is financially significantly liquid and holds an equally significant level of working capital, any liabilities incurred through excess duties are much easier to sustain and settle.

When computing financial ratios and when doing other financial statement analysis, always keep in mind that the financial statements reflect the accounting principles. This means that assets are generally not reported at their current value. It is also likely that many brand names and unique product lines will not be included among the assets reported on the balance sheet, even though they may be the most valuable of all the items owned by a company.

These examples are signs that financial ratios and financial statement analysis have limitations. It is also important to realise that an impressive financial ratio in 1 industry might be viewed as less than impressive in a different industry.

The explanation of financial ratios and financial statement analysis is organised as follows:

- **Balance sheet:**
  - General discussion;
  - Common-size balance sheet;
  - Financial ratios based on the balance sheet.
- **Income statement:**
  - General discussion;
  - Common-size income statement;
  - Financial ratios based on the income statement.
- **Statement of cash flows.**

General Discussion of the Balance Sheet

The balance sheet reports a company's assets, liabilities and stockholders' equity as of a specific date, such as 31 December 2020, 31 March 2021, etc.

The accountants' cost principle and the monetary unit assumption will limit the assets reported on the balance sheet. Assets will be reported:

(1) Only if they were acquired in a transaction; and
(2) Generally in an amount that is not greater than the asset's cost at the time of the transaction.

This means that a company's creative and effective management team will not be listed as an asset. Similarly, a company's outstanding reputation, its unique product lines, and brand names developed within the company will not be reported on the balance sheet. As you may surmise, these items are often the most valuable of all the things owned by the company. (Brand names purchased from another company will be recorded in the company's accounting records at their cost.)

The accountants' matching principle will result in assets such as buildings, equipment, furnishings, fixtures, vehicles, etc. being reported at amounts less than cost. The reason is that these assets are depreciated. Depreciation reduces an asset's book value each year, and the amount of the reduction is reported as depreciation expense on the income statement.

While depreciation is reducing the book value of certain assets over their useful lives, the current value (or fair market value) of these assets may actually be increasing. (It is also possible that the current value of some assets – such as computers – may be decreasing faster than the book value.)

Current assets such as cash, accounts receivable, inventory, supplies, prepaid insurance, etc. usually have current values that are close to the amounts reported on the balance sheet.

Current liabilities such as notes payable (due within 1 year), accounts payable, wages payable, interest payable, unearned revenues, etc. are also likely to have current values that are close to the amounts reported on the balance sheet.

Long-term liabilities such as notes payable (not due within 1 year) or bonds payable (not maturing within 1 year) will often have current values that *differ* from the amounts reported on the balance sheet.

Stockholders' equity is the **book value of the company**. It is the difference between the reported amount of assets and the reported amount of liabilities. For the reasons mentioned above, the reported amount of stockholders' equity will therefore be different from the current or market value of the company.

Example:

Company Balance

Sheet 31 December 2014

ASSETS		**LIABILITIES**	
Current Assets		**Current Liabilities**	
Cash	$2,100	Notes Payable	$5,000
Petty Cash	$100	Accounts Payable	$35,900
Temporary Investments	10,000	Wages Payable	8,500
Accounts Receivable – net	40,500	Interest Payable	2,900
Inventory	31,000	Taxes Payable	6,100

Supplies	3,800	Warranty Liability	1,100
Prepaid Insurance	1,500	Unearned Revenues	1,500
	-----------		----------
Total Current Assets	**89,000**	**Total Current Liabilities**	**61,000**
	-----------		----------
Investments	36,000	Long-Term Liabilities	
	---------	Notes Payable	20,000
		Bonds Payable	400,000
Property, Plant and Equipment			----------
Land	5,500	Total Long-Term Liabilities	420,000
Land Improvements	6,500		----------
Buildings	180,000	**TOTAL LIABILITIES**	**481,000**
Equipment	201,000		----------
Less: Accumulated Depreciation	(56,000)	**STOCKHOLDERS' EQUITY**	
	------------	Common Stock	110,000
Property, Plant and Equipment – net	337,000	Retained Earnings	229,000
	------------	Less: Treasury Stock	(50,000)
Intangible Assets			-----------
Goodwill	105,000		
Trade Names	200,000	**TOTAL STOCKHOLDERS' EQUITY 289,000**	

Total Intangible Assets	305,000	**TOTAL LIABILITIES and STOCKHOLDERS' EQUITY**	**770,000**

Other Assets	3,000		----------

TOTAL ASSETS	**770,000**		

By definition, the current assets and current liabilities are "turning over" at least once per year. As a result, the reported amounts are likely to be similar to their current value. The long-term assets and long-term liabilities are *not* "turning over" often. Therefore, the amounts reported for long-term assets and long-term liabilities will likely be different from the current value of those items.

The remainder of our explanation of financial ratios and financial statement analysis will use information from the following balance sheet.

Financial Ratios Based on the Balance Sheet

Financial statement analysis includes financial ratios. The following are 3 financial ratios that are based solely on current asset and current liability amounts appearing on a company's balance sheet.

FINANCIAL RATIO	HOW TO CALCULATE IT	WHAT IT TELLS YOU
Working Capital Ratio	= Current Assets – Current Liabilities = **$28,000**	An indicator of whether the company will be able to meet its current obligations (pay its bills, meet its payroll, make a loan payment, etc.). If a company has current assets exactly equal to current liabilities, it has no working capital. The greater the amount of working capital, the more likely it will be able to make its payments on time.
Current Ratio	= Current Assets / Current Liabilities = $89,000 / $61,000 = **1.46**	This tells you the relationship of current assets to current liabilities. A ratio of 3:1 is better than 2:1. A 1:1 ratio means that there is no working capital.
Quick Ratio (Acid Test Ratio)	= [(Cash + Temp. Investments + Accounts Receivable) / Current Liabilities] : 1 = [($2,100 + $100 + $10,000 + $40,500) / $61,000] : 1 = [$52,700 / $61,000] : 1 = **0.86 : 1**	This ratio is similar to the current ratio except that Inventory, Supplies, and Prepaid Expenses are excluded. This indicates the relationship between the amount of assets that can quickly be turned into cash versus the amount of current liabilities.

Four financial ratios relate balance sheet amounts for Accounts Receivable and Inventory to income statement amounts. To illustrate these financial ratios, the following income statement information is used.

Example Enterprise

Income Statement

Year ended 31 December 2014

Sales	$500,000
Cost of Goods sold	380,000

GROSS PROFIT	120,000

Operating Expenses	
Selling Expenses	35,000
Administrative Expenses	45,000

	80,000

Operating Income (120,000–80,000)	40,000
Interest Expense	12,000

Income before Taxes	28,000
Income Tax	5,000

Net Income after Taxes	$23,000
	========

FINANCIAL RATIO	*HOW TO CALCULATE IT*	*WHAT IT TELLS YOU*
Accounts Receivable Turnover	= Net Credit Sales for the Year / Average Accounts Receivable for the Year = \$500,000 / \$42,000 (a computed average) **= 11.90**	The number of times per year that the accounts receivables turn over. Keep in mind that the result is an average since credit sales and accounts receivable are likely to fluctuate during the year. It is important to use the average balance of accounts receivable during the year.
Days' Sales in Accounts Receivable	= 365 Days in Year / Accounts Receivable Turnover in Year = 365 Days / **11.90 = 30.67 Days**	The average number of days that it took to collect the average amount of accounts receivable during the year. This statistic is only as good as the Accounts Receivable Turnover figure.
Inventory Turnover	= Cost of Goods Sold for the Year / Average Inventory for the Year = \$380,000 / \$30,000 (a computed average) **= 12.67**	The number of times per year that inventory turns over. Keep in mind that the result is an *average*, since sales and inventory levels are likely to fluctuate during the year. Since inventory is at cost (not sales value), it is important to use the Cost of Goods Sold. Also, be sure to use the average balance of inventory during the year.
Days' Sales in Inventory	= 365 Days in Year / Inventory Turnover in Year = 365 Days / 12.67 **= 28.81**	The average number of days that it took to sell the *average* inventory during the year. This statistic is only as good as the Inventory Turnover figure.

The next financial ratio involves the relationship between 2 amounts from the balance sheet: total liabilities and total stockholders' equity.

Common-Size Balance Sheet

One technique in financial statement analysis is known as vertical analysis. Vertical analysis results in common-size financial statements. A common-size balance sheet is a balance sheet where every dollar amount has been restated to be a percentage of total assets. We will illustrate this by taking Example Company's balance sheet (shown above) and dividing each item by the total asset amount of $770,000. The result is the common-size balance sheet for Example Company.

Example:

Company Common-Size Balance

Sheet 31 December 2014

ASSETS		**LIABILITIES**	
Current Assets		**Current Liabilities**	
Cash	0.3%	Notes Payable	0.6%
Petty Cash	0.0%	Accounts Payable	4.7%
Temporary Investments	1.3%	Wages Payable	1.1%
Accounts Receivable – net	5.3%	Interest Payable	0.4%
Inventory	4.0%	Taxes Payable	0.8%
Supplies	0.5%	Warranty Liability	0.1%
Prepaid Insurance	0.2%	Unearned Revenues	0.2%
	-----------		----------
Total Current Assets	**11.6%**	**Total Current Liabilities**	**7.9%**
	-----------		----------
Investments	4.7%	Long-Term Liabilities Notes Payable	2.6%
	---------	Bonds Payable	52.0%
Property, Plant, and Equipment			----------
Land	0.7%	Total Long-Term Liabilities	54.6%
Land Improvements	0.8%		----------
Buildings	23.4%	**TOTAL LIABILITIES**	62.5%
Equipment	26.1%		----------
Less: Accumulated Depreciation	(7.3%)	**STOCKHOLDERS' EQUITY**	
	------------	Common Stock	14.3%
Property, Plant, and Equipment – net	43.7%	Retained Earnings	29.7%
	------------	Less: Treasury Stock	(6.5%)
Intangible Assets Goodwill	13.6%		----------
Trade Names	26.0%	**TOTAL STOCKHOLDERS' EQUITY**	**37.5%**

Total Intangible Assets	39.6%	**TOTAL LIABILITIES and STOCKHOLDERS' EQUITY**	**100.0%**

Other Assets	0.4%		----------

TOTAL ASSETS	**100.0%**		

The benefit of a common-size balance sheet is that an item can be compared to a similar item of another company regardless of the size of the companies. A company can also compare its percentages to the industry's average percentages. For example, a company with Inventory at 4.0% of total assets can look to its industry statistics to see if its percentage is reasonable. (Industry percentages might be available from an industry association, library reference desks, and from bankers. Many banks have memberships in Risk Management Association (RMA), an organisation that collects and distributes statistics by industry.)

A common-size balance sheet also allows 2 business-persons to compare the magnitude of a balance sheet item without either revealing the actual dollar amounts.

General Discussion of Income Statement

The income statement has some limitations since it reflects accounting principles. For example, a company's depreciation expense is based on the cost of the assets it has acquired and is using in its business. The resulting depreciation expense may not be a good indicator of the economic value of the asset being used up. To illustrate this point let's assume that a company's buildings and equipment have been fully depreciated, and therefore there will be no depreciation expense for those buildings and equipment on its income statement. Is zero expense a good indicator of the cost of using those buildings and equipment? Compare that situation to a company with new buildings and equipment, where there will be large amounts of depreciation expense.

The remainder of our explanation of financial ratios and financial statement analysis will use information from the following income statement.

Example Corporation

Income Statement

Year ended 31 December 2014

Sales	$500,000
Cost of Goods sold	380,000

GROSS PROFIT	120,000

Operating Expenses	
Selling Expenses	35,000
Administrative Expenses	45,000

	80,000

Operating Income (120,000–80,000)	40,000
Interest Expense	12,000

Income before Taxes	28,000
Income Tax	5,000

Net Income after Taxes	$23,000
	========
Earnings per Share	$ 0.23
(based on 100,000 Shares outstanding)	========

Common-Size Income Statement

Financial statement analysis includes a technique known as vertical analysis. Vertical analysis results in common-size financial statements. A common-size income statement presents all of the income statement amounts as a percentage of net sales. Below is Example Corporation's common-size income statement after each item from the income statement above was divided by the net sales of $500,000.

Example Corporation

Common-Size Income

Statement Year ended 31 December 2014

Sales	100%
Cost of Goods Sold	76%

GROSS PROFIT	24%

Operating Expenses Selling Expenses	7%
Administrative Expenses	9%

	16%

Operating Income (120,000–80,000)	8%
Interest Expense	2.4%

Income before Taxes	5.6%
Income Tax	1.0%

Net Income after Taxes	4.6%
	======

The percentages shown for Example Corporation can be compared to other companies and to the industry averages. Industry averages can be obtained from trade associations, bankers, and library reference desks. If a company competes with a company whose stock is publicly traded, another source of information is that company's "Management's Discussion and Analysis of Financial Condition and Results of Operations" contained in its annual report to the Securities and Exchange Commission (SEC). This annual report is the SEC Form 10-K and is usually accessible under the "Investor Relations" tab on the corporation's website.

Financial Ratios Based on the Income Statement

FINANCIAL RATIO	*HOW TO CALCULATE IT*	*WHAT IT TELLS YOU*
Gross Margin	= Gross Profit / Net Sales = $120,000 / $500,000 **= 24.0%**	Indicates the percentage of sales dollars available for expenses and profit after the cost of merchandise is deducted from sales. The gross margin varies between industries and often varies between companies within the same industry.
Profit Margin (after tax)	= Net Income after Tax / Net Sales = $23,000 / $500,000 **= 4.6%**	Gives the profit per sales dollar after all expenses are deducted from sales. This margin will vary between industries as well as between companies in the same industry.
Earnings per Share	= Net Income after Tax / Weighted Average Number of Common Shares Outstanding = $23,000 / 100,000 **= $0.23**	Expresses the corporation's net income after taxes on a per-share of common stock basis. The computation requires the deduction of preferred dividends from the net income if a corporation has preferred stock. It also requires the weighted average number of shares of common stock during the period of the net income.
Times Interest Earned	= Earnings for the Year before Interest and Income Tax Expense / Interest Expense for the Year = $40,000 / $12,000 **= 3.3**	Indicates a company's ability to meet the interest payments on its debt. In the example, the company is earning 3.3 times the amount it is required to pay its lenders for interest.
Return on Stockholders' Equity (after tax)	= Net Income for the Year after Taxes / Average Stockholders' Equity during the Year = $23,000 / $278,000 (a computed average) **= 8.3%**	Reveals the percentage of profit after income taxes that the corporation earned on its *average common* stockholders' balances during the year. If a corporation has preferred stock, the preferred dividends must be deducted from the net income.

Statement of Cash Flows

The statement of cash flows is a relatively new financial statement in comparison to the income statement or the balance sheet. This may explain why there are not as many well-established financial ratios associated with the statement of cash flows.

The following cash flow statement for Example Corporation is used to illustrate a limited financial statement analysis.

Example Corporation

Statement of Cash Flows for the Year Ended 31 December 2014

Cash Flow from Operating	
Activities Net Income	$23,000
Add: Depreciation Expense	$4,000
Increase in Accounts Receivable	$(6,000)
Decrease in Inventory	$9,000
Decrease in Accounts Payable	$(5,000)

Cash provided (used) in operating activities	$25,000

Cash Flow from Investing Activities	
Capital Expenditures	$(28,000)
Proceeds from Sale of Property	$7,000

Cash provided (used) by Investing Activities	$(21,000)

Cash Flow from Financing Activities	
Borrowings of Long-Term Debt	$10,000
Cash Dividends	$(5,000)
Purchase of Treasury Stock	$(8,000)

Cash provided (used) by Financing Activities	$(3,000)

Net Increase in Cash	$1,000
Cash at the beginning of the year	$1,200
Cash at the end of the year	$2,200
	=======

FINANCIAL RATIO	*HOW TO CALCULATE IT*	*WHAT IT TELLS YOU*
Free Cash Flow	= Cash Flow provided by Operating Activities – Capital Expenditures = $25,000 – $28,000 **= ($3,000)**	This statistic tells you how much cash is left over from operations after a company pays for its capital expenditures (additions to property, plant and equipment). There can be variations of this calculation. For example, some would only deduct capital expenditures to keep the present level of capacity. Others would also deduct dividends that are paid to stockholders since they are assumed to be a requirement.

The cash flow from operating activities section of the statement of cash flows is also used by some analysts to assess the quality of a company's earnings. For a company's earnings to be of "quality", the amount of cash flow from operating activities must be consistently greater than the company's net income. The reason is that under accrual accounting, various estimates and assumptions are made regarding both revenues and expenses. When it comes to cash, however, the money is either in the bank or it isn't. And it is likely that the company does not hold vast reserves of cash in its corporate safes on-site.

FINANCIAL RATIO	*HOW TO CALCULATE IT*	*WHAT IT TELLS YOU*
Debt to Equity	= (Total Liabilities / Total Stockholders' Equity) : 1 **= 1.66.1**	The proportion of a company's assets supplied by the company's creditors versus the amount supplied by the owner or stockholders. In this example, the creditors have supplied $1.66 for each $1.00 supplied by the stockholders.

For companies such as importers and distributors, large amounts of stock held in storage are classed as liabilities, not assets. They have been purchased but have not yet been sold, and the longer they stay on storage shelves, the more they depreciate in value, meaning that the sales value diminishes, leading to less actual sales revenue. This also means that any Import Duty paid on such stocks amounts to "dead" money, in that it may not be redeemed for some time, thus resulting in long-term liabilities. Import Duties must be added to the cost of sales on the Profit and Loss Account, thus resulting in lower gross profits. For imported consignment stocks, the importer, i.e. the stockholder or distributor, does not own the goods at the time of import, and therefore cannot reclaim any Import VAT incurred on the import given that the company in question still acts as importer of record and must declare the goods to the Customs Authority and hence pay Import Duty and VAT on the consignment unless they are approved for Customs Warehousing. In such cases, Import Duty and VAT are suspended until the goods are released to the customer, and such Import Duty and VAT are assigned to each customer at the point of release from the warehouse, given that the goods are actually sold to the respective customers in the warehouse prior to release into Free Circulation.

Liquidity

Liquidity is a very critical part of a business and is required for a business to meet its short-term obligations. Liquidity ratios are a measure of the ability of a company to pay off its short-term liabilities.

Liquidity ratios determine how quickly a company can convert its assets and use them for meeting the dues that arise. The higher the ratio, the easier is the ability to clear the debts and avoid defaulting on payments.

This is a very important criterion that creditors check before offering short-term loans to the business. An organisation that is unable to clear dues results in creating an impact on its creditworthiness and also affects the credit rating of the company.

Types of Liquidity Ratio

There are the following types of liquidity ratios:

1. Current ratio or working capital ratio;
2. Quick ratio, also known as acid test ratio;
3. Cash ratio, also known cash asset ratio or absolute liquidity ratio;
4. Net working capital ratio.

Current Ratio or Working Capital Ratio

The current ratio is a measure of a company's ability to pay off its obligations within the next 12 months. This ratio is used by creditors to evaluate whether a company can be offered short-term debts. It also provides information about the company's operating cycle. It is also popularly known as working capital ratio. It is obtained by dividing the current assets by current liabilities.

Current ratio is calculated as follows:

Current ratio = Current Assets / Current Liabilities

A higher current ratio around 2 is suggested to be ideal for most industries, while a lower value (less than 1) is indicative of a firm having difficulty in meeting its current liabilities.

Quick Ratio or Acid Test Ratio

Quick ratio, also known as acid test ratio, is used to determine whether a company or a business has enough liquid assets that can be instantly converted into cash to meet short-term dues. It is calculated by dividing the liquid current assets by the current liabilities.

It is represented as

Quick Ratio = (Cash + Marketable securities + Accounts receivable) / Current liabilities

The ideal quick ratio should be 1:1 for a financially stable company.

Cash Ratio or Absolute Liquidity Ratio

Cash ratio is a measure of a company's liquidity that assesses whether the company has the ability to clear off debts solely using the liquid assets (cash and cash equivalents such as marketable securities). It is used by creditors to determine the relative ease with which a company can clear short-term liabilities.

It is calculated by dividing the cash and cash equivalents by the current liabilities.

Cash ratio = Cash and equivalent / Current liabilities

Net Working Capital Ratio

The net working capital ratio is used to determine whether a company has sufficient cash or funds to continue its operations. It is calculated by subtracting the current liabilities from the current assets.

Net Working Capital Ratio = Current Assets – Current Liabilities

Liquidity Ratio Formula

The following are the important liquidity ratio formulas in a tabular format.

Liquidity Ratios	*Formula*
Current Ratio	Current Assets / Current Liabilities
Quick Ratio	(Cash + Marketable securities + Accounts receivable) / Current liabilities
Cash Ratio	Cash and equivalent / Current liabilities
Net Working Capital Ratio	Current Assets – Current Liabilities

Importance of Liquidity Ratio

Here are some of the important aspects of liquidity ratios:

1. It helps to understand the availability of cash in a company, which determines the short-term financial position of the company. A higher number is indicative of a sound financial position, while lower numbers show signs of financial distress;
2. It also shows how efficiently the company is able to convert inventories into cash. It determines the way a company operates in the market;
3. It helps in organising the company's working capital requirements by studying the levels of cash or liquid assets available at a certain time.

CHAPTER 5

Exporting and Importing Consignments

Essential International Trade Risk

As part of an analysis of risk management in Customs and international trade, it is useful to examine the overall risks involved in the process of international trade, prior to looking specifically at Customs and compliance issues. International trade is regarded as the overall process of trade-related activities, i.e. exporting (international sales) and importing (international purchases). However, it is also fraught with a number of risks. Some of these risks include:

1 – Buyer's insolvency/credit risk;
2 – Buyer's acceptance risk;
3 – Knowledge inadequacy;
4 – Seller's performance risk;
5 – Documentation risk;
6 – Economic risk;
7 – Cultural risk;
8 – Legal risk;
9 – Financial risk;
10 – Foreign exchange risk;
11 – Interest rate risk;
12 – Political/sovereign risk;
13 – Transit risk;
14 – Customs risk.

1 – Buyer's insolvency or credit risk. Buyer's insolvency or credit risk refers to the inability of the buyer to honour full payment for goods or services rendered on the due date. This is a risk on the seller associated with selling or supplying a product or service without collecting full payment or experiencing late payment.

2 – Buyer's acceptance risk. Buyer's acceptance risk refers to the buyer's non-acceptance of goods delivered or services rendered. Unaccepted goods

 DOI: 10.4324/9781003341345-6

or services may create difficulty for the seller to dispose the goods to another buyer or encounter working capital problem.

3 – Knowledge inadequacy. A buyer or seller who intends to expand his business into another product/service/industry/country may not have adequate knowledge of the risk of the new product/service, local market situation or demand for the goods. The lack of knowledge increases the chances of business failure.

4 – Seller's performance risk. A seller may fail to carry out his obligations in a sales contract due to 1 or more reasons, and such non-performance by the seller may have adverse consequential impacts on the buyer's business. It could be expensive for the buyer to take legal action against the seller in his country.

5 – Documentation risk. Documentation risk is the risk of non-conformance to specific documentation requirements under a sales contract or documentary credit, where a Letter of Credit is used to secure payment. Failure in fulfilling documentation requirements may result in the seller's inability or delay in obtaining payment for goods delivered or service rendered.

6 – Economic risk. Economic risk refers to unfavourable economic conditions in the country of the buyer or seller which may affect both parties in fulfilling their obligations. On the buyer side, economic risk may result in the buyer's insolvency or inability to accept the goods or services. On the other hand, the seller may experience difficulty in producing or shipping the goods to the buyer.

7 – Cultural risk. Different countries have their unique language and culture. The inability to appreciate/accept cultural differences and/or language barriers may result in conflicts and non-completion of the sales contract.

8 – Legal risk. Legal risk is the potential for financial loss arising from uncertainty of legal proceeding or change in legislation, such as a foreign exchange control policy. A sales contract could be frustrated due to changes in laws and regulations.

9 – Financial risk. An exporter or importer must always ensure that they are financially solvent and liquid. Credit Terms can vary, but in general range from 30 days to 90 days. That means that there is a likelihood that the exporter will not be paid for at least 1 month following the transaction. Unless the exporter is being paid on Cash in Advance terms, they will have to ensure that they have sufficient financial reserves to ensure full commercial operations without the need to borrow money from the bank until when they are paid by the customer. For importers, there is the need to pay Import Duties and VAT on all imported consignments, and if the importer is using facilities such as Duty Deferment or even Import Duty Reliefs, they have to convince the national revenue authorities that they are sufficiently financially liquid to pay not only the Import Duty and VAT per transaction but also the bank guarantees imposed by the revenue department where actual or potential Customs debts are concerned, i.e. the aforementioned Customs facilities.

In general, financial liquidity is measured by either the acid test or quick ratio, or the liquidity ratio. These ratios are derived by the calculation of current assets divided by current liabilities, with or without inventory and stocks inclusions, based on 3 years' worth of annual accounts, in particular the balance sheets for each of these annual accounts. The acid test ratio subtracts the inventory stocks from the current assets and then divides this figure by the total current liabilities. The liquidity ratio adds the inventory stocks to the current liabilities (or includes them in the current liabilities) and then divides the current assets by the current liabilities. With any of these formulae, as long as the ratio exceeds 1.2:1, then the company is sufficiently liquid to carry out the above activities. Anything below these ratios infers that the company is not sufficiently liquid, and could encounter financial problems in the future. If the ratio exceeds 1.5:1, then the company is in a strong financial position, and therefore will satisfy the requirements laid down by the revenue authorities concerning the use of Customs facilities and associated bank guarantees.

10 – Foreign exchange risk. A buyer or seller may deal with foreign currencies in their daily course of business. This implies that they are exposed to fluctuations in the foreign exchange market which may result in paying more (by the buyer) or receiving less (from the buyer) in terms of the local currency, especially where there is pronounced or extreme currency exchange fluctuation. Forward planning and contracts are essential for this kind of business, as the contract with the bank for foreign exchange needs to take into account any forward fluctuations in the exchange rate, and thus build these in to the actual exchange rate used for the fulfilment of the international transaction.

11 – Interest rate risk. Interest rate risk is the risk borne by an interest-bearing asset, such as a floating rate loan. An increase in interest rate will result in buyer or seller paying more interest for their floating rate loan.

12 – Political/sovereign risk. Political/sovereign risk refers to the complications that buyer or seller may expose due to unfavourable political decisions or political changes that may vary the expected outcome of an outstanding contract. Examples of political/sovereign risk are changes in fiscal/monetary policy, war, riots, terrorism, trade embargoes, etc.

13 – Transit risk. Transit risk is the risk of goods being damaged during shipment from the place of origin to the place of destination. Failure in addressing transit risk may result in heavy replacement cost or performance risk.

14 – Customs risk. Customs risk involves anything related to the clearance of goods through Customs controls, at both export and import stages. This may involve a variety of factors, namely documentation, cargo information, international controls such as sanctions and, of course, international and national Customs compliance factors. It also involves the use of the national import tariff, Customs Duty Relief regimes, Customs Warehousing, trade preferences and any other forms of Customs controls and facilities.

How to Mitigate Risks in International Trade

For the Buyer (Importer)

1 – Deal with seller with sound reputation or established track record;
2 – Request for performance guarantee to avoid non-performance risk;
3 – Agree on more secure methods of payment such as documentary credit or open account;
4 – Acknowledge and respect cultural differences with the seller;
5 – Buy and sell in same currency to minimise foreign exchange risk. Alternatively, the buyer can hedge against foreign exchange risk by entering a forward or option foreign exchange contract with a bank;
6 – If financing is needed, enter into a fixed interest rate loan or interest rate swap agreement to militate against interest rate risk;
7 – Ensure sufficient insurance coverage against transit risk;
8 – Always have a contingency plan against unfavourable events;
9 – Ensure all documentation and information is correct for the purposes of import clearance through Customs. Failure to do so can result in costly delays as well as follow-up action by Customs to recover any Customs debt.

For the Seller (Exporter)

1 – Deal with buyer with sound reputation or established track records;
2 – Engage a reputable credit agency or credit insurer to minimise buyer's insolvency or credit risk;
3 – Engage on more secured methods of payment such as documentary credit or advance payment;
4 – Avoid granting excessive credit period or limit to the buyer;
5 – Ensure that the sales contract or documentary credit does not contain ambiguous or erroneous terms and conditions that are subject to future disputes;
6 – Acquire sufficient knowledge in document preparation to mitigate against documentation risk;
7 – Acknowledge and respect cultural differences with the buyer;
8 – Buy and sell in same currency to minimise foreign exchange risk. Alternatively, the buyer can hedge against foreign exchange risk by entering a forward or option foreign exchange contract with a bank;
9 – If financing is needed, enter into a fixed interest rate loan or interest rate swap agreement to mitigate against interest rate risk;

10 – Ensure sufficient insurance coverage against transit risk;
11 – Engage a representative in the buyer's country to deal with the goods or relevant parties in case of non-payment or non-acceptance by the buyer and always have a contingency plan;
12 – Ensure all documentation and information is correct for the purposes of export clearance through Customs. Failure to do so can result in costly delays.

The International Supply Chain

The first main area of the International Supply Chain to be considered is always the relationship between suppliers and customers. For many companies, both suppliers and customers may be located outside their own country, which means importing and exporting goods. To this extent, any company located within the Supply Chain must therefore establish the geographical location of both suppliers and customers, as this will affect logistics considerations and costs, especially transport and fiscal costs. Greater distances between the elements of the Supply Chain will affect transport costs, as well as determining how goods should be moved, i.e. as small consignments or in bulk consolidations.

The next consideration is that of the function of the International Commercial Terms of Delivery, otherwise known as the INCOTERMS. All too often, companies use terms such as EXW (Ex Works – used for export) or DAT (Delivered At Place – used for import), on the grounds that they do not want to take responsibility for arranging transport for the goods. Much of the time, savings can be made by an importer or an exporter arranging some, if not all, of the transport, on the grounds that they can negotiate better freight rates for full or consolidated loads. It is often the case that consolidations work out cheaper than small one-off consignments, as a carrier wants to fill a container or a trailer. Indeed, full sea container rates are often cheaper than part loads or even trailer and Ro-Ro (Roll-On/Roll-Off) loads, and the shipper needs to be aware of this.

Transport methods, too, are a crucial issue. All too often, urgency requires express shipments, usually by the quickest form of transport, namely air freight. Even road freight can often be a reasonably quick method af carriage. However, if the consignment is planned well in advance, then the most can be made out of cheaper forms of transport, especially sea freight, where maritime transport becomes a necessity or can be considered part of the international transaction. Movements by container are still seen as the cheapest form of international transport, especially full container loads, which are ideal for the carrier. Indeed, full container loads can be arranged directly with the carrier and do not necessarily require the services of a freight forwarder, especially within the European Union and through the Mediterranean and short sea routes to Northern Europe. They may take longer to reach their destination, but they cost much less than either road or air transport.

Rules of Origin are vital to the international trade process. The European Union has a variety of Free Trade Agreements with many parts of the world, including the other Mediterranean countries, Africa, including South Africa, parts of the Middle East, the EFTA, Eastern Europe and beyond. Trade preferences with developing countries elsewhere in the world also mean reduced costs, and all these preferences ultimately mean reduced rates of Import Duty, often at zero rates.

This then leads nicely into the whole issue of fiscal controls and Import Duties. In the International Supply Chain, it is often assumed that every importer needs to pay Import Duties on all of their imports. If a consignment which is imported from outside the European Union is destined for consumption in the country of import, then this is so, but if there is any likelihood that the consignment will be re-exported to another non-EU country, especially if it has been re-processed in any way, then Import Duty and Value-Added Tax can be avoided. The principle of Inward Processing Relief, where duty and VAT is suspended, can be used under such circumstances. If the importer supplies the construction or maintenance of sea-going vessels, then they can use what is known as Shipwork End-Use Relief, which also avoids Import Duty liability where materials are imported from outside the European Union.

Another useful facility is that of Customs Warehousing. Many companies import large quantities of goods from outside the European Union and store them before distributing them to their customers. They pay Import Duty at the time of import on the full consignment. If their have their own storage warehouse, then this procedure is not necessary. They can apply to the Customs Authority to have the warehouse brought under Customs control, which then means that they can import the goods directly into the warehouse and kept them there under Customs control, until they are going to draw off materials to send to their customers. With an approved Customs Warehouse facility, they only pay Import Duty and VAT on what they are releasing from the warehouse at the time. The rest of the goods in the warehouse remain under Customs control. Furthermore, if the goods are destined for another EU country, then Import Duty is paid, but VAT is zero-rated under the Intra-EU INTRASTAT procedure. And if the materials are for re-export or inclusion in ship activities under the Shipwork End-Use facility, or Continental Shelf Offshore End-Use Relief, both of which are now covered by the more extensive Inward Processing facility as Entry In Declarant's Records (EIDR), then no Import Duty is liable. Another advantage is that of items stored in a Customs Warehouse become obsolete before they are sold, the company can scrap them or sell them off at a much lower price and have much less Import Duty to pay on them, if at all.

Warehousing is itself a major issue. Many companies store massive quantities of materials in the anticipation that if they purchase now, the cost will be less. The risk is that some items may become obsolete and cannot be used. The FIFO (First In, First Out) technique is becoming increasingly useful for this. Lower warehouse inventories are much more manageable, and cost less to operate. They can also be controlled better, using Just-in-Time (JIT) or KanBan techniques. Another increasingly important measurement tool is **Six Sigma**, where a set of benchmarks and parameters is obtained, and then performance is measured according to these controls. The purpose of the Six Sigma approach is to reduce time spent in various activities, as well as cost. It can be achieved by the following basic procedures:

- **D**efine;
- **M**easure;
- **A**nalyse;
- **I**mplement;
- **C**ontrol.

Or DMAIC, for short. The US and other countries have been using these techniques for some time to reduce costs and inefficiencies in many industries, including manufacturing and logistics, and the results include increased efficiencies and cost reductions. These principles are examined in greater detail later in this text.

A key factor in deciding upon the transparency of information submitted to Customs is the availability of information emanating from the supplier of a consignment of goods. If the supplier or the agency concerned does not convey accurate or detailed information to the carrier, then it cannot be expected that the carrier can in turn convey such information to the relevant authorities of the country of destination.

The basic process of the Supply Chain can be illustrated as follows:

The simplified international supply chain.

The information flow within the Supply Chain commences at the door of the exporter (the supplier). As shown in the previous chapter, in order to facilitate such a flow of information, there are 13 recognised International Terms of Delivery – the INCOTERMS – which are occasionally revised to account for changes in international market conditions or to clarify the varying degrees of risk and responsibility incurred by either the seller (supplier) or the buyer (customer) in each of the stages of any international shipment. The very basic term used by the exporter is EXW, where the exporter does no more than make the consignment ready for collection from the exporter's premises by the buyer. The buyer takes total responsibility for the shipment right up to their own premises. It would be normal practice to expect the exporter to inform the buyer of the nature of the shipment by way of a Commercial Invoice or a Packing List.

Groupage or Consolidation is 1 of the principal enemies of the accuracy of information pertaining to marine cargo reporting. Where the freight agent has accurate detailed knowledge of the consignment to be shipped, that information should be adequately transmitted via the carrier to the port of arrival, and any extra precautions required in the case of the reporting of hazardous goods will be taken. But if such information is not known, then such precautions cannot be taken and the result is a compounding of risks pertaining to both cargo insurance and the provisions for the handling of hazardous goods under the IMO Codes, especially under the IMDG and FAL requirements. In this respect, there is a clear need for the freight agent to be absolutely aware of the nature of the consignment at the time that consignment is loaded into the container, so that the correct information concerning the cargo can be passed to the carrier, i.e. the Shipping Line, prior to the container being loaded aboard vessel. Failure to provide such information could result in several compromises, as follows:

- Failure to adhere to the requirements of the SOLAS, IMDG and FAL regimes laid down by the IMO;
- The nullification of the Cargo Insurance policy under the provisions of the Maritime Insurance Act 1906;
- Failure to provide accurate cargo information to the relevant Customs Authority.

There is therefore the need for a fully transparent system of the transmission of cargo information to the Customs Authority in the multimodal system long before the container or trailer is loaded aboard the vessel. The nature of the International Supply Chain demands that information pertaining to cargoes is passed down the line from supplier to customer in order to ensure the smooth and efficient despatch and delivery of the consignment, and that all authorities and parties within the Supply Chain, especially from a transportation and national control perspective, are fully informed as to the nature and risk of the consignment in question. Even where no international frontier controls are involved, such as within the European Union, there is still a significant need for such flows of information, especially where mixed forms of transport are involved, such as road and sea, either from a Ro-Ro perspective or a Short Sea Container perspective. These flows start at the point of the exporter or seller, and progress through the freight agents, the Road Trucking Companies and Shipping Lines and the Port Authorities, as well as any Customs Authorities, to the importer or buyer. Such information flows should show the full extent of the consignment as well as the risks involved in handling and transporting it between the seller and the buyer.

Given the complexities of the Supply Chain, the manufacturer may not necessarily know where many of the materials involved in the manufacturing process originate, or to what extent Import Duties have been included in the Supply Chain costs. Indeed, the customers may also require evidence of origin for Customs and quality purposes There is therefore the need for significantly greater levels of transparency in the Supply Chain, in order to determine origin by way of long-term supplier declarations and Certificates of Origin, especially where international trade preferences and Free Trade Agreements apply.

Supply Chain Risk Management (SCRM)

Supply Chain Risk Management (SCRM) is defined as "the implementation of strategies to manage both frequent and exceptional risks along the Supply Chain based on the principle of continuous risk assessment with the objective of reducing vulnerability and ensuring continuity". It is a systematic process which involves the identification, assessment and prioritisation of risks associated with a company's Supply Chain. In other words, SCRM is to work collaboratively with partners in a Supply Chain or on one's own, apply risk management process tools to deal with risks and uncertainties caused by, or impacting on, logistics-related or supply-related activities or resources in the Supply Chain, especially the International Supply Chain.

SCRM attempts to reduce Supply Chain vulnerability by way of a co-ordinated holistic approach, involving all Supply Chain stakeholders, which identifies and analyses the risk of failure or weakness points within the Supply Chain. Risks to the Supply Chain range from unpredictable natural threats to counterfeit products, as well as international security and Customs issues, and reach across quality and security, to resiliency and product integrity. Mitigation plans to manage these risks can involve logistics, cybersecurity, finance and risk management disciplines, with the ultimate goal being to ensure Supply Chain continuity in the event of a scenario which otherwise would have interrupted normal business and thereby profitability.

Sometimes, it is possible for Supply Chain logistics techniques such as Supply Chain optimisation to prejudice or compromise contingency planning which would otherwise reduce the overall risk level for that particular Supply Chain. It's also becoming more common among businesses especially manufacturers to employ a supplier quality management software, which integrates all phases of the Supply Chain cycle. This approach is shown to increase transparency, reduce overhead costs, and improve operational efficiency.

Supply Chain risk management typically involves 4 processes, namely:

- Identification;
- Assessment;
- Controlling; and
- Monitoring of Supply Chain risks.

However, due to the complexity of many Supply Chains, these processes might not be sufficient to ensure that all eventualities are prepared for. Therefore, the concept of Supply Chain Risk Management, which is based on cause rather than effect, is often combined with the concept of Supply Chain resilience, which aims to ensure that the Supply Chain can bounce back from risks irrespective of their cause.

Some options which can ensure an acceptable risk level include:

- Cost management;
- International trade management;
- Customs management;
- Managing stock;
- Considering alternative sourcing arrangements;
- Business interruption/contingency insurance;
- Risk assessments and audits;
- Awareness campaigns and training programmes;
- The use of business intelligence from big data analytics and continuous monitoring for predictive security measures versus clean up;
- Redundancy optimisation;
- Postponement;
- Collaboration.

ISO 28000/ISO 28001

As well as initiatives introduced by organisations such as the IMO and the World Customs Organisation (WCO), the International Standards Organisation (ISO) has endeavoured to introduce a series of international standards in order to maximise their security potential and thus minimise levels of security risk in the International Supply Chain. The ISO 28000 initiative was introduced to apply a security standard to the International Supply Chain, by implementing a set of procedures and checklists for all exporters and importers when shipping consignments of goods overseas. The standard requires each exporter to ensure that all consignments being exported are subjected to a series of checks prior to the goods being packed and containerised for security purposes, based on a security risk assessment, and in the form of a security management system. The purpose of the implementation of such a set of procedures is to anticipate any potential risk and reduce or eliminate it at the point of the goods being dispatched from the exporter's premises. The drawback in the system is that it refers to the actual goods themselves, and the ability of the exporter to control the shipment. It does not necessarily relate to the details contained in the documentation accompanying the consignment.

However, the initiative does include details concerning both upstream and downstream movements, which cover responsibility for the integrity of the cargo and ensuring that adequate steps are taken to account for every item being included in the cargo being shipped. This would include supervising the loading of vehicles, trailers and containers, and ensuring that an account is made on the load list pertaining to the vehicle load, of every item scheduled to be loaded aboard that means of transport.

Downstream refers to the actions, processes and movements of the cargo in the Supply Chain that occur after the cargo leaves the direct operational control of the organisation, including, but not limited to, insurance, finance, data management, and the packing, storing and transferring of cargo. Downstream thus refers to the despatch process for the goods when they are no longer in the custody of the organisation in the Supply Chain, e.g. the exporter.

Upstream refers to the actions, processes and movements of the cargo in the Supply Chain that occur before the cargo comes under the direct operational control of the organisation, including but not limited to insurance, finance, data management, and the packing, storing and transferring of cargo. Upstream thus refers to the arrival process for the goods before the organisation in the Supply Chain, e.g. the importer, takes custody or possession of the goods.

Much of the issue concerning upstream and downstream operations concerns the extent to which the shipper is fully aware of the nature, description and quantity of the consignment being shipped. On many occasions, little attention is paid to the consignment at the time of loading aboard vehicle at the seller's premises, hence the problems which can arise concerning the accuracy of manifests and shipping documentation. Under ISO 28000/1, it is the express responsibility of the seller to ensure that adequate supervision is exercised over the despatch process, to the point of tallying off the load list referring to the vehicle load prior to its despatch.

One of the main points of ISO 28000 is the security management system. It states the following:

- An organisation must establish, document, implement, maintain and continually improve an effective security management system for identifying security risks and controlling and mitigating their consequences;
- An organisation must define the scope of its security management system;
- Where an organisation outsources any processes affecting conformity with these requirements (including Ex Works shipments), the organisation must ensure that these processes are controlled, and that the necessary controls and responsibilities of such outsourced are identified within the security management system.

Under the EXW principle this may be a vague area, as the exporter bears no legal responsibility for the actual shipment. However, it is pointed out in the INCOTERMS book that EXW can lead to difficulties proving export compliance, especially form a Customs angle, and therefore another term such as FCA should be used for the purposes of Customs compliance. Within the security management system there are 5 main action elements, which are:

- Policy;
- Security risk assessment and planning;
- Implementation and operation;
- Checking and corrective action;
- Management review.

This implies that a constant self-corrective action plan should be drawn up by the organisation and adhered to at all times, suggesting more responsibility being placed on the organisation for ensuring that it does have control over all its shipments, both inward and outward. In itself, this is a worthy solution, and it can be used effectively, depending upon the transparency of information provided by all parties in the shipping process. Indeed, much of the process behind the ISO 28000 and 28001 benchmarks has also been included in the Authorised Economic Operator (AEO) status initiative being implemented by HM Revenue and Customs, which will apply as much to shipping agencies as much as it does to the shippers themselves, and indeed the AEO status is included in the provisions of ISO 28000/1.

According to ISO 28001 (ISO 28001, Section 3.3), the Authorised Economic Operator is a party involved in the international movement of goods in whatever function that has been approved by or on behalf of a national Customs administration as complying with WCO or equivalent Supply Chain security standards.

AEOs can include exporters, importers, manufacturers, brokers, carriers, consolidators, intermediaries, ports, airports, terminal operators, integrated operators, warehouses and distributors. Indeed, any organisation concerning with the manufacture, supply, handing and movement of goods on an international basis may seek to be approved as an Authorised Economic Operator.

Any assessment of security risk, audit trails and accountability takes into account all aspects of transport, including ocean shipping, short sea shipping, Ro-Ro and inland waterway transport, as well as the other forms of international transport. It details all aspects of handling, including:

- Loading;
- Manufacturing;
- Storage (including intermediate storage);
- Transfer;
- Unloading;
- Consolidation/Groupage;
- Deconsolidation/Breakbulk.

The assessment also concerns the level of competence and training of company employees, as well as the handling or processing of information concerning cargo or transport routes. There must be full awareness and competence in dealing with these issues, and they concern the overall compliance of the company concerning international operations.

The Integrated Supply Chain Network Model: A Customs Perspective

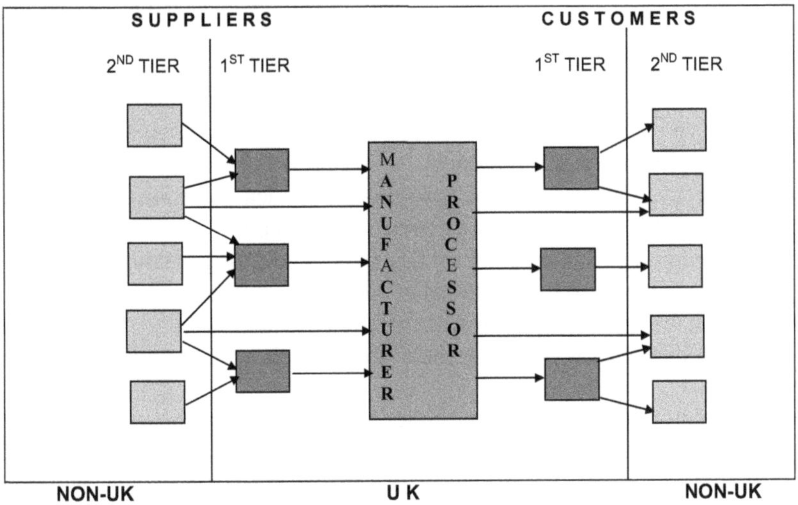

1. The suppliers at **2nd tier level** outside the UK Union supply those within the UK at **1st tier level** with raw materials;
2. The **1st tier suppliers** in turn supply the manufacturer/processor with semi-processed components for incorporation in the finished product;
3. The processor supplies the finished product to the **1st tier customer**, which in turn may act as a distributor (or as an onward processor) and supply the finished product to the end-customer, or the end-user, located at **2nd tier level**.

Given the above scenario, as long as the manufacturer knows that some or all of the raw materials (and hence the **2nd tier suppliers**) originate outside the UK, and that some or all of their **2nd tier customers** are located outside the UK, then they may use a Duty Relief Facility mechanism, in particular **Inward Processing Relief (IPR)**, to ensure that they can minimise Import Duty liability on the products they manufacture. The only time where Import Duty becomes liable is where the finished product is destined for the UK or EU market under Free Circulation conditions. In using an IPR facility, the manufacturer may also ensure that their **1st tier suppliers and customers** are authorised to use the same IPR authorisation or their own IPR authorisation in order to complete the minimisation of Import Duty and Tax liabilities.

ISO 28001

Security incidents against International Supply Chains are threats to international trade and the economic growth of trading nations. People, goods, infrastructure and equipment, including means of transport, need to be protected against security incidents and their potentially devastating effects. Such protection benefits the economy and society as a whole.

International Supply Chains are highly dynamic and consist of many entities and business partners. This International Standard recognises this complexity. As a result, the ISO benchmark 28000/28001 has been developed to allow an individual organisation in the Supply Chain to apply its requirements in conformance with the organisation's particular business model and its role and function in the International Supply Chain.

This International Standard provides an option for organisations to establish and document reasonable levels of security within International Supply Chains and their components. It will enable such organisations to make better risk-based decisions concerning the security in those International Supply Chains.

This International Standard is multimodal and is intended to be in concert with and to complement the World Customs Organization's SAFE Framework of Standards (detailed later in this text) to secure and facilitate global trade. It does not attempt to cover, replace or supersede individual Customs agencies' Supply Chain security programmes and their certification and validation requirements.

The use of this International Standard will help an organisation to establish adequate levels of security within those part(s) of an International Supply Chain which it controls. It is also a basis for determining or validating the level of existing security within such organisations' Supply Chain(s) by internal or external auditors or by those government agencies that choose to use compliance with this International Standard as the baseline for acceptance into their Supply Chain security programmes. Customers, business partners, government agencies and others might request organisations which claim compliance with this International Standard to undergo an audit or a validation to confirm such compliance. Government agencies might find it mutually agreeable to accept validations conducted by other governments' agencies. If a third-party organisation audit is to be conducted, then the organisation needs to consider employing a third-party certification body accredited by a competent body, which is a member of the International Accreditation Forum.

It is not the intention of this International Standard to duplicate governmental requirements and standards regarding Supply Chain security in compliance with the WCO SAFE Framework. Organisations that have already been certified or validated by mutually recognising governments are compliant with this International Standard.

To undertake the security assessment needed to produce the security plan, an organisation using this International Standard will:

- Identify the threats posed (security threat scenarios);
- Determine how likely persons could progress each of the security threat scenarios identified by the security assessment into a security incident.

This determination is made by reviewing the current state of security in the Supply Chain. Based on the findings of that review, professional judgement is used to identify how vulnerable the Supply Chain is to each security threat scenario.

If the Supply Chain is considered unacceptably vulnerable to a security threat scenario, the organisation will develop additional procedures or operational changes to lower likelihood, consequence or both. These are called counter-measures. Based upon a system of priorities, counter-measures need to be incorporated into the security plan to reduce the threat to an acceptable level.

Annexes A and B are illustrative examples of risk management based security processes for protecting people, assets and International Supply

Chain operations. They facilitate both a macro approach for complex Supply Chains and/or more discrete approaches for portions thereof.

These annexes are also intended to:

- Facilitate understanding, adoption and implementation of methodologies, which can be customised by organisations;
- Provide guidance for baseline security management for continual improvement;
- Assist organisations to manage resources to address existing and emerging security risks;
- Describe possible means for assessment of risk and mitigation of security threats in the Supply Chain from raw material allocation through storage, manufacturing and transportation of finished goods to the market place.

Annex C provides guidance for obtaining advice and certification for this International Standard if an organisation using it chooses to exercise this option.

Scope

- The International Standard ISO28000/28001 provides requirements and guidance for organisations in International Supply Chains to:Develop and implement Supply Chain security processes;
- Establish and document a minimum level of security within a Supply Chain or segment of a Supply Chain;
- Assist in meeting the applicable authorised economic operator criteria set forth in the World Customs Organization Framework of Standards and conforming national Supply Chain security programmes.

Note: Only a participating National Customs Agency can designate organisations as AEOs in accordance with its Supply Chain security programme and its attendant certification and validation requirements.

In addition, this International Standard establishes certain documentation requirements that would permit verification.

Users of this International Standard will be able to:

- Define the portion of an International Supply Chain within which they have established security;
- Conduct security assessments on that portion of the Supply Chain and develop adequate counter-measures;

- Develop and implement a Supply Chain security plan;
- Train security personnel in their security related duties.

It should be noted that the ISO28001 Benchmark has been included in the SAFE Framework of Standards as established by the World Customs Organisation, and therefore constitutes a major part in determining and measuring import/export compliance on the part of international traders.

Customs Risk Areas

There are several areas of risk in terms of Customs management, and these are defined as follows:

- Valuation;
- Commodity Codes;
- Customs Procedure Codes;
- Origin;
- Import Duty Reliefs;
- Anti-Dumping Duty.

These areas have been determined by the World Customs Organisation, and are constantly monitored by the relevant Customs Authority in terms of imports of goods from overseas.

Customs and Tax Administration – The Vietnamese Case

A cost–benefit analysis conducted in 2007 on behalf of the World Bank into Customs and Tax affairs in Vietnam yielded some interesting observations.

Some quantifiable economic benefits expected from tax administration reform projects were as follows:

Macroeconomic Benefits

Trade liberalisation will result in lower revenues from trade taxes. If this trend were not accompanied by an increase in domestic tax revenue or lower expenditures, deficits would ensue. The negative social and economic effect of these options could be avoided if increases in domestic tax revenues were to make up for the loss in trade tax revenue. This represents economic benefits for a project that increases domestic revenue mobilisation. Their quantification depends on:

(i) The benefits derived from retaining the expenditures that would be scaled down if no additional taxes were raised; and
(ii) Avoiding the economic costs of deficit financing.

These benefits need not necessarily be quantified, yet they are certainly positive, suggesting that the calculated benefits represent a lower bound estimate.

Reduction in Administrative Costs of Collecting the Taxes

The modernisation of tax administration should lead to lower costs per amount of revenue raised as:

(i) The tax administration is streamlined;
(ii) Tax officials are better trained; and
(iii) Taxpayers become more compliant as a result of enhanced taxpayer education, and the establishment of taxpayer support centres, process simplification and improved automation.

If the project results in a simpler tax policy, this would also add to the economic and fiscal benefits.

Reduction in Compliance Cost for the Taxpayer

These costs, which tend to be higher than the cost of administering the tax itself, include the cost individuals and enterprises incur in preparing their tax declaration, and dealing with tax audits (*Chris Evans: Studying the Studies; 2003*). Some of these costs are in-house costs, whereas others result from fees paid to tax preparers and outside advisers, as well as the bribes paid to convince tax officials to reduce their tax liability, speed up the tax audits, and influence the results of these audits. In a static sense these bribes are merely transfers from taxpayers to tax officials and thus not an economic cost to the economy. In a dynamic sense they adversely affect economic behaviour; their reduction would benefit the economy. The design and targets of the revenue enhancing project will have an impact on the benefits generated. Based on good knowledge of local circumstances, basic assumptions can be reflected in the estimates. Results are likely to increase the awareness of taxpayers and tax authorities of the burden of compliance costs. A few pointers:

- Compliance costs for domestic taxes have been estimated at 2–10% of the revenue of these taxes, up to 2.5% of GDP (Evans 2003);
- Some taxes yield cash flow benefits (time lapse between the occurrence of tax liability and tax payment), and can substantially reduce the net compliance cost;
- Compliance costs tend to be higher for small and medium-sized enterprises than for large enterprises that are better equipped to deal with tax authorities;
- Projects that aim at simplifying the tax system, thus making it more predictable, enhancing the accountability of tax officials, improving tax payer services, speeding up appeals and audits, and introducing

automation, are likely to reduce compliance costs more than projects that include none of these elements;

- Compliance costs relate to wage costs for in-house and outside advisers, and for this reason are expected to be lower in low-wage countries than in high-wage countries. Yet, studies on compliance costs done for India do not corroborate this reasoning.

Support Trade Liberalisation

Trade taxes distort consumption choices and resource allocation. In fact, this is often the purpose of these taxes as they intend to protect domestic producers at the expense of higher cost to the consumer. Trade liberalisation policies will result in the reduction of trade-related taxes over time, a process that could be undermined if the revenue authorities were unable to make up for this trend by raising more domestic tax revenue. Benefits from trade liberalisation would be slower in coming. These benefits have been estimated for the period 1997–2015 by the World Bank in its annual report of 2002 at US$500 billion (1997 dollars), 3/4 of which would result from the dismantling trade barriers in low- and middle-income countries (World Bank 2002). When account is taken of endogenous productivity gain, the benefits increase to 2/3. The revenue generation of the project under consideration would better ensure that the country shares in these benefits. Quantification of this would need to be based on country-specific estimates.

Customs Export Requirements

The export element of Customs control, especially with regard to maritime movements, has become more automated and electronic with the implementation in 2002 of the NES (New Export System) means of Export Declarations, although there is still the requirement for the submission of the full cargo manifest to Customs by the Ship's Agents prior to the vessel being cleared by Customs for sailing. In this respect, the cargo manifest is based on the load list for each consignment, coupled with the raising of NES Export Declarations by the Clearing Agent/Freight Forwarder. However, the submission of each set of documents rests with different parties, as the following summary shows:

- The cargo manifest is submitted to Customs by the Ship's Agents or the Port Agents;
- The Export Declarations are submitted by the Freight Agents;
- The Bills of Lading are raised by the carrier (the Shipping Line).

The Bills of Lading are submitted by the Shipping Line to the Freight Forwarder responsible for arranging the shipment, and copies may also be held by the Ship's Agent, who submits the cargo manifest on behalf of the Line to Customs. Cases arise where there is uncertainty over who is responsible for the loading of cargo aboard vessel, owing to the absence of a specific INCOTERM in the contract of delivery, with the result that in some cases Bills of Lading are not submitted to a freight agent, and consequently no cargo manifest is submitted concerning the specific consignment to Customs. Customs are therefore unaware that the consignment in question has been loaded aboard vessel, and consequently has not been correctly declared. In the case of hazardous or dangerous cargoes, this failure to correctly record and declare a consignment could prove disastrous in the event of an accident aboard vessel or a collision, as a trader, i.e. the exporter or importer, could ultimately be held liable for the consequences of such an accident. A further consequence of a failure to correctly declare a consignment to Customs is that the trader is liable for VAT on the value of the consignment and equally a civil penalty on the grounds of a false declaration being made to Customs.

In the case of the UK, it is worthwhile noting the following procedure concerning the issue of NES Export Declarations since the procedures involved influence how quickly the vessel can be cleared by Customs for departure:

- The Export Pre-Shipment Advice Declaration (PSA) is entered into the CDS Customs computer and a Declaration Unique Consignment Reference (DUCR) for the individual consignment is raised;
- The computer acknowledges the Declaration and clears the consignment for movement to the Port of Loading;
- The consignment arrives at the Port and the Declaration Unique Consignment Reference (DUCR) is input into the Customs computer;
- The Customs computer selects 1 from 3 possible clearance routes for the consignment:
    1. Route 6 Electronic Clearance Without Examination;
    2. Route 1 Documentary Check;
    3. Route 2 Consignment Examination.
- Upon satisfactory checks being made, especially in cases of either Routes 1 or 2, the Customs computer clears the consignment for loading aboard vessel;
- The departure message is sent to the agents signifying that the vessel is ready to depart;
- The final message is sent to the agents signifying that the vessel has sailed and that the cargoes have left UK waters (EU waters until 31 January 2020).

In all instances of loading aboard vessel, it is imperative that all steps are taken to ensure that all cargoes are correctly entered on shipping documentation so that correct Export Declarations can be raised and submitted to Customs in advance of the cargo being loaded aboard vessel, as well as the cargo manifest being submitted to Customs prior to the vessel's departure. Theoretically, failure to correctly declare a cargo to Customs could result in the refusal by Customs to allow the loading of the cargo aboard vessel, although in reality there are few physical checks of export cargoes made at the port owing to a lack of physical resources and manpower on the part of Customs at the port, thus allowing the port authority to carry out loading formalities without physical Customs checks on the consignment concerned. However, in the European Union, the exporter is required by law to have a valid hard copy of the Export Customs Declaration (**Commission Regulation 2454/93 Articles 205.3 and 288**) for each export made to a destination outside the European Union. This is also enshrined in UK Customs law, in the 1979 Customs and Excise Management Act (CEMA), and is referred to in Section 167(1) of the Act.

With the transfer of most reporting mechanisms to electronic means, the structure of the maritime reporting regime with regard to Customs controls has also changed. Although Customs still maintain control over all seaports, there is no longer the same degree of physical presence of Customs Officers at many seaports. The CDS Customs computer relies on the details of the export consignment in the form of the DUCR to ensure that the correct details of each consignment have been entered into the computer by the exporter or, more likely, the freight agent. However, in cases where the consignment is shipped EXW and especially in a groupage arrangement, the exporter is very unlikely to see a copy of the Export Declaration, and in many cases, a DUCR may not be raised by the Clearing Agent as the consignment is part of a larger consolidated consignment arranged by the overseas buyer, and thus the only declaration raised at export will be the Master UCR which covers the whole LCL groupage container load. In this respect, the details shown on the declaration will show the agent/consolidator as the exporter, and hence their VAT details will be entered, rather than those of the individual exporters whose consignments are contained in the consolidation. In this respect, there is no compliance for each exporter, and this not only distorts statistical information pertaining to export consolidations, given that the Customs Authority places full responsibility for an export at the door of the exporter, but also masks and distorts information concerning the true contents of the container at the time of export. Such omissions contravene US Customs regulations under the CT-PAT initiative, and also compromise safety regulations concerning the carriage of cargoes by sea, especially concerning the nature of the FAL 2 Cargo Manifest and its requirements under the IMO FAL Convention.

In the same way that all Import Declarations for maritime cargo have been rendered electronic, so too have Export Declarations for maritime cargo and ship's stores. Electronic initiatives driven by the EU have resulted in many EU countries implementing electronic Export Declaration procedures, and the UK implemented its own electronic export regime, the NES in 2002 for all seafreight Export Declarations. The CUSCAR Cargo Manifest is submitted electronically by the Port Agent to Customs in advance of the vessel being loaded, especially in the case of shipments destined for the US, where Cargo Manifests must be submitted to US Customs officers based in the UK 48 hours prior to the vessel's departure under the US CT-PAT initiative. The NES Export Declaration is submitted to the CDS Customs computer as a Pre-Shipment Advice (PSA) once the cargo is ready for shipment (usually no more than 24 hours before the consignment is due to be loaded aboard vessel), and this declaration is acknowledged by the computer. Once the consignment has been loaded aboard the container and reaches the Port of Loading, another message (the Arrival Message) is entered by the agent into the CDS Customs computer stating that the consignment has arrived at the port and awaits clearance instructions. The CDS Customs computer issues the appropriate message (Route 6 Automatic Clearance/Route 1 Documentary Check, etc.) for the export consignment in question. Once the consignment has been cleared by the CDS Customs computer, the consignment is loaded aboard vessel and a Route 7 Departure Message is issued by CDS Customs computer. A further Route 8 message clears the vessel to sail, and departure is completed. At this point, the Marine Bills of Lading for each export consignment are issued to the party arranging the shipment.

The same electronic initiative which controls inward IMO FAL declarations is also used for outward movements. The suppliers of ship's stores must also submit electronic declarations based on the UN/EDIFACT Inventory Report (INVRPT) for all ship's stores loaded aboard the vessel prior to its departure. These declarations can be submitted electronically online in the same manner that inward ship's stores declarations are submitted at the time of the arrival in port of the vessel. Thus, the electronic arrangement of Customs Export Declarations is as follows:

- NES Export Declaration (Exporter/Freight Forwarder/Port Agent);
- IMO FAL Form 2 Cargo Manifest (CUSCAR);
- IMO FAL Form 3 Ship's Stores Declaration (Ship's Master, supplier or agent).

However, given that an IMO Ship's Stores Declaration requires a signature by either the Ship's Master or the Ship's Agent, there is still the need for a hard copy to be made available to a Customs Officer where required. The same is true of both the FAL Form 2 Cargo Manifest and the NES Declaration. A hard copy of the Export Declaration plus supporting departure messages must be kept by the exporter for presentation to a Customs Officer where and when required for VAT zero-rating or Excise suspension purposes.

Customs Import Requirements

Although the UK's trade with the EU is substantial, much of UK external trade is still conducted with non-EU countries, and once the UK has left the EU all external trade will be outside UK Customs jurisdiction and therefore subject to Customs controls. In the same way, in North America, although the NAFTA accounts for a large amount of intra-continental trade, a large amount of trade is carried out with the EU, Latin America and the Pacific Rim. Such trade is conducted either subject to Preferential Trading Agreements or on the basis of WTO Normal Trading Relations subject to full rates of Import Duty being liable on all non-Preference Imports. Over the last several years, the World Trade Organisation has sought to reduce tariff levels on a variety of items, particularly in the area of industrial goods, and in this respect there are less duty liabilities associated with the import of many products than there used to be. In many cases, Import Duty levels have been reduced to zero, and this has resulted in a much freer worldwide movement of many products, particularly those connected with the consumer sector.

The main factors concerning the import of products and materials are as follows:

- Price;
- Availability;
- Quality;
- Quantity.

The importer must ensure that the documentation reflects such a movement, and that the correct Customs clearance methods are employed to ensure that the Import Declaration is still submitted in the right way.

Home Use and Free Circulation

The definition of Home Use is the consumption or sale of a product or item in one's own domestic territory. Even in the case of the offshore oil and gas sector, some of the materials imported by suppliers in the sector will not be shipped offshore, but will be used for onshore installations, such as Supply Base operations. In the case of the UK, this has come to imply consumption in the European Union as a whole, given the existence of the EU as a Single Unified Customs Territory. The definition of Free Circulation is that an item may pass freely without Customs control within such a territory, and will not be subject to any duty liability while doing so. This also implies that once an imported item has passed through Customs control upon entry into the UK and has had Import Duty and VAT paid upon it, it may pass freely throughout not only the

UK but also anywhere else within the territory of the EU. Since the EU is a Customs Union, the rate of Import Duty applicable to the item concerned is exactly the same as that in any other of the EU Member States. In reality, such an item is within Free Circulation as far as Customs Import Duty is concerned, but in terms of VAT, such tax liability varies according to which country the items is destined for. VAT will only be paid at the point of ultimate arrival. Because of the rules concerning Import Duty liability, unless the imported item concerned has not been assessed for Import Duty at the time of importation, it cannot be considered as being in Free Circulation in the EU. If an item is for temporary importation, storage for onward shipment or is to be included in a process approved under any of the Duty Relief Facilities, then Free Circulation would not be required, as duty liability would be waived. But if such a product is subsequently destined for Home Use, then in order to achieve Free Circulation status, it must have Import Duty paid on it. The only other way in which an incoming item would not be subject to Import Duty liability is if it originated in a country which enjoyed the status of Free Trade Preference as a result of a Free Trade Agreement between the EU and another country.

The C88 Customs Declaration (UK) (EX1/IM1 – EU)

In the UK, the main Customs Declaration document for all non-EU imports and exports is still classed as the SAD (Single Administrative Document), known in the UK as the C88, although it is now processed as an electronic submission, and is confirmed by the CDS Customs computer with the issuing of an E2 Entry Acceptance Advice. The C88 in its original form covered both imports and exports, but has now been replaced in the UK by the Entry Acceptance Advice for Imports and the NES Export Declaration for Exports. In the EU, the document is known as the **EX1** (Exports) and **IM1** (Imports) Declaration. Similar documentary submissions exist in all other countries.

In the case of plain paper entries submitted to Customs by agents using Direct Trader Input computerised methods, then the C88 format changes slightly given that there is no specific numbered copy procedure. The Plain Paper Entry still contains all the same details as a conventional C88 Declaration, but can be reprinted or photocopied at will depending upon how many copies will be required and for what purpose. The Plain Paper Entry, i.e. the **E2 Entry Acceptance Advice**, is submitted for import purposes alone, and not for export purposes. In this manner, it replaces copies 6–8 of the conventional C88 Declaration, and a hard copy of it must be retained by the importer for record-keeping purposes under the terms of Commission Regulation 2913/92, replaced in 2016 by the Union Customs Code.

Although the format between conventional C88 and plain paper declarations may differ, the essential information contained therein is still basically the same. The information provided on the Declaration or Customs Entry as it is also known is processed in the Customs CHIEF (**C**ustoms **H**andling of **I**mport **E**xport **F**reight) system. Each entry is assigned a specific serial number which comprises the 3-digit code of the HM Revenue and Customs Entry Processing Unit (EPU) where the entry is processed, a 6-figure serial number (usually followed by a letter suffix) and the date the entry is processed.

The following information must be completed by the agent on the entry declaration prior to submission to the EPU:

- Consignor;
- Consignee;
- Consignee's VAT Registration Number (plus that of the agent, if the agent pays Import Duty and VAT on behalf of the importer);
- The Clearing Agent/declarant;
- Description of the consignment;
- Marks and numbers of packages;
- Gross and net weight/mass of the consignment (kg);
- Mode of transport;
- Country of origin;
- Pace of loading;
- Value of consignment;
- Value of freight plus insurance;
- Rate of exchange;
- Supplementary information (Duty Relief Authorisation, if appropriate);
- Calculation of taxes;
- Signature and name of declarant.

The Calculation of Taxes usually refers to 2 specific Tax Codes. These are:

- **A01** (Import Duty);
- **B01** (VAT).

Although the Codes may not necessarily be evident on a conventional C88 Entry declaration, they will be evident on a Plain Paper Entry. In this way, anyone analysing a Plain Paper Entry will be able to quickly ascertain the amount of Import Duty and VAT payable against the particular value of the item declared on the entry. As from 1 January 2021, Import VAT is now taken care of by the Postponed VAT Accounting (PVA) facility, which allows importers to account for the Import VAT by way of a monthly online Import VAT statement, the VAT amounts shown on which are transferred to the following VAT Return rather than being paid outright at the point and time of import. This amounts to a huge cash saving for UK importers, given that they can avoid having to physically pay the Import VAT at the time of import, and simply account for it on the following VAT Return.

Rates of Exchange are liable to fluctuation on the open market, and thus HM Revenue and Customs publishes its own recommended list of Rates of Exchange to be used when calculating values of consignments in Pounds Sterling a the time the entry is being submitted for processing. Lists of Rates of Exchange are normally produced weekly, and are available from Customs Advice Centres or from the Entry Processing Units themselves. All calculations of value must be completed in Pounds Sterling for Entries processed in the UK, regardless of the original currency used or quoted when the consignment is being shipped. The other reason for the Official Rates of Exchange used by HM Customs is where there may be a sudden fluctuation in the Rate of Exchange between the Pound and any other currencies which was not taken into account by HM Revenue and Customs.

Calculations for Import Duty and VAT will also be done by the agent, but these figures will be checked by HM Revenue and Customs against the Tariff Code used and the correct rate. If there are found to be any discrepancies between the calculations used by the Clearing Agent and HM Customs, the Post Clearance Section at HM Customs will pick up the discrepancy and will issue a C18 assessment to the importer for the outstanding balance.

Upon submission by the Clearing Agent to the EPU, the import entry details pass through the computer system which checks all details on the entry. The computer database holds details of importers and their Trader's Unique Reference Number (TURN). There are occasions where importers have had problems with Customs matters, and it is often the case where import consignments for such importers will be selected for examination, or at least a documentary check by an officer. There are 3 selection routes in the CDS Customs computer system – Route 1, Route 2 and Route 3.

Route 6 is the most simple – it clears the entry through the system without any need to check any details whatsoever, and the Goods Release Note is sanctioned by the Customs Office for the agent to collect the consignment. **Route 1** means that an import entry is selected by the computer for a documentary check, by a Control Officer and this can result in a slight delay to Customs clearance of the consignment. Once the documents are checked and found to be in order, then the Goods Release Note will be signed and the consignment cleared. **Route 2** is the most complex route – the consignment will have been selected for full examination, which means that a Customs Officer must be present to physically examine the contents of all the cartons used to ship the consignment. Once the officer has satisfactorily completed the examination and has issued the appropriate report on 1 copy of the entry, the Goods Release Note will be signed and the consignment cleared. The Route 1 procedure is normally applied on a random 1 in 10 selection of import consignments passing through the EPU at a particular time or on a particular day. The only time that a selection for examination will be issued by the computer is if the importer's details on the database show problems encountered with the department on previous occasions.

Import Duty and VAT Calculations

Import Duty on the consignment is calculated according to the Tariff Code used and its corresponding *ad valorem* percentage rate. This calculation is also based on the CIF (Cost, Insurance, Freight) value declared on the C88 Declaration, otherwise known as the landed cost. This figure, however, does not include inland freight to ultimate destination. Import VAT is charged on the following:

- CIF cost **plus**;
- Import Duty **plus**;
- Inland freight costs.

Thus, in the case of the UK, Import VAT is charged on the total of the above at 20%.

Example:

An importer is importing a consignment of valves for supply to an oil company. The consignment is consigned as a Full Container Load (FCL), and has a total CIF value of £25,000. Inland freight is £500. Valves have an *ad valorem* Import Duty rate of 2.5%.

Thus, the calculation for Import Duty and VAT would be:

CIF Cost of Widgets	£25,000
Import Duty @ 3%	**£625**

SUBTOTAL:	£25,625
Plus: Inland Freight	£500

VALUE FOR VAT:	£26,125
Plus: VAT @ 20%	**£5,225.00**

Thus, the total liability to the importer for Import Duty and VAT in this instance is **£5,850.00 (£625 + £5,225).**

Note how the addition of Import Duty and VAT adds some 20% to the total value of the goods. In reality, the importer can claim back the VAT through the normal VAT accounting procedure, but he remains liable for Import Duty on the consignment which cannot be claimed back. However, in order to be able to reclaim the VAT, the importer must receive a monthly copy of the **C79 Import VAT Certificate**, which details all the Import Entry Declarations submitted for the month in question, and the Import VAT paid against each entry. It is the responsibility of the importer to check each item on the Import VAT Certificate against each Import Declaration to ensure the accuracy of all details, before they input all the Import VAT on the appropriate VAT return for the period.

Valuation Declarations

Every time a new import is made for the first time, it is advisable to submit a Valuation Declaration stating the value of the imported consignment to Customs. This declaration generally uses the Transaction Value method, namely the value of the goods based on the sale and therefore the commercial invoice. In cases where this method cannot be accurately ascertained, the next method is that of the equivalent price for the product concerned in the market of import.

In the case of the European Union, the reason for Valuation Declarations is that under EU Regulations, a declaration of value is required for goods liable to *ad valorem* Import Duty when imported into the European Union. It is normal, however, that once an initial Valuation Declaration has been submitted to Customs concerning the import of a new product or the import of a product for the first time by an importer, there will be no need for further Valuation Declarations on similar items, unless the trader imports further items new to the EU.

The Legal Implications of Importing and Liability for Import Duty and VAT

In the era of extensive outsourcing of the logistics function to an outside third-party operator, it is often all too easy to forget that an overseas sale is not simply a question of selling the goods and absolving all other responsibility for the shipment. The sale also includes the shipment to the customer and obtaining payment with respect to the sale. It implies that the customer receives the goods in good quality and condition, and that the customer pays duty and VAT based on such principles.

The Commercial Invoice should include the appropriate International Term of Delivery (INCOTERM) as agreed by the seller and the buyer. This INCOTERM should thus reflect the degree of responsibility each party is prepared to take in order to ensure that the consignment is correctly delivered to its destination. If Free Carrier (FCA), then the buyer takes charge of the whole international shipment, and undertakes all risks associated with that shipment. If DAP (Delivered At Place), then all the importer has to do is to pay Import Duty and Tax on the imported consignment.

In between, the terms FOB (Free on Board) and CIF are widely used, and refer specifically to seafreight consignments. They are not, however, simply International Terms of Delivery, as they also have distinct legal implications for buyer and seller dependent upon which term is used. Indeed, there are equally distinct legal implications for both EXW and DAP contracts, give the nature of multimodal, door-to-door and express shipments.

In logistics terms, the difference between FOB and CIF lies in which party is responsible for bearing the risk of the shipment and where title to the goods passes. In the case of FOB, the importer arranges the shipment from the Port of Loading and pays for not only the freight costs but also the insurance of the cargo, as well as all associated shipping and handling charges and Import Duty and Tax liabilities. In the case of CIF, the exporter arranges the international shipment, inclusive of insurance, and will also pay all shipping and handling charges at the despatch end. The importer would be responsible for handling charges at the point of unloading, as well as all Customs clearance charges and Import Duty and VAT liabilities.

But the legal implications go much further than simply logistics implications. There is a definitive legal implication concerning both FOB and CIF Contracts, as liability for shipment and loss or damage is also considered. In a FOB Contract, the exporter is liable for all aspects of the shipment until it is loaded aboard ship. At that time, liability and responsibility for the shipment passes to the importer, who must accept such liability up to the point of receipt at his premises. An FOB Contract assumes that title for the consignment passes at the time the goods are loaded aboard ship. If the cargo is damaged during the international shipment, then the importer must accept and bear such consequences, and cannot reject the goods at the point of import. If, however, the importer has reason to believe that, prior to loading aboard ship at the point of despatch, the goods suffer some form of damage or the contract was not carried out in any specific way, e.g. the nature or quality of the goods differed from the terms of the contract, then they can reject the consignment prior to it being loaded. However, the purpose of a Bill of Lading is that the carrier accepts responsibility for the goods at the point of loading aboard ship, and this responsibility is written into the Bill of Lading as the following statement:

> "*Received in apparent good order and condition*".

In this respect, the Bill of Lading is a legal document, as well as its status as a Document of Title, passing title from seller to buyer once the correct payment has been made from buyer to seller. It also confers responsibility for safe carriage of the consignment on to the carrier for the duration of the international journey, or up to the point specified under the conditions of carriage as arranged between seller and buyer, as in the case of an multimodal shipment. The carrier is thus responsible to whichever party, seller or buyer, arranged the contract of shipment. Under an FOB Contract, the buyer can submit a claim against the carrier in the event of damage sustained during the international journey. Furthermore, the Bill of Lading is a means of evidence to HM Customs and Excise that, in the case of export, there is an international shipment involved, and if the Bill is endorsed as a Certificate of Shipment, then VAT is exempted in the case of non-EU shipments. In the case of import, the Bill shows the amount of freight charges applicable to the consignment, and thus contributes to the landed cost of the consignment liable for Import Duty and VAT.

In a CIF Contract, 2 main issues occur. Title cannot pass to the importer until payment has been made to the exporter and documents have been transferred from seller to buyer. And the buyer can reject the consignment at the time of importation if the documents or the consignment itself do not comply with the terms of the contract. The exporter has effectively borne responsibility for the safe passage of the consignment, although risk has passed to the importer at the time of loading aboard ship, as with an FOB Contract. The exporter, however, passes the insurance documents to the importer who can claim against the policy should loss or damage to the consignment occur during the international journey.

The legal aspects of rejection of a consignment under a CIF Contract can have considerable implications on the relationship between buyer and seller. If a buyer rejects the consignment at the point of importation, they can claim for repayment of the amount paid to the seller, either by way of insurance or through legal redress. The importer can also claim repayment of any Import Duties and Taxes paid to the Customs Authority on the grounds of rejected goods. The exporter is obliged either to repay the amount in question or to replace the consignment free of charge, with added freight and insurance costs payable by the exporter. Under a FOB Contract, no such privilege or redress is available to the importer, who would not only pay for the consignment and all other freight and insurance costs but also any Import Duty and Tax liabilities as well. In the case of loss or damage, this burden could prove costly to the importer, unless he makes a claim against the carrier as allowed in the insurance policy. The exporter, however, is not legally bound to replace the consignment free of charge in such a case, although the importer may be able to claim a refund of Import Duty or Tax from the Customs Authority under specific circumstances where specific items are being scrapped or are being disposed of because of no commercial worth. The importer would, however, need to pay for further items to be shipped in order to replace or make good the loss.

Under a CIF Contract, the buyer can reject the consignment at the time of importation if the terms of the contract have not been adhered to by the exporter. Such terms include documentary compliance, condition of the consignment, date of shipment or means of shipment. As long as the importer was not aware of any changes to the conditions of contract following the time it was agreed, and that such changes were not acceptable under the terms of the contract, the importer may thus reject the consignment. This has distinct inferences for the means by which HM Revenue and Customs allows the importer to waive payment of Import Duty and VAT. **Customs Notice 266** details all the ways in which Customs will facilitate such avoidance of liability for Import Duty and VAT, but the main principles are detailed as follows.

Import Duty, Excise Duty and VAT on goods imported from outside the EU can be claimed back on items rejected, because they:

- Are defective (without prior knowledge of the importer to this effect);
- Do not comply with the terms of the contract; or
- Were damaged before being cleared by Customs.

Further conditions apply. These assume that:

- The goods are those entered for free circulation;
- The goods have not been used more than was necessary to establish that they were defective or did not comply with the contract; and
- The goods have not been sold after they have been found to be defective or not to comply with the contract.

All claims for duty or VAT refunds must be made within 12 months of the original importation, although Import Duty and VAT will not have been paid if the goods are still under Customs control, i.e. they have not been cleared for Free Circulation at the time the importer is made aware of the discrepancies in contractual terms or that they arrived damaged at the place of Customs clearance. In many cases, the carrier or the agent may well make the importer aware of such a situation prior to any clearance documents being issued, in order to give the importer the opportunity to reject the consignment prior to physically receiving it, and thus the importer may make a claim to HM Revenue and Customs requesting exemption from liability for duty and VAT based on the physical rejection of the consignment prior to receiving it.

Goods which have been rejected in such a manner can be disposed of by any of the following methods:

- Exportation outside the Customs Territory of the EU;
- Destruction at the expense of the importer;
- Destruction by order of a public authority; or
- Placing in a Customs Bonded Warehouse or a Free Zone when all the other rules for repayment have been met. This must be with a view to re-export of the goods, but in certain situations a request may be made for re-entry of the consignment into free circulation or another Customs procedure as an alternative to re-export.

Disposal of the consignment must take place under Customs control. If disposal occurs before HM Customs is notified, then the claim for duty refund or exemption could be jeopardised, as there is no concrete evidence of the nature of the rejection of the consignment in the first instance.

It is also worthwhile noting that it is the responsibility of the buyer to ensure that all documents necessary for Customs clearance are provided by the seller. It is often the case that goods are seized by the Customs Authority or Import Duty is levied on goods which otherwise might be eligible for duty-free preference because incorrect documentation as provided by the seller or documents were missing. Under the terms of a Letter of Credit, certain documents will be required in order to successfully complete the transaction, and the same is true of Customs clearance. If a contract clearly states the provision of a Certificate of Origin or a Movement Certificate, then this must be provided, as without certain documents or uncertain information on the invoice, goods can be seized by Customs and held for indefinite periods until the matter is resolved to mutual satisfaction on the part of all concerned. This delay in clearance can result in further financial penalties to the importer because the original contract was not adhered to properly.

A DAP Contract extends such responsibilities to the importer's premises. The importer does not need to inspect the goods at the port of discharge, but can wait until the point of arrival at his premises. And assuming such premises are bonded under Customs control, then no Import Duty or Tax need be paid on any rejected goods, since the goods remain under Customs control at the time of inspection and would be disposed of under Customs supervision. There would thus be no fiscal liability to the importer given their unsuitability for commercial sale.

If the buyer uses the services of a distributor, then under such circumstances it is the distributor who bears responsibility for the arrangement of such contracts rather than the ultimate buyer. If the distributor uses bonded premises, then Import Duty and Tax liability would only apply on all goods accepted by the distributor for onward sale to the customer. The distributor could, under the terms of a CIF or DAP contract, reject all goods damaged or non-compliant with the terms of the Contract of Sale without any fiscal liability and could use the procedure stated above for exemption from Import Duty or for a claim of Import Duty refund. They could also send such items back to the exporter, have them destroyed or otherwise disposed of as scrap, and simply request a replacement consignment without the need to pay Import Duty and Tax on the original consignment, thus avoiding added liability to their customers. The exporter would be obliged to replace the consignment to the distributor free of charge. Only when the replaced goods were correctly received and dispatched to the customer would any Import Duty and Tax be liable, thus enabling the distributor to retain all profits without any form of added cost owing to loss or damage.

Hence the importance of the correct use and application of International Contracts. It is important to understand why each form of contract is so vital in ensuring that each party is aware of their rights and responsibilities prior to the contract being made. Any uncertainty or omission of vital contractual details could severely prejudice the efficiency and worth of the sale, and ultimately the relationship between the buyer and the seller. Furthermore, uncertainties or omissions also prejudice the relationship between the importer and HM Customs and Excise, as failure to supply the correct information concerning the value of the consignment can result in the importer being liable for more Import Duty and VAT than originally anticipated. Where an international contract is not adhered to, then the importer may be obliged to pursue the inconvenience of claims through HM Customs for duty and VAT refund or exemption on goods rejected.

Roles of the Importer, Exporter and Clearing Agent

International Supply Chain and Logistics

For much of Britain's history as a trading nation, it has been considered crucial that the country should make much of its money from exports in order to boost its economic fortunes. Britain has never been self-sufficient in most of its economic needs, and has always needed to import certain commodities in order to satisfy the ever-increasing demands of its population. Indeed, in the 18th and 19th centuries, much of the world's wealth was as a direct result of buying manufactured articles produced in Britain, from textiles to railway locomotives. However, manufactured articles result from raw materials, and in this respect Britain needed to import such materials from overseas. Hence the concept of the so-called "Triangular Trade" of the 18th century. British ships transported slaves from West Africa to the Caribbean and America, to work on the cotton and sugar plantations. The sugar and cotton produced on these plantations was exported to the UK to be made into manufactured items, particularly in the textile industry. Cloth and garments were then exported to other nations, including Africa.

Other products were imported from other nations, owing to increasing demand for luxury items in the growing British economy which could not be obtained from the domestic market. Such items included spices, textile fineries, wines and spirits, tobacco and other sought-after goods. It was on the basis of such trade that Adam Smith and David Ricardo were to formulate their respective theories of Absolute Advantage and Comparative Advantage in international trade. As time has progressed, however, the comparative advantage once enjoyed by Britain in many commercial areas has greatly diminished, as the cost of production of many items imported from overseas has diminished. The reality of the economic equation is that Britain can no longer afford to manufacture many items for the overseas market, let alone its own, as costs of production have either physically increased or have increased relative to the costs of overseas production. As a result, it is cheaper in many cases to import from overseas than to produce locally. Such practice has further increased with the existence of the European Single Market, created at the beginning of 1993. Britain can now import duty-free a wide range of products from the European Union which would otherwise be more expensive to produce in the UK. And, in other cases, even considering Import Duties on items imported from outside the European Union, it is still more cost-effective for many companies to procure purchases from overseas.

This does not mean, however, that Britain exports nothing. Much of Britain's export activity relates to the production of items made from imported components for re-export. Thus much of the British International Supply Chain revolves around importing raw materials or components for assembly into finished products which will then be re-exported. Many of the companies investing in the British economy are overseas-owned and which exist to supply the rest of Europe with products imported into the UK from overseas. Such companies include the automotive and electronics sectors, which have made considerable inroads into the British economy and have in many cases overwhelmed indigenous British industries.

Thus, the International Supply Chain involves the following processes:

IMPORT >>>>>>>>>>>>> MANUFACTURE >>>>>>>>>>> EXPORT

The overseas customer relies on the British manufacturer, which relies in turn on the overseas supplier. The reality is that if 1 element fails, the whole Supply Chain fails. And furthermore, as the cost of imports rises, then so too does the export price.

Import costs can rise due to a variety of reasons. These include:

- Import Duties;
- Exchange rate fluctuations;
- Increased overseas production costs;
- Increased logistics costs.

Thus, as the cost of supply increases, so does the ultimate cost to the customer. Within this equation, certain elements may be controlled. These include:

- The cost of procurement, i.e. the seeking of more cost-effective supplies;
- Suppliers closer to the UK, hence reduced logistics costs;

- Customs Import Duty Reliefs, where products are being exported to non-EU countries.

Within the International Supply Chain, the main aim of the exercise is to reduce costs within the Supply Chain by as effective a means as possible without prejudicing the structure and efficiency of the Supply Chain itself. Hence the need to control and monitor areas such as logistics costs and Import Duties wherever possible.

The whole definition of logistics revolved around the principles of the supply of required items to a population. The term "logistics" is derived from the French word *logis*, meaning a lodging. Lodging, as well as residing, sheltering or sojourning, also implies feeding and generally being looked after. The great Napoleonic Army of Imperial France relied heavily on the principle of *logistique* to support its Europe-wide military campaigns at the beginning of the 19th century. As a result, the logistics discipline of today has come to represent every aspect of the Supply Chain, from the supply of raw materials to the manufacturer and the supply of the finished product to the customer, to all elements of transport, storage and distribution. From an international aspect, such elements also imply the control of such a process to ensure the speedy and efficient movement of goods across international borders, and hence the satisfaction of border and fiscal controls imposed by national governments on such movements. International transport is facilitated by freight forwarders, whose responsibility includes the submission of Customs documentation on behalf of their customers. Freight forwarding may also imply the temporary storage in bonded premises of goods intended for trans-shipment and onward distribution, and this involves further satisfaction of Customs requirements to ensure that certain tax liabilities may be avoided in the process. HM Customs and Excise, therefore, has a considerable influence in the process of international logistics as far as the UK is concerned, and this policy is no different elsewhere in the European Union or the rest of the world. The effects on the economics of logistics can be greatly influenced by the efficiency or otherwise of Customs management within the commercial system, and a prudent trading company seeks to ensure that it pays no more Customs duties than absolutely necessary in the course of its international business transactions. It is also evident, however, that many commercial organisations are not aware of the facilities available to them in order to achieve such efficiencies and achieve considerable cost savings in the form of the waiving of various tax and duty liabilities. If they were, then the international logistics process within the scope of the International Supply Chain would be a much more efficient affair.

The policy of global sourcing and procurement within the International Supply Chain has become an issue widely used throughout the globe today.

Multinational companies, especially those within the automotive and electronic sectors, seek to exercise a policy of vertical investment, choosing to procure components from 1 country, sub-assemblies from another and fully assembled products from another. This infers that 1 part of the world, such as South-East Asia, will be used to produce components, which will be shipped to Eastern Europe for inclusion in sub-assemblies, which will in turn be shipped to North America or the European Union for inclusion in the fully-assembled product. Given the variety of stages in the process, costs will be incurred at successive stages on areas such as logistics and Import Duties. Import Duties can be waived if the company in question is using an authorisation for Import Duty relief, a measure used to increasing effect worldwide. But not every company is aware of such facilities, hence the relatively high costs incurred in some cases throughout the Supply Chain. The more use made of duty-free facilities on a worldwide basis within the organisation in question, the greater the likelihood of reducing costs within the Supply Chain. The only time that Import Duty and other associated tax should be paid on any item is when it reaches its ultimate destination, and not at any other time during the Supply Chain process. All too often, taxes are being paid on items passing through a variety of countries during the Supply Chain process without any understanding on the part of the corporate management why this is so. No checks or audits are made to establish ways of reducing such costs during the supply chain process, and as a result there is often a significant leakage of expenditure through the system in the form of unnecessary tax liability. Quite naturally, no national government is going to refuse revenue for its coffers, but it does welcome requests for duty exemption when the product is not being consumed on a national basis in that country.

The ENS System

At the beginning of 2011, the European Union implemented a regime to ensure that cargoes shipped by sea from around the world into EU ports would have their information submitted to the EU Customs computer in advance of the container being loaded aboard ship, by means of the Entry Summary Declaration (ENS), in a similar fashion to the C-TPAT (Customs–Trade Partnership Against Terrorism) initiative implemented by the US authorities. This initiative is called the Import Control System (ICS), and the system works in such a way that information concerning all cargoes being shipped to the European Union must be entered into the EU Customs computer at least 24 hours before the computer is dispatched to the Port of Loading and loaded aboard the vessel (http://ec.europa.eu/ecip).

In each non-EU load port, the transmission must be carried out no later than 24 hours prior to start of loading to the vessel bound for an EU port. To comply with this regulation, the shipping line will require complete and correct shipping instructions. The documentation closing times will follow the same timelines as other "advance manifest" 24-Hour Rule locations such as the US, Canada or Mexico. They are stipulated in the marine carrier's booking confirmation.

Transmission of ENS is obligatory for all cargo discharged in an EU port (including trans-shipment cargo) as well as FROB cargo (Foreign Cargo Remaining on Board), i.e. cargo which is discharged in a port outside the EU after the vessel has called an EU port.

In many cases, the advance notification which is issued at the Port of Loading needs to be given by the ship operator, carrier or his representative, such as the Ship's Agent. At present there is no distinction within the regulations as to whether, in the case of a chartered vessel, the charterer or the owner is considered to be the operator/carrier for the purposes of submission of the required declarations. However, it is expected that the charterer will be defined as the operator/carrier under a time charter, and the owner will be the operator/carrier under a voyage charter party. In containerised shipping, a freight forwarder, or Non Vessel Operating Common Carrier (NVOCC), will normally issue the advance notice, although this can also be carried out by the shipping agency at the Port of Loading. However, in the case of submission by a freight forwarder or NVOCC, this submission can only be carried out with the ship operator's full knowledge and consent. In the case of combined transport operations where trucks are driven on to a Ro-Ro ferry, it is the duty of the haulage company, its representative or the truck driver, to submit the advance notification prior to arrival at the Port of Loading. With regard to vessel-sharing arrangements such as slot carrier agreements in the container trade, the declaration is to be issued by the carrier issuing the Bill of Lading rather than the ship operator.

If the information is submitted by a nominated third party, such as an agent or freight forwarder, the ship operator will still be held responsible if notice is not delivered in advance or on time, and this delay may result in a penalty being imposed. However, the third party will still be liable for the accuracy of the information provided. Regardless of who provides the advance cargo declaration, the responsible party must also provide their Economic Operator Registration and Identification Number (EORI), which is essentially the trader's VAT Number plus an additional set of digits, in the case of the UK "000". For example, if a UK-based trader's VAT Number is 123 4567 89, their EORI will be 123456789000. The use of an EORI has been mandatory within the EU since 1 July 2009. Once advance notice of the cargo movement has been submitted, a confirmation will be issued containing a unique 18-digit number called a Movement Reference Number (MRN), used hitherto for Community Transit movements. The entire system is electronic, and therefore the person giving notice to Customs requires a computer system which can interface with the national Customs system. However, at the present time there is no system that is common throughout the EU capable of handling the new declarations, and for the present each Member State retains its own national system.

The information submitted in the various declarations is used by Customs to conduct a risk assessment of the cargo from a viewpoint of security and safety. As a result of this assessment, the cargo will then be classed as either risk type A, B or C, which in turn determines how the Customs Authority will respond. For example, if the Customs Office identifies a serious safety and security risk in relation to cargo to be loaded onto a deep sea container ship and classifies it as risk type A, it will issue a "Do Not Load" (DNL) or "Customs Hold" message preventing the carrier from shipping the cargo. DNL is the message returned by the EU Customs Office of first entry in receipt of the ENS in the place of an MRN. It means that analysis has been carried out on the declaration and that an unacceptable risk exists concerning the goods covered by the ENS declaration. This risk level may be further compounded by a lack of information entered on the cargo manifest with relation to details of the cargo. In the same way that the US and Canada outlawed the terms FAK (Freight of All Kinds) and "Said to Contain ...", the ENS system allows for a similar level of controls applied to scrutiny of the entry declaration, hence the risk assessment carried out by the relevant EU Customs Authority on each declaration.

The shipper is therefore required to submit an accurate and detailed set of shipping instructions to the carrier or their agent in order to facilitate an entry summary declaration. The required data elements for the entry summary declaration are:

- Full name and address of shipper and consignee;
- Full name and address of notify party where goods are carried under a negotiable "to order" Bill of Lading (B/L);
- Container number;
- Acceptable goods description (general terms for example "consolidated cargo", "general cargo", "Freight All Kinds", "Said to Contain", cannot be accepted);
- Minimally, the first 4 digits of the HS Commodity Code, although the 6-digit HS Code is recommended;
- Marks and numbers of packages;
- Cargo gross weight (in kilograms);
- Seal number;
- UN Dangerous Goods Code and IMDG Classification Code, where applicable;

- Method of payment for transport charges in case of "Freight Prepaid" (CFR, CIF, CPT, CIP), for example, payment in cash, payment by cheque, electronic credit transfer, etc.

The ENS will be sent to the Customs Office of the first port of entry (first port of call) in the EU, and this Customs Office will carry out a security risk assessment.

In the event that a risk is identified, subsequent ports of arrival and ports of loading will be informed:

- Risk Type A = Do Not Load;
- Risk Type B = Interception of a suspicious shipment at the first port of entry;
- Risk Type C = Interception of a suspicious shipment at the port of discharge.

In addition to submitting an ENS, an operator must also advise the national Customs Authority of a vessel's arrival by the submission of an *Arrival Notification* (AN) by a means acceptable to the Customs Office in that particular Member State. The AN may comprise of a list of MRNs relating to the vessel, or what is termed an "Entry Key", which consists of information about the vessel and the cargo (e.g. mode of transport, the vessel's IMO number, expected date of arrival).

There are certain drawbacks with the new entry summary declaration system. First, each national Customs Authority in the EU still retains its own national control system, which, as explained earlier, may not be compatible with those of other national Customs Authorities within the EU. This implies that information submitted in the form of an ENS to 1 Customs Authority cannot necessarily be transmitted to other Customs Authorities, especially in the case of the diversion of a vessel from 1 EU port to another port in another EU Member State, owing to a perceived lack of compatibility in systems used by each authority.

Second, the information provided for each cargo as contained within the ENS is only transmitted to the Customs Authority and not to any other national organisation. This means that any information deemed as being sensitive or prejudicial to national security may not necessarily be passed to other security authorities, such as other government departments, e.g. Defence or Interior. In this sense, the effectiveness of such information may be reduced, as it cannot be disseminated amongst the parties which ultimately may still have an interest in it, and thus leading to the risk of prejudicing national security interests.

In itself, this is not a problem insofar as the information provided is vetted by the EU Customs computer and will be authorised for entry into the EU on a *prima facie* basis, i.e. its face value. However, there is an increasing incidence of scams and fraudulent activities concerning the issue of fraudulent and false Bills of Lading concerning non-existent cargoes and either fictitious containers or containers which are in reality nowhere their purported route and which do not contain the supposed cargo. This trend casts grave doubt on the effectiveness of such a regime, especially where no official verification is made of the actual cargo inside the container by means of physical examination, or even a detailed scrutiny of the load list referring to the cargo stuffed inside the container, assuming that such a load list for the container actually exists in the first place. It is unfortunate that the days of cargo being physically scrutinised as it is stuffed into the container no longer exist. It has been common practice for the carrier or their agent to rely on the shipper to provide information concerning the containerised cargo for the purposes of the creation of the container manifest, hence the common usage of the term "Said to Contain …", which under the regimes of both ENS and C-TPAT is no longer allowed. However, although this term is no longer allowed and absolute details of the cargo must be submitted to the Customs computers, there is still no attempt by port or other national authorities to verify the exact details and accuracy of the cargoes being shipped by container, hence the alarming case of the radioactive container sitting isolated at the Port of Genoa. This may appear to be an isolated case, but it demonstrates and illustrates the alarming ease by which cargoes may be shipped across the oceans without adequate scrutiny and enter a country without a significant degree of vetting. In short, the information submitted through the ENS system may not necessarily equate with the actual cargo occupying the container.

It should be noted that the UK is subject to these cargo pre-clearance requirements for cargo exported form the UK to the EU since the exit of the UK from the EU on 31 December 2020.

Import/Export Compliance Summary

As a summary, the main elements of risk that should be addressed in terms of import and export documentation and procedures are the following:

Import Documentation

- Import Commercial Documentation (Invoices, Packing Lists);
- Import Transport Documentation (Bills of Lading, Air Waybills, CMR Consignment Notes);
- Customs Documentation (Certificates of Origin, Import Customs Declarations).

All Customs Import Declarations must be retained and filed by the importer according to each import transaction, as they are legal documents and must be retained by the importer for compliance purposes.

Export Documentation

- Export Commercial Documentation (Invoices, Packing Lists);
- Export Transport Documentation (Bills of Lading, Air Waybills, CMR Consignment Notes);
- Container/Trailer Manifests (for pre-clearance purposes);
- Customs Documentation (Certificates of Origin, Export Customs Declarations).

All Customs Export Declarations must be retained and filed by the importer according to each import transaction, as they are legal documents and must be retained by the importer for compliance purposes.

Documented Procedures Manuals

Although process flowcharts are an illustrative solution, Customs Authorities require documented Import and Export Procedures manuals as Standard Operating Procedures (SOPs). These explain, in a step-by-step basis, the requirements for the management and execution of individual import and export transactions, from the purchase order through the despatch of the consignment to the delivery of the consignment at the buyer's premises, including the documentation required for such activities. There must be a complete and transparent audit trail to cover such activities, and indeed the benchmarks ISO 28000 and 28001 deal with these issues in detail. Indeed, such is the depth of the ISO 28000/28001 benchmarks that they are included in requirements for AEO approvals.

Import and Export Transaction Record-Keeping

- Import transaction spreadsheet records;
- Export transaction spreadsheet records.

These must be maintained on a regular basis, as they are a requirement for import and export procedural compliance following the exit of the UK from the EU Customs Union at the end of 2020.

Other compliance requirements relate to:

- Origin;
- Commodity Codes;
- Customs Procedure Codes;
- Import Duty Reliefs (Special Procedures), e.g. Customs Warehousing, Inward Processing Relief;
- VAT;
- Duty and VAT Management.

These areas are covered in Customs Notices, but are part of the overall global World Customs Organisation remit, and affect importers and exporters globally. There is also the need for regular management checks and audits, both internal and external, as well as regular risk assessments, in order for the importer/exporter to maintain a low-risk status. Risk is an area constantly reviewed by any Customs and Tax Authority, and its crucial for the importer or exporter to recognise this and act upon it accordingly.

CHAPTER 6

Tariffs, Quotas, Sanctions and Other Trade Restrictions

Tariffs, quotas and other trade restrictions discourage imports of foreign products into a country. Tariffs are taxes on imported products. Quotas are limits on the amount of imported products. The ultimate quota is an embargo, which is a complete stop on the import or export of a certain product. Other measures that restrict international trade include standards and licenses. For example, some governments impose health and safety standards for imported products that are higher than for products made domestically. Governments can also require import and export licenses. This makes it more expensive and sometimes impossible for firms to engage in international trade. Some countries manipulate their currency values as a form of protectionism. If a country's currency decreases in value (relative to foreign countries' currencies), its exports become cheaper and its imports become more expensive. The Chinese government has been accused of artificially lowering its currency in order to encourage its exports and discourage foreign imports.

Tariffs, quotas and other trade restrictions discourage imports of foreign products into a country. Tariffs are taxes on imported products. Quotas are limits on the amount of imported products. The ultimate quota is an embargo, which is a complete stop on the import or export of a certain product. Other measures that restrict international trade include standards and licenses. For example, some governments impose health and safety standards for imported products that are higher than for products made domestically. Governments can also require import and export licenses. This makes it more expensive and sometimes impossible for firms to engage in international trade. Some countries manipulate their currency values as a form of protectionism. If a country's currency decreases in value (relative to foreign countries' currencies), its exports become cheaper and its imports become more expensive. The Chinese government has been accused of artificially lowering its currency in order to encourage its exports and discourage foreign imports.

 DOI: 10.4324/9781003341345-7

Quotas

What Is a Quota?

A quota is a government-imposed trade restriction that limits the number or monetary value of goods that a country can import or export during a particular period. Countries use quotas in international trade to help regulate the volume of trade between them and other countries. Countries sometimes impose quotas on specific products to reduce imports and increase domestic production. In theory, quotas boost domestic production by restricting foreign competition.

Government programmes that implement quotas are often referred to as protectionism policies. Additionally, governments can enact these policies if they have concerns over the quality or safety of products arriving from other countries.

In business, a quota can refer to a sales target that a company wants a salesperson or sales team to achieve for a specific period. Sales quotas are often monthly, quarterly or yearly. Management can also set sales quotas by region or business unit. The most common type of sales quota is based on revenue.

Key Points

- Countries use quotas in international trade to help regulate the volume of trade between them and other countries;
- Within the US, there are 3 forms of quotas: absolute, tariff-rate and tariff-preference level;
- Tariffs are taxes 1 country imposes on the goods and services imported from another country;
- Because tariffs increase the cost of imported goods and services, they make them less attractive to domestic consumers;
- Highly restrictive quotas coupled with high tariffs can lead to trade disputes and other problems between nations.

How a Quota Works

Quotas are different from tariffs or Customs, which place taxes on imports or exports. Governments impose both quotas and tariffs as protective measures to try to control trade between countries, but there are distinct differences between them.

Quotas focus on limiting the quantities (or, in some cases, the cumulative value) of a particular good that a country imports or exports for a specific period, whereas tariffs impose specific fees on those goods. Governments design tariffs (also known as Customs duties) to raise the overall cost to the producer or supplier seeking to sell products within a country. Tariffs provide a country with extra revenue, and they offer protection to domestic producers by causing imported items to become more expensive.

Quotas are more effective in restricting trade than tariffs, especially if domestic demand for something is not price-sensitive. Quotas may also be more disruptive to international trade than tariffs. Applied selectively to various countries, they can be utilised as a coercive economic weapon.

Import Quota Regulatory Agencies

In the US, the US Customs and Border Protection Agency, a federal law enforcement agency of the US Department of Homeland Security, oversees the regulation of international trade, collecting Customs and enforcing US trade regulations. Within the United States, the 3 forms of quotas are absolute, tariff-rate and tariff-preference level:

1. An absolute quota provides a definitive restriction on the quantity of a particular good that may be imported into the United States, although this level of restriction is not always in use. Under an absolute quota, once the quantity permitted by the quota is filled, merchandise subject to the quota must be held in a bonded warehouse or entered into a foreign trade zone until the opening of the next quota period;
2. Tariff-rate quotas allow a country to import a certain quantity of a particular good at a reduced Import Duty rate. Once the tariff-rate quota is met, all subsequently imported goods are charged at a higher rate;
3. A separate set of negotiations creates tariff-preference levels, such as those established through Free Trade Agreements (FTAs).

In the UK, the Department of International Trade, as part of HM government, is largely responsible for the imposition of quotas, although HM Revenue and Customs (HMRC) and the UK Border Force also maintain trade controls through Customs controls and scrutiny. Examples of UK-based quotas are the safeguard quotas imposed against imports of steel from overseas to protect steel manufacturers in the UK. These are based on Import Duty rates and amount to additional rates of 25% *ad valorem* duty imposed on such imports, usually for a specific period during the year, after which quotas may be temporarily suspended depending upon import levels of steel and steel products.

Goods Subject to Tariff-Rate Quotas

Various commodities are subject to tariff-rate quotas when entering the United States. These eligible commodities include, but are not limited to, milk and cream, cotton fabric, blended syrups, Canadian cheese, cocoa powder, infant formula, peanuts, sugar and tobacco. Such measures can conflict with the USMCA (US–Mexico–Canada) Free Trade Agreement.

Real World Example

Highly restrictive quotas coupled with high tariffs can lead to trade disputes, trade wars and other problems between nations. For example, in January 2018, President Trump imposed 30% tariffs on imported solar panels from China. This move signalled a more aggressive approach toward China's political and economic stance. It was also a blow to the US solar industry, which was responsible for generating US$18.7 billion of investment in the American economy and which at the time imported 80% to 90% of its solar panel products.

Price and Quality Effects

Trade restrictions generally raise the price of imported products and lower the quantity purchased. Consequently, buyers are more attracted to competing domestic products. In the short run, domestic firms benefit from trade restrictions.

However, the decrease in foreign competition provides the domestic producer with less incentive to produce a high-quality and low-cost product. The domestic firm typically raises its price, albeit less than the price increase of the foreign good. In the long run, the lower quality and higher price of the domestic firm's products harm the domestic firm. Consumers purchasing the product suffer as well, because they pay a higher price and face a more limited variety of competing products.

Tariffs and quotas are alike in that they both lower the quantity sold and raise the price of the foreign goods sold in this country. The difference is that in the case of a tariff, the imposing government generates revenue, whereas in the case of a quota, the higher price can benefit the foreign manufacturer (revenue and profit can increase depending on the elasticity of the product). Japanese automakers were not entirely unhappy with the quotas on their car sales to the United States. They sold fewer cars, but they received higher prices for them. Thus, their revenue decreased very little (depending on the elasticity of cars, revenue might have even increased).

Retaliation

Foreign countries often retaliate against countries imposing trade restrictions. Thus, export industries in all countries suffer. While trade restrictions may benefit domestic industries competing with foreign industries, they hurt export industries affected by retaliation. The economy as a whole suffers because, on balance, no jobs are gained and prices are higher due to the lost opportunities to specialise and benefit from absolute and comparative advantages.

In 2010, the United States imposed tariffs on tyre manufactured in China and imported into the United States. As retaliation, China imposed tariffs on chickens and auto parts purchased from the United States. In the end, taxes (tariffs) increased and, therefore, prices increased. On balance, no country gained employment. Competition, consumers, economic efficiency and the overall standard of living suffered.

The recent trade war between China and the United States is hurting both countries' productivity and economic growth. One of the US administration's justifications for imposing tariffs on China is to punish China for unfair trade practices and the illegal copying of products and intellectual information. China also has very restrictive rules for foreign companies doing business (direct investments) inside China. If these punitive tariffs lead to China liberalising its trade practices (implementing unrestricted free trade), the current tariffs may eventually have a positive outcome. However, if higher tariffs imposed by both countries remain, it will hurt economic growth and consumers in both countries.

Economic Sanctions

Economic sanctions are instruments of foreign policy that are imposed by countries or international organisations on other countries, or on entities and individuals within those countries. They are designed to penalise illegal activities, including financial crimes, humanitarian crimes and terrorism, or to achieve diplomatic objectives. Economic sanctions specifically prevent firms and individuals from doing business in, or with, countries named on a sanctions list.

Types of sanctions: Depending on diplomatic and political objectives, economic sanctions may be implemented as:

- Embargoes, preventing the provision of goods and services to another country;
- Tariffs on imported goods;
- Quotas on imports and exports;
- Non-tariff barriers, such as licensing or packaging requirements or standards for imports;
- Asset freezes on goods and funds.

Economic sanctions can be imposed comprehensively, meaning that they target entire countries, or they can be imposed as selective economic sanctions, meaning that they are targeted against individuals, entities or groups. Economic sanctions are devised by governments or international authorities, such as the United Nations Security Council, and enforced by domestic financial authorities. In the United States, for example, sanctions are enforced by the Office of Foreign Assets Control (OFAC).

AML and Economic Sanctions

The complexities of cross-border banking and financial systems and the diversity of global regulatory environments mean that countries and individual criminals are often able to exploit vulnerabilities to launder money and finance terrorist activities. By restricting and preventing business relationships with and within these countries, economic sanctions have become a foundation of anti-money laundering policies in jurisdictions across the world. Accordingly, financial institutions must integrate economic sanctions searches as part of their risk-based anti-money laundering (AML) policies: an obligation that requires firms to screen and monitor their customers and transactions.

Non-compliance with economic sanctions may result in fines and criminal charges. In 2019, OFAC issued around US$1.29 billion in penalties against 22 firms for sanctions breaches – up from US$71.5 million against 7 firms in 2018.

Importance of Sanctions Screening and Monitoring

Sanctions screening and monitoring can be complex and challenging. While many money launderers use pseudonyms or aliases, it may also may be difficult for firms to verify customer identities due to duplicate names, missing information or unfamiliar naming conventions. In many cases, sanctions screening can generate false positives and, worse, false negatives, so it is important that each institution implements a solution that delivers a satisfactory level of compliance performance.

In 2019, the OFAC issued a framework to help US companies implement and shape their economic sanctions compliance programmes. The document includes guidance on meeting compliance obligations, setting up internal controls and auditing for vulnerabilities. With that in mind, when devising a sanctions programme, firms should consider several important principles, including:

- **Regular updates:** Economic sanctions are issued and withdrawn frequently, so firms should also ensure that their screening and monitoring measures are responsive enough to adapt to these changes.

- **Geographic location:** Firms should ensure their sanctions screening measures are relevant to the jurisdiction in which they operate and can distinguish between comprehensive and selective sanctions.
- **Data analysis:** In order to screen sanctions lists and monitor changes in risk, firms must verify a range of data. Data collection and analysis software must be able to facilitate that process efficiently and accurately to create rich customer profiles.
- **Accuracy and fuzzy logic:** Screening and monitoring processes must take naming conventions, nicknames and pseudonyms into account when searching sanctions lists. Similarly, screening software should be capable of using fuzzy logic to identify duplicate entries on lists or to fill in gaps of missing data.

Companies must dedicate technology, resources and expertise to their AML and economic sanctions compliance needs, including training staff to manage the growing sanctions burden. Where an in-house compliance programme is not possible or prudent, firms should seek third-party support to find a solution that meets their needs and risk profile.

Trade Sanctions

Trade sanctions are laws passed to restrict or abolish trade with certain countries.

A type of economic sanction, **trade sanctions** are implemented to restrict trade activities with certain foreign targets, usually as part of a wider sanctions programme intended to achieve political or diplomatic goals. Trade sanctions set out prohibitions that may apply to target industries and individuals, or broadly to entire countries: the prohibitions make it a criminal offence for persons in the issuing country to do business with persons that fall under their scope.

Trade sanctions are a cornerstone of foreign policy for governments around the world and are used to punish violations of international law and human rights abuses or to enhance national security. Accordingly, trade sanctions are strictly enforced by regulators, meaning that banks, financial institutions and other service providers should carefully monitor their compliance to ensure they do not incur significant penalties or criminal charges.

Trade sanctions may be imposed unilaterally or target specific forms of trade, or even individuals and organisations. Individual countries may impose trade sanctions as part of autonomous sanctions regimes or, alternatively, groups of countries acting as members of international organisations, such as the United Nations, may impose trade sanctions collectively.

The different categories of trade sanctions include:

- **Tariffs:** The application fees or taxes on the import of goods and services from a target country;
- **Quotas:** The imposition of limits on the trade of goods and services to and from a target country;
- **Asset freezes:** Governments may restrict trade by freezing the assets of countries, organisations, or individuals, when those assets are located within their jurisdiction.
- **Non-tariff barriers:** The imposition of peripheral trade restrictions, such as packaging requirements, humanitarian labour requirements, or animal welfare requirements.

Embargoes

While trade sanctions and embargoes occupy the same regulatory space – in the sense that they both involve economic restrictions against a third country – there are practical *differences* between the 2 measures. Whereas sanctions may target specific trading activities or individuals, embargoes are applied much more broadly, often comprehensively prohibiting trade with a target country, or instead prohibiting all imports from, or exports to, that country. In some cases, an embargo may restrict only the import and export of certain types of goods, such as military end-use equipment.

Examples of Trade Sanctions and Embargoes

Trade sanctions are used frequently as a way to coerce or incentivise target countries to adhere to international law. Examples include:

- The US embargo on Cuba, imposed in 1963, prohibited all imports and exports between the US and Cuba. The embargo was adjusted in 2000 to allow for the export of medical and agricultural goods;
- The OPEC oil embargo on the US, imposed between 1973 and 1974 in response to the US's support for Israel during the Arab–Israeli War;
- Embargoes from multiple countries against Apartheid South Africa – which lasted until the end of apartheid in 1994;
- US trade sanctions against North Korea prohibit the export of goods to, and any investment in, North Korea;
- EU sanctions against Turkish individuals in response to Turkey's oil drilling activities off the coast of Cyprus.

US, UK and EU sanctions against Russia in response to the 2014 invasion of Crimea, oppression of pro-democracy protests and the arrest of opposition leader Alexei Navalny. These have been further reinforced because of the Russian invasion of Ukraine in late February 2022, without any sign of withdrawal by the Russian forces. As a result, trade sanctions against Russia have been significantly increased by the aforementioned countries.

Trade Sanctions Enforcement

Most governments have established enforcement authorities to manage the implementation of trade sanctions. In the United States, sanctions enforcement is the responsibility of the **Office of Foreign Assets Control**, which maintains the US's **Specially Designated Nationals (SDN)** and **Blocked Persons List**. The SDN list sets out the individuals and companies that are currently targeted by US trade sanctions.

Trade sanctions can take various forms such as:

- Complete embargo on specific types of trade;
- Tariff barriers: Higher taxes on imports of goods. If the tariffs are sufficiently high, they may stop imports completely;
- Quotas limiting the amount of trade.

Trade sanctions could be implemented for political or economic reasons.

- For example, the US imposed a trade embargo with Cuba from 1963, in protest at the Communist government. From 2000, the embargo was lifted on medical and agricultural items but remained on others;
- After the First Gulf War, the United Nations imposed trade sanctions on Iraq to put pressure on allowing weapon inspectors;
- Trade sanctions may be imposed on countries engaging in unfair trading practices. For example, domestic subsidies may give domestic firms an unfair competitive advantage. Brazil imposed trade sanctions against the US in response to the US government subsidising US cotton farmers.

Trade Barriers

Definition: Trade barriers are government policies that place restrictions on international trade. Trade barriers can either make trade more difficult and expensive (tariff barriers) or prevent trade completely (e.g. trade embargo).

Examples of Trade Barriers

- **Tariff barriers.** These are taxes on certain imports. They raise the price of imported goods, making imports less competitive;
- **Non-Tariff barriers.** These involve rules and regulations which make trade more difficult. For example, if foreign companies have to adhere to complex manufacturing laws, it can be difficult to trade;

- **Quotas.** A limit placed on the number of imports;
- **Voluntary Export Restraint (VER).** Similar to quotas, this is where countries agree to limit the number of imports. This was used by the US for imports of Japanese cars;
- **Subsidies.** A domestic subsidy from the government can give the local firm a competitive advantage;
- **Embargo.** A complete ban on imports from a certain country. For example, US embargo with Cuba.

Real-World Examples of Trade Barriers

- **Chinese import tariffs.** This link shows that China is reducing its import tariffs on luxury foreign goods such as Scottish Whiskey from 10% to 5%. It is a sign the Chinese government wants to encourage consumer spending.
- **50% tariff on imports of washing machines.** The US trade body has recommended tariffs of 50% on imports of washing machines – especially from South Korean manufacturers LG and Samsung. The Trade body is concerned LG is selling washing machines below cost and dumping surplus supply on the US market. US manufacturer Whirlpool brought the case.
- **Customs Duties post-Brexit.** Since the UK left the EU Single Market as part of the Brexit process, there are Customs Declarations and regulations to meet on exports and imports. These rules and regulations provide significant controls on trade, despite the UK–EU Trade and Co-operation Agreement (TCA).
- **Quotas on low-tariff food.** The EU has a quota for allowing a certain number of food items to enter without attracting tariffs.
- **VER.** In 1981, the US implemented a Voluntary Export Restraint (VER) agreement that limited the Japanese to exporting 1.68 million cars to the US per year. This limited the import of cars, though ironically made it more profitable for Japanese exporters. With a limit on the quantity, they could increase prices. Another consequence of this was that Japanese firms began assembling cars in the US and entering into partnerships with American car companies to get around the export restrictions.
- **Subsidies.** The EU gives €39 billion to farmers in direct subsidies. Indirectly, this makes EU agricultural exports more competitive and gives EU farmers an advantage in trade.
- **Embargoes.** Embargoes are usually implemented for political reasons. After Fidel Castro came to power, the US imposed a trade embargo on Cuba, which was strictly enforced.

CHAPTER 7

Anti-Dumping and Countervailing Duties

Dumping

Dumping, in economics, is a kind of injuring pricing, especially in the context of international trade. It occurs when manufacturers export a product to another country at a price below the normal price with an injuring effect. The objective of dumping is to increase market share in a foreign market by driving out competition and thereby create a monopoly situation where the exporter will be able to unilaterally dictate price and quality of the product.

A standard technical definition of dumping is the act of charging a lower price for the like product in a foreign market than the normal value of the product, for example the price of the same product in a domestic market of the exporter or in a third country market. This is often referred to as selling at less than "normal value" on the same level of trade in the ordinary course of trade. Under the World Trade Organisation's (WTO) Anti-Dumping Agreement, full name *Agreement on Implementation of Article VI of the General Agreement on Tariffs and Trade 1994*, dumping is not prohibited unless it causes or threatens to cause material injury to a domestic industry in the importing country. Dumping is also prohibited when it causes "material retardation" in the establishment of an industry in the domestic market.

If a company exports a product at a price that is lower than the price it normally charges in its own home market, or sells at a price that does not meet its full cost of production, it is said to be "dumping" the product. It is a sub-part of the various forms of price discrimination and is classified as third-degree price discrimination. Opinions differ as to whether or not such practice constitutes unfair competition, but many governments take action against dumping to protect domestic industry. The WTO agreement does not pass judgement. Its focus is on how governments can or cannot react to dumping – it disciplines anti-dumping actions, and it is often called the "Anti-dumping Agreement". It should be noted that this focus only on the reaction to dumping contrasts with the approach of the subsidies and countervailing measures agreement.

 DOI: 10.4324/9781003341345-8

The legal definitions are more precise, but in general the WTO agreement allows governments to act against dumping where there is genuine, i.e. "material", injury to the competing domestic industry. To a certain degree, Section 201 of the US 1974 Trade Act covers this element. To do so, the government has to show that dumping is taking place, calculate the extent of dumping (how much lower the export price is compared to the exporter's home market price), and show that the dumping is causing injury or threatening to cause injury.

While permitted by the WTO, the General Agreement on Tariffs and Trade (GATT) Article VI allows countries the option of taking action against dumping. The Anti-Dumping Agreement clarifies and expands Article VI, and the two operate together. They allow countries to act in a way that would normally break the GATT principles of binding a tariff and not discriminating between trading partners – typically, anti-dumping action means charging extra Import Duty on the particular product from the particular exporting country in order to bring its price closer to the "normal value" or to remove the injury to domestic industry in the importing country.

There are many different ways of calculating whether a particular product is being dumped heavily or only lightly. The agreement narrows down the range of possible options. It provides 3 methods to calculate a product's "normal value." The main one is based on the price in the exporter's domestic market. When this cannot be used, two alternatives are available: the price charged by the exporter in another country, or a calculation based on the combination of the exporter's production costs, other expenses and normal profit margins. The agreement also specifies how a fair comparison can be made between the export price and what would be a normal price.

Detailed procedures are set out on how anti-dumping cases are to be initiated, how the investigations are to be conducted, and the conditions for ensuring that all interested parties are given an opportunity to present evidence. Anti-dumping measures must expire 5 years after the date of imposition, unless a review shows that ending the measure would lead to economic injury.

In general, an anti-dumping investigation usually develops along the following steps: domestic producers make a request to the relevant authority to initiate an anti-dumping investigation. Then, an investigation of the foreign producer is conducted to determine if the allegation is valid. It uses questionnaires completed by the interested parties to compare the foreign producer's (or producers') export price to the normal value (the price in the exporter's domestic market, the price charged by the exporter in another country, or a calculation based on the combination of the exporter's production costs, other expenses and normal profit margins). If the foreign producer's export price is lower than the normal price and the investigating body proves a causal link between the alleged dumping and the injury suffered by the domestic industry, it concludes that the foreign producer is dumping its products. According to Article VI of GATT, dumping investigations shall, except in special circumstances, be concluded within 1 year, and in no case more than 18 months after initiation. Anti-dumping measures must expire 5 years after the date of imposition, unless a review shows that ending the measure would lead to injury.

Anti-dumping investigations are to end immediately in cases where the authorities determine that the margin of dumping is *de minimis*, or insignificantly small (defined as less than 2% of the export price of the product). Other conditions are also set. For example, the investigations also have to end if the volume of dumped imports is negligible (i.e. if the volume from 1 country is less than 3% of total imports of that product – although investigations can proceed if several countries, each supplying less than 3% of the imports, together account for 7% or more of total imports).

The agreement states that member countries must inform the Committee on Anti-Dumping Practices about all preliminary and final anti-dumping actions, promptly and in detail. They must also report on all investigations twice a year. When differences arise, members are encouraged to consult each other. They can also use the WTO's dispute settlement procedure.

Duties

Anti-dumping duty is an Import Duty charged in addition to the normal Customs Duty and applies across the UK and the whole EU. It allows the UK and EU to take action against goods sold at less than their normal value, defined as the price for "like goods" sold in the exporter's home market.

An anti-dumping duty is, therefore, a protectionist tariff that a domestic government imposes on foreign imports that it believes are priced below fair market value. Dumping is a process wherein a company exports a product at a price that is significantly lower than the price it normally charges in its home (or domestic) market.

Key Points

- An anti-dumping duty is a protectionist tariff that a domestic government imposes on foreign imports that it believes are priced below fair market value;
- In order to protect their respective economy, many countries impose duties on products they believe are being dumped in their national markets; this is done with the rationale that these products have the potential to undercut local businesses and the local economy;
- While the intention of anti-dumping duties is to save domestic jobs, these tariffs can also lead to higher prices for domestic consumers;

- In the long-term, anti-dumping duties can reduce the international competition of domestic companies producing similar goods;
- In the US, the International Trade Commission (ITC) – an independent government agency – is tasked with imposing anti-dumping duties;
- The World Trade Organization – an international organisation that deals with the rules of trade between nations – also operates a set of international trade rules, including the international regulation of anti-dumping measures.

In order to protect their respective economy, many countries impose duties on products they believe are being dumped in their national markets because these products have the potential to undercut local businesses and the local economy.

The actions of the US international Trade Commission (ITC) are based on recommendations which it receives from the US Department of Commerce and investigations by the International Trade Commission and/or the Department of Commerce.

In many cases, the duties imposed on these goods exceed the value of the goods. Anti-dumping duties are typically levied when a foreign company is selling an item significantly below the price at which it is being produced.

While the intention of anti-dumping duties is to save domestic jobs, these tariffs can also lead to higher prices for domestic consumers. In the long-term, anti-dumping duties can reduce the international competition of domestic companies producing similar goods.

The World Trade Organization, based in Geneva, Switzerland, is the main international organisation that deals with the rules of trade between nations. The WTO also operates a set of international trade rules, including the international regulation of anti-dumping measures. The WTO does not intervene in the activities of companies engaged in dumping. Instead, it focuses on how governments can – or cannot – react to the practice of dumping. In general, the WTO agreement permits governments to act against dumping "if it causes or threatens material injury to an established industry in the territory of a contracting party or materially retards the establishment of a domestic industry".

This intervention must be justified in order to uphold the WTO's commitment to free-market principles. Anti-dumping duties have the potential to distort the market. In a free market, governments cannot normally determine what constitutes a fair market price for any good or service.

Example of an Anti-Dumping Duty

In June 2015, American steel companies United States Steel Corp., Nucor Corp., Steel Dynamics Inc., ArcelorMittal USA, AK Steel Corp., and California Steel Industries, Inc. filed a complaint with the US Department of Commerce and the ITC. Their complaint alleged that several countries, including China, were dumping steel into the US market and keeping prices unfairly low.

After conducting a review, 1 year later the US announced that it would be imposing a total of 522% combined anti-dumping and countervailing Import Duties on certain steel imported from China. In 2018, China filed a complaint with the WTO challenging the tariffs imposed by the Trump administration. The Trump administration continued to use the WTO to challenge what it claimed were unfair trading practices by the Chinese government and other trading partners.

Countervailing Duties

Countervailing duties (CVDs), also known as **anti-subsidy duties**, are trade Import Duties imposed under WTO rules to neutralise the negative effects of subsidies, especially export subsidies. They are imposed after an investigation finds that a foreign country subsidises its exports, injuring domestic producers in the importing country. According to WTO rules, a country can launch its own investigation and decide to charge extra duties, provided such additional duties are in accordance with GATT Article VI and the GATT Agreement on Subsidies and Countervailing Measures.

Since countries can rule domestically whether domestic industries are in danger and whether foreign countries subsidise the products, the institutional process surrounding the investigation and determinations has significant impacts beyond the countervailing duties.

Countervailing duties in the US are assessed by the International Trade Administration (ITA) of the US Department of Commerce, which determines whether imports in question are being subsidised and, if so, by how much. If there is a determination that there is material injury to the competing domestic industry, the Department of Commerce will instruct the US Customs and Border Protection (US CBP) Agency to levy duties in an amount equivalent to the subsidy margins.

Petitions for remedies may be filed by domestic manufacturers or unions within the domestic industry, but the law requires that the petitioners represent at least 25% of the domestic production of the goods for which competition is causing material injury.

Countervailing duties (CVDs) are, therefore, tariffs levied on imported goods to offset subsidies made to producers of these goods in the exporting country. CVDs are meant to level the playing field between domestic producers of a product and foreign producers of the same product who can afford to sell it at a lower price because of the subsidy they receive from their own national government.

Key Points

- Countervailing duties, or CVDs, are tariffs on imported goods that are imposed to offset subsidies given by the exporting country's government;
- CVDs help offset any negative domestic impacts that producers of the same good might experience due to foreign competition, who in this case, would receive a subsidy to export the same good;
- The WTO only permits countervailing duties to be charged after the importing nation has conducted an in-depth investigation into the subsidised exports.

CVDs are special measures meant to neutralise the negative effects that subsidies for the production of a good in 1 country have on that same industry in another country, where the production of that good is not subsidised.

If left unchecked, such subsidised imports can have a severe effect on the domestic industry, forcing factory closures and causing huge job losses. As export subsidies are considered to be an unfair trade practice, the World Trade Organisation, which deals with the global rules of trade between nations, has detailed procedures in place to establish the circumstances under which countervailing duties can be imposed by an importing nation.

The WTO's "Agreement on Subsidies and Countervailing Measures", which is contained in the General Agreement on Tariffs and Trade 1994, defines when and how an export subsidy can be used and regulates the measures that member nations can take to offset the effect of such subsidies.

These measures include the affected nation using the WTO's dispute settlement procedure to seek the withdrawal of the subsidy or imposing countervailing duties on subsidised imports that are hurting domestic producers.

Example of Countervailing Duties

Consider the following example of countervailing duties. Assume Country A provides an export subsidy to widget makers in the nation, who export widgets *en masse* to Country B at US$8 per widget. Country B has its widget industry and domestic widgets are available at US$10 per widget.

If Country B determines that its domestic widget industry is being hurt by unrestrained imports of subsidised widgets, it may impose a 25%

countervailing duty on widgets imported from Country A, so that the resulting cost of the imported widgets is also US$10. This eliminates the unfair price advantage that widget makers in Country A have due to the export subsidy from their government.

Special Considerations

The definition of "subsidy" in this regard is quite broad. It includes any financial contribution made by a government or government agency, including a direct transfer of funds (such as grants, loans and infusion of equity), potential direct transfers of funds (for example, loan guarantees), fiscal incentives such as tax credits, and any form of income or price support.

The WTO only permits countervailing duties to be charged after the importing nation has conducted an in-depth investigation into the subsidised exports. The agreement contains detailed rules for determining whether a product is being subsidised and calculating the amount of such subsidy, criteria for establishing whether these subsidised imports are affecting the domestic industry, and rules for the implementation and duration of countervailing duties, which is typically 5 years.

Anti-dumping duty is imposed on imports "dumped" in the UK and EU – that is, sold at a price substantially below their normal value, usually their domestic market price. Anti-subsidies and "countervailing" measures apply duties or other actions, such as import quantity restrictions, to imports that benefit from specific subsidies in their country of origin. Safeguards are actions temporarily imposed on imports expected or likely to cause serious damage to a domestic industry competing with the imported goods.

This guide provides an overview of the 3 measures and explains how to check when they apply. It also covers investigations, defences and other practices. For detailed information, see the guide on using trade preferences.

Anti-Dumping Duty Measures

The Anti-Dumping Agreement is 1 of 3 World Trade Organization principal trade defence agreements. The UK and the EU are party to the agreements, which are applied across the UK and all EU Member States.

Anti-dumping duty (ADD) is imposed in addition to any normal Customs Duty for which the goods being imported are liable. It enables the UK and EU to take action against goods sold at considerably less than their "normal value". This is defined as a price that is lower than the price of similar goods in the country from which they originate.

The UK or any EU member state can unilaterally apply anti-dumping measures after an investigation shows that the imported goods infringe the ADD agreement and that the dumped imports are causing material injury to a domestic industry producing a similar product. The same is true of any nation adhering to the rules imposed by the WTO.

ADD measures usually take the form of additional duties, calculated at rates to account for the discrepancy in the relevant values of the products imported.

Anti-dumping investigations are resolved by the exporters of the product agreeing not to sell that product below a certain price. If the trader has observed dumping that has caused, or threatened to cause, material injury to their domestic industry, they should report it.

If it is believed that an EU member state has not complied with all the requirements before imposing ADD measures, the affected trader can take their case to the WTO's Dispute Settlement Body.

Anti-Subsidies and Countervailing Measures

The Agreement on Subsidies and Countervailing Measures (ASCM) is 1 of 3 WTO principal trade defence agreements. The UK and the EU are party to all the agreements, which are and can be applied across the UK and all EU member states.

ASCM covers 2 separate but closely related topics:

1. Anti-subsidy measures allow importing countries to take banning action against certain kinds of subsidised imports. "Subsidies" are defined as financial assistance from the government of a third country to a company or group of companies in that country;
2. Other types of subsidy that are "actionable". This means that the importing country must investigate and be able to demonstrate how the subsidised imports have caused damage to domestic industry before it imposes any countervailing duties on the subsidised products.

The issue of subsidies is complex and is handled at the government level, with disputes being settled by the WTO. A system of notification and reviews of measures allows for transparency.

The agreement does not apply to trade in agricultural products, where export subsidies are common in some countries.

There are also special rules for developing countries to provide some scope for maintaining export subsidies under certain conditions.

Safeguard Measures

The Safeguards Agreement is 1 of 3 WTO principal trade defence agreements. The UK and the EU are party to all the agreements, which are and can be applied across the UK and all EU Member States.

This agreement differs from the other 2 as countries are entitled to take action in cases of unfair foreign competition arising from either anti-dumping, anti-subsidy, or both. The UK and EU use an independent mediator to guarantee fairness and the right of defence in trade proceedings.

Safeguards do not cover traders' allegations that the competition is unfair. They allow a WTO member to temporarily restrict imports of a product to protect a specific domestic industry, e.g. steel. This could occur because unforeseen surges in imports cause or threaten to cause serious damage to that particular industry. The recent safeguard quotas imposed on steel imports into the UK and the EU came about largely because of the sheer quantities of steel being imported into the UK and the EU at low prices, a scenario that was deemed to be causing economic harm to domestic steel producers in both the UK and the EU.

Measures can be applied under the Safeguards Agreement, provided that all the following conditions prevail and apply during the term of the measures:

- They only apply for a temporary period;
- They are only imposed when the imports are found to cause or threaten serious injury to a competing domestic industry;
- They are applied to imports from all sources on a non-selective basis;
- The measures are progressively liberalised while in effect – the member imposing the safeguards may be required to compensate the members whose trade is affected.

Goods imported from outside the UK and EU may be subject to Import Duty, depending on the type of goods and their country of origin. Details are given in the UK Trade Tariff, where traders can find the specific classification for imports. The classification also explains whether duty is payable, but traders should also check for updates.

Imports of some types of goods from particular countries may be subject to the following additional Customs Duties:

- Anti-dumping duties (ADD) may be imposed if the goods are being dumped in the UK or EU at below their normal commercial value;
- countervailing duties can apply to imports that have been subsidised by the authorities of the exporting country from which they originate – note that this isn't the same as countervailing charges, which can apply to agricultural products subject to the Common Agricultural Policy;
- if the UK or EU suspect dumping is taking place, traders may have to pay provisional duty while an investigation is being carried out.

Once goods imported from outside the UK and EU clear Customs, they are normally in Free Circulation within the UK and EU. This means they can then be traded within the UK and EU without any further duty (except for excise goods such as tobacco, which are subject to Excise Duty). This page explains when any anti-dumping or countervailing charges must be paid and includes notes on special cases such as duty suspension schemes and registration.

Any import, anti-dumping and countervailing duties are payable when the goods are put into free circulation in the UK and EU.

Duty Suspension Schemes

Special rules apply in some cases. The point of free circulation may be deferred when placing goods under Customs Warehousing, Inward Processing, and other duty relief procedures that may benefit traders. For more detailed information, see the guide on importing your goods from outside the UK and EU.

Sometimes, as a result of European Commission regulation, Customs Officers may suspect that goods may be subject to anti-dumping or countervailing duty, but need to investigate further.

In these circumstances, the imports may be registered before being released by Customs. Traders may be required to pay additional duties later if it is confirmed that the goods in question are being dumped.

Anti-dumping and countervailing duties are applied at an EU-wide level, rather than just in the UK. Complaints of unfair trade practices are investigated either by the Trade Defence Section of the EU or, in more serious cases, by the European Anti-Fraud Office (OLAF).

Investigations are only undertaken if there is sufficient evidence of a negative impact on UK and EU producers. Specifically, you need to show that:

- Imports from a particular country (outside the UK or EU) are being dumped or subsidised for sale in the UK or EU;
- Import volumes are significant, and producers representing at least 25% of total UK or EU production of the particular goods are affected.

This means that complaints are usually started by UK or European trade associations rather than single companies.

Provisional anti-dumping or countervailing duty may be charged while suspected dumping is investigated. If a definitive duty is not imposed at the end of the investigation, any provisional duty paid is refunded automatically.

In some circumstances, a full or partial refund can be claimed on any additional duty that has been paid. A full refund can be claimed if it can be shown that the goods on which duty was charged were not, in fact dumped. If it can be shown that too much duty was charged, a partial refund can be claimed. For example, anti-dumping duty might be based on the difference between the price charged in the UK, or EU, and the price charged in the exporter's home market. If it can be shown that the home market price is, in fact, higher than suggested, especially in cases of inefficient production of the material concerned, the duty could be reduced.

In the case of the UK, repayment claims are dealt with by the Department of International Trade (DIT) Trade Defence Unit. Claims must normally be made within 6 months of the regulation coming into force. Traders have the right to appeal against decisions to impose anti-dumping duty made by HMRC. For example, a trader might appeal if they feel the amount of duty charged has been incorrectly calculated. Normally, the duty must be paid before an appeal can proceed.

Investigations

When it is suspected that goods are being dumped in the UK or EU at an unfairly low price, an investigation can be started. Once the UK and EU decide to investigate, an investigation typically lasts a maximum of 15 months. The UK and EU can impose provisional duties for up to a maximum time of 9 months after the investigation has commenced if this is justified. A final decision is made on whether to make the measures definitive within a further 6 months. If the investigations show that dumping is not occurring, no additional duties are imposed. Any provisional duties that have already been paid are refunded.

Definitive duties can then be imposed for a period of up to 5 years. After this period has expired, this regulation will normally be reviewed to see if an extension is warranted.

Provisional anti-dumping or countervailing duty may be imposed while the investigation is being carried out. If the investigation shows that the goods are being dumped, a definitive duty is then imposed.

More serious cases and investigations, known as missions, are usually carried out by the anti-fraud office of the EU, OLAF, sometimes with a delegate from HMRC in attendance. Usually, it is exporters who are investigated, although manufacturers and agents can be subject to investigation too.

An investigation can be stopped if a particular exporter of the suspect goods gives a satisfactory undertaking to stop the suspected dumping. For example, the exporter can increase the price to a fair level or stop exporting the goods to the areas where they were being dumped. The exporter must also provide evidence of doing this and allow Customs to carry out any required checks.

Circumvention

Anti-dumping and countervailing duties are imposed on goods from a particular country. Sometimes traders try to avoid the duties by diverting goods so that they seem to come from somewhere else. For example, goods could be sent to another country, repackaged, and then exported to the UK or EU. Another form of circumvention is the use of an inappropriate commodity code that is not affected by anti-dumping duties. These issues are considered high risk by HMRC concerning import practices. If the Customs authority detects this form of circumvention, all imports of the goods in question may be investigated by the authorities of the UK and the EU.

If the goods are later proven to have originated in the country that is subject to anti-dumping duty, then the UK and EU are likely to extend any regulations to cover such imports, regardless of where they originate. This means that all imports of the affected goods from the "transit" country could have anti-dumping duty imposed, regardless of their origin.

In the UK, the DIT is responsible for trade policy and legislation, including trade defence measures such as anti-dumping and countervailing duties. HMRC is responsible for collecting anti-dumping and countervailing duties.

CHAPTER 8

Excise Duty

Domestic duties are consumption-based taxes, i.e. based on the consumption of specific products, and are levied on the specific strength or nature of the product concerned, i.e. tobacco, fuels or alcoholic beverages. These also include several other taxes and duties, from landfill tax and air passenger duty, through vehicle excise duty and gambling and gaming taxes to specific Excise Duties on hydrocarbon-based products such as vehicle fuel, namely petrol or diesel, ethanols and bioethanols, tobacco and alcoholic goods. However, the main source of revue, especially for the UK and the EU, comes from alcoholic goods, tobacco products and fuel duty. In the case of alcoholic goods, the main sources are:

- Spirits (gin, whisky, rum and spirit-based liqueurs);
- Wines (including fortified wines such as port and sherry);
- Beers and ciders.

Excise Duties are much higher than other duties, such as Import Duty, and have their own due diligence requirements, for both domestic and import purposes, including the domestic production of alcoholic beverages, including beer, cider, wines, liqueurs and spirits. In turn, this generates even more risk concerning possible compromises to revenue generation based on such duties, and requires traders to exercise much more due diligence concerning the control and management of such duties. HMRC in the UK have published such due diligence guidelines, namely EDDC 01010, and resulting from this, EDDC 1030. EDDC 01010 covers overall Excise due diligence.

In the UK, due diligence, in relation to alcohol duty fraud, became a condition of approval on 1 November 2014 for breweries approved to trade in duty suspension under section 41A of the Alcoholic Liquor Duties Act 1979 and on the following approvals registered under section 100G of the Customs and Excise Management Act 1979:

- Authorised Excise Warehousekeepers;
- Registered Owners of Goods (within an Excise warehouse);

 DOI: 10.4324/9781003341345-9

- Registered Tax Representatives (this applies to Northern Ireland businesses only);
- Registered Commercial Importers (this applies to Northern Ireland businesses only);
- Temporary Registered Consignees (this applies to Northern Ireland businesses only);
- Registered Consignees (this applies to Northern Ireland businesses only);
- Registered Consignors (this applies to Northern Ireland businesses only).

The same regulations apply to distilleries of gin and whisky and bonded maturation premises, as well as trade facility activities such as blending and bottling of alcoholic beverages. Given that the UK was part of the EU at the time, these measures were commensurate with those within the rest of the EU, although Excise Duties differ throughout the EU.

Due diligence also became a condition of approval on 1 January 2016 for businesses approved under the Alcoholic Liquor Duties Act (ALDA) 1979 part 6A section 88c as wholesalers of alcohol under the Alcohol Wholesaler Registration Scheme (AWRS). It is aimed at those who are dealing in alcoholic liquor goods as their main business.

In general terms, due diligence is the appropriate reasonable care which a business must exercise when it enters into business relationships or contracts with other businesses. It is a series of checks to identify and manage any risk that a business may have within a transaction or Supply Chain. These risks could be anything from not being paid to handling illegally sourced goods. The approach will differ from business to business, with different tests applied, depending on where the business is within a Supply Chain and the nature of the transactions under consideration.

Due diligence is not static but is an ongoing, dynamic process that develops as the relationship between the trading parties evolves. Reasonable care is based on the use of sound judgement or acting in a sensible manner. The actual due diligence carried out by a business should be proportionate to the level of risk it identifies. This means that the greater the potential, perceived or actual risk, the greater the level of due diligence required, and all HMRC approvals and authorisations require the applicant company to show that they maintain an acceptable level of due diligence in their activities.

According to EDDC 1030, the due diligence condition is an anti-fraud measure to help address UK alcohol fraud. To introduce illicit goods into legitimate markets, criminals capitalise on the demand for popular brands, and use complex supply routes (with sophisticated finance, procurement and logistics arrangements) to mask the origin of goods.

The due diligence condition places a requirement on Excise-registered businesses at all key stages of a Supply Chain to:

- Consider tax fraud risks;
- Make checks in relation to those risks;
- Establish the level of risks and whether they are acceptable to their business;
- Take effective action to reduce exposure to fraud risks identified.

This ensures that due diligence is carried out within each alcohol supply route. Where registered businesses identify and react appropriately to fraud risks, this will help reduce criminals' access to, and restrict avenues for onward sale of, illicit goods. It also reduces the risk of legitimate businesses unwittingly handling illicit goods. Therefore, risk assessments and due diligence checks must be carried out to a reasonable standard across the sector. Where it is not, you should react robustly and consistently.

In the case of Excise management for alcoholic beverages, businesses must carry out due diligence to minimise their exposure to risks of goods they trade in or handle being linked to alcohol fraud. This same due diligence must be carried out in the case of fuel products, as there is a major issue with the misuse of rebated fuels such as red diesel, and regular checks carried out on traders and operators alike where such fuels are used. Businesses must carry out timely, reasonable and proportionate checks on intended transactions (and Supply Chains) before entering into new agreements. They should also carry out regular checks on existing arrangements they have. Where businesses properly carry out due diligence this will help ensure that:

- They have a good understanding of risks and overall market for the goods traded;
- They have a good knowledge and understanding about their customer;
- Their customers will pay for goods on time;
- Goods held out for sale physically exist and will arrive if ordered;
- Sellers have legal ownership of goods and are able to sell them on;
- Goods are as described and not counterfeit;
- Goods are of merchantable quality;
- Taxes and duties are correctly accounted for;
- Businesses holding Excise approvals do not become unwittingly liable for duty or penalties;
- Risk of fraud or evasion is minimised.

Each business should have appropriate management controls for these checks. Where a third party carries out due diligence checks, the registered person remains responsible for ensuring that adequate due diligence and risk assessment procedures are in place.

A key element in tackling alcohol and fuel fraud is to ensure that the Excise due diligence condition is applied properly and consistently across the sector, from production to consumption. Although a large number of businesses will carry out reasonable due diligence, others may choose to ignore risks or carry out cursory checks to appear compliant. We should challenge robustly those who are not applying due diligence properly, reminding them of their obligations. It is these businesses who may, unwittingly or otherwise, become involved with the illicit alcohol trade. Of particular risk are those in key positions, such as warehousekeepers, and those trading in significant volumes of Excise goods.

Due diligence is also a requirement in other tax areas, for example, VAT; in the case of HMRC, VAT Notice 726 (GOV.UK) provides more detail, and similar provisions exist with other national Revenue Authorities globally. Where Excise due diligence concerns are identified, you should also consider whether there are any wider "cross tax" implications to your findings and share your concerns with appropriate teams.

The effective management of indirect taxes is crucial to a company's successful operation in the present-day global marketplace. As Supply Chains grow longer and become more international and more complex, understanding the impact of VAT/GST, Excise Duties, Customs Duties and export controls is not just an issue for the tax function. Indirect taxes must be actively managed throughout the business if they are to work with, not against, any international trading company's strategic agenda.

Considerations include:

- Cost base – avoiding irrecoverable VAT, Excise Duties and Customs Duties;
- Cash flow – delayed VAT refunds and pre-financed duty payments;
- Compliance burden – managing Customs and Excise warehouses, applications for incentives, VAT returns and VAT registrations, VAT invoicing, Excise returns, Customs documentation requirements, managing export compliance obligations;
- Corporate risk – reputational risk, penalties, fines and criminal liability for errors and omissions;
- Growth opportunities – incentives for setting up new productive activity, intelligent sourcing from or producing in markets where import preferential Customs Duty rates apply;
- Efficiency – Customs and Excise simplifications, goods held up or delayed at Customs, business disrupted by tax audits and new activities delayed for incentive grants.

Tax trends have been significantly changing in recent years. These can be identified as:

- Increasing VAT/GST rates;
- Broadening of the VAT/GST tax base;
- Refinement and consolidation of consumption tax systems;
- Increased focus by tax administrations on compliance and tax avoidance, using advanced technology and more efficient risk assessment/management methods;
- A continuing rise in Excise Duties;
- Decreasing Customs Duties from increasing free trade and the number of Free Trade Agreements throughout the world, as well as Import Duty reductions resulting from changes to national import tariffs.

Due Diligence for Excise Businesses

Due diligence is the appropriate reasonable care a company takes when entering into business relations or contracts with other companies, and how it responds to trading risks identified.

Without effective safeguards in place, there are considerable risks to all businesses along alcohol Supply Chains of becoming implicated in illicit trading.

As an Excise-registered business operating in the alcohol sector, you must consider the risk of Excise Duty evasion as well as any commercial and other risks when you are trading. This will help get rid of illicit trading from alcohol Supply Chains, and reduce the risk to businesses of financial liabilities associated with goods on which duty has been evaded.

It is a condition of the trader's approval as an Excise warehousekeeper, registered owner, duty representative or registered consignor that they must carry out the following actions:

- Assess the risks of alcohol duty fraud within the Supply Chains they operate in;
- Put reasonable and proportionate checks in place in their day-to-day trading to identify transactions that may lead to fraud or involve goods on which duty may have been evaded;
- Have procedures in place to take timely and effective mitigating action where a risk of fraud is identified;
- Document the checks they intend to carry out and have appropriate management governance in place to make sure that these are, and continue to be, carried out as intended.

Assessing Risks and Checks to Carry Out

The trader will need to consider the full range of trading relationships you have established and the potential for fraud in each.

The main risks within the alcohol sector include:

- Involvement in the supply of goods for fraud;
- Receiving goods that have been smuggled or diverted into the UK;
- Unintentionally facilitating fraud by providing import or warehousing services.

A key feature of the smuggling or diversion of alcohol to the UK market is the ability to source products either where the Excise Duty has been suspended or it has been refunded under drawback provisions.

To assess the trader's exposure to this risk they need to assess if there is potential for duty evasion resulting from their trading activity. They will therefore need to:

- Know who they are selling to;
- Where the goods are destined for;
- Understand the market for these products.

Without these checks, there is a risk of supplying goods directly or through a third party into illicit Supply Chains and thus compromising the revenue.

Import and warehousing procedures are often exploited to provide cover for the illicit movement of goods. Fraudsters will seek to distribute duty evaded goods as well as counterfeit alcohol into legitimate retail Supply Chains. To assess the trader's exposure to this risk, they will need to consider whether the Supply Chain and trading activity is credible which includes knowing from whom they source goods and to whom they provide a service.

High level indicators of risk include goods being received from unusually complex or apparently uneconomic supply routes, for example, regular supplies of UK produced goods that have been shipped out to an EU member state and then re-imported. If the trader is sourcing duty paid goods they will also need to consider the credibility of suppliers and the level of evidence which they you can obtain to demonstrate the origin and duty status of goods.

Once the trader has established the main risks of fraud that they may be exposed to, their regular checks during trading should be of a type and level sufficient to establish the integrity of the Excise transactions and Supply Chains which they are trading in. This level needs to be reasonable and proportionate to the risk.

Depending on the nature of the trader's business and complexity of your transactions, checks will need to be individually tailored. In particular, they must be sufficiently sensitive, yet robust enough, to pick up potential fraud risks. These checks should provide protection from the threat of fraud or the trader becoming inadvertently involved in fraudulent activity.

Responses to Identified Risks

Where checks made by the trader indicate concerns, the revenue authority (in this case HMRC) would normally expect aspects of the trader's Supply Chain to be changed to address this. For example, the trader's concern may be with the supplier or the destination of the goods. A decision of whether or not to trade with another party remains a commercial decision for the business to take.

If, during company checks, duty fraud is suspected, this should be reported to the Revenue Authority (in the case of the UK, HMRC).

Example: HMRC Enforcement and Audit

As part of HMRC's enforcement and general audit programmes, they will consider whether or not the steps which the trader has taken to embed anti-fraud due diligence into their trading activity are sufficient and timely to address fraud risks in their Supply Chains.

HMRC will aim to establish whether the trader has assessed the risks in their Supply Chain. The trader must be able to show that they have put reasonable and proportionate checks in place and set up procedures to respond to risks when they arise.

If HMRC considers the trader's due diligence procedures are insufficient, the Department will consider the facts of the case before taking further action. Where appropriate, HMRC will help the trader to strengthen their procedures.

Serious Cases

In more serious cases such as a failure to consider the risks, undertake due diligence checks or respond to clear indications of fraud, HMRC will apply appropriate and proportionate sanctions. For serious non-compliance, such as ignoring warnings or knowingly entering into high risk transactions, we may revoke Excise approvals and licenses.

Handling Goods

Handling goods liable to Excise Duty held outside a duty suspension arrangement may also cause the trader to become liable for any Excise Duty due on those goods and an Excise penalty. Any of those goods currently held by the trader could also be liable to forfeiture.

Examples of Due Diligence Checks

Where the trader identifies 1 or more of the following indicators in both suppliers and customers, they should be concerned, and they may need to make further enquiries. This is not a full list, but indicators can include the following:

- Financial health, i.e. financial liquidity, of the company which the trader intends trading with (this can be ascertained by financial ratio analysis);
- Identity of the business;
- Terms of contract, payment and credit agreements;
- Transport and transit security;
- Existence or provenance of goods, i.e. where are the goods coming from;
- The transaction itself.

Once the trader has established the most appropriate due diligence tests for their business, these should be used to test both new and existing transactions and Supply Chains linked to the trader's business. Some checks may be more appropriate to their business than others.

Financial Health of the Company Which the Trader Intends Trading With

In order to protect themselves financially, the trader needs to:

- Carry out credit checks or other background checks;
- Establish how the transactions will be funded – what security can be offered that the trader will be paid where they find a poor credit rating;
- Find out who is providing the credit facility, if credit is offered by the business;
- Find out what payment terms are offered and whether they are commercially viable.

Identity of the Business

The trader needs to:

- Check company details provided to them against other sources such as website, letterheads, telephone directories;

- Ask whether their customer or supplier is a member of a relevant trade association (e.g. the Scotch Whisky Association (SWA), the Bonded Warehousekeepers Association (BWA) in the UK);
- Obtain copies of certificates of incorporation, VAT registration certificates and Excise registration certificates where appropriate and where a trade class is quoted, check that it relates to the type of trade engaged in;
- Verify VAT and Excise registration details with HMRC, which recommends that the trader carries out these checks regularly for new trading arrangements and longer for trusted ones;
- Be satisfied that the owner of the goods is registered, in the case of the UK, under Warehousekeepers and Owners of Warehoused Goods Regulations (WOWGR) where required, if the trader is a warehousekeeper receiving duty suspended goods into their warehouse;
- Obtain signed letters of introduction on headed letter paper and references from other customers or suppliers;
- Insist on personal contact with a senior official of the prospective supplier and where necessary, make an initial visit to their premises to meet them – keep a record of the meeting;
- Establish what the customer's or supplier's history in the trade is;
- Obtain the prospective customer's or supplier's bank details – in the case of an import or export, does the supplier or recipient share the same country of residence as their bank;
- Establish who the trader will be paying – is it the same company as the one that they are dealing with;
- Find out who will be paying if the trader is providing a service.

Terms of Any Contracts, Payments and Credit Agreements

The trader needs to check:

- The terms of any contracts and credit agreements before entering into these and challenge anything that appear unusual;
- What recourse is there if the goods are not as described;
- If payment is to be made to or from a third party – is there a sound commercial reason for this;
- If payment is to be made to or from a third party – is it to or from an off shore account;
- That there are normal commercial arrangements in place for the financing of the goods;

- Where payment is made from an overseas business, how is that to be made;
- If your supplier referred you to a customer who is willing to buy goods of the same quantity and brand as being offered by the supplier;
- If your supplier offers deals that carry no commercial risk for you, for example, no requirement to pay for goods until the payment is received;
- That the goods are adequately insured;
- There are no high value deals offered with no formal contractual arrangements.

Where the trader is buying from a broker they need to check:

- What overall value does this link in the Supply Chain add;
- Is it possible to source directly;
- How competitive is the broker's pricing to those from a more direct route;
- How are the savings made in a longer Supply Chain to make it viable;
- Where transactions are being financed by a third party – is this person a regulated financial body such as a bank.

Transport

Checks can include:

- Finding out where the goods will be sourced from – if this is the country of production, then why the goods are being routed in this way;
- Determining who is responsible for the transport;
- Working out if the potential logistical costs make the unit price unrealistic, if the cost of the goods are inclusive of transport;
- Details of delivery vehicles, which should be kept and if necessary any variations to expected transport arrangements recorded.

Existence of Provenance

Checks can include:

- How the trader contacted you;
- Confirmation the goods exist;
- Inspection of the goods before purchasing them;

- That the goods are in good condition and not damaged;
- The quantities on offer should be credible for the type of business you intend trading with.

Where goods are said to be duty paid, find enough information to be satisfied that they are. This will be easier the closer you are in the Supply Chain to production. This is also important where you intend holding goods on behalf of a third party.

The Deal/Transaction

Check whether the deal includes the nature of the transaction, and:

- Whether it looks too good to be true;
- That the demand for the type of alcohol is credible and If the demand is said to be from abroad, what is the real market (consumption) for them in that country;
- If the alcohol has come from abroad but is of UK origin, find how this occurred and why;
- Where incentives are offered, does this make the overall deal seem too good to be true;
- Why it is being offered;
- Have normal commercial practices been adopted in negotiating prices;
- Does the price compete with offers from competitors;
- Check the age of the goods – if the stock is old, ask for an explanation;
- Does the price seem realistic – be aware of unit cost when duty and VAT values are removed.

If the trader is already established in a trading agreement, the revenue authority would also recommend that the trader continues to monitor correspondence and business paperwork to identify changes in those arrangements and take any follow up action as necessary.

CHAPTER 9

Value-Added Tax (VAT)

As a prelude to the analysis of Customs and international trade risk management, it is worthwhile mentioning something of the VAT situation, as in international trade, VAT is linked to Customs management in the form of Import VAT, which is reclaimed by the import trader as long as they are VAT-registered, and can be zero-rated as long as the goods in question are sold to a customer outside the national domain, i.e. exported. In this respect, VAT is a **Non-Cascading** indirect tax, as it is reclaimable at each stage in the purchase process within the Supply Chain, whereas Customs and Excise Duties are **Cascading** indirect taxes, in that they cannot be reclaimed by the importer, and must be passed on to any customer involved further down the Supply Chain as part of the overall sales costs. In the case of Excise Duties, Drawback is available if the products are subject to specific conditions, such as non-combustible products such as greases and lubricants which are not subject to Excise Duty and are thus subject to Excise Duty Reliefs.

What Is VAT?

Value-Added Tax, or VAT, is a general, broadly based consumption tax assessed on the value added to goods and services. It applies more or less to all goods and services that are bought and sold for use or consumption in the countries applying the tax.

Thus, goods that are sold for export or services that are sold to customers abroad are normally not subject to VAT, i.e. they are zero-rated for VAT purposes, as long as documentary evidence of the export can be verified and obtained by the exporter. Conversely, imports are taxed to keep the system fair for producers so that they can compete on equal terms in the market with suppliers situated outside the country.

Value-Added Tax is:

- A general tax that applies, in principle, to all commercial activities involving the production and distribution of goods and the provision of services;

DOI: 10.4324/9781003341345-10

- A consumption tax because it is borne ultimately by the final consumer. It is not a charge on businesses;
- Charged as a percentage of price, which means that the actual tax burden is visible at each stage in the production and distribution chain;
- Collected fractionally, via a system of partial payments whereby taxable persons (i.e. VAT-registered businesses) deduct from the VAT they have collected the amount of tax they have paid to other taxable persons on purchases for their business activities;
- This mechanism ensures that the tax is neutral regardless of how many transactions are involved;
- Paid to the Revenue Authorities by the seller of the goods, who is the "taxable person", but it is actually paid by the buyer to the seller as part of the price. It is thus an indirect tax.

What Is a Taxable Person?

For VAT purposes, a taxable person is any individual, partnership, company or whatever entity supplies taxable goods and services in the course of business. However, if the annual turnover of this person is less than a certain limit (the threshold), which differs according to the Member State, the person does not have to charge VAT on their sales.

How Is It Charged?

The VAT due on any sale is a percentage of the sale price, but from this, the taxable person is entitled to deduct all the tax already paid at the preceding stage.

Therefore, double taxation is avoided, and tax is paid only on the value added at each stage of production and distribution. In this way, as the final price of the product is equal to the sum of the values added at each preceding stage, the final VAT paid is made up of the sum of the VAT paid at each stage.

Registered VAT traders are given a number and have to show the VAT charged to customers on invoices. In this way, the customer, if they are a registered trader, knows how much they can deduct in turn, and the consumer knows how much tax they have paid on the final product. In this way, the correct VAT is paid in stages, and to a degree the system is self-policing.

VAT Coverage and VAT Rates

In the case of the EU, given that EU law only requires that the standard VAT rate must be at least 15% and the reduced rate at least 5% (only for supplies of goods and services referred to in an exhaustive list), the actual rates applied vary between Member States and between certain types of products. In addition, certain Member States have retained separate rules in specific areas.

The most reliable source of information on current VAT rates for a specified product in a particular Member State is that country's VAT Authority. Nevertheless, it is possible to get an overview of the different rates applied from the VAT rates in the European Union information document.

VAT on Imports and Exports

For the purpose of exports between the Community and non-Member countries, no VAT is charged on the transaction and the VAT already paid on the inputs of the goods for export is deducted – this is an exemption with the right to deduct the input VAT, sometimes called "zero-rating". There is thus no residual VAT contained in the export price.

However, as far as imports are concerned, VAT must be paid at the moment the goods are imported so they are immediately placed on the same footing as equivalent goods produced in the Community. Taxable people registered for VAT will be allowed to deduct this VAT in their next VAT return.

VAT on Goods Moving Between Member States

No frontier controls exist between EU Member States, and therefore VAT on goods traded between EU Member States is not collected at the internal frontier between tax jurisdictions. It is zero-rated at source and accounted for by both the seller and buyer using the INTRASTAT VAT Reverse Charge system on the VAT return.

Goods supplied between taxable persons (or VAT-registered traders) are exempted with a right to deduct the input VAT (zero-rated) on dispatch if they are sent to another Member State to a person who can provide a VAT number in another Member State. This is known as an "intra-Community supply". The VAT number can be checked using the VAT Information Exchange System (VIES).

The VAT due on the transaction is payable on acquisition of the goods by the taxable customer in the Member State where the goods arrive. This is known as "intra-Community acquisition". The customer accounts for any VAT due in their normal VAT return at the rate in force in the country of destination.

VAT on Services

VAT on services is paid at the place where the service has been supplied. This will most often, but not always, be where the service supplier is established.

The trader will, in those cases, account for VAT on his services in the Member State where he is established, applying the VAT rate of that country.

Depending on the nature of the service, VAT may need to be paid in another Member State other than that where the supplier is established. This is, for example the case with services connected to immovable property; transport of passengers or goods; cultural, artistic, sporting, scientific, educational and entertainment services.

How Do the EU Member States Apply VAT?

The detailed application of VAT varies according to the administrative customs and practices of each EU Member State within the framework set out by Community legislation.

Why Do All Member States Use VAT?

At the time when the European Community was created, the original 6 Member States were using different forms of indirect taxation, most of which were cascade taxes.

These were multi-stage taxes that were each levied on the actual value of output at each stage of the productive process, making it impossible to determine the real amount of tax actually included in the final price of a particular product. As a consequence, there was always a risk that Member States would deliberately or accidentally subsidise their exports by overestimating the taxes refundable on exportation.

It was evident that if there was ever going to be an efficient, Single Market in Europe, a neutral and transparent turnover tax system was required which ensured tax neutrality and allowed the exact amount of tax to be rebated at the point of export.

As explained in "VAT on imports and exports," VAT allows for the certainty that exports are completely and transparently tax-free.

The History of VAT in the European Union Until 1993

On 11 April 1967, the first 2 VAT Directives were adopted, establishing a general, multi-stage but non-cumulative turnover tax to replace all other turnover taxes in the Member States.

However, the first 2 VAT Directives laid down only the general structures of the system and left it to the Member States to determine the coverage of VAT and the rate structure. It was not until 17 May 1977 that the Sixth VAT Directive was adopted, which established a uniform VAT coverage.

On 1 January 2007, the Sixth Directive was replaced by the EU VAT Directive (Directive No. 2006/112/EC). It brings together the various provisions into 1 piece of legislation, providing a clearer overview of EU VAT legislation currently in force.

The VAT Directive guarantees that the VAT contributed by each of the Member States to the Community's own resources can be calculated. It still, however, allows Member States many possible exceptions and derogations from the standard VAT coverage. Moreover, it does not set out the rates of VAT to be applied in Member States, only a minimum rate of 15% fixed until 31 December 2010. This means that VAT rates differ widely. Currently, Member States apply a standard rate of between 15% and 25%. They may also apply 1 or 2 reduced rates of at least 5%.

There are a number of temporary derogations, e.g. zero-rates in the United Kingdom (no longer part of the EU) and Ireland. The VAT coverage also still differs from 1 Member State to another.

VAT and the Single Market – 1993 to Now

The realisation of the Single Market in 1993 resulted in the abolition of controls at fiscal frontiers. To achieve this, the Commission proposed moving from the pre-1993 "destination-based" system, where VAT is effectively charged at the rate of VAT applicable where the buyer is established, to an "origin-based" system, with VAT being charged at the rate in force where the supplier is established.

This would have effectively abolished fiscal frontiers within the EU. This was, however, not acceptable to Member States as rates of VAT were too different, and there was no adequate mechanism to redistribute VAT receipts to mirror actual consumption.

Therefore, until the conditions were right, the Community adopted the Transitional VAT System which maintains different fiscal systems but without frontier controls. The intention is still eventually to have a common system of VAT where VAT is charged by the seller of goods – an origin-based VAT system.

The transitional system is an origin-based system for sales to private persons who can go and buy tax-paid goods anywhere they like in the Union and take the goods home without having to pay VAT again. There are some exceptions to this general rule, however (e.g. the purchase of new means of transport and distance selling).

For transactions between taxable persons, it is still a destination-based VAT system.

Over the past few years, between 60–70% of European Union Member States have increased their VAT rates at least once, including the UK, and the assumption that no state would go over 25% has ended with Hungary's VAT raise to a rate of 27%. The overall aim of the EU is to ultimately raise

VAT rates in all Member States to the highest level of VAT in any Member State. These rate increases will continue because when governments urgently demand more revenue they often turn to indirect taxes, especially VAT or GST, because this broad-based tax produces significant revenue with each rate increase. And even if governments slow their spending growth, they will have to confront their accumulated debt and to do so they will need more revenue. Since the beginning of 2010, governments have not only been demanding more revenue, but they have been demanding it quickly. The Italian government even announced a 1 percentage point increase in VAT effective from the following day. It has been suggested that the aim of the EU is to eventually raise VAT rates in the whole of the EU to the highest level of VAT applicable in any of the Member States, which at present is Hungary with 27% VAT.

VAT compliance mistakes are more costly when the rate is higher, and mistakes are more likely when companies have so little notice. Even governments not in such dire financial straits as Italy are expecting taxpayers to react with uncommon alacrity to tax changes. At the end of 2011, China introduced a complex VAT pilot in Shanghai with only 8 weeks' notice, replacing to a degree its Business Tax system, and this led to the adoption of this system throughout China as a whole in 2015.

Value-Added Tax complexity and controversy related to indirect taxes are growing at a quick pace as tax legislators constantly adjust the base and raise the tax rate. However, this can lead to more frequent errors such as:

- VAT paid to suppliers (input VAT) is not reported and recovered on the VAT return;
- VAT paid to suppliers is reported but not recovered because tax authorities find the supplier's VAT invoice to be invalid;
- A "missing trader" purchases goods from a supplier based in another EU Member State, zero-rates the VAT on the purchase, then fails to pass on to his own Tax Authority the VAT charged on supplies to customers in his own country (Acquisition Fraud);
- VAT is charged to customers but is not paid to the tax authorities, as the supplier disappears (carousel fraud);
- The goods are sold to another broker who re-exports the goods to either an overseas non-EU country or to a customer elsewhere in the EU, or, in the case of the UK, to another country. The broker claims back the VAT on the purchase of the goods from the "missing trader" (which was never paid to the national Customs Authority in the first place) and then zero-rates the international transaction for VAT purposes, thus compounding the anomaly (extended carousel fraud);

- VAT paid to suppliers is recovered when it does not qualify for recovery, including Import VAT paid on imported consignment stock. Tax policymakers, including the OECD, have stated that they expect indirect taxes to be their leading source of new revenue over the next decade, while tax administrators and taxpayers view indirect taxes as a key source of risk over the next 3 years. Indeed, the OECD has implemented a system called SAF-T (Standard Audit File – Taxation), which will ultimately replace the VAT return as used at present with a spreadsheet-based Tax Return, which will show all elements of VAT payable and recoverable. This system is presently being used in several European countries and will eventually be operated globally.

Another area that is subject to significant HMRC scrutiny, indeed the scrutiny of most Revenue Authorities, is that of traders who make net VAT reclaims on a consistent basis owing to their import and export activities. Where exports dominate a trader's sales business, these exports are zero-rated for VAT purposes. However, the same trader will also reclaim VAT on purchases, be they materials procured from their own country or from overseas. This means that the trader concerned is not submitting significant levels of output tax to the national Revenue Authority because of their volume of exports, and instead is submitting net VAT reclaims every time they submit their VAT returns. This means that the Revenue Authority is constantly refunding VAT to such companies. On this basis, the Revenue Authority will see these traders as of a higher risk and will conduct more frequent audits to determine the validity of these VAT returns. Such audits will encompass close scrutiny of import and export documentation, procedures and absolute compliance with the regulatory requirements of the Revenue Authority, and will concentrate on the evidence of export, as well as the accounting procedures used by the company, including the SAGE accounting system.

In the case of the UK, HMRC has published guidance (VAT Notice 726, available on the GOV.UK website) on the types of checks that a business should carry out in order to avoid being unwittingly liable under the principles of VAT fraud. HMRC has recommended that the following issues should be regularly checked:

- The legitimacy of customers or suppliers (e.g. their trade history);
- The commercial viability of the transaction (e.g. the existence of a market for the goods);
- The viability of the goods (e.g. the existence and condition of the goods).

To remain competitive in the present-day global market, companies need to closely address their Supply Chains and their duty and tax liabilities, and make their Supply Chain procedures, especially cross-border transactions, as cost-effective as possible while limiting the accumulation of unnecessary inventory and the costs associated with it.

The demands for internal controls, risk management and overall competitiveness require companies to leverage and control their financial, accounting, and business systems more effectively. In this way, they can have access to the data necessary to properly manage and plan for Customs Duties and VAT, manage export control licenses, regularly screen and monitor transactions, and report international trade data in an efficient and compliant manner. Companies require specific trade experience to help them select, implement, and customise effective trade automation solutions.

The efficient integration of import and export processes into overall business objectives, tax planning, and Supply Chain management is crucial to the present-day success of a multinational company. It is clear that savings in Customs Duties have a direct impact on a company's bottom line, as they increase profit, as well as having an indirect positive effect on their customers. However, high-volume global traders wishing to achieve such savings face critical issues, such as:

- Shortcomings in an organisation's international trade planning, internal controls and compliance processes may cause the business to overpay duties, overlook compliance issues, and incur penalties and unnecessary costs;
- Changes in Supply Chain, sourcing, and the structuring of transactions may impact a company's Customs Duty and VAT position, both significantly and negatively. However, individuals in functions outside the Customs function often make decisions without taking these changes into consideration, possibly because of their lack of knowledge, understanding or consideration of Customs issues. Building compliance and planning into existing business processes and systems helps to determine cross-functional communication and co-operation.

Types of VAT Fraud

VAT fraud is a scheme through which businesses avoid paying VAT and even claim refunds for VAT they never pay. Such businesses actualise their criminal intents using different established methods. Thus, different types of VAT fraud can be identified, on which the governments of VAT-administering countries have spent and indeed are spending huge amounts of money to investigate and combat.

Inflated Refund Claims

This is a VAT fraud scheme through which traders acquire invoices for purchases they never make. Their intent is to claim more refunds from tax-collecting authorities than they deserve. Such traders acquire fake invoices because invoices are needed to claim refunds. (Invoices give evidence of merchandise purchases which traders have made and on which they have paid refundable VAT.) There is an established crime network dealing in such fabricated invoices, which business-people purchase to defraud the government.

Underreported Sales

Traders conceal their actual amount of sales from domestic markets in order to evade their obligation to charge VAT on these sales. Such fraud is designed to enable them to claim more refunds (credits) than they deserve. In addition, this scheme has the natural potential of boosting the business of such traders because it will encourage patronage on account of the relatively cheap goods and services the traders offer buyers.

Fictitious Traders

Traders set up unreal enterprises and register them for VAT, thus creating fictitious traders. They make fake commodity purchases and sales, defrauding the authorities by registering their non-existent business transactions. Their aim is to have grounds for VAT refund claims. In addition to setting up fake enterprises, they create fake export invoices. To avoid being exposed, they try to make fast profits and disappear quickly.

Domestic Sales Disguised as Exports

Under this scheme, traders sell goods and services on a domestic market but claim to have sold them on an export market. For this purpose, the sellers acquire fake export invoices or even actual "export" invoices. Fake export invoices contain claims about the amount of purchases greater than the actual amount such traders made. Such fabricated invoices apparently justify their claims to greater VAT payments and therefore to greater VAT refunds.

Indeed, the sellers may actually have sold the goods to an overseas trader, but the overseas trader immediately sells these goods back to UK customers without the goods leaving the UK. Export invoices are raised and submitted, but the goods do not actually leave the country of export. The buyer immediately raises invoices to each individual onward customer for the goods concerned, and the goods are sent from the original seller directly to the onward customer located in the same country as the original seller.

An example is as follows:

> Company A is based in the UK. They sell goods to a Spanish distributor, Company B, which sells the goods onwards to a series of UK-based customers. The goods never leave the UK, but are dispatched to the onward UK customers on the instructions of the Spanish distributor. Company A zero-rates the export invoice to Company B as if the goods had been dispatched to Spain, which they have not. Company B also zero-rates its invoices to the onward customers in the UK. The goods are dispatched from Company A direct to the UK onward customers, thus implying that VAT should be liable on the goods as they are subject to a domestic movement.

Missing Trader Intra-EU Fraud

This fraud allows traders to evade their VAT obligations in 2 different EU countries by capitalising on goods or services that are in high demand in a particular EU country. For instance, after registering for VAT in 1 EU country, e.g. France, they can purchase goods and services that are in high demand in Ireland, on which they cleverly avoid paying VAT. They then return to France to quickly sell such goods or services at VAT-inclusive prices (having registered for VAT there). Thereafter, they quickly disappear without paying their VAT.

Missing trader fraud (also called **missing trader intra-community fraud** or **MTIC fraud**) involves the theft of VAT from a government by fraudsters who exploit VAT rules, most commonly the EU VAT Rules which provide that the movement of goods between EU Member States is VAT-free (i.e. zero-rated). There are different variations of the fraud, but they generally involve a trader charging VAT on the sale of goods and absconding with the VAT (instead of paying the VAT to the government's taxation authority). The term "missing trader" is used because the fraudster has gone missing with the VAT.

A common form of missing trader fraud is **carousel fraud**. In carousel fraud, VAT and goods are passed around between companies and jurisdictions, similar to how a carousel revolves.

The usual operation of VAT is as follows: a business that buys and sells goods charges VAT to those to whom it sells ("output tax") and is charged VAT by those from whom it purchases ("input tax"). Subject to various rules, it can reclaim the VAT it pays by subtracting the input tax from the output tax, and so passes to the government the net VAT it collects (being output tax less input tax). In this way, a business acts as a tax collector on behalf of the government.

Within the European Union, Member States charge VAT at differing rates on goods as a form of indirect taxation. However, all exports of goods within the EU are tax-free, i.e. zero-rated, as VAT zero-rating is conditional for export transactions on the provision of documentary proof of export, i.e. transport documents and documentary proof of receipt of the consignment by the customer, such as a copy of the transport document endorsed by the customer as proof of receipt of the consignment by the customer, and returned to the supplier. In other words, a business does not charge VAT on the sale of goods to buyers in another Member State according to the fulfilment of these conditions. This leads to the situation where an exporter will be able to reclaim VAT from the government, as it will have been charged VAT by the business from which it purchased the goods, and will owe the government nothing because it has sold the goods tax-free to a buyer in another Member State. However, this activity also attracts more in-depth scrutiny by the national Revenue Authority, as the government is under obligation to protect its revenue collection and therefore requires full compliance by the trader.

Although missing trader fraud is most common in the EU, it is also seen in other jurisdictions that have a Value-Added Tax regime, such as Singapore.

Acquisition Fraud

The simplest missing trader fraud is where a trader (Company A) imports some goods that are zero-rated in the country of origin; VAT on the goods should be paid in the country into which they have been imported. After importing, Company A sells the goods to another trader (Company B), charging the price of the goods plus VAT, but does not pay the VAT collected to the government; Company A becomes a "missing trader". The buyer, Company B, who has paid the VAT to Company A, can then reclaim the VAT paid from the tax authorities on its VAT return. Company B then sells the goods to Company C, which reclaims the VAT charged to it by Company B and declares the VAT it charges to its customer, Company D. Company D then sells the goods to the general public, reclaiming the VAT charged to it by Company C and declaring the VAT it charges.

In this situation, the fraudsters have obtained the value of the VAT charged by Company A to Company B. This situation, where the goods are made available for consumers in the importer's home market, is often known as "acquisition fraud".

The trader defaulting on its VAT liability (Company A in this example) is described as a "missing trader" or "defaulting trader", whereas the other traders in the transaction chain (Companies B, C and D) are "buffer traders". The role of the buffer traders is to distance the missing trader from the end consumer and make it harder for the taxation authorities to detect the fraud.

Carousel Fraud

Carousel VAT fraud is a complicated and highly sophisticated process that is very difficult to detect. Here, we explain the missing trader fraud process in 5 steps:

1. Carousel fraud involves a chain of events, starting with the purchasing of goods from the missing trader, who has purchased these goods from a supplier in another EU Member State;
2. The missing trader then sells the goods to another national business, charging VAT. It should then be the role of the missing trader to pay the VAT to HMRC, but fraudsters disappear without doing so;
3. The business that has bought the goods then sells them to another business, charging VAT but then also paying the VAT received from the business before, to the HMRC;
4. This process can continue, but eventually, a broker sells the goods to an EU customer. As this transaction from the broker to customer is within the EU, the customer is not charged VAT;
5. As the broker paid VAT in purchasing the goods, the broker then reclaims the VAT from HMRC. This amount is the VAT not paid by missing traders, which solidifies the losses experienced by HMRC.

As can be seen, carousel VAT fraud can operate in continuous cycles, which is why it is described as a carousel, i.e., going round and round in circles.

Carousel fraud is like acquisition fraud, except that the goods or services do not end up with an end consumer. Instead, they are sold from 1 trader to another. Using the example in the previous section, say Company D (instead of selling the goods to the general public) sells the goods to Company E located in another Member State of the European Union. Company D reclaims the VAT charged to it by Company C, but because the sale is zero-rated, it declares no output tax.

In this scenario, Company D is known as the "broker". The broker is able to claim back from the government all the VAT that should have been paid on the goods (as exports are zero-rated). However, because there is a "missing trader" further back in the chain of sales, part of this VAT would never have been paid in the first place.

The goods will now carousel through other traders in Member States. The above process begins again, sometimes with different companies and sometimes with 1 or more of the same companies. The process can repeat many times, with the goods going around as if in a carousel.

Contra-Trading

Contra-trading fraud is the further evolution of carousel fraud. The fraudsters evade government detection by using 2 carousels of traded goods where

1 carousel is legitimate and the other is not. The contra-trader's output tax from 1 chain is designed to offset the input tax incurred on the other chain.

The 2 types of transaction chains are:

- "Tax loss chains", where the contra-trader based in Country A incurs input tax on its purchases in Country A and makes zero-rated supplies of those goods to customers in other Member States or exports to customers outside the EU; and
- "Contra chains", where the contra-trader typically acquires goods from another Member State and sells them on to traders in Country A, acting as an acquirer and generating an output tax liability from the onward sale.

The tax loss chains will trace back to a defaulting trader or occasionally to another contra-trader (known as "double" or "multiple" contra-trading). The contra chains will end up with a broker (Company D in the example given in the previous section) who will sell the goods to traders located in another Member State, allowing it to reclaim the VAT that should have been paid on the goods. The benefit of introducing contra-trading is that it makes it more difficult for the tax authorities to detect a connection between the VAT reclaim by the broker and the default by the missing trader, which now occurs in a different Supply Chain.

EU Triangulation – How Do We Prove VAT Zero-Rating?

Many UK companies trade within the EU, even though the UK left the EU at the end of 2020. The UK company acts as an intermediary between EU sellers and buyers, but in order to ensure VAT zero-rating on these transactions, the UK company must have an EU VAT Number. If not, VAT must be charged on each element of the EU transactions, and given that the UK company is not VAT-registered in the EU, the input VAT cannot be easily reclaimed by any participants in the transaction, especially as the UK would have to charge VAT on the last (second) sale element of the transaction based on UK VAT rates, i.e. 20%.

For the purposes of EU Triangulation and Simplified VAT procedures, all companies involved in the transactions must have EU VAT Numbers.

Although the invoice (including the VAT Numbers of Company A and Company C) goes from A to C, the movement of the consignment is the essential element of VAT zero-rating. Company A must obtain a Consignment Note for the movement of the consignment from A to B, and this must also show the VAT Number of Company B, which receives the consignment. Therefore:

Goods move from A to B (VAT zero-rating).

Invoice moves from A to C.

The EC Sales List should, therefore, show the VAT Numbers of Companies B and C, and the INTRASTAT Declaration should show Company B as the recipient.

The Principle of EU Triangulation

The EU Revenue Authorities state that Triangulation involves 2 supplies of goods between 3 VAT-registered traders in 3 different European Union Member States. For example, a trader established in 1 Member State (MS1) sells goods to a trader established in a second Member State (MS2). The goods, however, are delivered to a trader in a third Member State (MS3).

To reduce the administrative and compliance burdens on traders and the tax authorities associated with such triangular transactions, there is a simplification measure. This simplification measure can only operate when the 3 traders involved are all registered for VAT in the European Union.

In general, the simplification measure works as follows:

- There is a zero-rated intra-community supply (ICS) from Company A to Company B;
- The supply is listed in the VAT Information Exchange System (VIES) return by Company A to Company B;
- As company B has quoted its VAT number, it has made an intra-community acquisition (ICA). Company B accounts for this ICA in its VAT return;
- Company B makes a VAT-free supply to Company C. Company C accounts for this transaction in its VAT return as a received supply. In this way, Company C is deemed to have accounted for Company B's VAT liability in Member State 3.
- Where Company C is entitled to reclaim VAT, it takes a simultaneous credit for this transaction in the relevant VAT return.

Scenario

Where Company A (UK) is the intermediary/facilitator, the goods move between B and C (e.g. 2 companies in the EU, where B is the supplier in 1 EU Member State and C is the customer in another EU Member State). The process operates in the same way, with the evidence of movement of the materials required for the movement between B and C. A is invoiced by Supplier B (country in the EU) and, in turn issues an invoice, including mark-ups, to Customer C (based elsewhere in the EU). The goods move from B to C. As long as the CMR Consignment Note is issued for that movement and copies are retained by B and C, the invoices for the consignment can be VAT zero-rated.

The main condition for this is that A, B and C must be VAT-registered in the EU. This means that even after Brexit, A can use its EU VAT Number to facilitate this simplified procedure as sanctioned by HMRC and other EU Revenue Authorities.

Call-Off and Consignment Stock VAT

The European Union has created a special set of VAT rules for companies holding their stocks in foreign territories, and the same rules have been applied by HMRC in the UK. They provide guidance on when VAT should be charged, and if a company needs to register for VAT as a non-resident trader in another country where it is warehousing its goods.

The treatment of foreign stock for VAT is split into 2: call-off stock and consignment stock. They are separated based on who controls access and use of the stock, which triggers the VAT Point and compliance rules.

VAT on Call-Off Stock

Call-off stock refers to goods sent from your home country to a warehouse or client's storage facility in another country. The title of the goods still remains with the seller. If a customer has control of the storage, is aware of stock movements, and may take stock at will, then it is categorised as call-off stock and does not generally require the seller to VAT register in the foreign country as a non-resident trader.

For VAT purposes, any eventual sale is treated as an intra-community VAT supply. This means the sale is recorded under the seller's domestic VAT number and return, and there is no VAT charged. The customer only has to register the sale as an acquisition in its local VAT returns. In the case of the EU, reporting under INTRASTAT and EC Sales Listing may still be required.

VAT on Consignment Stock

If the stock is initially sent to the seller's warehouse, which is under their control (including rented storage), then the setup is treated as consignment stock. Typically, there are multiple potential customers for consignment stock.

This has a different treatment for VAT purposes than call-off stock. The movement of goods to the warehouse is treated as a supply. This means the seller almost certainly has to register for VAT in the country of destination, as it is liable for Import VAT at the point of import of the stock into the country concerned, as well as VAT on the onwards sales to each customer. The movement is treated as a self-sale (acquisition). INTRASTAT reporting will be required at this point, too. When the goods are sold to the customer, the local VAT is charged and recorded in the seller's foreign VAT registration.

Postponed VAT Accounting

This section is also included later in the text concerning imports and exports, but it is prudent to detail the facility in this initial chapter because of its importance as an element of VAT liability. Import VAT is levied on imported consignments at the time of import, and in most cases, it must be paid outright on the import consignment or deferred by way of the importer's deferment account. However, changes to the UK's Import VAT regime as a result of the UK's exit from the European Union have meant positive implications for the cash flow of UK importers. On 1 January 2021, the UK government introduced the facility of Postponed VAT Accounting (PVA), where importers can account for Import VAT levied on Import Declarations by way of monthly online Import VAT statements, with the monthly Import VAT then transferred to the following VAT return using the Reverse Charge mechanism. This effectively replaces the previous system of paying the Import VAT against the Import Declaration either outright or through the importer's deferment account. However, the PVA system has not yet been made automatic and still gives UK importers the choice between the 2 systems. The PVA regime has positive effects concerning corporate cash flow, as it means that Import VAT is accounted for on the VAT return rather than being physically paid at the point of import. The same PVA facility is also in operation in the Republic of Ireland, also from 1 January 2021.

UK VAT-registered importers will be able to use PVA on their Customs Declaration. PVA will not, ordinarily, be mandatory, and it will be possible for importers to continue to use the current process to pay, defer or, if appropriate, secure the VAT on importation if they so wish. They can then choose to start using PVA at any time after 11 pm on 31 December 2020. It will also be possible for importers to use PVA for some imports and existing means of payment for others.

The introduction of PVA will enable importers to account for and recover Import VAT as input tax on the same periodic (usually quarterly) VAT return, rather than having to pay it up-front and recover it on a subsequent return using the C79 VAT certificate as evidence of entitlement. Indeed, the PVA system allows for the use of online Import VAT statements rather than a hard copy of the C79 Import VAT certificate.

These changes will not affect non-VAT-registered importers and individuals, who must continue to pay (or defer) Import VAT on imported goods at the same time as Customs Import Duty, as they do now.

All UK VAT-registered importers are eligible to use PVA, and no prior authorisation is required. They simply make the appropriate import entry and provide their EORI and/or VAT registration number (VRN) on their Customs Import Declaration, but need to put the letters "PVA" on the entry or instruct their clearing agents to do so. This process, which is subject to Customs clearance, allows the goods to enter into free circulation without up-front payment of the Import VAT and is shown under the MOP box as the letter "G". The Import VAT is shown on the monthly online Import VAT statement and is consequently entered on the following VAT return using the Reverse Charge mechanism, where the importer charges themselves the Import VAT in the appropriate box on the VAT return and then claims it back using the appropriate box also on the VAT return. In the Republic of Ireland, the letters PVA are also inserted on the VAT return, which acts as a supplementary facility showing the PVA facility in operation using the Reverse Charge system for VAT Accounting on the VAT return. The Customs Declaration generates an online Monthly Postponed Import VAT Statement (MPIVS) that is the evidence required to account for and recover the Import VAT as input tax on their next VAT return. (Note: The C79 continues to be produced for those entries where any VAT is physically paid on importation).

PVA is only available on declarations where Import VAT would ordinarily be due and where goods are being declared to free circulation. Where goods are placed into a Customs special procedure, e.g. Customs Warehousing, PVA is available on the declaration that removes them from the special procedure concerned and places the goods into free circulation. Since the risk of non-payment of Import VAT is minimal, the facility is available to the majority of importers.

No matter the size of the business organisation, be it a small-to-medium enterprise (SME) or a large multinational organisation, any business involved in international trade has some form of Supply Chain or is involved in 1, and therefore needs to address its entire international business strategy to ensure that it not only does it make money in the form of profit generation but that it also ensures that its duties and taxes are correctly managed. However, duty management also requires absolute compliance with Customs requirements, and this requires planning and monitoring to lower the potential of compliance risk. The challenge lies in how to achieve this in the form of, in this case, Customs and VAT Compliance and Risk Reduction. This text is designed to put these issues into perspective and show how and why Risk Assessment and Management play such a large part in managing the International Supply Chain and, in particular, import and export management from a Customs and VAT perspective.

CHAPTER 10

Customs and VAT Risk Management

Customs or Border Control Officers have an increasingly difficult job in detecting fraud. Human resources are restricted, the complexity of Customs tariffs is high and Customs fraud volumes are rising. Few people know exactly how much Customs fraud takes place. Most agree that it is a small yet persistent percentage of the global export market. Of a global total of US$19.7 trillion global export trade, about US$6.9 trillion in goods will be imported into the EU. That volume of freight traffic creates a hugely complex task for Customs Authorities charged with identifying which truck to stop or container to open, with the emphasis on keeping the trade flowing without creating bottlenecks.

There are large profits to be made by avoiding duty or importing illegal goods and the chances of detection are small, so it's no surprise this is a target area for organised crime. To spot criminals, Customs Authorities have moved from manual searching, and reliance on officers' detective skills, to rule-based systems and database searching. However, these systems are now also under pressure as smugglers become more sophisticated and better at out-manoeuvring existing systems.

Officials require detailed information about each shipment in order to so as to scrutinise its nature. A skilled Customs expert will investigate beyond the immediate shipment and search for identifying links, such as details of high-risk companies, directors and known fraud cases, as well as being aware of what has been declared and whether it poses a specific risk. However, conducting this manually is time-consuming. To conduct risk management thoroughly, agencies must gather data from multiple sources, including the business itself, other Customs and tax agencies and the police. To compound their difficulties, they face human resource issues, but at the same time they need to act fast to respond to information that is often received late. Automated systems are available, but they are often expensive and time-consuming to implement and use to full effect, and in many cases they may only be affordable by the fully developed nations, while lesser-developed nations cannot afford them.

 DOI: 10.4324/9781003341345-11

All this means that Customs officials can often only check a small percentage of goods and must therefore carefully target their approach. Today, most Customs Authorities, at best, are only armed with systems that automate the separate Customs management processes they run. First generation rule-based solutions often lack the advanced analytics necessary to optimise their rules. They typically generate large volumes of false positives resulting in wasted time, reduced operational efficiency, increased costs, mistrust and ultimately system atrophy and stagnation. Coupled with this, there is a lack of information sharing between government agencies, due to political and cultural issues; concerns about privacy and security; poor policies and inadequate technologies.

Fortunately, a new breed of risk management solutions is emerging, offering a range of operational advantages over its predecessors. Advanced risk management systems enable agencies to rank import transactions and manage associated information to create risk scores. Field offices can plan the deployment of staff to best match threat priorities. The new systems also need to provide graphic user interfaces that help the Customs Officer understand why they should stop a specific consignment. The systems should also pinpoint the most relevant data, so officers can target this or ask the right questions. This ability to view summarised data enables investigators to make faster decisions.

Another key benefit is that they deploy self-learning advanced hybrid analytics to reduce false positives. With false positive rates minimised, Customs Officers can focus their time on fraudulent shipments rather than on unwarranted alerts, thereby becoming more efficient. Furthermore, and more critically, the latest solutions can score and assess imports and exports in real time. This allows 24/7 monitoring and accelerates the decision and detection process.

The versatility and flexibility of these next generation solutions also extends to the creation, testing and deployment of new detection rules. Unlike first generation Customs solutions, the latest systems can quickly assess the transactional data history of all risk patterns, identify new rules to mitigate these risks and complete the process in just a few minutes. By embracing new "scale free" technologies, benefits can be further extended, by allowing interaction with other border control systems, or by enabling use of the same solutions across associated departments such as Customs and Tax, facilitating data sharing and reducing total cost of ownership.

The days of expensive in-house fraud management projects built from scratch are coming to an end. The cost of managing and maintaining these systems on-site is frequently prohibitive, and, in many cases, unaffordable. Increasingly, governments are looking to pre-packaged solutions which offer low risk and costs, scalability and a high level of future-proofing, i.e. reliability for future activities, as well as being user-friendly. Advanced risk management technologies are the right solution to real problems and, far from costing a country significant financial resources, should easily be seen as a valuable return on investment, especially where they increase revenue to the national government without incurring massive costs along the way. The automated approach that these technologies offer to risk management is definitely here to stay. These technologies are already operational and profitable within a few Customs departments globally. They cut costs, increase Customs revenue and perhaps most critical of all, bring more criminals who perpetrate the frauds to justice.

Risk management in any Customs organisation involves much of the above, but does not or at least should not create any new work. Instead, it combines or restructures existing programmes to maximise resources. It also seeks to mitigate, i.e. control levels of risk where there is seen to be a significant degree of vulnerability in areas such as potential tax fraud, errors on Customs Entries and Declarations, valuation errors, misuse of Tariff Commodity Codes and mis-declaration of origin, all considered major high-risk areas by all Customs Authorities.

According to Standard 6.3 of the Revised Kyoto Convention (RKC) and the corresponding guidelines, risk management is defined as the systematic application of management procedures and practices which provide Customs with the necessary information to address movements or consignments that present a risk.

According to the *HMRC Customs Risk Manual*, the objective of the national Customs administrations of the Member States and DG XXI of the European Commission in the risk programme is to achieve equivalent levels of control at the Community's external frontiers. Risk analysis aims to concentrate controls on areas of highest risk while at the same time leaving the majority of trade to flow relatively freely through Customs. Principles concerning risk analysis and profiling need to be established on a Community-wide basis. Guidelines for implementation and improvement in the use of risk analysis can now be defined at Community level. Even once the UK has fully exited the EU, it is likely that this policy will be maintained by the UK Revenue Authorities.

Customs regulations are designed to ensure payment of Customs Duties, observance of prohibitions and restrictions and the application of special rules on quotas, preferences and other trade measures. Every regulation has a corresponding risk. Traders may breach it, deliberately or unintentionally. Risk analysis techniques try to identify and quantify these risks in order to develop control procedures, for example, selection for documentary check or physical examination and to concentrate control effort by Customs Officers on risk areas where breaches of the regulations are most likely to occur-whether deliberate or not.

Customs Definition of Risk Management

"Risk" means the likelihood that something will prevent the application of Community or national measures concerning the Customs treatment of goods.

To minimise the occurrence of risks, Customs can use risk management as a technique to more effectively set priorities and more efficiently allocate resources necessary for maintaining a proper balance between controls and facilitating legitimate trade.

Risk management can therefore be defined as a technique for the systematic identification and implementation of all the measures necessary to limit the likelihood of risks occurring. International and national strategies can be effectively implemented by collecting data and information, analysing and assessing risk, prescribing action and monitoring outcomes. For Customs purposes, this technique is based on a mixture of post-clearance and trader audits, as part of the HMRC policy of regular management checks. However, increasing reliance is being made by Customs on the ability of the trader to conduct their own self-assessment audits and checks, and this is becoming especially common where traders are applying for specific types of Customs facilities, such as Import Duty Reliefs.

According to Standard 6.3 of the Revised Kyoto Convention and the corresponding Guidelines, risk management is defined as the systematic application of management procedures and practices which provide Customs with the necessary information to address movements or consignments that present a risk. The preamble to the RKC lists the application of risk management as one of seven key principles of trade facilitation embodied in it, and the following five main steps are described as follows:

Monitor and Review

1. Establish context;
2. Identify risks;
3. Analyse risks;
4. Assess and prioritise risks;
5. Address risks.

These apply to documentation, communication and consultation.

Standard Customs Risk Management Process

This diagram also appears in Chapter 8.

There are five main steps in the standard Customs risk management process as defined by the World Customs Organization:

1. "Establish context": Importation of goods, export controls, passenger traffic, etc.;
2. "Identify risks": Revenue protection (e.g. under valuation, origin, classification), prohibitions and restrictions (e.g. drug trafficking, IPR, fire arms, etc.);
3. "Analyse risks": Likelihood of a risk occurring (less likely, likely, highly likely);
4. "Assess and prioritize risks": Assess impact and consequence of risks occurring (e.g. high, medium, low);
5. "Address risks": Define counter-measures and assign to the appropriate risk options (e.g. tolerate, treat, transfer or terminate).

In addition to these five steps, risk management requires constant monitoring and review in order to eliminate false negative as well as false positive risk assessments. Throughout the process proper documentation, communication and consultation with all relevant stakeholders is key, as risk management is a corporate task involving the entire organisation and not one dedicated unit only.

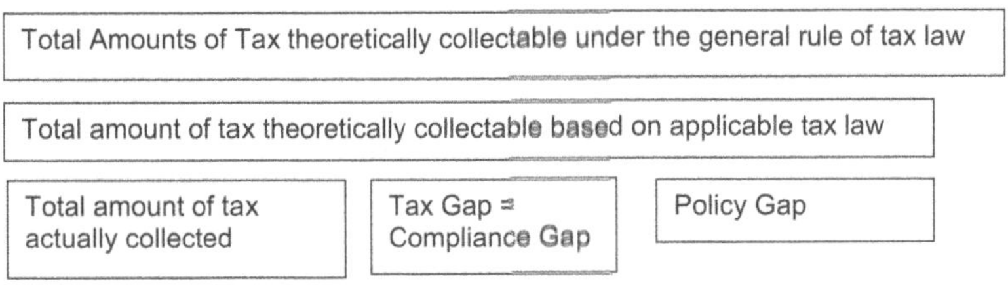

The tax gap (Source: HMRC).

The tax gap equals the total amounts of tax theoretically collectable *minus* the total amount of tax actually collected. This also equates to the policy gap, i.e. the gap caused by the weaknesses in policy relating to tax collection.

(Source: World Customs Organization)

Revenue/Tax Gap Analysis

The tax or revenue gap is the difference between the amount of tax that should, in theory, be paid to HMRC, and what is actually paid. The tax gap provides a useful tool for understanding the relative size and nature of non-compliance.

Tax administrations collect a certain amount of tax in a given period. However, the amount of tax collected is likely to be less than the amount of tax due. This raises the question of the measurement of what is the amount of tax which is not collected and, therefore, can be seen as the amount of revenue loss.

In general, the revenue loss can be described as the amount of tax liability incurred but not paid in a given period. The tax liability incurs as a result of the occurrence of a taxable event and is payable by a due date, as determined by tax law. This tax liability constitutes the tax due, which can be perceived as the theoretically collectable amount of tax. Accordingly, the tax gap can be estimated as the difference between the total amounts of tax theoretically collectable, based on the applicable tax law and the total amounts of tax actually collected in a given period.

This understanding can be applied in many different ways:

- It provides a foundation for the strategy of the Revenue Authority – thinking about the tax gap helps the department to understand how non-compliance occurs and how it can address the causes and improve the overall health of the tax system;
- Drawing on information on how other countries manage their tax gaps, the revenue department's tax gap analysis provides insight into which strategies are most effective at reducing the tax gap;
- Although the tax gap is not sufficiently timely or precise enough to set performance targets, it provides important information which helps the Revenue Authority to understand its long-term performance.

A definition of the tax gap is as follows:

The International Monetary Fund (IMF) developed the Revenue Administration Gap Analyses Program (RA-GAP) to quantify and understand compliance gaps. In the IMF's approach, the overarching framework is one in which a gap arises between actual receipts from some tax and receipts under some perfectly enforced benchmark tax system. This overall gap can then be decomposed into the compliance gap (i.e. imperfect compliance with the current tax system) and the policy gap (i.e. deviations of current tax rules from the benchmark). The following figure shows graphically the differences between the "policy gap" and the "compliance gap" in this approach, where the former is included in rectangle "D–G–H–E" and the latter by the area "B–C–G–F".

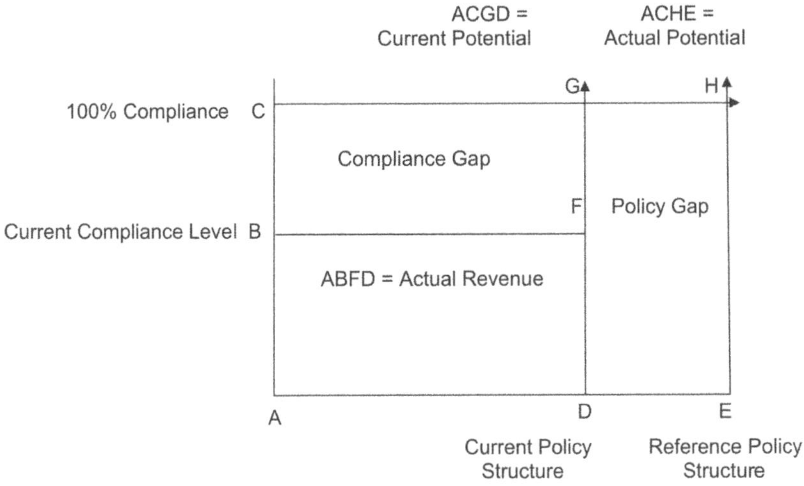

Source: IMF

The tax gap arises for a number of reasons. Some taxpayers make simple errors in calculating the tax that they owe, despite their best efforts, while others don't take enough care when they submit their returns. Legal interpretation, evasion, avoidance and criminal attacks on the tax system also result in a tax gap. It is impossible to collect every penny of tax that is owed – for example, we cannot collect outstanding tax from businesses that become insolvent.

For example, the HMRC Customs revenue gap for 2017–2018 was 4.1%, conglomerated within the category of "Other Taxes", while the VAT revenue gap was much higher, at 9.1%, significantly high enough to warrant a greater level of VAT investigations on the part of HMRC, as well as measures taken to collect outstanding VAT debts and implement a much greater level of compliance on traders, especially in the area of imports and exports. This also raised the risk level of many traders owing to non-compliance in the area of import and export.

Tax avoidance is the process of bending the rules of the tax system to gain a tax advantage that government never intended. It often involves contrived, artificial transactions that serve little or no purpose other than to produce a tax advantage, including the use of offshore tax havens. It involves operating within the letter, but not the spirit, of the law, and therefore is legal, although it may be unethical.

The avoidance tax gap was estimated at £1.8 billion for 2017–2018. This estimate reflects the laws that were in place at the time and does not include any subsequent changes to the tax law to prevent further use of avoidance. VAT and Customs accounted for approximately 3% of total revenue, quantified at £0.2 billion.

VAT, Customs and Excise tax gaps are estimated using a predominately "top-down" approach, by comparing the implied tax due from consumer expenditure data with tax receipts. Most other components are estimated using a "bottom-up" approach, building up from the Revenue Authority's own operational data and management information. The way that the Revenue Authority, e.g. HMRC, estimates each tax gap component and the data that it uses is set out in the relevant chapters, with additional information in the "Methodological annex".

The "top-down" estimate is set out as follows:

- Independent, external data on consumption is used to estimate the tax base;
- This tax base is used to calculate a theoretical value of tax that should be paid;
- The actual amount of tax paid is subtracted from this theoretical value to estimate the tax gap.

This is therefore a simple formula of:

Tax Payable *less* Tax actually paid = **Tax Gap**.

The tax gap percentage is therefore:

$$\frac{\text{Tax Payable } \textit{less} \text{ Tax actually paid}}{\text{Tax Payable}} \times 100\%$$

From this, the very fact that tax gaps exist mean that government needs to remedy these anomalies as a priority. Given that much of the issue concerns non-compliance on the part of traders, any trader falling foul of Customs and VAT investigations may not only have to pay tax penalties as well as excess duty and tax, but will also be registered on a high-risk assurance list. This means that they will be monitored and vetted until they have shown evidence of the ability to be more compliant with Customs and VAT requirements, usually by documentary and procedural evidence. Once this has been proven, their risk status will be progressively reduced until they are considered to be low risk.

Customs Risk Analysis

The following text sets out an agreed approach to the development of a standardised framework for risk management by the Customs administrations of the EU. It was developed in partnership between the EU Member States and the EU Commission (Directorate General Taxation and Customs Union) under the Customs 2002 programme, and has since been used as the basis for the 2007 Customs programme and the Union Customs Code of 2016. Its structure still applies to the UK since the withdrawal of the UK from the EU at the end of 2020.

Using the risk data, and assessment of the risks in each aspect of the context should be undertaken. There are two main ways to view this, by analysing **proven risk** and by analysing **potential risk**.

Proven risk is historical fact, an irregularity has occurred and the organisation has a record of the incident and the facts surrounding the case. Lists of these risks can be analysed against current data to see if conditions surrounding the risk currently exist. If yes, an assessment of the likelihood and consequence of the risk should be undertaken (see below).

Potential risks are risks that have not yet been uncovered but are suspected. For example the development of a new commodity to which the owner assigns their Trade Mark, may become the target of others wishing to breach the owners intellectual property rights. These risks should also be analysed against current data and if the conditions for the risk exist, an assessment of the likelihood and consequences should be undertaken. Exchange of risk information between Member States is an additional source of information, this is an important aspect to help equivalence of controls and to counter emerging threats rapidly.

The risks should be analysed in terms of likelihood and consequence. The analysis should consider how likely an event is to happen and, if it were to happen, what are the potential consequences and their importance. Combining these elements will produce an estimated level/weighting of the risk in the next step of this element.

There are different types of ranking systems. The assessment into high, medium and low is widespread. Although ranking in three levels is widespread, it can be defined in only two levels (high and low) or if desired it can be more than three levels. The output of this element in the risk management process should be a prioritised list of risks and the future treatment action specified.

High risks are generally likely to arise and have severe effects. Treatment actions for these risks should be highly visible to senior management and possibly agreed in control plans. In exceptional cases where a control is not acted upon, the reasons for not acting should be documented and made transparent to those responsible for assessing the risk.

Medium risks may be less likely to arise, or have less severe effects, but not necessarily both. Also with medium risks it is recommended to document the reasons for not acting.

Low risks are acceptable risks that can be assessed by standard or routine procedures or even where no action is necessary.

A consistent strategic approach, based on common criteria, understanding, methodology and procedures that applies across all areas of the risk management exercise should minimise unnecessary subjectivity in the decision process. The consistent use of inputs including criteria, procedures and data will promote the production of comparable outputs, such as identified risks that are prioritised according to a common measurement scale. Logical categorisation of risks is considered necessary to set level of priority for assessing the identified risks.

In a frontier environment the levels of risk could be treated as follows:

1. **Dynamic parameters:** Profiles based on information from various sources such as the Risk Information Form (RIF), AM-fiches, etc., can be introduced into a clearance system. Parameters can be inserted which cause the consignments to be selected for checking based on data of the single administrative document If the consignments are selected, based on the inserted parameters, the document will mostly be assessed as *a high risk* because the information on which the profiles are drafted are based on concrete risks;
2. **Fixed parameters:** These are where there is a mathematical selection based on pre-determined risk values for every procedure code, country code, product code and company number. A total score value is calculated and can be assessed by a score table resulting in high, medium or low risk;
3. **Random selection:** Local Customs officials have to be in a position to undertake random checks on consignments otherwise not selected. This can be done by a statistical random selection run in a computer programme or by manual system based on an agreed technique that eliminates individual's subjectivity. The output of this element in the risk management process should be a prioritised list of risks and definition future actions needed.

Risk Treatment

Develop and implement treatment of selected risks. Control actions can be (documentary and physical) on the spot or at the trader's premises. It could be decided to undertake *a posteriori* controls such as audit to minimise the burden on the trade at the frontier or for more detailed checks.

Accept low-priority risks with minimal further treatment. For risks in other categories, develop and implement treatment as specified in management plans.

Whenever a transaction is selected for control, a control form can be provided with the control advice including explanatory notes so that the local officer has information of the risk assessment. The result of the controls can also be recorded on the control form (on paper or electronically).

A local officer could also report if he has taken no action and the reason why no action has been taken. This is important input in the next element of monitoring and review. It might result in deleting existing profiles or introducing new ones.

Knowing the effectiveness of the strategy, implementing changes to procedures and the improvement of controls are best achieved with the use of an effective monitoring system. Monitor and review the performance, effectiveness and efficiency of the risk management system and changes that might affect it. Evaluation and review should be carried out by a regular mechanism.

The review must use information feedback from the process and lead to updating the analysis and prioritisation of control work. A distinction should be made between feedback, which leads to changing and updating the risk profiles and monitoring, which is a process to evaluate the effectiveness of the system.

In both cases IT-support is considered important. Most Member States are seeking better systems to deal with monitoring and review of the risk management process. Sharing experiences is considered useful in this area.

Specific Areas of Risk

The *Internal HMRC Risk Manual* highlights several specific areas of risk, and these are as follows:

- Valuation;
- Commodity Codes;
- Duty Reliefs;
- Origin.

These can be given more detail, as each area presents significant challenges to both traders and the Customs/Revenue Authority.

Valuation

Valuation for import purposes is a crucial issue, as it affects Import Duty liability as well as Import VAT. When a consignment is imported and an Import

Declaration is submitted to Customs, there are 3 main elements which must be inserted for the purposes of the calculation of Import Duty. These are:

- Purchase Cost of Consignment (Cost);
- Insurance of the Consignment (Insurance);
- International Freight Cost (Freight).

These three elements constitute the CIF (Cost Insurance Freight) Import Landed Cost, and are essential to the calculation of Import Duty on the consignment, along with the correct Commodity Code(s) for the consignment.

The valuation of the consignment is vital as part of this calculation, as the valuation must reflect the market price of the country of import. However, in many cases the valuation for import purposes is based on the export value of the consignment, which may in many cases be less than that of the market of import. This is often encompassed in the system of Transfer Pricing, where the export market value is directly transferred to the import market value without taking into considerations differences between the two values on the same product. Where the export value may be less than the expected import value, this may be construed by the Import Revenue Authority as a means of deliberately undervaluing the product in order to deliberately reduce the Import Duty liability on the product concerned.

In accordance with the Agreement on Implementation of Article VII of the General Agreement on Tariffs and Trade 1994, Article 1 – Rules on Customs Valuation, Articles 1–17, HMRC apply 6 methods of valuation, and these same methods are generally applied globally for Import Duty purposes. These same methods have been adopted by all other national Revenue and Customs Authorities for the purposes of Customs Valuation.

Method 1

This is called the "transaction value", and it is the normal method of valuation which applies to over 90% of importations liable to *ad valorem* Customs Duty.

The transaction value is the price paid or payable by the buyer to the seller for the goods when sold for export to the UK adjusted in accordance with specific rules explained in detail in the following paragraphs. This value takes into account the export price of the product based on all production costs (materials, production costs such as labour and machining, overheads and profits) plus ancillary costs such as packaging and packing.

The Customs value is based on the price actually paid or payable by the buyer to the seller for the goods. This means the total payment made or to be made by the buyer to or for the benefit of the seller for the imported goods. It includes all payments made or to be made as a condition of sale of the imported goods by the buyer to the seller or by the buyer to a third party to satisfy an obligation of the seller. Thus, periodic payments (such as monthly, quarterly, annually) or "one off" payments by the buyer to the seller for the imported goods must be taken into account, for example, tooling charges, engineering fees and development costs.

The following items must also be added to the price paid by the importer (unless they are already included):

(a) Delivery costs. The costs of transport, insurance, loading or handling connected with delivering the goods to the UK border must be included, but must be itemised separately on the commercial invoice, depending upon the INCOTERM used. The INCOTERMs C&F, CIF, CPT, CIP, DAP and DPU would include such itemised international delivery costs, whereas in the case of EXW, FCA, FAS and FOB, these costs would not be included on the export commercial invoice but would be paid and accounted for separately by the importer;

(b) Commissions. Certain payments of commission and brokerage, including selling commission, must be included;
However, buying commission can be excluded if it is shown separately from the price paid or payable for the goods (see paragraph 3.16(f) and section 34).

(c) Royalties and license fees. These payments must be included when they relate to the imported goods and are paid by you as a condition of the sale to you of those goods;

(d) Goods and services provided free of charge or at reduced cost by the buyer. If you provide, directly or indirectly, any of the following, you must include in the Customs value any part of the cost or value not included in the price charged to you by the seller:
    (i) Materials, components, parts and similar items incorporated in the imported goods including price tags, kimball tags, labels;
    (ii) Tools, dies, moulds and similar items used in producing the imported goods, for example, tooling charges – there are various ways of apportioning these charges;
    (iii) Materials consumed in producing the imported goods, for example, abrasives, lubricants, catalysts, reagents etc which are used up in the manufacture of the goods but are not incorporated in them;
    (iv) Engineering, development, artwork, design work and plans and sketches carried out outside the UK and necessary for producing the imported goods – the cost of research and preliminary design sketches is not to be included.

It must be noted that if the importer makes any payments (periodically or "one off") to the seller for any of the above goods and services, they must include the amounts in the Customs value (see paragraph 3.4).

(e) Containers and packing, include the cost of:
Containers which are treated for Customs purposes as being one with the goods being valued (that is not freight containers the hire-cost of which forms part of the transport costs);
Packing whether for labour or materials;
Where containers are for repeated use, for example, reuseable bottles, you can spread their cost over the expected number of imports. If a number of the containers may not be re-exported, this must be allowed for.

(f) Proceeds of resale. If the importer is to share with the seller (if directly or indirectly) the profit on resale, use or disposal of the imported goods, they must add the seller's share to the price paid. For example, if the seller is to have 30% of the profit which you receive, this is to be added to the price paid or payable. If at the time of importation the amount of profit is not known, the importer must request release of the goods against a deposit or guarantee;

(g) Export Duty (very rare) and taxes paid in the country of origin or export. When these taxes are incurred by the buyer they are dutiable. However, if the importer benefits from tax relief or repayment of these taxes they may be left out of the Customs value.

Method 2

This is the second method you must try. It is based on the Customs value of identical goods exported to the EC at or about the same time as the goods to be valued.

Identical goods are goods produced in the same country as those being valued. They must also be the same in all respects, such as physical characteristics, quality and reputation. Minor differences in appearance do not matter. If the producer of the Method 2 goods does not produce Method 1 goods, another producer's goods may be used for comparison.

Method 2 is based on a Customs value of identical goods already accepted by UK Customs under Method 1. Where there is a sale at the same commercial level and in the same quantity this must be used. If more than one value is available, the lowest value should be used.

Method 3

This is the third method that should be used. It is based on the Customs value of similar goods exported to the UK at or about the same time as the goods to be valued.

Similar goods are those goods which differ in some respects from the goods being valued but they:

- Are produced in the same country;
- Can carry out the same tasks;
- Are commercially interchangeable.

Where similar goods are not made by the producer of the goods to be valued, the importer can use similar goods produced by a different person or supplier.

Method 4

This is the fourth method that can be used. It is based on the selling price of the goods in the UK.

It should be pointed out that Method 5 can be tried before Method 4 if wished by the importer.

The Customs value is based on the price of each item (unit price) at which:

- The imported goods;
- Identical imported goods;
- Similar imported goods.

are sold in the UK in the condition as imported to customers unrelated to the seller. The unit price must relate to sales in the greatest aggregate quantity at or about the time of the importation of the goods to be valued.

The importer must be able to produce details of the sales in the greatest aggregate quantity at the time of entry into Free Circulation. In the UK this is known as "Method 4(a)".

Method 5

This method is the fifth method that can be used, and it is based on the costs of production of the goods. Usually, it can only be used where the importer and supplier are related. It is possible to try this method before Method 4 if wished.

The Customs value is a built-up value, and is based on the sum of the following:

- The cost or value of materials and fabrication or other processing used in producing the imported goods including:
- The items supplied by the buyer, directly or indirectly, even if the work listed earlier in the valuation notice is carried out in the UK,

the importer must include the value of the work in the Customs value if they charge the producer of the goods to be valued for that work;

- Containers and packing;
- An amount for the producer's profit and general expense;
- The cost of transport, insurance and loading or handling connected with delivering the goods to the UK border.

Method 6

This is the final method and is called the "fall-back" method.

For this method, the importer must arrive at the Customs value by using reasonable means consistent with the WTO valuation principles. They do this where possible by adapting Methods 1 to 5 flexibly to fit unusual circumstances:

Examples:

Methods 2 or 3. The Customs value could be based on the transaction value of identical or similar imported goods produced in a country other than the country of exportation of the goods being valued.

Method 4(b). The 90 days limit for sales could be extended.

The Customs value could be based on the price that would have been paid for the goods if they had been purchased (perhaps by reference to the export price list for sales to the UK issued by the supplier). This approach would be consistent with WTO valuation principles.

In terms of evidence required, the importer must be able to get information about the cost or value of the items included in Method 5. This information must be based on the producer's commercial accounts. These accounts must follow the general principles of accounting, which apply in the country where the goods are produced.

Commodity Codes

Commodity Codes are considered to be a high area of risk, in that they can be used or manipulated to attempt to pay less Import Duty than defined by the Customs Authority, including instances where anti-dumping duties (ADD), countervailing duties (CVD) or safeguard duties may apply. It is commonplace for importers to deliberately use Commodity Codes where the definition of the product may be somewhat vague, or where the product is referred to but not necessarily its parts or spare parts, which may attract a higher rate of Import Duty. In cases where parts of an item attract higher rates of Import Duty, the finished product is declared, whereas it may not have been fully assembled at the time of import, and may thus be assessed by the Customs Authority as parts relating to the product but not the full product itself.

If, however, the company is approved to use an Import Duty Relief facility to import the parts or components under Import Duty suspension, and then declare the finished product into Free Circulation once it has been manufactured in the country of import, then the finished product may indeed be declared through Customs using the Commodity Code of the finished product attracting the lower Import Duty rate rather than those Commodity Codes pertaining to the parts or components, which attract higher Import Duty rates. This technique is known as **Tariff Inversion** or **Reversed Cascading**, but still requires Customs approval to be used.

Import Duty Reliefs

These are known as Special Economic Procedures in the present Customs regime, and are subject to application to Customs by the importer and approval accordingly. They encompass three main areas, namely Inward Processing (IP), Outward Processing (OP) and Customs Warehousing (CW). Other Duty Reliefs such as Returned Goods Relief or Duty Relief for Testing purposes are also available, but do not require prior approval by the Customs Authority.

Such reliefs require absolute compliance with Customs requirements, and are often contravened because of a lack of control of import and export procedures on the part of the importer/exporter. A particular example of this is the misuse of the INCOTERMS, where an importer/processor imports material under Import Duty Relief using the correct Customs Procedure Codes on the Import Declaration, but fails to take control over the corresponding export of the processed product, owing to the use of the EXW (Ex Works) INCOTERM, where the customer takes full control over the shipment of the consignment from the point of the consignment being made available for collection at the processor's factory gate. With the term EXW, the exporter has no control over the export shipment, including the raising and submission of the Export Declaration to Customs, and it is very probable that the customer was not made aware that the consignment was subject to Inward Processing controls, which require specific Customs Procedure Codes (CPCs) being inserted on the Export Declaration. In many cases, the CPCs used refer to export under Free Circulation, which contravenes Inward Processing Relief requirements, and thus make the consignment subject to Import Duty as a result.

Origin

Much can be written about the subject of origin and trade preferences. Trade preferences result from the implementation of Free Trade Agreements between two or more countries and encompass the issue of duty-free trading between these countries on a preferential basis. However, such duty-free trade is conditional on the products being exported within Free Trade bloc originating in the countries concerned, subject to the Rules of Origin pertaining to the specific Free Trade Agreement.

It is often the case that materials imported into one country under Free Circulation conditions and then re-exported without any significant transformation or processing to another country in the Free Trade Bloc to which that country belongs are declared as originating in that country, which they clearly do not. The rule is that entry into Free Circulation does *not* mean originating. In this respect, Import Declarations allow for two specific boxes, namely country of origin and country of dispatch. Where the country of dispatch is the same as the country of origin, then the goods being exported do originate in the country of dispatch, and therefore qualify for duty-free import into the country of ultimate destination. However, where the country of origin is not the same as the dountry of dispatch, then the consignment concerned does not originate in the country of dispatch, and therefore the goods do not originate there and therefore cannot be imported duty-free into the ultimate country of import.

Actual Debt versus Potential Debt

Much of the above issues result from the issue of Actual Customs Debt versus Potential Customs Debt. An Actual Debt is a Customs debt, i.e. Import Duty and VAT, incurred by an importer on a consignment at the point of import. This debt, specifically Import Duty, can be paid outright or by way of a Duty Deferment Account. Import VAT can be presently accounted for in the UK and Ireland by way of Postponed VAT Accounting, a facility which allows the importer to account for the Import VAT on their VAT Returns rather than paying it at the point of import. Elsewhere in the EU and overseas, Import VAT must be paid outright at the point of import or deferred through the importer's deferment account and paid at by direct debit to the Revenue Authority at a fixed future date in the month following the import transaction(s).

Potential debt, however, is a debt deemed by the Revenue Authority to be potential, in that it is not automatic but may become liable based on default or compliance error on the part of the importer when using an Import Duty Relief facility such as Inward Processing, as detailed in the above section on Import Duty Reliefs. Where compliance with Customs requirements is breached, such Import Duty and VAT liability becomes applicable, and the Duty and VAT is taken to account from the importer by the Revenue Authority.

Customs Audit and MSS

In the Customs environment, audit risk is taken very seriously, especially where the import and export records of a trader are being examined. At first instance, any investigation is carried out electronically by way of the Customs computer, with any discrepancies being highlighted by the computer prior to any further in-depth analysis being undertaken by an auditing officer.

In general, the Customs computer provides details of all import and export transactions for any trader based on the trader's EORI (Economic Operator Registration Identifier) details, which correspond to the trader's VAT Registration Number, and which are recorded on an Excel spreadsheet. In the UK, this spreadsheet, using the Microsoft Excel system, is known as the HMRC MSS (Management Support System), and contains all the information derived from Customs import and export entries.

When a Customs audit takes place, the local officer holds records of actual data entered and will raise assessments against traders on duties for imports not recognised by the trader's records but actually declared to Customs. This mainly arises where an appointed agent has inadvertently failed to make a correct declaration. It is the importer who is responsible for correctly declaring goods and only negligible liability is placed upon the agent, unless there is clear evidence of negligence or incompetence. Larger traders with multi-site operations have particular difficulty in keeping administrative records of their imports due to the number of different locations employing different agents.

Depending upon the gravity and history of the errors, the trader may be put onto a high-risk assurance list by HMRC. This means that the trader will be audited more frequently and their declarations scrutinised more frequently to establish any pattern in perceived errors or to ensure that the trader does not continue to make consistent errors in Import or Export Declarations, especially where HMRC revenue may be compromised.

Providing records to traders means their work would be simplified and they would have a better chance of getting it right, especially in terms of the scrutiny of import and export data. Customs would need to spend less time chasing cases of inadvertent non-compliance. Traders' own management information and administration systems would also benefit, for example, by giving accurate figures for the total amount of duty paid against the value of goods entered, as well as the use of Import Duty Reliefs. Furthermore, the use of such records means that the trader can spend more time in control of their import or export activities with the confidence of knowing that they have a robust verification mechanism in the form of MSS to ensure that all import and export transactions are carried out correctly and efficiently, and that they have the power to challenge the clearing agents should any errors occur.

Four standard reports are available covering the following:

- Import item;
- Import entry;

- Import tax lines;
- Export item data.

These import and export item reports are able to meet the requirements of the majority of HM Revenue and Customs customers.

HMRC supplies the following information:

- Entry Number;
- Entry Date;
- Tariff Commodity Code;
- Customs Procedure Code;
- Value of Consignment;
- Country of Origin;
- Country of Dispatch;
- Country of Destination;
- Import Duty; and
- VAT.

These items of information are derived directly from the Import Declarations. Other items of data, such as country of origin or country of destination, and the Agent's Reference Number, are also included on the spreadsheet. Export Declarations do not contain details of Import Duty and VAT, but other information detailed above is common to both Import and Export Declarations.

This data can then be transmitted in Excel spreadsheet format by e-mail on a monthly basis to a named responsible person of the business. The request should clearly indicate whether import data, export data or both is required, and provide an e-mail address for receipt of the data.

Not all data items available on Management Support System (MSS) are available for purchase in reports, since there is information on the system which cannot be released to traders because it could compromise HMRC control activities.

Customs Risk Management Best Practices

Over the last several years, global international best practices for Customs have evolved from a series of standards and agreements such as the World Customs Organisation (WCO) Framework of Standards to Facilitate and Secure Global Trade (SAFE) and the WCO's Columbus Program for Customs Modernisation and Capacity Building. By conforming to these existing standards, a national Customs service can promote and encourage integrity, responsible enforcement and good governance within its Customs programmes. However, it must also seek to become more efficient and effective in its primary roles of revenue collection and protection, and the prevention of illicit trade.

A key component of best practices for Customs modernisation is effective risk management. Risk management has emerged as the guiding principle for border management to allow the focusing of resources on high-risk shipments while promoting pre-approved and/or low-risk trade. In other words, this means providing a balance between effective Customs controls and efficient trade facilitation.

International best practices for Customs have evolved from standards and agreements such as the Revised Kyoto Convention on the Simplification and Harmonization of Customs Procedures, the World Customs Organisation's Framework of Standards to Facilitate and Secure Global Trade (SAFE), and the WCO's Columbus Program for Customs Modernization and Capacity Building.

In line with the WCO SAFE framework, modern Customs administrations have begun adopting the use of automated risk management systems to improve their ability to identify high-risk shipments and promote trade facilitation. These systems have evolved to become the core of the Customs risk management regime in those countries. Performance is measured by increased enforcement, enhanced security, more trade, and a surge in the movement of trans-shipments, resulting in increased revenue and economic and social development.

Border control agencies, including Customs Authorities, face major challenges balancing a country's need for controls with the benefits of facilitating cross-border traffic in people and goods. To better manage the growing volume of travellers and trade, a significant number of leading Customs administrations have adopted a risk management strategy as the guiding principle for border management. The systematic implementation of risk management at strategic, operational and tactical levels ensures that Customs administrations best deploy resources to protect their citizens from threats to health, safety, and security, while simultaneously supporting economic growth by maintaining efficient and predictable cross-border transit times. In some cases, Border Agencies have been separated from Customs administrations, thus requiring increased levels of communication between the two authorities and thus requiring increased levels of intelligence and the efficient flow of important information concerning cross-border movements.

Many developing Customs services currently use risk-adverse approaches requiring a full inspection of many/all shipments, conveyances, crews and passengers. However, this approach has several shortcomings, including the following:

- Costly in resources, as it applies the same degree of intensity to all threats;

- Constrained, in that it forces a lower degree of inspection intensity overall due to a uniform treatment of all cargo and passengers;
- Creates a high incidence of officer errors due to higher workloads;
- Achieves fewer enforcement results;
- Encourages normally law-adhering entities to circumvent the system to hasten the cross-border transit of their goods;
- Creates opportunities for criminals to circumvent and avoid interception and interdiction by rendering Customs reactions predictable;
- Slows and impedes the Supply Chain;
- Obstructs and limits economic growth;
- Does not scale or make distinctions;
- Fails ultimately to achieve efficient, secure border management.

However, it should be noted that frontier examinations can reduce the risk of non-declaration or mis-declaration because of the ability to verify consignments at the time they cross the frontier, thus reducing a degree of the threats posed to national fiscal control. Furthermore, such examinations can also reduce the level of illicit trade, namely smuggling and contraband, as well as the illegal trafficking of human beings across borders.

In moving away from such risk-adverse approaches, many large Customs administrations have demonstrated that technology is a key factor in enabling efficiency. The *WCO SAFE Framework of Standards to Secure and Facilitate Global Trade* specifically mentions that Customs administrations should develop or procure automated electronic risk management systems. Based on international best practices, risk assessment systems use standard data sets and strategic intelligence to support identification of high-risk shipments and travellers.

Adopting an automated risk assessment system is a significant step towards successfully adopting risk management practices strategically, operationally and tactically. Border control processes that use risk assessment systems help ensure that Customs resources are always focused on the highest-risk shipments and people in real time.

Automated targeting and risk assessment systems process electronic pre-arrival data in an analytical workflow to identify the shipments or passengers of most interest. Low-risk shipments and passengers are facilitated and high-risk ones are set aside for additional scrutiny, up to and including physical inspections or orders not to load cargo or fly passengers. When combined with random inspections, pre-arrival data can significantly augment threat identification and interdiction, thus improving an administration's effectiveness in meeting national economic and security mandates.

The successful implementation of risk assessment systems requires the mandated use of electronically submitted pre-arrival data. Many Customs administrations use real-time pre-arrival data in the form of pre-submissions of cargo manifests for a variety of purposes, including:

- Increasing cargo control;
- Recovering lost or evaded revenue;
- Gathering intelligence;
- Profiling risks;
- Setting lookouts;
- Identifying potential security threats;
- Enhancing end-to-end Supply Chain or travel visibility in order to identify anomalous behaviour in relation to people, entities, commodities and routings.

Pre-arrival data from such manifests provides Customs administrations with the ability to extend the border on a virtual basis and decide whether to facilitate or intercept cargo or people before they reach the physical border. This is generally carried out in the form of pre-examination of cargo manifests, often at the point of loading aboard vessel or aircraft, as in the cases of the EU's ENS system, the Canadian ACI (Advance Commercial Information) system and the US C-TPAT (Customs-Trade Partnership Against Terrorism) system, enabling the Customs computer in the country of arrival to pre-select specific cargoes for import examination, or even to prevent the loading of cargoes based on a risk level of low, medium or high, according to a perceived risk level depending upon the information provided by the export or import trader.

It is therefore prudent to adopt a risk management-based strategy as the core foundation to any Customs or border modernisation activity, with due attention paid to the following specific tasks:

- *Update* Customs and Trade legislation, regulations, standard operating procedures and directives to provide authority to field personnel to adopt and use risk-based decisions for all travellers and trade entering or leaving the country;
- *Adopt* a simple, clear, and unified framework and approach to risk management at strategic, tactical, and operational levels;
- *Perform* a detailed analysis and ranking of threats;
- *Acquire* human and technical resources to enable the following:

    1. Separation of duties to enhance integrity;
    2. Collection of pre-arrival data;
    3. Implementation of trusted trader and registered traveller programmes;

4. Expansion of available inspection types to allow for varying intensities of inspections;
5. Establishment of control processes throughout the pre-arrival, arrival and post-clearance stages of the Customs process;
6. Capture of all outcomes in automated systems;
7. Establishment of a post-clearance audit and analysis unit to continually validate, monitor and review the above.

The adoption of border risk management at strategic levels within an administration is the first step towards this objective. The transition to a risk-managed decision-making process at all levels requires a multi-faceted organisational change involving a mixture of new policy, clear and continuous communication, technology and training, as well as a continuous improvement approach based on cyclical monitoring and improvement. Indeed, training needs to be provided for both Customs officials and traders, in order to ensure that all parties are fully aware of both the changes to Customs strategy and procedures, and the need for the adoption of specific Customs procedures on the part of import and export traders. Above all, this transition requires persistence, dedication and patience at all levels. Technology adoption is often the most significant catalyst for establishing a risk management framework within any Customs or border organisation. The acquisition of new technology provides momentum for change, and also allows an administration to modernise itself to the most current and leading-edge solutions while avoiding many development hurdles borne by other Customs administrations. The use of systems already adopted by other administrations can cut time and cost by leveraging the best practices and benchmarks already incorporated in tested technology, but this does not mean a one-size-fits-all approach, as each national Customs administration differs from others in terms of size and complexity, as well as its development status and its ability to adopt this transition.

One of the key capabilities required from Customs risk management strategy is risk profiling and targeting. As a result, data mining techniques are used regularly to identify risk profiles. Data mining often uses machine learning and statistical methods to classify and group the high-risk profiles and target groups. Though, it has scientific roots, it is based on a few assumptions which can be flawed if not clearly understood. Data warehousing, although a comprehensive means of data mining, is subject to issues such as continuous maintenance and updating, which can prove a costly process.

It is important to understand that data mining is not a front-end selectivity function used by end-users such as Customs Officers. Generally, data mining techniques, such as historical trend analysis, forecasting, correlation, business intelligence, etc., are used to identify risk profiles by intelligence analysts working in a strategic intelligence environment, especially as they are often associated with retrospective or historic data stretching back several years. These profiles are often turned into risk indicator rules (high, medium, low) in front-end decision support systems such as targeting and risk assessment systems for selectivity decisions by Customs Officers based on historic evidence of errors or anomalies. Selectivity decisions eliminate low-risk shipments for trade facilitation, which in turn promotes economic growth, and scrutinise, inspect, or intercept high-risk shipments that may pose a significant threat to a nation or region of the globe. Such selectivity means that fewer resources are spent on dealing with low-risk shipments, where the potential yield in terms of the recovery of fiscal revenue may be extremely low, especially where there are very low rates of Import Duty involved.

While Customs administrations collect regulatory declarations and submissions from carriers (e.g. cargo declarations, manifests) exporters and importers (Export and Import Declarations), the growing volume of this information has become difficult to manage, resulting in the need for constant updates to Customs computers. While the volume of global trade continues to grow at the rate of about 10% each year, the data expands at the same rate. As such, Customs administrations should be anticipating data volumes to double every ten years and should therefore update their systems to accommodate this increase. The effective use of this data in an operational environment for selectivity decisions to determine highest-risk shipments is key to successful management of the system, yet many vendors in today's market place will promote retrospective historical trend analysis tools using business intelligence and data mining and processing techniques to identify anomalous behaviour in the data that may suggest nefarious or illegal activity. However, such an approach, important as it may be, does not necessarily transfer to an operational environment where a decision support system is paramount. Data mining and processing identifies profiles based on strategic analysis of large data sets, as exemplified by data warehousing facilities used by some Customs administrations, whereas targeting and selectivity solutions use risk indicator rules, based on these profiles, in a front-end decision support system. Risk indicators identify specific companies or individuals based on (non-)compliance history, or where such entities have shown a propensity to breach Customs regulations on a regular basis. This means that a Customs computer will automatically be able to identify high-risk traders, and will immediately highlight them for further scrutiny based on this high-risk status, usually by selective analysis and identification of their tax reference numbers.

A key component of international best practices for Customs modernisation, risk management has emerged as the guiding principle for border management to allow the focusing of resources on high-risk shipments while promoting pre-approved and/or low-risk trade. In line with the WCO SAFE framework, the majority of Customs administrations have already adopted the principles of risk management, and the rest will doubtless follow.

In line with this, modernised Customs administrations have begun to adopt the use of automated electronic risk management systems as well as internal tax compliance risk manuals to improve their ability to identify high-risk shipments, overall trader compliance and the promotion of trade facilitation. Indeed, the use of these systems has evolved to become the core of the Customs risk management regime in these countries, with performance measured by increased enforcement, enhanced security, increased international trade, and a surge in the movement of trans-shipments resulting in increased revenue, and economic and social development.

Risk

Risk can be defined as what is at stake. In the context of Customs freight control, risk is a chance that the collection of revenue or the enforcement of controls may be adversely affected.

Risk Analysis

Risk analysis in the context of Customs control is a working method that aims to maximise the use of Customs resources while minimising the risk. This is achieved by:

- Identification of risks;
- Assessment of the level or degree of risk;
- Expression of the risk; and
- Allocation of resources to target the risks.

Risk Assessment

Risk assessment can be identified as the estimated degree of risk inherent in any Customs activity. Depending on agreed parameters, a risk can be:

HIGH = (H)
MEDIUM = (M)
LOW = (L)

Another method to estimate the degree of risk may consist in allocating a numerical value to each identified risk.

By the use of risk assessment, Customs resources can be more effectively allocated and should result in goods or traders with the same quantified risk receiving similar resources and priorities.

Areas of Risk

Risk areas in Customs freight control are those Customs or Customs-related regimes and procedures that involve revenue collection or enforcement functions (for example, VAT, Customs and/or Excise Duties, CAP, common commercial policy measures, environment. public health). Risk areas can extend to Customs regimes with economic impact and also traders who fail to comply with the conditions of Customs regimes.

For an effective risk analysis programme to be followed, the following criteria need to be met:

- Policy and operational objectives are clearly set out;
- Accountability both to management and auditors is clearly identified;
- The existence of a satisfactory management information system in place to enable performance to be measured; and
- Local Customs managers with the right information to enable any risk analysis to be effective.

Risk Indicators

Risk indicators are those factors that can increase or decrease the level or degree of risk to the revenue or enforcement function within each risk area. Depending on the risk area, several risk indicators can be used for risk assessment. In the case of Customs freight, risk indicators include the following:

- Tariff Commodity Code;
- Country of origin;
- Country where the consignment was dispatched;
- Licensing indicator;
- Value of the consignment;
- Trader compliance;
- Financial consequences;
- Means of transport;
- Financial situation of the trader.

Risk Profile

A risk profile is the means by which a Customs Office puts risk analysis into practice concerning import and export traders. It is a practical means of replacing random examination of documents and consignments with a planned and targeted working method, making maximum use of Customs resources. A risk profile is a document that can be set out in any number of ways but should be comprehensive and relevant to the Customs locations. The risk profile should:

- Be a source of information which Customs managers can use as a basis for allocating resources;
- Identify the risk areas in freight for the Customs location;
- Express the risk areas in agreed terms, for example, high (H), medium (M), or low (L) (or numerically where this approach is chosen); and
- Test the effectiveness of the counter-measures taken.

In order to maintain effectiveness, the risk profile must be flexible enough to allow for the identification and testing of new risks, and establish that where risks have been tested, they have been found to be satisfactory record as low risk.

A risk profile can be kept in a suitable hard-copy file or on a local computer and should be as accessible as possible to all Customs Officers. A risk profile can have a number of sections dealing with different types of freight – general cargo, CAP goods and goods liable to Excise Duties. Different risk profiles will apply to imports and exports.

The risk profile should contain a description of the risk area, an assessment of the risk, the counter-measures to be taken, an action date, the results and an evaluation of the effectiveness of the action taken.

(Source: HMRC INCHP08050 – Risk Analysis)

Additional Risk Indicators

Additional risk indicators could be:

- The basis for tax;
- The time (for tariff quotas);
- Any particular conditions, such as:
  - Licenses;
  - Reliefs;
  - Origin certificates;
  - Diversions (lost in transit).

In some cases, the extent to which simplified procedures are used could be an indicator of risk in a certain area. Most of the above risk indicators are product or transaction related.

The trader or economic operator is an important factor that will influence the overall risk assessment and risk profiling at several stages. Unusual behaviour in trade, any change of habits relating to the import or export of goods such as new types of goods, new places of operating or new commercial partners may be risk indicators according to the particular case. Generally, the fact that they have or have not already been guilty of infringements or irregularities against the Customs or fiscal law has to be taken into consideration. Solvency will also be an important factor.

Risk Profiles

General

The building of risk profiles follows the basic cycle of the "system approach". Information allows the assessment of the risk, leading to the decision to be taken in order to choose the control: this decision will be followed by an action, itself giving some information; in the background, feedback is essential at all stages.

Information is the first stage in risk profiling and is a condition for all other stages to be successful; to collect as much information as possible is crucial in order to make correct assessments and sound decisions.

Qualitative, quantitative and statistical data on the product or consignment, on the trader and the trade flow needs to be collected and studied for the construction of relevant and comprehensive risk profiles.

Assessment of the degree or level of the risk in a specific case is the second stage; the level or degree of risk can be assessed during the planning process as high, medium or low (or a numeric value may be assigned). It expresses the probability that an adverse situation can have when some conditions are met. It is a function of quantitative (volume of trade, value of consignment, level of duties or levies, frequency and number of locations of a specific import/export activity, etc.) also qualitative elements (past activity of the trader, relationships with other traders, variability in the range of goods of the purchase and sales prices, presence of goods that are susceptible to fraud, etc.). It can be based on the appropriate combination of several data items in the SAD and the other accompanying documents of the specific Customs procedure involved.

Depending on the assessment results, the decision stage will define the type of control (physical, documentary, etc.) taking into account resources and other constraints, including burdens on trade.

Action, the last stage, will consist in studying all types of control, ensuring their execution and reporting on the controls carried out in order to redefine the risk analysis and to complete the last profile.

Feedback is essential at all stages, in order that constant validation can take place and the necessary updating can be applied. The correct and most appropriate course of action can be documented and monitored as to their relative success.

It is also essential to keep the risk profile accurate, relevant and up-to-date and to rid the system of unnecessary information.

Therefore, risk profiles may be considered to have at least 4 functions:

1. To be a source of information on import and export activity/freight that can be used in the optimal allocation of resources;
2. To identify risk areas;
3. To express those risk areas in terms of high, medium or low (or in numerical terms); and
4. To test the effectiveness of controls.

In the context of the Internal Market, not only exchange of experience in risk profiling is necessary, dissemination and communication or risk profiles to other locations that may be concerned must be possible. Continuous updating of risk profiles and of the risk profiling methods are vital for the correct functioning of the system, especially when new EU or national legislation is developed, or new trade activities or trade policies are introduced.

Information and Intelligence

Sources of information are an essential part of the tools that can be used in the risk analysis-based system of Customs controls. Available sources of information can be:

- At the central headquarters;
- Other government departments and public institutions (Ministry of Agriculture, of Trade, of Transport, the Police, etc.);
- Fiscal controls, a varying proportion of which are carried out by the same administration in most Member States as Customs controls;
- Trade (airlines, shipping lines, agents, airport/port operators, competitors);
- Commission sources of information;
- Other Member States and international sources;
- Specialised newspapers and magazines; and
- Trade and professional organisations.

The completion of the EU Internal Market has made it imperative that information on trends and risk areas across the EU should be available to all Customs services.

Operational Customs information or "tactical intelligence" (which includes information on trends detected by Customs services, such as new smuggling routes) can be transmitted and received via the Customs Information System (CIS), managed by the EU's DG XXI, although since the exit of the UK from the EU, HMRC is presently working on its own intelligence system in accordance with the Revised Kyoto Convention and the ensuing SAFE Framework of Systems. This system is available at 250 locations throughout the Community including all major ports and airports, and incorporates a database continuing the information exchange via the system once the legal basis for this has been adopted under a regulation that will replace the current Council Regulation (EEC) No. 1468/81 on manual assistance. In addition, access is available via the CIS/SENT/fiscal SCENT network to specialised databases both within the Commission (Comext. for foreign trade statistics, Celex for Community legislation) and outside it (Dun and Bradstreet, for company information; Lloyds Seadata for shipping data; and Piers, for certain ships' manifests). A database ("IRENE") on irregularities and recoveries notified to the Commission by Member States under various provisions (FEOGA, 1468/81, 1552/89) has been operating on an experimental basis within UCLAF.

Information is raw data that may have been subject to minimum analysis processing. It is basic statistical data used principally as management information or on such areas as volume of traffic, total numbers of import entries and total value of imports in a given period. General trends, e.g. increase/decrease in traffic, can be identified to enable management decisions to be taken on staffing numbers at specified locations, etc.

Information becomes intelligence when it is analysed to identify trends in specific risk areas or areas of potential fraud, when it is collected or collated as applying specifically to those areas, or when it is used to build up a case against a fraudulent or potentially fraudulent individual/organisation.

It is this intelligence that will play a major part of the identification and prioritisation of the more universal indicators. Intelligence can be tactical, operational or strategic.

Tactical intelligence is actionable information on the current or imminent location and movements of, for example, a suspect consignment arriving from a third country for Customs clearance at a specific port. It requires an immediate enforcement response to effect detection and seizure; tactical intelligence if often time critical and applies to areas of fraud and smuggling in general.

Operational intelligence refers to information gathered to provide analytical support to the investigation and prosecution process. Information relating to individuals or organisations is collected and analysed. Analysis reveals the identity and activity or organisations, established relationships and uncover conspiracies.

Strategic intelligence is evaluated information on broad patterns and trends to be used by Customs policy planners and management on order to identify problem areas and make appropriate resource and legislatives decisions. Strategic intelligence includes information on smuggling methods and trends and the identification of fraud trend patterns in Customs.

Within HMRC the Risk and Intelligence Service (RIS) provide an assessment writing service, using all-source intelligence analysis. RIS Intelligence Assessment provide strategic assessments a national level (for policy makers) and will provide operation and tactical support on more localised issues for local managers.

In this framework, system-based controls (SBC) must also be taken into account.

Freight Declarations

Risk assessment and targeting strategy builds on and refines the processing of freight declarations. All freight declarations are processed in some way, either manually or electronically, to calculate and collect duties/levies, collect trade statistics, ensure that appropriate control documents are attached, endorsed, removed, returned or scrutinised to decide whether the goods should be checked.

Freight declarations can be divided into two categories:

1. Where Customs must intervene on every occasion because EU legislation required it or because without such intervention the control regime would not function; and
2. Where Customs intervention is not necessarily systematic but may vary according to assessment of risk.

Depending on the level of sophistication of risk assessment techniques, this second category may be subject to a minimum mandatory low interception rate to ensure and check general levels of compliance. Beyond this, Customs intervention can be based on risk assessment.

Authorised Economic Operators (AEOs) who have met the required criteria, are entitled under Regulation 1875/06 to fewer physical and document based controls. Goods may still be selected for examination but AEOs should be given priority treatment.

The existence of interactive computerisation processing of declarations greatly assists by automatically selecting consignments for either documentary or physical checks if required.

The Freight Team Concept

UK Border Agency/HMRC Officers can be organised to reflect the risk-based approach. Sufficient staff must naturally be deployed to carry out mandatory processing of declarations, low-level compliance checks and any routine risk-based selections. There can also be a dedicated resource within the team, relatively small in number, free of demand-led work that is able to test areas of risk, identify targets and build up expertise in special areas. This freight team concept combines the role of intelligence (information gathering, analysis and dissemination) with being the forefront operationally by selecting its own targets following risk assessment exercises.

This approach can be helped by the computerised selections. Adequate selection facilities are crucial, particularly when applying trade characteristics: the EU level can be considered too, as DG XXI can provide appropriate intelligence.

Routine Selection

Special selection parameters can be used to impose short-term controls. They may be used to assess the risk of a particular type of importation or identify particular suspect consignments.

Random selections can be utilised over and above the two previous types of selection. This can provide a control mechanism for identifying new routine and special selection and possibly reduce the risk of the declarant being able to avoid selection by acquiring knowledge of the selection parameters of the system. This concept is equally valid for exports.

To carry out its identification and testing role, the freight team needs to draw on a number of information sources. Information can be received from national headquarters that receives information from similar teams across the country, collates it, analyses trends and disseminates this information as appropriate. A database may be used to record and retrieve information on agent/trader performance, offence action taken and particular risk factors. Past declarations and their supporting documents can be recalled from filing. Commercial documents and historic records can also play a part.

For a freight team to be effective, it must identify and determine the relative importance of the risk indicators present in its area of responsibility. This returns to the need for audit work, as this is the method by which this task is performed. It is therefore essential that freight staff be trained to do this work. The freight team management must recognise that the audit work itself will need considerable resources in the short terms, but without this, greater resources will be lost in the longer term without the necessary checks being applied.

System-Based Control (SBC)

The SBC system is a systematic and flexible working method based on the fact that each operator has his own system of functioning, from the simplest to the most complex to be used for the elaboration of risk indicators. Techniques will differ between the small, one-man business and the larger company heavily involved in several Customs regimes.

Quantifying risks helps determine resource allocation and drives the future system-based control programme. A system-based control confined to documents and accounts cannot be fully effective, selective physical checks will be needed to test and evaluate these systems.

System audits are a tool in the development of risk profiles. "Universal" indicators, for example, all imports from a given country of origin or of goods under a specific Commodity Code, can generally be determined from historical data.

The more a Customs administration co-operates with a company in order to establish its internal system, the more checks can efficiently be based on the operator's systems.

The objective of SBC is to:

- Obtain assurance that a system contains the checks and controls necessary to account for the right amount of revenue at the right time and any reliefs are properly applied; and
- Ensure that the checks and controls are operating effectively.

SBC achieves this through a structured and systematic approach to control that encompasses several stages:

- Establish and record manual and/or computer operations within the system;
- Identify the revenue risks within the system by evaluating the key controls and weaknesses; and
- Carry out tests and controls (physical and documentary).

SBC largely relies on auditing the trader's records, but a vital part is testing the credibility of the record produced.

The advantage of the SBC approach is by targeting resources and tests to the potential risk within the system, it will identify any errors within it that prevent revenue being accounted for correctly. If there are no errors, assurance is obtained that the system is producing the desired result. The outcome of audit tests, are to inform any analysis of future risk and should determine the need and frequency of future control.

Systems-based controls are also used to identify the relative importance of the more specific risk indicators for building a risk profile. For example, in the area of simplified import procedures, where the control system operates by the relevant administration matches the initial and supplementary declarations submitted by the trader, then the risk that initial entries will not be accounted for on the supplementary declaration is very small. If this matching process were not performed by the administration, the same risk would be much greater.

In order to develop accurate risk profiles, the ways each of the risk areas are managed in each Member State will need to be controlled. Often the amount of revenue is used as the major criteria: if the value of the revenue is greater than €5,000, then the risk must be high. This is not always the case as, for example, an audit of the system used to control the risk area may indicate that the "audit assurance" is high and therefore the risk is low however great the amount of money at stake.

The degree of reliance that can be placed on the trader's accounting systems is another factor influencing the relative importance of risk indicators. Such systems play a major revenue-accounting role in some risk areas, e.g. simplified entry procedures, inward/outward processing, CAP, etc. By doing a full audit on these systems, the importance of risk can be accurately determined. This also means that, when developed to their full potential, risk profile can be trader specific.

One of the methods that can be used may consist of individually assessing the risk of each company and allocating a number to each of them.

Risk Indicators

Risk indicators are the key areas of concern for Customs Authorities in terms of potential fraud or mis-declaration in terms of revenue collection and protection.

Risk indicators: six main risk indicators are identified as:

- Origin: False declaration of origin;
- Value: False declaration of the value in order to reduce the amount of duty;
- CN Code (Commodity Code): False declaration of the product to another code where no duty is applied (84 71 99 10 "other peripheral units", as opposed to articles used in the manufacture of computers but found in other chapters of the tariff where items are subject to Import Duty rates, such as Chapter 39 – Articles of Plastic – EU duty rate 6.5%; UK duty rate 6%);
- Anti-dumping duty (ADD) evasion;
- Quantity same as value;
- Place of consignment: False declaration based on country of despatch to facilitate falsification of origin (e.g. products made in China (no tariff preference) but dispatched from Malaysia (GSP Preference)).

Risk assessment (to determine the level or degree of risk to each one of them): a comparative analysis of the flow of imports of goods under the above mentioned CN codes for the period before and after the application of the anti-dumping duty is carried out, based on statistical data on enterprises on: number of declarations, declared values, Customs Offices. The analysis of both product and trader based as it focuses on the study of trends in business strategies for the activity concerned (import of specific product). Results of this risk analysis can show:

- A possible mis-declaration of goods liable to the Commodity Code 8471 9290 being declared to 8471 9910;
- An unexpected change in the Customs Officers' office or Member State where the goods are imported;
- An unusual change in the unit price of the commodity; and
- An unusual declaration of origin for goods under code 8471 9290.

According to the results of the analysis, a high, medium or low degree of risk will be applied to each one of the risk indicators for selection operators; different "profiles" will be constructed which will determine the framework of control at each specific Customs Office according to its particular situation (resources, volume of trade, etc.). When all four indicators prove to be of low risk, no control might be necessary. Results of the controls could be used to update the risk analysis sheet.

In general terms, once the risk assessment is completed in each case, the (x) in the checklist will appear as (h) = high risk, (m) = medium risk, (l) = low risk; they can also be numbers, for example x = 1, n, to show ranged priorities for control according to risk. They can also be assigned a letter in addition to show the type of control that is needed, for example: (d) = control of documents accompanying the goods, (p) = a later control in the business premises, or (h) = physical control of goods.

More risk areas can be identified in the above case of anti-dumping measures; in fact, the economic procedures (temporary admission, warehouses or free-zones, IP and OP) and transit procedures may be involved in the operators' trade activities for the goods in question. Risk analysis of these areas as well would result in different levels of the same indicators, whereas additional ones can be identified (e.g. destination).

ADD and CD (countervailing duty) risks from all sources are assessed and disseminated to Regional risk teams and frontier staff.

The following are suggested as the Top 10 ADD/CD risks:

1. Goods misdescribed by traders to avoid a tariff heading that attracts ADD or CD;
2. Incorrect country of origin declared by the trader to avoid ADD or CD;
3. Incorrect country of consignment/dispatch declared by trader to avoid ADD or CD;
4. Technical specification of goods misdescribed to avoid ADD or CD within a specific tariff heading or obtain a lower duty rate;

5. Incorrect supplier's name given to avoid ADD or CD, or to obtain a lower rate they are not entitled to;
6. Components imported for assembly in EU to avoid ADD on finished article. The components could be liable to ADD if the assembled article enters into the EU;
7. Goods overvalued on invoice in order to exceed a Minimum Import Price (MIP) to avoid ADD or CD;
8. Under-declaration of weight when ADD or CD is levied at a specific rate based on import weight;
9. Satisfactory security not held subject to provisional ADD or CD and;
10. Retrospective revenue not secured once measure is made definitive.

(Source: HMRC INCHP 08000 Risk Analysis)

It should be noted that the above information relates to HMRC activities, but generally applies to all Revenue Authorities, as the issues at stake refer to global activities and are therefore accounted for by the World Customs Organisation (WTO).

Risk management requires clear responsibility and accountability for each programme or action. Some of the programmes that are currently being used to manage risk include compliance measurement, compliance assessment, selectivity, and account management. Risk management also shows field personnel how their individual work affects the overall work and operation of the national Customs Authority.

According to the WCO, the main steps in the risk management process are:

1. Establishing the context;
2. Risk assessment;
3. Risk identification;
4. Risk analysis (i.e. likelihood and consequences);
5. Risk evaluation and prioritisation;
6. Risk treatment.

Establishing the Context

Any effort to manage risk must begin by first establishing what needs to be managed. This stage defines the context in which risk management will take place, and aims at clearly articulating and clarifying the objectives and what risks are being examined. Determining what needs to be managed helps set the parameters for the rest of the risk management process.

The following questions can be used to establish context, outlining both the internal and the external aspects:

- What are the objectives in the context where the risk management process takes place?

- What is the operating environment?
- What capabilities and resources are available for managing risk?
- What criteria are used to assess risks and to determine if additional control is needed?
- What are the scope and limits of risk management?
- What are the expectations of stakeholders such as the government, affected communities, traders and other private sector groups?
- What other details are known about the process or activity?

An outcome of this phase should be a statement of the environmental operating context which includes a clear indication of the objectives ("risk to what") and the risk areas, and defines the criteria and parameters for the risk assessment phase.

Risk Identification

Risks cannot be analysed or managed until they are identified and described in an understandable way. The risk identification phase identifies and records all potential risks by using a systematic process to identify what risks could arise, why, and how, thus forming the basis for further analysis.

Some of the questions asked in this phase could include:

- What are the sources of risk?
- What risks could occur, why and how?
- What controls may detect or prevent risks?
- What accountability mechanisms and controls – internal and external – are in place?
- What, and how much, research is needed about specific risks?
- How reliable is the information?

Risk identification activities at various levels of the organisation must be closely linked to each other. Once an administration's strategic risks have been identified they are delegated to managers, who then further refine the broad strategic risks and determine priority areas for action within their areas of influence. Once these decisions have been taken and priorities assigned, operational line management can begin the process of identifying specific cases from within their areas of influence for further action. At each step in the process, the extent of the risk being managed is progressively reduced and the risk is managed at an appropriate level within the organisation.

The outcome of the risk identification process is a register of risks, which documents the risks and ensures that the entire risk spectrum is considered. There are many different ways to construct a risk register. Annex 1 of this book outlines examples of risk register templates.

Risk Analysis

Risk analysis is principally about quantifying risk, and requires consideration of the sources of identified risks, an assessment of their potential consequences in terms of achieving objectives, and judgement as to the likelihood that the consequences will occur (in the absence of any specific treatment with the existing controls in place). It relies upon the use of data and information to substantiate the consequences that are likely to be incurred if the risk occurs and/or remains unaddressed. Even though risk analysis should be evidence-based to the extent possible, it needs to be remembered that it is not an exact science. Knowledge about the business environment, expert judgement and common sense should never be overlooked when analysing risks.

In short, the analysis considers:

- How *likely* is an event to happen; and
- What are the potential *consequences* and their magnitude.

Combining these elements produces an estimated level of risk. Risk estimation can be quantitative or qualitative, or a combination of the two. Based on tolerance judgements using a 3 × 3 Matrix (high, medium, low), the following diagram suggests possible descriptions and indicators for estimating the likelihood of a risk occurring.

LIKELIHOOD	DESCRIPTION	INDICATORS
High (Probable)	Likely to occur or more than a 20% chance of occurring	Has occurred in the last 12 months
Medium (Possible)	Could occur, but less than 20% chance of occurring	Has occurred between 1 year and 3 years ago Has occurred in another country within the last 2 years
Low (Remote)	Not likely to occur and less than 5% chance of occurring	Has not occurred in the last 3 years or more (In the case of the EU, has not occurred in a Member Country within the last 2 years.

Based on tolerance judgements using a 3 × 3 Matrix (high, medium, low), the next diagram suggests possible descriptions and indicators for estimating the consequences of a risk occurring.

CONSEQUENCE/IMPACT	DESCRIPTION	INDICATORS
High (Serious)	If adverse risk occurs then there could be a severe community, economic or political crisis	Long-term ramifications for government or organisation
Medium (Manageable)	An adverse risk occurring would obstruct workflows and harm community or business	Damage to ability to meet organisational goals and commitments to government, community and business
Low (Treatment within existing workflows)	An adverse risk would cause minor delays to service delivery	Adverse risk event can be absorbed within existing standard operating procedures

Repeating this exercise on a regular basis (annually in the organisational and business unit context) is required, and normally results in changes to the estimated level of risk. These changes occur because of the treatments and preventative measures put in place. For example, the amendment of ambiguous legislation would leave less room for interpretation and therefore decrease the likelihood of an adverse event occurring. This in turn would lead to a lower risk level compared to the time before the preventative measure was implemented, etc.

Risk Evaluation and Prioritisation

This step entails comparing the assessed risks against a pre-determined significance criterion. By considering the risk level of each of the risks as described by the relevant management team in the matrix, it is possible to evaluate and prioritise the key risks that need to be analysed in more detail. This will then lead to the deployment of proportionate resources in order to prepare for, prevent or respond to the risk.

The evaluation enables Customs to better understand the risks. The process consists of deciding whether the risk is tolerable (acceptable), and assists in determining how imminently the risk event may occur. Decisions about which risks to respond to and which to monitor will potentially be impacted by many different issues, including:

- Internal capability;
- Internal capacity;
- Is there an effective capability to implement the treatment;
- Risk rating/level;
- Return of treatment;
- Effects to reputation; and
- The cost–benefits of proposed treatments.

These issues form the basis on which the effectiveness of treatment strategies will ultimately be evaluated. Note that it may be necessary to group a tolerability result and add specific response criteria for different categories. The outcome of the risk evaluation and prioritisation process should be a risk register that has been quantified and prioritised according to the risk level, linking risks with the risk owners responsible for their mitigation and monitoring.

Risk Treatment

Risk treatment refers to the decisions or actions taken in response to identified risk. There are four generic types of responses that can be applied. These are the so-called “4 Ts”, as stated earlier in the text:

- Tolerate;
- Treat;
- Transfer; or
- Terminate.

Tolerating risk would be acceptable in many instances, for example where resources are scarce or the risk is considered to be as well managed as possible with existing controls in place, or without expending too much in terms of money or resources to reduce the impact or consequence only marginally. Tolerating or accepting a risk does not mean that the risk would not be controlled and monitored. Monitoring is often done through standard operating procedures to see whether there are any changes to the level of risk.

Treating risks is often the most used option by Customs in terms of managing the risks it faces in its operations. This means reducing the likelihood or consequence of risks occurring by putting in place control measures and actions that are intended to modify the level of risk to fit the organisational tolerance. Depending on the type of risk, there are often many available treatments including preventative, detective and enforcement measures. When deciding on treatments, it is important to understand the causes of risks instead of concentrating only on the symptoms. A better understanding of the risks and the causes behind them enables more informed decisions to be made about the best treatment strategy or mix of strategies to mitigate them.

Risk transfer means transferring a risk to a third party for mitigation. Risks can be transferred internally or externally. For example within a Customs administration, a risk could be transferred from Operations to IT or from human resources to operations, etc. External transfer of risks may occur in operational and non-operational environments and even at strategic levels. Operationally, risks may be transferred to another law enforcement agency, or to a sub-contractor – where subcontractors are involved the risk transfer often entails having a legal contract or agreement in place for the work. It is important to remember that transferring risk does not necessarily mean transferring responsibility. In the first example above, if the risk is realised the senior manager in operations may still be held responsible for the risk even though the IT department is dealing with it. Termination means avoiding a risk by deciding to discontinue or no longer pursue an activity that may cause the risk to be realised.

Monitoring and Review

Monitoring and review should include all aspects of the risk management process, including the performance of the risk management system, the changes that might affect it and whether the original risks remain static. Some of the questions asked at this stage could include:

- Are assumptions about risks still valid?
- Are there any new or emerging risks?
- Are treatments for minimising risks effective and efficient?
- Are the treatments cost-effective?
- Are management and accounting controls adequate?
- Do the treatments comply with legal requirements and government and organisational policies?
- How can the system be improved?

To monitor and review the results and progress with the treatments implemented, a robust evaluation framework is needed, with criteria against which the outcomes are compared. The framework may include various measures aimed at outlining the direct and related results and effects of the chosen actions, enabling comparison of the pre- and post-treatment results. Different compliance measurement activities such as campaigns, random checks or other types of statistically valid analysis methods or surveys can all be potential tools for measurement in the operational context.

Documentation, Communication and Consultation

Communication and consultation with internal and external stakeholders should be conducted as appropriate at each stage of the risk management process, and for the process as a whole. Communication and consultation should be planned and ongoing activities addressing not just the process, but any issues that may arise. Good governance requires decision-making that is accountable and transparent. To ensure accountability it is important that the documentation indicate why decisions were made and actions were taken. Therefore, risk management activities at all different stages of the process need to be well recorded and stored in a way that enables their retrieval:

- Assumptions;
- Methods used;
- Sources of Data;
- Logic and analysis;
- Results; and
- Decisions made and the reasoning behind them.

Customs risk management is generally carried out using a 4-step process:

1. Collection of Data and Information:

Proper risk management requires a structured approach to collecting data.

2. Analyse and Assess Risk:

Analyse the data and determine the likelihood of non-compliance.

3. Prescribe Action:

Once the potential risk has been identified and analysed, it is time to design the appropriate action and dedicate the necessary resources.

4. Track and Report:

Once the appropriate action is designed, ownership for the action must be assigned and its results tracked and fed back into the risk management process.

This process is cyclical, and relates in many ways to the basic principles of the Six Sigma process of **DMAIC** – Define, Measure, Analyse, Improve/Implement and Control.

These steps can be described as the following:

Define – Define the project goals and internal and external deliverables
Measure – Measure the process to determine current performance
Analyse – Analyse and determine the root cause(s) of the defects or problems
Improve/Implement – Improve the process by eliminating defects and implementing control measures
Control – Control future process performance

In many ways, the Improve/Implement step is very similar to the Treat element of the 4 risk options. The purpose of the exercise to treat or mitigate higher risks, in order to reduce the risk level as much as possible.

Customs compliance is about risk management and being commercially effective. A compliance system can make the difference between having a reliable Supply Chain in a profitable business or an unreliable Supply Chain plagued with delays and penalties. The following pages will provide observations respecting how to plan a Customs Compliance Programme.

Compliance

Compliance is an area which demands significant scrutiny on the part of the trader, and generally involves continuous monitoring and review of documentation, practices and procedures. It is defined by the regulatory authority, in this case the government fiscal authority, through a series of regulations and requirements supported by national (and perhaps) supranational) statute and legislation, and is therefore imposed on the commercial and private sector in order to maintain fiscal accuracy and protection. Compliance management is linked to risk management techniques, and can therefore vary according to the ability of the trader to ensure compliance with fiscal requirements at all times. It is also linked to the concept of Regulatory Risk Differentiation, which is the process used by a regulatory authority (the regulator) to systemically treat entities differently based on the regulator's assessment of the risks of the entity's non-compliance. Regulators can include law enforcement agencies, while the word entities applies to all those under the authority of the regulator – in most cases ranging from individuals to companies to synthetic entities to multinationals operating within the regulator's jurisdiction.

The process requires the regulator to directly link a robust risk assessment to a suggested regulatory response (e.g. financial penalties, criminal imprisonment). Regulatory risk differentiation is also referred to as **the compliance model** in some regulatory agencies.

According to the Australian Taxation Office (ATO), the compliance model is a structured way of understanding and improving taxpayer **compliance**. It helps us to understand the factors that influence taxpayer behaviour and to apply the most appropriate compliance strategy. Taxpayer compliance behaviour is influenced by many factors – business, industry, sociological, economic and psychological.

The compliance model describes a continuum of taxpayer attitudes towards compliance. At the base of the continuum, taxpayers have the desired attitude of being "willing to do the right thing". This results in a more lenient approach from the Revenue Authority. At the other extreme, taxpayers have decided not to comply – choosing to evade or opt out of the tax system. This results in a much more radical and punitive approach from the Revenue Authority, resulting in fines and prosecutions.

The compliance model also summarises the different sorts of support and intervention that may be needed to provide to collect the required revenue. The model suggests that the ATO has the ability to influence taxpayer behaviour through our response and interaction.

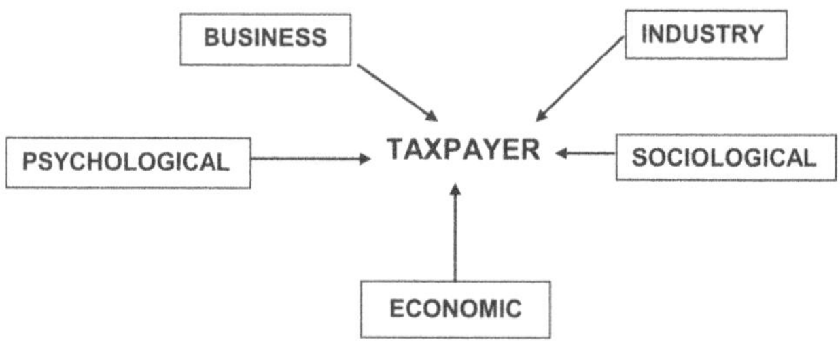

Compliance factors

From this model, the compliance pyramid is derived. It is similar to the compliance model, but it provides more specific detail concerning trader behaviour and corresponding action on the part of the government regulatory authority.

When the reaction of the regulator is tied to the behaviour, it is known as a **responsive compliance model**. The responsive compliance model was suggested by Ian Ayres, Professor at Yale University and John Braithwaite, Professor at the Australian National University, in their book *Responsive Regulation: Transcending the Deregulation Debate* which built on earlier work by John Scholz, and which was represented by a compliance pyramid, as shown below.

The pyramid is designed in such a way as to show from bottom up the levels of action taken depending upon the attitude or behaviour of a trader in response to compliance requirements and enforcement. If the trader has committed an error and is aware that the error has been committed inadvertently, then all that is required is a gentle warning or notification by the regulatory authority in the belief that remedial action will be taken by the trader, illustrated by the lowest level of the pyramid. If, however, the trader wilfully or recklessly commits a compliance-based error, then the next level up of the pyramid applies, in the form of a warning letter coupled with some form of monitoring on the part of the regulatory authority, as part of a higher-risk strategy. If the behaviour of the trader hardens, then succeeding higher levels of the pyramid apply to the point that any licenses held by the trader insofar as Customs activities or facilities are concerned will be revoked and full prosecution and litigation proceedings initiated. This regulatory action is, however, very much of a last resort given the use of resources by the regulatory authority, and is rarely used. However, depending upon the Customs

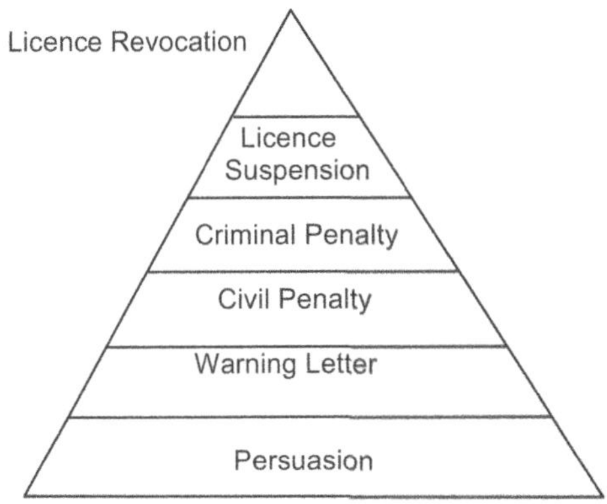

ATO compliance pyramid (Ayres & Braithwaite/ATO).

control, prosecution can very much be an option, especially concerning trader controls such as trade sanctions, where export licenses such as OGELs (Open General Export Licences) and SIELS (Specific Individual Export Licences) are required.

Given the extent to which the regulatory framework operates, it is essential for any import/export trader to create some form of Customs Compliance Plan. This may take several forms, but it should be created in such a way as to be easily understood, effective and useable.

The Bow-Tie Risk Approach

The bow-tie risk approach is a more specialist approach, but it takes into account a series of causes or threats, all of which lead to an adverse event, and hence lead to a series of adverse consequences which can have severe effects on an organisation. The diagram below shows a simplified version of this.

In terms of the application to Customs compliance, the diagram can be used to show the following set of threats (left) and consequences (right).

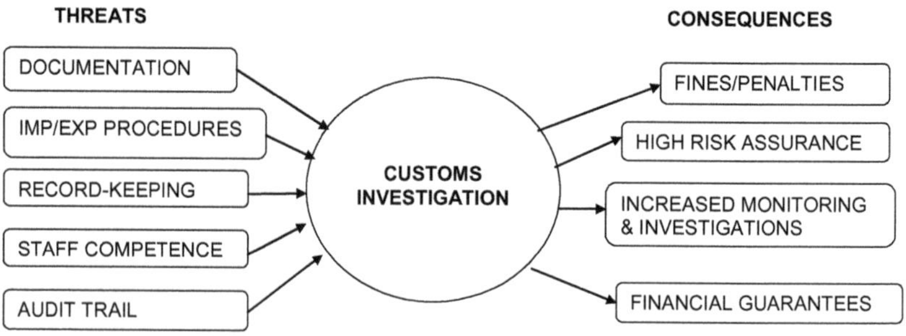

The Bow-Tie Risk Assessment

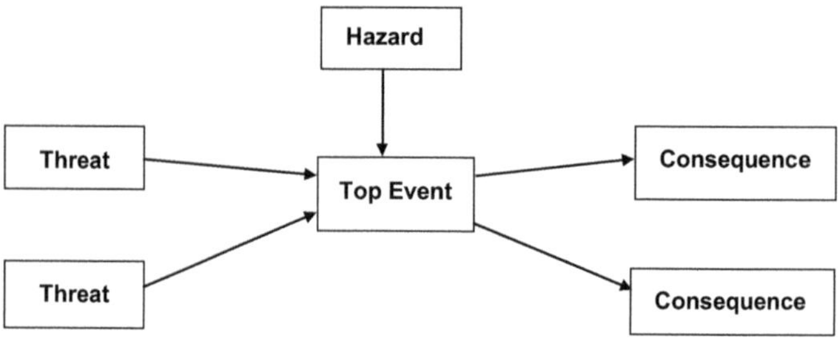

Each threat carries in itself a raw and actual risk. The higher the risk (raw risk), the more likely the resulting event and consequences will be. Where mitigating action is taken by the organisation, the residual risk (consequential risk) will be much lower and will result in far fewer adverse consequences. This can mainly be achieved by the use of the Risk Register detailed in Chapter 1. Where a risk register is applied, the factors contributing to a high-risk status can be addressed and their raw risk reduced by way of mitigating action per factor, which not only reduces the inherent risk to a much lower level but also reduces the prevalence of the bow-tie risk approach. Indeed, the application of the bow-tie risk analysis alongside the risk register as a pre-emptive action can result in an organisation ensuring that its risk appetite is reduced, and that it is much more sensitive to factors which could increase its risk status in terms of its import/export management and relationship with the national revenue or Customs Authority. This approach also increases the level of compliance based on the anticipatory analysis of all the factors influencing compliance with Customs and Tax requirements and regulations.

Import/Export Trade Compliance

It would be interesting to know when the last time was that any import/export trader took a long, hard look at their compliance programme or strategy. What compliance programme? What compliance strategy? Perhaps the company concerned employs people in multi-tasking roles, e.g. purchasing, logistics and, of course, taking care of Customs matters as well, which may be a recipe for disaster. Customs Authorities require specific personnel to be responsible for Customs activities, including import and export controls. Priorities may depend on the company's reporting structure. In the case of logistics, the priority is usually to get the freight here quickly. In the case of Finance, the priority is usually to get the product here the most cost-effective way. In the case of legal, someone somewhere might be concerned with compliance, which is definitely the case in the US corporate sector because of US CBP (Customs and Border Protection) and Tax requirements.

Trade compliance should be the goal of every importer and exporter to ensure all personnel know the rules and regulations, how to abide by them, and how to manage them. Compliance promotes integrity within the company and upholds your company standards. It is necessary to think of a compliance programme as a security blanket that protects the company and its employees by having a structure in place.

According to US Customs advisers and experts, here are the top three reasons for the need to review (or worse, implement) the company's import and/or export trade compliance programme:

1. **A trade compliance programme lays the groundwork for how the company needs to behave and ensures that the company is meeting its legal obligations with Customs and other government agencies.** How would anyone know if their company is adhering to what it is supposed to do? Have personnel been adequately advised or trained in import or export compliance matters? Compliance can be a moving target with constant regulatory changes in economic, industry, and operating conditions, and that is why a continuous process is needed;
2. **Not having a compliance programme in place increases company exposure to penalties.** An established compliance programme goes a long way towards mitigating any penalties which the company receives. Any company should never wait for a violation to occur! The larger the company, the greater the expectation by Customs that the company has a functioning programme in place. In the US, a first Importer Security Filing (ISF) offence can cost the company US$5,000 per Bill of Lading. A second offence can cost US$10,000. On this basis, it is not difficult to calculate how many errors it would take to put the company out of business. That's just one type of penalty, and there are many more;
3. **A compliance programme will also save the company money.** It will help to avoid audits, penalties, and border delays. When a shipment is held up for an examination by Customs, it can affect the company's cost margin and its relationship with customers when a delivery is delayed, which directly impacts the company's bottom. It may also be possible for the company to take advantage of duty savings under duty reduction programmes such as GSP, Inward Processing, Customs Warehousing and Free Trade Agreements. Not having regulatory impediments to the company's business will lower your costs and ensure your product moves to market faster and more effectively.

Trade compliance should never be an afterthought, and it will not happen on its own. In most cases, the company should consider outsourcing this function so that experts can put the pieces of the compliance puzzle together for the company. Compliance experts can advise the company what its obligations are as an importer and/or exporter and show it how to comply with them. By understanding the regulatory risks the company faces, it is possible to put into place the necessary policies and procedures. This should be the foundation of any compliance programme. The only way to know if the company's compliance programme is working is to assess it and evaluate it. Lowering risks and ultimately lowering costs will be the end result.

Unfortunately, many importers and exporters do not even consider hiring outside assistance with their compliance programme. Why is this? While it may be hard to understand, here is a compilation of the comments that have emerged over the years – and here are the reasons why these are *myths* and not *facts*:

- **It is too expensive.** The cost of penalty actions will far outweigh the costs of putting a compliance programme into place. Remember that ISF penalty previously mentioned? It is useful to know that level of penalty is on the (very) low side. Penalties for negligence and gross negligence have been issued in terms of millions of US dollars. Export penalties easily reach 7 or more figures;
- **It takes too much time (1).** There is the need for a time investment to establishing a compliance programme, but once it is in place, shipments will move more quickly and that is where one will see the time savings. Once the programme is implemented, the company only needs to maintain it;
- **It takes too much time (2).** It should also be noted that in the US, a Customs audit, known as a Focused Assessment, takes about six months ***when no issues are found.*** If there is no compliance programme in place, it should be expected that an audit will take much, much longer with Customs auditors spending lots of time in the company's office. In order to understand how painful a Focused Assessment really is, talk to an importer that has been through it. Customs audits can be a traumatic experience, and that comes from a former Customs Officer with significant experience in these issues. Training Courses on "Preparing for a Customs Audit" are always useful;
- **Customs doesn't bother us.** They soon will. No company can remain undetected forever. Most major Customs Authorities have a programme of Quick Response Audits that can target any size importer on a single issue, and it is surprising to see how many penalties are issued to long-established importers. Complacency is no excuse. Nor is ignorance of the law or the regulations;
- **Our Broker/Clearing Agent takes care of everything.** This is the classic cop-out of all time, and, unfortunately, applies as much in the UK as it does in the US. As the importer of record under any Customs law, the importer or exporter holds the legal responsibility for all aspects of the entry/declaration. The broker is only a conduit to Customs on the importer's behalf, in that the broker completes Customs entries and submits them to Customs on the importer's behalf, thus acting on the specific Customs clearance instructions

of the Importer. The broker is simply an agent acting on behalf of the importer, and indeed can only act on the importer's instructions. Therefore, the importer cannot absolve themselves of or outsource the responsibility of ensuring that all information contained in the Customs Entry/Declaration is absolutely correct. In the event of discrepancies, Customs will investigate the broker; they will investigate the importer.

If the company does not have a compliance programme, now is the time to start and initiate one. If the company does have one in place, it is essential to make sure that it is reviewed by an expert. If the company works with a Customs Broker, they could be a great resource for this type of consulting. However, there are also many Customs specialist consultants around, either independent or working for the main management consultants. Some companies go as far as evaluating the services of a Customs attorney, especially in the US. However, in the US and Canada, Customs brokers are licensed by US/Canadian Customs by necessity and are usually more cost effective. The company may even be able to find companies that will carry out an assessment of its compliance programme and advise on whether the company needs further help.

Principal Features of a Compliance Plan/Programme

A good Customs Compliance Programme should meet the following priorities:

1. **Effectiveness:** A system should be able to make accurate and useable information available to the manager and to custom authorities in a timely way. This is critical in times where regulatory investigations, verifications, audits or enforcement activity takes place. Being able to access documents and correct information in a timely way signals that the business is being run in a compliant manner;
2. **Efficiency:** A system should provide information in the most productive and economical manner (e.g. using electronic rather than paper processes when possible). The advantages to using electronic processes may be self-evident. Electronic documents and information may be easier to store, easier to access and retrieve, and may be easier to send to the Customs or Border Control Authority in response to verification or audit questionnaires;
3. **Confidentiality:** A system should protect information from unauthorised disclosure. Unauthorised disclosure may be a big concern for certain clients who wish to protect such things as: (a) the cost

of goods; (b) the profit margin on goods; (c) supplier's names and locations; (d) purchaser's names; (e) ingredients in goods; and (e) method of fabrication of goods;

4. **Integrity:** A system should provide true, accurate and complete declarations and reports. Accurate and complete declarations are required at the time of Customs accounting. It is also absolutely critical to be true, accurate and complete when dealing with a Customs verification or other audits. The provision of inaccurate information can quickly dampen the rapport that a business has with a verification officer or auditor;
5. **Availability:** a system should be able to provide information now and for the required record retention period, in general between 3 and 5 years, although this may vary from country to country;
6. **Ability to address all regulations:** a system should ensure that the requirements of all laws, regulations and contractual arrangements are met. Where a business has global operations it is necessary to keep track of the Customs compliance requirements for each country. This may be a challenge for companies with Customs transactions occurring on a world-wide basis. In such case, it may be necessary to work with local Customs brokers to identify Customs requirements and to monitor Customs compliance;
7. **Reliability:** a system should provide reliable information. A system that it prone to, for example, intermittent breakdowns, can lead to disaster especially if the breakdowns occur at peak business periods or while a Customs verification or other audit is underway;
8. **Practicality:** A good Customs Compliance Plan should address all import and export issues, including documentation, documented procedures, INCOTERMS, valuations, logistics costs, Tariff Commodity Codes, origin, Duty Reliefs, record-keeping and staff competence and awareness. This list is not exhaustive, but it encompasses the main crucial areas of concern.

With the introduction of the Authorised Economic Operator initiative, the above form of plan has become essential in ensuring Customs compliance in any company involved in international trade.

Priority Compliance Issues

In many cases, importers and exporters may wish to reduce budgets for items that are not perceived as revenue-producing. Budget limitations may make Customs compliance more challenging. Compliance managers or Customs brokers may be forced to identify immediate priorities. In such cases it may be most effective and efficient to identify the issues that may most commonly arise and which may present the most risk if the business was the subject of a Customs verification or audit. The following is a list of potential priorities:

1. **Valuation:** Establish the method for determining how to value goods. Some importers have been surprised that post-importation adjustments must be made to the value for duty of goods;
2. **Classification:** Establish the method to determine how to classify goods;
3. **Origin:** Establish the method for determining the origin of goods;
4. **Anti-dumping and countervailing duties:** Determine whether or not goods are subject to anti-dumping or countervailing duty or other special levies;
5. **Programme eligibility:** Determine, for example, whether or not goods are eligible for preferential tariff treatment under a Free Trade Agreement for duty relief;
6. **Special levies or taxes:** Determine whether or not goods are subject to a special import or export charge, manufacturing processing fee, value added tax or other levy;
7. **Certification requirements:** Determine whether or not the goods must meet country-specific or international safety, environmental or other standards;
8. **Export controls, embargos:** Determine whether or not goods are subject to export controls and regulations;
9. **Import controls:** Determine whether or not goods are subject to import controls or regulations;
10. **Permits:** Determine whether or not a permit is required in order to import or export the goods;
11. **Unique country-specific requirements:** Determine whether or not there are unique considerations applicable to particular countries (e.g. Brazil Customs Authorities may have a particular interest respecting the declaration of the weight of goods).

Best Compliance Practices

Customs compliance planning may also include the following:

1. The establishment of good lines of communication with the Customs Officers responsible for the administration and enforcement of programmes that apply to the business. Global Customs managers may need to establish a rapport with Customs Authorities in various countries. For example, there may be a programme manager responsible for a particular Customs programme (for example,

duties relief under the Exporters of Processing Services). Further, contacts should be established with officers and with other government authorities (e.g. Environmental Agencies, for the transportation of hazardous recyclable materials, or the Export Controls Organisation for export controls established pursuant to the country's Export Control List);

2. Understanding any country-specific laws and policies that affect goods or technology that will be imported or exported. For example, the exports of all goods and technology as defined in any specific item in the country's Export Control List, regardless of their nature and destination, require permits;
3. Conducting regular periodic self-audits to determine compliance levels. Compliance audits may focus on the high-risk priorities and may follow the methodology set out by CBSA verification officers or other auditors responsible for the administration and enforcement of particular programmes (e.g. the Export Controls Division);
4. Creating a compliance committee involving a compliance manager and representatives for the regions or countries in which the company or group of companies does business. The responsibility of the compliance manager may include the following:
    a. Identify applicable Customs laws and policies;
    b. Establish business systems and controls to ensure that those requirements are met;
    c. Establish a Customs compliance team, including representatives of the importer or exporter and its service providers. For example, an importer may create a centralised electronic information and document sharing system via cloud computing. In this way the importer can obtain up-to-date information respecting the status of purchase orders, shipment date, reports (such as advance reporting of goods by carriers), permits (for example any import or export permit) and declarations from submitted forms such as Import or Export Customs Declarations filed by Customs clearance agents);
    d. Establish contact with the officials responsible for the administration and enforcement of applicable laws and policies;
    e. Monitor compliance.
5. Create a Customs Compliance and Procedures Manual which sets out a record of past decisions and current procedures. A compliance manual is to record the decisions made in respect of transactions that may be the subject of verification and the procedures which should be followed to ensure that the business is compliant.

Planning for Verification and Audit Compliance

Many countries have established a self-reporting and self-assessing Customs scheme. To some extent, self-reporting and self-assessing schemes rely upon the honesty and integrity of the declarations provided by importers and exporters. However, officers conduct verifications and audits to:

a. Audit or verify compliance;
b. Correct non-compliance;
c. Assess or re-assess duties, taxes and charges; and
d. Assess interest, penalties and other consequences for non-compliance.

A Customs verification or audit can be a confusing, difficult and time-consuming experience in the absence of compliance planning. Disorganised, incomplete or inaccurate responses to Customs authorities may lead to findings of non-compliance and assessments of duty, penalties and interest. With compliance planning, an importer or exporter may stand a better chance of obtaining a successful verification or audit result. Some steps that importers or exporters can take in order to plan for verification and audit compliance include the following:

a. Ensure that a business representative is responsible for receiving and responding to correspondence, verification letters, Detailed Adjustment Statements and other similar Customs related documents in a timely way. Many audits result in the assessment of Administrative Monetary Penalties for failure to respond to the requests issued by Customs Officers;
b. If a Customs Officer (UK: HMRC; Canada: CBSA – Customs and Border Security Agency; US: CPB – Customs and Border Protection) conducts a verification or an auditor conducts an audit, it is necessary to ensure that only one person is responsible for communicating with the verification officer or auditor. Also ensure that all other relevant personnel are advised of the purpose of the verification or audit and the identity of the business point person;
c. Ensure that the business leaders, i.e. Managers, Directors or Vice-Presidents, understand the consequences for failing to respond to Customs correspondence, verification questionnaires, Detailed Adjustment Statements and the like;
d. Obtain the resources (internal staff, Customs brokers, consultants, legal counsel) necessary to deal with requests that are issued by the Customs Authority. For example, the Customs Authority may issue a verification questionnaire relating to 25 sample transactions. The Customs Officer may request relevant supply documents including the purchase orders, invoices and Customs Declarations (In Canada: *B3 Canada Customs Coding Forms*). The Customs Officer may also

request related documents such as royalty agreements in order to verify whether or not royalty payments should be included in the value for duty. It may be necessary to obtain assistance from persons within the verification team in order to comply with the request.

Summary

This outline has provided information respecting how to plan a Customs Compliance Programme. Desirable features of a Customs Compliance System include: effectiveness, efficiency, reliability, confidentiality, integrity, availability, the ability to address all regulatory requirements. Customs managers may find it more effective and efficient to identify high-risk or most common substantive issues. In addition, best compliance planning practices include establishing a rapport with relevant government officials and setting up a compliance team. Further, compliance planning should include measures for dealing with a Customs investigation or other audit. It must be understood that takes time to plan for Customs compliance. However, the reward is the improvement of business operations and cost savings. After all, business leaders like to avoid penalties, protracted audits and appeals. However, they may not like to have to completely restructure their fiscal system to implement documentary procedures and record-keeping systems, despite that they are required to do so by the national revenue department.

CHAPTER 11

Customs and VAT Compliance Management

Customs and VAT compliance is a paramount issue, especially given the changes in Customs controls scheduled in 2016 as part of the overall initiative implemented by the Revised Kyoto Convention of 2005. The subsequent SAFE Framework of Standards highlighted several issues designed to maximise the efficiency of the Customs function from both government and commercial perspectives, in particular more efficient Customs controls, and far more stringent controls over commercial trader, especially concerning issues of compliance, competence and due diligence. Although VAT *per se* was not covered in the Revised Kyoto Convention, it still operates alongside Customs issues, especially concerning import and export compliance, as Import VAT is still a major issue concerning imports, while VAT zero-rating on exports is conditional, as it is still subject to export documentary compliance. VAT may be charged on exports where the INCOTERM EXW (Ex Works) is used, given that the exporter may have no documentary evidence of the exported consignment, and in such cases, the national revenue authority states that VAT must be charged by the exporter to the buyer as if the transaction were conducted on a domestic basis. The VAT can only be refunded to the buyer if the buyer sends documentary evidence to the exporter showing the exporter as the legal Exporter of Record.

The impact of Customs and VAT issues on any business that is involved in the international movement of tangible goods across borders can be considerable and is certainly significant, as it requires a high level of competence and due diligence on the part of the trader, especially with regard to the audit trail and the transparency of international transactions with regard to documentary evidence of shipment, namely the transport document and the Export Customs Declaration.

The management of duties and taxes associated with the importing of goods is a critical element of the issues of compliance, responsibility and cost in the International Supply Chain. While responsibility and roles are shared between the purchasing company, supplier, Customs Clearance Broker and government, Customs Declarations, both import and export, involve the highest degree of transparency over the exact nature of the commodity entering

DOI: 10.4324/9781003341345-12

the country, its value and where it was made, i.e. origin, especially where preferential trade within a Free Trade Agreement is concerned. With this information in hand, in addition to the requisite commercial and licensing documentation, the trading community can meet the entry process requirements through a variety of methods such as direct entry into free circulation, bonded goods, free zones, as well as addressing the re-exportation of goods and recovery of duties paid by means of drawback or where duty suspension is involved.

Customs issues can have implications for the following international trade issues:

- Whether goods can be traded;
- The nature, content, specification, source, origin, cost, selling price, and marketing of goods;
- The terms on which they are sold and purchased;
- The location of manufacturing operations;
- The design of physical distribution facilities and systems; and
- The international structure of companies.

The fundamental principles of Customs planning are, therefore, to identify all potential commercial transactions that may have Customs implications and then to arrange those transactions in such a way as to obtain the optimum treatment under Customs and international trade regulations and practices. It is vital that Customs issues are covered in any proposed international trade transaction at the outset. Otherwise, it may be too late to incorporate them once goods have been purchased. It could even be too late once they have been manufactured.

The Customs Compliance Management Approach

According to the *WCO Risk Management Compendium*, modern risk-based compliance management is built on several key foundations, which can be broadly grouped into 4 main categories: a country's legislative framework, and the administrative, risk management and technological frameworks adopted by Customs administrations. Collectively, these 4 categories represent the key determinants of the manner in which cross-border flows may be expedited and the way Customs control may be exercised over such flows.

Risk-based compliance management starts with robust legislation that incorporates areas such as acknowledgement of the respective responsibilities of government and industry, i.e. the international commercial sector, includes regulations for electronic communication, provides sanctions for non-compliance and provisions to break the nexus between physical movements of goods across international borders and processing, reporting and revenue liability, and, finally, allows for flexible and tailored business solutions.

This approach also requires administrative arrangements, including initiatives such as the introduction of a client service approach, education and awareness raising, technical assistance and advice, consultation and co-operation, the publishing of formal rulings, and formal appeal mechanisms. The adoption of a risk management framework introduces risk-based decision-making and procedures into the organisation that enable a balance between control, facilitation and Supply Chain security to be maintained. The introduction of risk-based procedures includes activities such as those associated with the early and accurate lodgement of information for risk assessment, intervention as early as possible in the Supply Chain for high-risk transactions, self-assessment and post-entry verification for lower risk, and investigative capability where non-compliance or fraud is detected. The available technology represents an enabler that serves to significantly enhance an administration's ability to adopt such an approach.

Automation enables vast amounts of information to be processed in practically no time; it allows the effective and efficient screening of information against predetermined risk criteria, and assists with the making of decisions on both high and low risks. In the same way, modern non-intrusive inspection technologies, when used based on the basis of risk assessment, can lead to more effective inspection activity and reduced delays. All the above is consistent with the standards and guidelines of the Revised Kyoto Convention, the SAFE Framework of Standards and the WCO's Customs in the 21st Century Strategy, which together provide the key building blocks for modern Customs administration.

According to the Customs in the 21st Century Strategy, the expanding responsibilities facing Customs require a more sophisticated understanding of the risk continuum and how scarce resources can be better targeted towards the higher end. Therefore, it is useful to think of the risk continuum as a method to achieve client segmentation by risk categorisation. Conceptually, Customs clients, i.e. international traders, can be divided into 4 broad-based categories:

1. Those who are voluntarily compliant;
2. Those who try to be compliant but do not necessarily always succeed in their endeavours;
3. Those who will avoid complying if possible; and
4. Those who deliberately do not comply.

An effective risk-based compliance management strategy acknowledges that the client categories outlined require different responses. Incentives and simplified procedures should be applied to those who are voluntarily compliant (low risk), assisted compliance to those who try to be compliant but do not necessarily always succeed, directed compliance to those who try to avoid following the letter of the law, and enforced compliance to those who are deliberately non-compliant (high risk).

The key in relation to risk-based compliance management is to actively "steer" the client population towards the low-risk category. This can be achieved both by providing incentives for traders and travellers to comply, and by operating a credible enforcement regime that effectively and efficiently detects and punishes non-compliance. Affecting client behaviour and actively steering the population towards low risk will allow Customs to concentrate its control resources on high risks.

In the Customs context, control and risk management of goods, conveyances, i.e. the means of transport, or people commence at the export or departure point and continue with ongoing verification actions at the point of import or arrival and, in post-control audit circumstances, beyond. The term multi-layered is used to encapsulate the entire decision-making process and other activities that may be carried out by Customs along this Supply Chain continuum. A modern compliance management approach recognises that risk mitigation strategies can and should be applied throughout the Supply Chain. It also recognises that a combination of multiple measures often leads to better results and more effective use of resources. Where appropriate legal, technological and operational arrangements are in place, a multi-layered approach can also facilitate risk identification, response coordination and collaboration across and between governments, which is part of the overall SAFE Framework of Standards policy. At the operational level, a modern risk-based compliance management approach is increasingly enabled by intelligence support. Intelligence-enabled risk management brings together information and knowledge acquired by Customs with a systematic approach for identifying and treating risks of greatest consequence. This is a critical process, as high risks identified through the risk management process will often be greater in number than Customs' resources and ability to respond. This is the point where intelligence holdings inform decision-makers of a recommended priority order for intervention and assist decisions about where Customs resources should be mobilised and deployed.

The WCO Global Information and Intelligence Strategy (GIIS) sets out what intelligence is, how it is derived, for whom it is being produced and why it is needed. The GIIS also sets out the intelligence cycle and fundamental principles and processes that underpin all intelligence activity. Customs practitioners should be guided by the GIIS when developing their risk management approach.

The following diagrams illustrate an example of a compliance management model.

RISK LEVEL	*LOW*			*HIGH*
Client Categories	**Voluntary Compliance**	**Assisted Compliance**	**Directed Compliance**	**Enforced Compliance**
	People who want to comply	People who try to comply but don't always succeed	People who will avoid complying if they can	People who deliberately do not comply
Client Behaviours	Voluntary Compliance Informed Clients	Attempting to comply Uninformed Clients	Resistance to Compliance Will avoid if possible	Criminal Intent Illegal Activity

CUSTOMS COMPETENCES			*INTERVENTIONS*	
INFORMATION High quality, timely, and accurate information about the arrival and departure of all persons, goods, and craft	Advanced Cargo/ Passenger/Craft information (in and out) Monitoring of the physical movement of all people, goods, and craft activities across (in and out) the border	Patterns of non-compliance by • Industry, product, location, ethnicity, destination, or port of origin • Type of non-compliance (e.g. incorrect documentation)	Profile of individual non-compliant traders/travellers • Identification of specific compliance problems (e.g. bad systems, poor data entry, etc.)	Profile and ongoing intelligence (on and offshore) about offenders/ potential offenders and their associates
ASSESSMENT Assessment of the level of risk posed by arriving and departing people, goods and craft	Front Line Passenger/Goods staff intuition • Intelligence profiles • Statistically valid random checks	• Compile information on client behaviours • Identify and monitor compliance trends/ patterns	• Problem solving Approach to specific compliance problems • Investigation	• Assess risk and information needs in relation to seriousness of offence • Investigation
ACTION Actions required to mitigate identified risk(s) without unduly disrupting legitimate trade and travel	• Compliance programmes (e.g. Front Line, Call Centre) • Education and advice • Visible deterrence • Cargo and baggage screening	• Targeted compliance guidance • Punitive sanctions • Rolling audit programme • Increased attention	• Deter by detection and surveillance • Comprehensive audits • Prosecution	• Pre and post clearance interventions • Comprehensive audits • Passenger/ cargo searches • Prosecution

Detailed below is a checklist, albeit non-exhaustive, of what would be expected in a truly compliant organisation in relation to the management of the Customs function, covering both compliance and planning activities.

- **Administration of the Customs function.** A designated unit is clearly responsible for establishing, operating and maintaining processes and controls to ensure compliance with all Customs laws and regulations impacting the import and export of goods. It should be intranet-enabled and have active communication links with finance, purchasing, legal staff, internal controls, audit services, senior management and business planning. It should have documented processes for identifying and communicating changes in laws, regulations, or company operations that have, or may have, a Customs impact on all affected departments.
- **Proactive consultation.** Consultation with the designated business unit is embedded in all major sales and procurement processes in order to consider the impact that duties and Customs compliance costs will have on the proposed transaction.
- **Formally documented procedures.** Formal procedures for complying with Customs-related activities are extranet-enabled. These set forth instructions for all relevant parties, such as forwarders, carriers, brokers, banks, etc. These procedures are simple and easy to follow; they are integrated into the company's systems and other business processes, and are periodically reviewed and updated. These procedures are backed up by training for the purchasing staff and for other members of the company, as appropriate.
- **Suppliers.** Well before any shipments are made, the most compliant companies ensure that their suppliers are capable of providing electronic invoices with standardised information. These standards include all details required by Customs and provide an understandable description of the products sold, with separate identification of non-dutiable elements of value. They also ensure that issues, such as product labelling, marking and certification regarding compliance with local safety standards, etc., are properly addressed before the goods are shipped. Best-of-breed companies measure the success of their procurement departments against net margin achieved, rather than gross margin, which includes hidden costs.
- **Record-keeping procedures.** Records are maintained (within statutory timescales) to support all activity relating to the import of goods. The records retained normally will include Customs, shipping, purchase, cost, value, and origin documentation for all imported goods.

- **Internal audit.** A process is in place to ensure a risk-assessed proportion of Customs entries made on behalf of the company by its agents are audited on a periodic basis to establish and ensure: (a) goods have been entered with the correct HS classification code; (b) the Customs value of the goods has been calculated and entered properly; (c) the origin of the goods has been properly declared; (d) the amount of any duties has been calculated and reported properly to the Customs Authorities; (e) all supporting documents are provided. Periodic meetings are held with the agents for the purpose of discussing performance levels and targets, and opportunities to reduce costs.
- **Tariff classification.** Best-of-breed companies have a dedicated centre of classification expertise, regionally as appropriate, to check the tariff classification carefully before deciding upon the specification of the goods to be imported and also the condition in which to import them. They maintain a regularly updated global classification database on the material master.
- **Origin and preferences.** A best-of-breed business constantly assesses the scope for sourcing goods from countries that receive tariff preferences. Prior to an order, they would ensure that the goods will satisfy the origin rules and the necessary documentation will be available. They determine, in advance, whether they will be subject to any restrictions or quotas.
- **Customs valuation.** A best-of-breed business (using both indirect and direct tax specialists) strips out non-dutiable costs from a prospective transaction to assess the effects before making the purchasing decision, since the price for the goods often includes payment for items that should not attract duty. Examples of costs that can be unbundled include buying commissions; warranties; post-importation expenses such as erection and assembly, research and development expenditures, interest payments, and advertising costs, etc.
- **Duty Reliefs.** Customs Duty Reliefs, such as Inward Processing Relief, Outward Processing Relief, End-Use Relief, etc., are embedded and automated within commercial processes wherever practicable and efficient to do so.
- **Customs Warehousing.** The use of Customs procedures, such as Customs Warehousing (and Free Trade Zones) is system-based and fully automated. In particular, Type E "virtual" warehousing (and pan-EU Type E Customs Warehousing, for the most advanced best-of-breed companies) is considered the most efficient form of Customs Warehousing, in conjunction with the CFSP (Customs Freight Simplified Procedures) electronic system.
- **Simplified procedures.** Best-of-breed companies experience very few delays due to Customs at the ports, and no extra inventory is

held in anticipation of such delays. They are always looking to utilise cross-frontier Customs authorisations which are valid in more than 1 EU Member State. They also maximise, wherever possible, the use of simplified entry procedures and local clearance authorisations. All of this is underpinned by a robust accounting system and internal controls.

- **Terms of Trade.** Terms of Trade, presently referred to as INCOTERMS 2010, define a broad range of cost and shipping obligations, including the manner in which a product is packed, inland transportation costs on the seller's side, export clearance, international transport costs, insurance and inland transport costs on the buyer's side, etc. These obligations and costs need to be built into any international transaction. There are 11 INCOTERMS to choose from and each has a different effect on price and delivery. Selection of the correct INCOTERM has a huge impact on the risk and profitability of international trade. Indeed, it is virtually impossible to make an international sale until a specific INCOTERM has been chosen. The most compliant companies are familiar with all of the INCOTERMS 2010, particularly the multi-modal terms, and to this extent they would rarely use FOB, as it is a specific marine term, but would sooner use terms such as FCA (Free Carrier) or DAP (Delivered At Place).
- **Statistics.** At any given time, best-of-breed businesses know precisely how much duty they have paid and how much they have saved.
- **Cutting-edge planning.** The designated business unit is constantly striving to reduce the effective rate of Import Duty by way of the implementation of Import Duty reduction schemes. However, the use of these schemes is dependent upon the trader's compliance history, and under the conditions of the Union Customs Code (to be implemented in May 2016), 1 of the prime conditions for the use of Duty Relief schemes is the company's ability to be authorised for AEO (Authorised Economic Operator) status.

Trade Process Management

Much of the issue concerns the fact that Customs places a significant level of control over international trade. Detailed below is a non-exhaustive checklist of what would be expected from a fully compliant organisation with relation to the management of the Customs trade process/systems function, covering both compliance and planning.

- Duty planning systems should be comprehensively integrated into the purchasing decision systems;

- Full control should be evident over the system producing the transaction value purchase invoice (used for Customs clearance) for valuation planning purposes;
- Centralised methodical duty-minimisation orientated classification systems shared across divisions;
- Stock tracking systems should hold all Customs-relevant information for each consignment in order to provide a full audit trail;
- An intranet site with full, up-to-date details of contacts, processes and procedures for Customs control purposes;
- An intranet-based "early warning" and knowledge sharing procedure to help control and manage official audits and log correspondence and activity, etc., with internet access to/from advisers where appropriate;
- Fully integrated paperless Customs clearance procedures include simplified procedures;
- Monthly analysis and trend spotting for duty and VAT paid against various metrics, including SKU;
- Full use of automated systems-based duty planning (avoidance and delay) procedures post-importation where appropriate, e.g. Customs Warehousing, Import Duty Relief regimes.

It should be noted that much of the control of individual trader activities and transactions is carried out by scrutiny of the trader's VAT Number, or rather more specifically their Economic Operator Registration Identifier (EORI). In the UK, this is structured as the trader's VAT Number (comprising 9 digits) plus 3 zeros, e.g. 123456789000, plus the prefix "GB" in front of the registration number, thus making it GB123456789000. This system allows the CDS Customs computer to access the details of the international transactions of any VAT-registered UK trader engaged in international activities, and identify any possible discrepancies, errors, or inconsistencies. An Officer of HM Revenue and Customs (HMRC) may then conduct a more detailed examination of these transaction details and request more in-depth documentary information from the trader concerned. In general, computer checks are conducted on a random basis, but if the computer recognises a specific company because of a previous non-compliance history or systematic errors in Customs Declarations, it can automatically identify that trader's transactions on a more thorough and detailed basis.

International Freight Management

International freight management is itself a major influencing factor in how international goods are priced, especially in terms of import landed cost, in the form of the CIF (Cost Insurance Freight) basis, which is subject to Import Duty based on the CIF *ad valorem* (based on value) percentage of Import Duty derived from the Customs Import Tariff.

Detailed below is a non-exhaustive checklist of what would be expected from a fully compliant organisation with respect to their management of international freight costs and methods.

- **Negotiated group-wide freight rates for all trade lanes served.** Not only does global leveraged purchasing reduce shipping/logistics costs, but it also dramatically reduces the supplier base while improving Supply Chain coordination. However, this does depend to a degree on the method of freight utilised, as more negotiation can be exercised over sea freight rates than over air freight rates.
- **Metrics and internal cycle analysis.** The ability to measure operational efficiencies is known as "metricing". Metrics are essential because they allow organisations to monitor internal and external practices. The ability to gauge any system allows companies to utilise best practices and monitor red flags. Metrics are also useful in providing information to gauge actual vendor service levels against promised service levels. The ability to track shipments throughout the Supply Chain allows a company to verify that they are receiving the best overall service possible, at the best price. Results of these measurements, metrics, can be on a cycle time or cost basis. For metrics to be useful to an organisation, it must contain 4 characteristics:
  - *Validity* – concepts that are intended to be measured are actually being measured;
  - *Reliability* – the metric is constant. If circumstances do not change, results should stay the same;
  - *Practicality* – results are relevant to the processes of the organisation;
  - *Salience* – measurements must have meaning to those who will be implementing change and have importance to overall systems.
- **Minimised, and regularly reviewed supplier base.** In negotiating freight rates on a global basis, the supplier base can be vastly reduced to a core of specialist service providers; consequently, this enables a considerably greater degree of control and management of these vendors.
- **Continuous review and benchmarking.** To maintain a firm grip on overall shipping/logistics efficiencies and expenditure, it is essential that logistics processes and costs are reviewed regularly, not only to ensure best practices are being achieved but also to keep a tight

rein on freight expenditure, which can often increase dramatically before anyone really notices.

- **Global infrastructure.** Developing and maintaining a global shipping/logistics infrastructure to support the entire business is very important if you are to be successful in managing the global sourcing, transportation and distribution of goods anywhere in the world. There has to be an organised methodology on how the global logistics function is managed, clearly defining each individual's remit and responsibilities.
- **Information Technology.** Today's best-of-breed organisations cannot survive efficiently without utilising the latest technology available. The accessibility of the internet has changed the way the freight forwarding and logistics industries conduct their business. Today's IT solutions can dramatically accelerate the velocity of a Supply Chain. Whether you're supplying, buying or facilitating the movement of goods worldwide, you can now have complete electronic connectivity to your existing systems, internal and external customers, and transportation partners – international and domestic, across all modes.
- **Commercial.** In order to minimise the risk of commercial exposure, it is essential that all members of the global logistics team are trained logisticians with detailed working knowledge of international trade, particularly INCOTERMS 2000, International Letters of Credit, Marine Insurance, Hazardous Goods, and Export and Import Compliance. It is also essential that the best use of trade terms is employed when negotiating contracts to eliminate unnecessary costs.

Customs Compliance

Compliance-based regimes can help international trading companies identify *inter alia*:

- Potential Customs and international trade exposures and quantify their impact;
- Customs and international trade process inefficiencies; and
- Strategies to correct such inefficiencies and assist with implementation.

Such compliance regimes can also assist CEOs, CFOs and Audit Committees in complying with Section 404 of the US Sarbanes-Oxley Act, which requires all companies and divisions associated with US-based companies to uncover financial and commercial risk in the company's overseas markets, or to affirm the accuracy of financial provisions and liabilities. Tax directors should not perceive such an assessment as a critique of their performance, but rather, as an opportunity to:

- Justify changes in provisions for potential Customs exposures;
- Identify possible strategies to mitigate and/or eliminate duties and penalties associated with potential Customs exposures;
- Support an increase in staffing or avoid future workforce reductions;
- Develop and implement better Customs reporting controls and practices, along with improved Customs compliance procedures;
- Uncover potential duty refund opportunities;
- Gain a comprehensive understanding of the business's Customs and international trade position; and
- Obtain a comprehensive understanding of local Customs' record-retention requirements and uncover any existing deficiencies in corporate record-retention policies.

In engaging in the implementation of compliance-based regimes, companies can maintain a comprehensive analysis of their Customs and international trade operations, from the initial recording of each transaction to the completion of local import entry submissions and Customs returns.

CHAPTER 12

Customs Risk Strategy and Selectivity

Definition/Scope

According to Standard 6.3 of the Revised Kyoto Convention (RKC) and the corresponding guidelines, risk management is defined as the systematic application of management procedures and practices which provide Customs with the necessary information to address movements or consignments that present a risk. The preamble to the RKC lists the application of risk management as 1 of 7 key principles of trade facilitation embodied in it.

There are 5 main steps in the standard Customs risk-management process as defined by the World Customs Organisation:

1. **Establish context:** Importation of goods, export controls, passenger traffic, etc.;
2. **Identify risks:** Revenue protection (e.g. under valuation, origin, classification), prohibitions and restrictions (e.g. drug trafficking, IPR, firearms, etc.);
3. **Analyse risks:** Likelihood of a risk occurring (less likely, likely, highly likely);
4. **Assess and prioritise risks:** Assess impact and consequence of risks occurring (e.g. high, medium, low);
5. **Address risks:** Define countermeasures and assign to risk levels and options.

Risk options:

- Tolerate;
- Treat;
- Transfer; or
- Terminate.

In addition to these 5 steps, risk management requires constant monitoring and review in order to eliminate false negative as well as false positive risk assessments. Throughout the process proper documentation, communication

DOI: 10.4324/9781003341345-13

and consultation with all relevant stakeholders is key, as risk management is a corporate task involving the entire organisation and not 1 dedicated unit only.

Appraisal

In far too many countries, Customs still applies a 100% physical inspection regime, i.e. every shipment is stopped and physically examined (partially or completely), causing significant delays at border crossings, ports and airports. Such a 100% inspection regime also creates an enabling environment for informal payments to speed up the process, which in many cases may be seen as a form of bribery or undue influence. According to the Customs Capability Reports published in 2009 by the Global Express Association, only 37 out of 114 administrations surveyed applied a risk-based selectivity approach, 18 examined 100% of all shipments, and the remaining countries selected shipments for inspection randomly or at the sole discretion of the inspection officer, which would suggest a completely ineffective form of scrutiny.

Implementation Guidance

The application of risk management and the use of risk-based selectivity (red/green channel) allows Customs to allocate its scarce resources to the high-risk areas while increasing the efficiency of the clearance process for low-risk shipments. For example, enhancements made to Japan Customs' risk assessment capabilities since 1999 helped Customs keep the staffing levels nearly unchanged since 1999, while the number of import transactions increased by almost 60% (2007) and exports transactions increased by around 50% (2007).

By analysing and measuring the level of compliance related to individual traders, commodities or trading countries at the national, regional and local level, Customs can identify those cases in which further scrutiny in the form of physical examination and documentary review is necessary and will likely lead to results. By acknowledging the compliance level of a trader, in particular, authorised traders and Authorised Economic Operators (AEOs), leading to a lower inspection rate than that of other less-compliant traders, Customs creates incentives for traders to invest in compliance. In combination with pre-arrival processing of cargo and goods declarations, Customs gains the necessary time for conducting risk assessment and enabling immediate release of the goods upon arrival.

Risk-based selectivity operates more effectively in an automated environment, as computer-based risk-based selectivity can be applied consistently to all imports and exports and is significantly faster and more accurate in comparing a given set of data (e.g. from a goods declaration) against all currently active risk profiles. Also, information technology (IT) can significantly facilitate keeping all existing risk profiles up to date against the latest clearance and audit results. However, the lack of an IT-based risk assessment and targeting system should be no excuse for Customs not to apply this key trade facilitation principle.

Additional Information

The guidelines to Standard 6.3 of the Revised Kyoto Convention contain a detailed description of the risk-management process. The World Customs Organisation (WCO) has recently published a detailed risk-management compendium, which gives structured guidance on how to establish the organisational environment for successful risk management. Risk management also plays a critical role in a Single Window and cross-border management environment as well as in the area of Supply Chain security. The ICC Customs Guideline Number 14 also provide relevant business perspectives on aspects of selective examination.

Revised Kyoto Convention (RKC)

The International Convention on the Simplification and Harmonization of Customs procedures (Kyoto Convention) entered into force in 1974 and was revised and updated to ensure that it meets the current demands of governments and international trade.

The WCO Council adopted the Revised Kyoto Convention in June 1999 as the blueprint for modern and efficient Customs procedures in the 21st century. Once implemented widely, it will provide international commerce with the predictability and efficiency that modern trade requires.

The Revised Kyoto Convention promotes trade facilitation and effective controls through its legal provisions that detail the application of simple yet efficient procedures. The Revised Convention also contains new and obligatory rules for its application which all contracting parties must accept without reservation.

The Revised Kyoto Convention is the main trade facilitation Customs convention. It was developed by the World Customs Organization and entered into force on 3 February 2006. It is an update and revision of the International Convention on the Simplification and Harmonization of Customs Procedures (Kyoto Convention) adopted in 1973–1974. The RKC aims at facilitating trade by harmonising and simplifying Customs procedures and practices. To this end the convention provides standards and recommended practices for modern Customs procedures and techniques.

Countries wishing to become a contracting party to this international convention have to accept the Body and the General Annex to the RKC, which are binding. The General Annex of the RKC commits contracting parties to the following key principles:

- Transparency and predictability of Customs actions;
- Transparency and predictability of Customs actions;
- Standardisation and simplification of the goods declaration and supporting documents;
- Simplified procedures for authorised persons;
- Maximum use of information technology;
- Minimum necessary Customs control to ensure compliance with regulations;
- Use of risk management and audit-based controls;
- Co-ordinated interventions with other border agencies; and
- Partnership with the trade.

The WCO Secretary General is the depositary of the convention. Countries need to deposit their instrument of accession or ratification with the Secretary General of the Council. The convention is administered by the Management Committee to the RKC whose members are contracting parties. Only contracting parties have a vote, but all others can attend as observers. The Management Committee has no enforcement or dispute-settlement function in the case where a contracting party does not comply with the standards contained in the RKC. Countries having acceded to this convention have 3 years to implement the standards and 5 years to implement the transitional standards contained in the General Annex and in the specific annexes accepted.

The WCO promotes the implementation of the convention through awareness raising, training and capacity-building initiatives. As of October 2013 there were 91 contracting parties. The text of the convention and additional information on the Revised Kyoto Convention can be found on its website.

Standard 3.25 Revised Kyoto Convention

CHAPTER 3

CLEARANCE AND OTHER CUSTOMS FORMALITIES

Competent Customs offices

3.1. Standard

The Customs Authority shall designate the Customs offices at which goods may be produced or cleared. In determining the competence and location of these offices and their hours of business, the factors to be taken into account shall include in particular the requirements of the trade.

3.2. Standard
At the request of the person concerned and for reasons deemed valid by the Customs Authority, the latter shall, subject to the availability of resources, perform the functions laid down for the purposes of a Customs procedure and practice outside the designated hours of business or away from Customs offices. Any expenses chargeable by the Customs Authority shall be limited to the approximate cost of the services rendered.

3.3. Standard
Where Customs offices are located at a common border crossing, the Customs administrations concerned shall correlate the business hours and the competence of those offices.

3.4. Transitional Standard
At common border crossings, the Customs administrations concerned shall, whenever possible, operate joint controls.

3.5. Transitional Standard
Where the Customs Authority intend to establish a new Customs office or to convert an existing one at a common border crossing, they shall, wherever possible, co-operate with the neighbouring Customs Authority to establish a juxtaposed Customs office to facilitate joint controls.

The declarant
(a) Persons entitled to act as declarant

3.6. Standard
National legislation shall specify the conditions under which a person is entitled to act as declarant.

3.7. Standard
Any person having the right to dispose of the goods shall be entitled to act as declarant.

(b) Responsibilities of the declarant

3.8. Standard
The declarant shall be held responsible to the Customs Authority for the accuracy of the particulars given in the Goods declaration and the payment of the duties and taxes.

(c) Rights of the declarant

3.9. Standard
Before lodging the Goods declaration the declarant shall be allowed, under such conditions as may be laid down by the Customs Authority:

1. to inspect the goods; and
2. to draw samples.

3.10. Standard
The Customs Authority shall not require a separate Goods declaration in respect of samples allowed to be drawn under Customs supervision, provided that such samples are included in the Goods declaration concerning the relevant consignment.

The Goods declaration

(a) Goods declaration format and contents

3.11. Standard
The contents of the Goods declaration shall be prescribed by the Customs Authority. The paper format of the Goods declaration shall conform to the UN-layout key.

For automated Customs clearance processes, the format of the electronically lodged Goods declaration shall be based on international standards for electronic information exchange as prescribed in the Customs Co-operation Council Recommendations on information technology.

3.12. Standard
The Customs Authority shall limit the data required in the Goods declaration to only such particulars as are deemed necessary for the assessment and collection of duties and taxes, the compilation of statistics and the application of Customs law.

3.13. Standard
Where, for reasons deemed valid by the Customs Authority, the declarant does not have all the information required to make the Goods declaration, a provisional or incomplete Goods declaration shall be allowed to be lodged, provided that it contains the particulars deemed necessary by the Customs and that the declarant undertakes to complete it within a specified period.

3.14. Standard
If the Customs register a provisional or incomplete Goods declaration, the tariff treatment to be accorded to the goods shall not be different from that which would have been accorded had a complete and correct Goods declaration been lodged in the first instance.

The release of the goods shall not be delayed provided that any security required has been furnished to ensure collection of any applicable duties and taxes.

3.15. Standard
The Customs Authority shall require the lodgement of the original Goods declaration and only the minimum number of copies necessary.

(b) Documents supporting the Goods declaration

3.16. Standard
In support of the Goods declaration the Customs Authority shall require only those documents necessary to permit control of the operation and to ensure that all requirements relating to the application of Customs law have been complied with.

3.17. Standard
Where certain supporting documents cannot be lodged with the Goods declaration for reasons deemed valid by the Customs Authority, they shall allow production of those documents within a specified period.

3.18. Transitional Standard
The Customs Authority shall permit the lodgement of supporting documents by electronic means.

3.19. Standard
The Customs Authority shall not require a translation of the particulars of supporting documents except when necessary to permit processing of the Goods declaration.

Lodgement, registration and checking of the Goods declaration

3.20. Standard
The Customs Authority shall permit the lodging of the Goods declaration at any designated Customs office.

3.21. Transitional Standard
The Customs Authority shall permit the lodging of the Goods declaration by electronic means.

3.22. Standard
The Goods declaration shall be lodged during the hours designated by the Customs Authority.

3.23. Standard
Where national legislation lays down a time limit for lodging the Goods declaration, the time allowed shall be sufficient to enable the declarant to complete the Goods declaration and to obtain the supporting documents required.

3.24. Standard
At the request of the declarant and for reasons deemed valid by the Customs Authority, the latter shall extend the time limit prescribed for lodging the Goods declaration.

3.25. Standard
National legislation shall make provision for the lodging and registering or checking of the Goods declaration and supporting documents prior to the arrival of the goods.

3.26. Standard
When the Customs cannot register the Goods declaration, they shall state the reasons to the declarant.

3.27. Standard
The Customs Authority shall permit the declarant to amend the Goods declaration that has already been lodged, provided that when the request is received they have not begun to check the Goods declaration or to examine the goods.

3.28. Transitional Standard
The Customs Authority shall permit the declarant to amend the Goods declaration if a request is received after checking of the Goods declaration has commenced, if the reasons given by the declarant are deemed valid by the Customs.

3.29. Transitional Standard
The declarant shall be allowed to withdraw the Goods declaration and apply for another Customs procedure, provided that the request to do so is made to the Customs before the goods have been released and that the reasons are deemed valid by the Customs.

3.30. Standard
Checking the Goods declaration shall be effected at the same time or as soon as possible after the Goods declaration is registered.

3.31. Standard
For the purpose of checking the Goods declaration, the Customs Authority shall take only such action as they deem essential to ensure compliance with Customs law.

Special procedures for authorized persons

3.32. Transitional Standard
For authorised persons who meet criteria specified by the Customs Authority, including having an appropriate record of compliance with Customs requirements and a satisfactory system for managing their commercial records, the Customs shall provide for:

- release of the goods on the provision of the minimum information necessary to identify the goods and permit the subsequent completion of the final Goods declaration;
- clearance of the goods at the declarant's premises or another place authorized by the Customs Authority; and, in addition, to the extent possible, other special procedures such as:
- allowing a single Goods declaration for all imports or exports in a given period where goods are imported or exported frequently by the same person;
- use of the authorized persons' commercial records to self-assess their duty and tax liability and, where appropriate, to ensure compliance with other Customs requirements;
- allowing the lodgement of the Goods declaration by means of an entry in the records of the authorized person to be supported subsequently by a supplementary Goods declaration.

Examination of the goods

(a) Time required for examination of goods

3.33. Standard
When the Customs Authority decides that goods declared shall be examined, this examination shall take place as soon as possible after the Goods declaration has been registered.

3.34. Standard
When scheduling examinations, priority shall be given to the examination of live animals and perishable goods and to other goods which the Customs Authority accepts are urgently required.

3.35. Transitional Standard
If the goods must be inspected by other competent authorities and the Customs Authority also schedules an examination, the Customs shall ensure that the inspections are co-ordinated and, if possible, carried out at the same time.

(b) Presence of the declarant at examination of goods

3.36. Standard
The Customs shall consider requests by the declarant to be present or to be represented at the examination of the goods. Such requests shall be granted unless exceptional circumstances exist.

3.37. Standard
If the Customs Authority deems it useful, they shall require the declarant to be present or to be represented at the examination of the goods to give them any assistance necessary to facilitate the examination.

(c) Sampling by Customs

3.38. Standard
Samples shall be taken only where deemed necessary by the Customs Authority to establish the tariff description and/or value of goods declared or to ensure the application of other provisions of national legislation. Samples drawn shall be as small as possible.

Errors

3.39. Standard
The Customs Authority shall not impose substantial penalties for errors where they are satisfied that such errors are inadvertent and that there has been no fraudulent intent or gross negligence. Where they consider it necessary to discourage a repetition of such errors, a penalty may be imposed but shall be no greater than is necessary for this purpose.

Release of goods

3.40. Standard
Goods declared shall be released as soon as the Customs Authority has examined them or decided not to examine them, provided that:

- no offence has been found;
- the import or export license or any other documents required have been acquired;

- all permits relating to the procedure concerned have been acquired; and
- any duties and taxes have been paid or that appropriate action has been taken to ensure their collection.

3.41. Standard
If the Customs Authority is satisfied that the declarant will subsequently accomplish all the formalities in respect of clearance they shall release the goods, provided that the declarant produces a commercial or official document giving the main particulars of the consignment concerned and acceptable to the Customs, and that security, where required, has been furnished to ensure collection of any applicable duties and taxes.

3.42. Standard
When the Customs Authority decides that they require laboratory analysis of samples, detailed technical documents or expert advice, they shall release the goods before the results of such examination are known, provided that any security required has been furnished and provided they are satisfied that the goods are not subject to prohibitions or restrictions.

3.43. Standard
When an offence has been detected, the Customs Authority shall not wait for the completion of administrative or legal action before they release the goods, provided that the goods are not liable to confiscation or forfeiture or to be needed as evidence at some later stage and that the declarant pays the duties and taxes and furnishes security to ensure collection of any additional duties and taxes and of any penalties which may be imposed.

Abandonment or destruction of goods

3.44. Standard
When goods have not yet been released for home use or when they have been placed under another Customs procedure, and provided that no offence has been detected, the person concerned shall not be required to pay the duties and taxes or shall be entitled to repayment thereof:

- when, at his request, such goods are abandoned to the Revenue or destroyed or rendered commercially valueless under Customs control, as the Customs Authority may decide. Any costs involved shall be borne by the person concerned;
- when such goods are destroyed or irrecoverably lost by accident or *force majeure*, provided that such destruction or loss is duly established to the satisfaction of the Customs Authority;

- on shortages due to the nature of the goods when such shortages are duly established to the satisfaction of the Customs Authority.

Any waste or scrap remaining after destruction shall be liable, if taken into home use or exported, to the duties and taxes that would be applicable to such waste or scrap imported or exported in that state.

3.45. Transitional Standard
When the Customs Authority sells goods which have not been declared within the time allowed or could not be released although no offence has been discovered, the proceeds of the sale, after deduction of any duties and taxes and all other charges and expenses incurred, shall be made over to those persons entitled to receive them or, when this is not possible, held at their disposal for a specified period.

Standard 6.3 Revised Kyoto Convention

CHAPTER 6

CUSTOMS CONTROL

6.1. Standard
All goods, including means of transport, which enter or leave the Customs territory, regardless of whether they are liable to duties and taxes, shall be subject to Customs control.

6.2. Standard
Customs control shall be limited to that necessary to ensure compliance with the Customs law.

6.3. Standard
In the application of Customs control, the Customs Authority shall use risk management.

6.4. Standard
The Customs Authority shall use risk analysis to determine which persons and which goods, including means of transport, should be examined and the extent of the examination.

6.5. Standard
The Customs Authority shall adopt a compliance measurement strategy to support risk management.

6.6. Standard
Customs control systems shall include audit-based controls.

6.7. Standard
The Customs Authority shall seek to co-operate with other Customs administrations and seek to conclude mutual administrative assistance agreements to enhance Customs control.

6.8. Standard
The Customs Authority shall seek to co-operate with the trade and seek to conclude Memoranda of Understanding to enhance Customs control.

6.9. Transitional Standard
The Customs Authority shall use information technology and electronic commerce to the greatest possible extent to enhance Customs control.

6.10. Standard
The Customs Authority shall evaluate traders' commercial systems where those systems have an impact on Customs operations to ensure compliance with Customs requirements.

WCO Framework of Standards to Secure and Facilitate Trade (SAFE)

Alongside the initiatives concerning the US CT-PAT regime implementing the Automated Manifest System (AMS) and the Canadian Advance Cargo Information (ACI) systems, the World Customs Organisation introduced its own initiative, agreed in Brussels in June 2005, to establish a global system of security rendering the whole regime of cargo movements both transparent and accountable, and facilitate a safer world trade regime, entitled the "SAFE Framework of Standards". The document also included the Customs initiative to create the Authorised Economic Operator regime, whereby companies involved in frequent international trade activities would be able to apply for a specific authorisation to operate a simplified Import and Export Declaration regime based on their history of compliance with Customs import and export requirements. This authorisation would allow such traders to use fast-track export and import clearance procedures, thus resulting in savings of both time and costs. The AEO regime was initiated in 2007, with companies being invited to apply for the authorisation.

Although the essence of the AEO regime is largely concerned with overall Customs compliance, it requires the shipper to maintain a complete control over their inward and outward shipments, particularly in the maritime cargo sector. This means that the shipper must maintain a complete control over the management of all maritime cargo shipments, concerning both documentation and procedural issues.

The SAFE Framework has several principles, and these are as follows:

- To establish standards providing Supply Chain security and facilitation at a global level to promote certainty and predictability in the Supply Chain process;
- To enable integrated Supply Chain management for all modes of transport;
- To enhance the role, functions and capabilities of Customs to meet the challenges and opportunities of the 21st century;
- To strengthen co-operation between national Customs administrations to improve their capability to detect high-risk consignments;
- To strengthen Customs/Business co-operation;
- To promote the seamless movement of goods through secure International Trade Supply Chains.

There are 4 core elements within the SAFE Framework. These are:

1) The harmonisation of the advance electronic cargo information requirements on inbound, outbound and transit shipments;
2) Each country joining the SAFE Framework commits to employing a consistent risk-management approach to address security threats;
3) The requirement that at the reasonable request of the receiving nation, based upon a comparable risk targeting methodology, the sending nation's Customs administration will perform an outbound inspection of high-risk containers and cargo, preferably using non-intrusive detection equipment such as large-scale X-Ray machines and radiation detectors;
4) The definition of benefits that Customs will provide to businesses which meet minimal Supply Chain security standards and best practices.

There are also 2 pillars within the SAFE Framework. These are:

1) Customs-to-Customs;
2) Customs-to-Business.

Each pillar involves a set of standards which are consolidated to guarantee ease of understanding and rapid international implementation. Like the US and Canadian initiatives, the framework is designed to provide better security against terrorism, and increase the contribution of Customs and trade partners to the economic and social well-being of countries. It is designed to improve the ability of Customs to detect and deal with high-risk consignments and increase efficiencies in the administration of goods, thereby expediting the clearance and release of goods, as well as, in the words of the document setting out the principles of the SAFE Framework, securing and facilitating legitimate global trade, along with the facilitation of the modernisation of global Customs operations. A further aim is to improve revenue collection and the proper application of national laws and regulations.

The establishment of Customs-to-Customs network arrangements is designed to facilitate the efficient exchange of accurate information which is supposed to place Customs administrations in the position of managing risk on a more effective basis. This network would enable Customs to more easily detect high-risk consignments and to improve their controls along the International Supply Chain, thus leading to a more efficient allocation of Customs resources. Such Supply Chain controls would thus enable the Customs administration of an importing country to request the Customs administration of the exporting country to carry out controls earlier in the Supply Chain, for example examinations of export consignments before they are loaded aboard vessel, either at the shipper's premises or at the port of loading.

One of the main elements of the SAFE Framework as far as the shipper is concerned is the requirement for the submissions of advance electronic Export Declarations to Customs at export prior to the goods being loaded on to the means of transport, such as a sea container, in effect consolidating and developing the existing electronic Export Declaration systems used, inter alia, by shippers in Canada and the UK. The UK electronic Export Declaration system, the so-called "New Export System", was introduced in 2002 and now covers all exports to non-EU destinations from the UK. Where simplified electronic Export Declarations are submitted at first instance, these would have to be followed up at a later stage by supplementary declarations as required by the national legislation. Similarly, the carrier or their agent would have to submit an advance electronic cargo declaration to Customs at export and/or at import. For maritime containerised shipments, the advance electronic cargo declaration would have to be lodged prior to the consignment or container being loaded aboard vessel, and would be followed up by a supplementary cargo declaration as stipulated by national legislation.

Similarly, the same procedure would be carried out at the import stage, in that an advance import goods declaration would be submitted to Customs prior to the cargo being landed at the port of destination. In the case of a simplified declaration, this would be followed up by a supplementary declaration for the purposes of calculation of Import Duties and other local taxes. The proposed "Authorised Supply Chain" procedure would allow for the possibility to integrate the export and import information flows into 1 single unified declaration for export and import purposes, which could be shared between the Customs administrations concerned.

Time limits for the pre-lodging of goods and cargo declarations by both shippers and carriers would be imposed by each national Customs authority. These would be as follows for maritime shipments:

- Containerised cargo (including multimodal transport): at least 24 hours before loading at the port of departure;
- Bulk/Breakbulk: at least 24 hours before the arrival of the consignment at the first port in the country of destination.

The Authorised Supply Chain is a concept under which all participants in an international trade transaction are approved by Customs as observing specified standards in the secure handling of goods and relevant associated information, including export, import and shipping documentation. Consignments passing from origin to destination entirely within such a chain would benefit from an integrated cross-border simplified procedure, where only 1 simplified declaration with minimum information would be required for both import and export purposes.

In essence, the new framework simplifies the Supply Chain process, but it requires all parties to the process to be absolutely compliant in all their related activities, especially concerning the shipment of consignments. There is a need for a clear audit trail, as well as the complete transparency of information, in order to facilitate the smooth and efficient flow of information and the equally efficient means for shipping goods and facilitating quick and efficient clearance through all Customs controls at the point of export and import.

Summary

The SAFE Framework rests on 2 pillars: The Customs-to-Customs network and the Customs-to-Business partnerships. It is furthermore complemented by a capacity-building programme, the so-called Columbus Program. Core elements of the SAFE Framework are:

- The harmonisation of advance cargo information;
- The introduction of a risk-management approach;
- The sending country's Customs inspection of high-risk containers by Customs Authorities;
- A benefits programme for compliant traders.

The SAFE Framework of Standards is a set of recommendations to the Customs organisations, which include issues as:

- Integrated Customs control procedures for Integrated Supply Chain Management;
- Authority to inspect cargo, and use modern technology in doing so;
- Risk-management system to identify potentially high-risk shipments;
- Identification of high-risk cargo and container shipments;
- Advance electronic information on cargo and container shipments;
- Joint targeting and screening.

Since this historic occasion much has been done to encourage implementation of the SAFE Framework by WCO Members, including in 2007 the addition of a major section on the conditions and requirements for Customs and Authorised Economic Operators. On the 10th anniversary of the adoption of the SAFE Framework of Standards by the WCO Council, key improvements to the SAFE Framework of Standards 2015 encompass a new version of the SAFE Framework that includes a new Pillar 3 on Co-operation between Customs and other government and inter-government agencies.

To further support implementation, the WCO SAFE Working Group and other WCO bodies, along with the Private Sector Consultative Group (PSCG), have developed a number of instruments and guidelines. In order to bring together this important body of material in 1 convenient place, the WCO compiled a SAFE Package which incorporates all these instruments and guidelines.

As the SAFE Framework continues to be more fully implemented by WCO Members it is clear that a substantial amount of additional support material will be developed in the future and it is envisaged that the SAFE Package will be able to be readily updated and expanded. In 2015, in addition to the presentation of instruments and tools by pillar, the updated SAFE Package comprises the introduction of a new toolkit for Pillar 1, an update of the AEO Compendium, and an update of the guidelines for the Procurement and Deployment of Scanning/NII Equipment.

Post Clearance Audit

Definition/Scope

Post-clearance audit (PCA) or audit-based controls are defined by the Revised Kyoto Convention as measures by which the Customs satisfy themselves as to the accuracy and authenticity of declarations through the examination of the relevant books, records, business systems and commercial data held by persons concerned. Post-clearance audit is a critical control methodology for Customs and other border regulatory authorities as it enables them to apply a multi-layered risk-based control approach by moving from a strictly transaction-based control environment to a stronger audit-based administration.

Transaction-based controls are those controls applied to each individual shipment at the time of crossing the border, such as physical examination, verification of value, origin and classification of goods, sampling, verification of certificates, licenses and permits, etc.

Administrations that do not use audit-based controls usually concentrate their controls entirely at the border and at the time of import, and often apply a 100% physical examination approach. This leads not only to unnecessarily long delays at the border but is also a very ineffective and inefficient use of the limited control and inspection staff at the border. In addition, 100% physical examination creates an enabling environment for corrupt practices. Audit-based controls are a prerequisite for administrations to successfully apply other trade facilitation measures, such as segregation of release and clearance, simplified procedures for authorised traders and AEOs or the WTO Valuation Rules.

Implementation Guidance

Post-clearance audit allows reduction of control activities at a border and at the time of arrival of goods to only those necessary to determine the admissibility of the goods. This can lead to a significant increase in revenue collection, as PCA allows a more comprehensive and holistic evaluation of the particulars necessary for the calculation of duties and taxes. In Japan, for example, the increased use of PCA generated more than twice as much revenue in 2009 than in 1999.

PCA can have the form of supporting transaction-based controls at the border by verifying the classification, valuation and origin of the goods after release through an audit of the supporting commercial documentation such as an invoice. In this way, goods can be released upon arrival (usually against security or guarantee) and clearance be completed and duties paid after the PCA. This segregation of release and clearance is a very important measure to accelerate the movement of goods across borders. Modern Customs administrations may be in a position to grant release and clearance simultaneously upon arrival of the goods, as stipulated in the ICC Customs Guideline Number 9.

In addition, PCA can have the form of periodic and cyclic audits, usually at the premises of the importer or trader concerned, where Customs reviews imports over a given period and checks all relevant commercial records, including bank statements and contracts to verify the particulars given in a goods declaration. Both forms of PCA should be performed following a risk-based selectivity approach similar to that applied to individual transactions at the time of import or export.

PCA requires an enabling environment such as a dedicated PCA organisation within Customs, the legal powers to access commercial records and to enter traders' premises, properly trained staff, as well as the existence and proper application of accounting standards (e.g. based on the International Financial Reporting Standards (IFRS) as adopted by the International Accounting Standards Board) based on which companies keep their records. Only by following such accounting standards will Customs be in a position to introduce audit-based controls.

Customs Automation

Definition/Scope

Customs automation describes the application of information and communication technologies (ICT) for accomplishing the mission of Customs. It may support the entire clearance process – from lodging, acceptance and processing of cargo and goods declarations for import, export and transit, payment of applicable duties and taxes, to release of the goods from Customs control – or only part of it. Customs automation offers new possibilities to administrations such as pre-arrival processing and automated release of securities and guarantees. It can facilitate the use of risk management and risk-based selectivity and the collection of data for reporting external trade statistics.

There is a long list of problems associated with insufficient Customs automation or Customs automation projects. The most relevant problems affecting trade facilitation are:

1. The manual processing of paper-based cargo and goods declarations is very time consuming. Since such administrations lack a sufficient number of well-trained staff, such manual processing will not cope with growing volumes of international trade;
2. The many occasions for manual intervention and face-to-face over the counter touch points between traders/brokers and Customs officials, in addition to the payment of duties and taxes in cash, often create opportunities for corrupt practices thus hampering trade and development. Consequently, Customs administrations operating manually without automation hinder the economic development of a country;
3. Customs administrations which apply IT systems often still require the subsequent submission of a paper declaration, because they continue to require a handwritten signature. Instead of providing the benefits of a paperless environment, these administrations are duplicating the requirements (and cost) by asking for paper in addition to the electronic declaration;
4. Customs automation projects are very complex undertakings, requiring the necessary analytical and project management skills to properly specify and manage user and technical requirements, and

to develop an achievable implementation and roll-out plan and keep the overall project on track. In many countries Customs administrations lack the skills to manage well such large-scale transformation projects. Consequently, projects are often not completed and systems not operated on time and within budget.

Implementation Guidance

Standards 3.18 (supporting documents), 3.21 (declaration), 6.9 (Customs control) and 7.1 (general) of the Revised Kyoto Convention require the use of IT and electronic means for Customs operations. Standard 7.4 of the RKC also requires Customs to establish the necessary enabling legal framework, including electronic authentication methods (e.g. digital signatures). The Kyoto Convention ICT Guidelines provide great detail about Customs automation and project management. The list of topics covered in these guidelines includes: application areas of ICT (e.g. declaration processing, release, e-payment, transit, trade statistics, enforcement); system development process, project and change management; IT security; outsourcing in Customs; IT-related legal aspects; and many more. Any Customs automation project aiming to implement the Revised Kyoto Convention should also apply the WCO Data Model as the standard for electronic messages and data standards. Such a project will require a review and in most cases a redesign of existing Customs processes and procedures, as well as harmonisation of the various data requirements of all relevant national border agencies into a single national data set. Above all, these projects require leadership to manage the changes.

However, very few Customs administrations have the skills and technical manpower to conduct a Customs automation project on their own. It is indispensable for any Customs administration to establish a professional IT team that is in a position to manage the user and technical requirements and to have the necessary skills of project and contract management in order to provide the leadership and overall responsibility for the IT project. Also Customs should consider inviting stakeholders from the national and international IT industry and service provider markets to offer support for the timely development and implementation of a Customs IT system. A number of commercial off-the-shelf (COTS) Customs IT solutions are now available in the market. While these solutions may require some customisation to specific domestic requirements, they will help to reduce the significant project risks of "from scratch" developments.

There are many successful examples of increased performance due to Customs automation and modernisation. For example, the "e-Douane" project in Luxemburg started in 2007 and was completed in 2009/2010. During that time Luxemburg Customs has moved from 15th place in 2007 to 1st place in 2010 in the Logistics Performance Index of the World Bank.

Pre-Arrival Processing

Definition/Scope

Pre-arrival processing involves the (electronic) submission of the relevant goods and/or cargo declaration data to the relevant authorities prior to the arrival (for import) or prior to departure (for export) of goods. Authorities are then able to conduct risk assessment and to process the declaration with a view to prepare the release decision prior to the goods arriving at the port of entry/port of exit, thus enabling the release of the goods immediately upon arrival. This may include communicating the release decision to the persons concerned so that they can continue their Supply Chain and logistics planning.

Traditionally, Customs allows importers and their agents to declare the goods only after they have arrived in the country and are presented to Customs. Consequently, Customs and other relevant authorities only then start to check and examine the declaration and prepare a release decision. This significantly delays the release process, as Customs and the other relevant agencies do not make use of the time afforded by the sometimes long journey of the goods to the country of importation, for risk assessment and declaration processing purposes.

Also, in a growing number of countries, the pre-arrival declaration option is increasingly converted into an obligatory Supply Chain security regime, in some cases with time limits prior to the departure of the goods in the country of export. This practice is adversely affecting trade and just-in-time Supply Chains and adds significant cost to doing business.

Implementation Guidance

Voluntary pre-arrival declaration and processing arrangements are the solution to expedite release. According to Standard 3.25 of the Revised Kyoto Convention, Customs shall allow the lodging and registering of goods declarations and supporting documents prior to arrival of goods. According to a Time Release Study conducted by Japan Customs in 2009, (see chart), the time required to release sea cargo in a non-pre-arrival mode was 2.9 days compared to 2.2 days in a pre-arrival mode. In the case of air cargo, only pre-arrival declarations enabled Japan Customs to grant almost immediate release.

At the same time, as stipulated by Standard 3.23 of the RKC, if Customs sets a time limit for lodging the goods declaration (even in a pre-arrival mode), the time allowed shall be sufficient to enable the declarant to complete the goods declaration and to obtain the supporting documents/information required.

For authorised traders, authorities should also give due consideration to the possibility of releasing goods even prior to their arrival (so-called pre-clearance), in particular for trusted traders as stipulated in Paragraph 2.3 of the WCO Immediate Release Guidelines.

A pre-requisite for the introduction of pre-arrival processing are a Customs automation system that can receive and process the advance declaration and a risk-management system in place.

Cross-Border Management

In the area of international trade, goods have to undergo at least 2 sets of border formalities, 1 in the country of export and 1 in the country of import. Often goods cross more than 1 border. Trade facilitation is therefore not only the responsibility of each individual country, but also the collective responsibility of all countries concerned. The more countries base their individual Customs working methods, processes and procedures on relevant international standards such as the Revised Kyoto Convention and the Convention on the Harmonisation of Frontier Controls of Goods, the more cross-border co-operation and co-ordination can be facilitated. For example, joint border controls will help to eliminate redundancies in the clearance process at land border crossings. Also, complying with international risk-management standards will increase predictability in the entire door-to-door Supply Chain. International transit arrangements will ensure that goods can be delivered smoothly and rapidly to their final destination without having to undergo Customs clearance in every country they pass through.

The management of such bilateral, plurilateral and multilateral cross-border Customs co-operation can help to reduce the cost of trading significantly. APEC economies agreed in 2005 to reduce transaction costs by 2010 by another 5% after having achieved a reduction of 5% as agreed in 2001. This APEC Trade Facilitation Action Plan is a good practice example of what is achievable through greater economic integration and cross-border management.

Single Window for Trade

The most commonly accepted definition of a SW is the 1 provided by UNECE Recommendation No. 33. It describes the SW as "a facility that allows parties involved in trade and transport to lodge standardised information and documents with a single entry point to fulfil all import, export, and transit-related regulatory requirements". "If information is electronic, then individual data elements should only be submitted once".

Independently from its description as a platform, environment, or facility, a SW can best be understood by the service that it aims to provide to traders and government authorities alike. Such service is that it facilitates the exchange of trade relevant information between traders and government agencies, and amongst government agencies, for obtaining permits and licenses, certificates and necessary approvals. It does so by allowing traders, or their agents, to submit trade documents and data, in electronic or paper form, through a single entry point.

The most advanced Single Window systems also connect private sector actors such as commercial banks, Customs brokers and freight forwarders. An example is the Mozambican SW, launched in 2011.

Relevance for Trade Facilitation

A SW for trade can be an important facilitation tool. If implemented effectively, it can simplify procedures and formalities for document submission and data collection and can save precious time and money. The following are the main benefits that key stakeholders of a SW project can achieve:

- **Government:** Increase in government revenue, enhanced compliance with rules, improved efficiency in resource allocation, better trade statistics;
- **Traders:** Faster clearance times, a more transparent and predictable process and less bureaucracy;
- **Customs:** Improved staff productivity through the upgraded infrastructure, increase in Customs revenue, a more structured and controlled working environment, and enhanced professionalism;
- **Economy as a whole:** Improved transparency and governance and reduced corruption, due to fewer opportunities for physical interaction.

The Korea Customs service estimates that the introduction of its SW brought some US$18 million in benefits in 2010, part of the overall economic benefit that year of up to US$3.47 billion from the agency trade facilitation efforts. In Singapore, the national Single Window for trade called TradeNet, brings together more than 35 border agencies since 1989 and leads to big gains in government productivity. Singapore Customs claims that for every US$1 earned in Customs, it spends 1 cent – a profit margin of 9,900%.*

Supply Chain Security

Over many years, international trade and transport networks and infrastructures have been identified as potential targets for international terrorism and cross-border crime. While Customs have always been in charge of controlling international trade in terms of prohibitions and restrictions, the aspect of securing the international trade Supply Chain has put growing and additional burdens on Customs to manage this balance.

In response to this growing challenge, the World Customs Organisation adopted the SAFE Framework of Standards in 2005 to provide a stronger focus on those principles of the Revised Kyoto Convention that improve co-operation among Customs administrations, provide Supply Chain security and facilitation at a global level to promote certainty and predictability. It also provides an international framework for standardisation and harmonisation of authorised economic operator programmes.

As a government task for Customs, Supply Chain security puts additional pressure on Customs to find the right balance between control/security and trade facilitation. The SAFE Framework of Standards contains a number of important standards especially dedicated to trade facilitation. SAFE calls for the harmonisation of advance electronic cargo information requirements and the employment of a consistent risk-management approach to address threats. It established the concept of the Authorised Economic Operator as a way to provide legitimate trade with a mechanism to receive tangible benefits for their commitment to invest in and comply with Supply Chain security standards. In addition to the AEO, SAFE lays the foundation for mutual recognition of AEO programmes, which means that AEOs would not have to undergo time-consuming accreditation processes in every country again and again.

Finally, the SAFE Framework of Standards makes a strong recommendation for governments to apply the latest non-intrusive inspection technology, which can increase security, but at the same time can help to avoid unnecessary physical inspections.

The EU Perspective

EU Risk Management

The following text is derived from the EU's taxation web portal at http://ec.europa.eu, and explains in good clarity the essential features of the EU's initiative to create a comprehensive Customs Risk Management Framework.

The role of modern Customs services has become increasingly challenging, involving the management of the free flow of trade in support of trade policy and economic development while prioritising the security, safety and health of citizens and ensuring the correct collection of duties and taxes, in order to provide the necessary level playing field between economic operators and avoid distortions of competition.

Since the tragic events of 11 September 2001 ("9/11") in the US, and other terrorist attacks which followed, especially in the EU, security has become a top priority for European Customs, especially as no frontier Customs controls exist within the European Union following the Schengen Agreement of 1990. The recent terrorist attacks in EU Member States, in particular in Paris, Brussels, Nice and Berlin, and also in other countries across the world reiterated the important role that Customs are invited to play in border security through controls on the movement of goods and persons carrying goods and/or money by all means of transport. The security of the EU and its citizens depends on Customs controls along the EU's external borders.

In addition, the scale of trade with the EU has increased significantly over the past years. Between 2004 and 2014, despite the impact of the financial crisis, the value of EU external trade grew by more than 72%. The EU is at the centre of global trade and Supply Chain logistics. According to statistics of the World Trade Organisation the EU held in 2014 the second position in the international scale of leading exporters and importers with 15% (and a difference of only 0.5% from the first one). Furthermore, the EU is the number 1 trading partner for the US, China and other countries.

More than 90% of global trade (8.4 billion tonnes of merchandise) is carried annually by sea along more than 25,800 global trade lanes. More than 20% of this seaborne trade is unloaded in Europe. There are 25,400 transport nodes worldwide for cargo and passengers moved by air, a substantial proportion of which are linked to more than 250 international airports in the EU. The numerous parties involved in the management of these trade lanes add to the complexity of Supply Chain logistics. The eastern land border runs to 9,890 km, with 133 commercial road and rail entry points. Along the entire EU external border there are more than 1,000 Customs offices of entry.

Although the bulk of trade is lawful, a study by the World Economic Forum estimates illicit trade at between 8% and 15% of the global GDP. The scale of illicit trade is, by nature, difficult to quantify. Its cost to the global economy is considerable and estimated to over $3 trillion (> €2.5 trillion), all aspects combined.

The challenge to stop an explosive device, a consignment of contaminated food or smuggled goods amongst all this volume of EU trade and to ensure the correct collection of duties and taxes is therefore tremendous.

It was established that in 2014, EU Customs processed 41.5 million pre-arrival cargo declarations (entry summary declarations), 152.6 million Import Declarations, 109.8 million Export Declarations and 16.4 million transit declarations. These figures represent an average of 609 declarations per minute handled by the Member States' Customs administrations.

The work load of Customs Authorities is in the process of constant evolution. In the space of only 3 years, namely 2011–2014:

- The number of ENS submissions increased by 15.2%;
- The number of Import Declarations by 9%;
- The number of Export Declarations by 14.38%;
- The number of Transit declarations by 16.4%;
- Due to the scale of the traffic 100% controls is not a realistic option for the EU.

The EU thus favoured the use of risk management with the control regime and tools used determined on the basis of risk assessment of Supply Chain data and related risk information and intelligence available to Customs including from other relevant authorities and through improved international co-operation. The real challenge for EU Customs risk management is to focus and target traffic on the basis of factors that indicate there may be something "wrong, unusual, abnormal, uneconomic" or otherwise giving rise to suspicion in the trade flow or in relation to particular consignments. The identification and determination of those factors is a daily process based on exchange of information with other authorities, in-depth analysis of fraud trends and screening of available information on traffic flows and trade patterns. Another important element of these analyses is the identification of reliable operators and the possibility for them to have access to procedural simplifications.

Customs Risk Management Framework (CRMF)

A sophisticated common Customs Risk Management Framework (CRMF) is nothing new as far as EU Customs management exists, as it was introduced into the previous Customs legislation as provided by the Community Customs Code of 1992, along with the provisions as laid down by the SAFE Framework of Standards, and is now covered by Article 46 of the Union Customs Code (UCC).

The CRMF is based on the recognition of the need to establish an equivalent level of protection in Customs controls for goods brought into or out of the EU and to ensure a harmonised application of Customs controls by the MS. It aims to support a common approach so that priorities are set effectively and resources are allocated efficiently with the aim of maintaining a proper balance between Customs controls and the facilitation of legitimate trade.

The CRMF therefore comprises:

- The identification and control of high-risk goods movements using common risk criteria;
- The identification of priority control areas subject to more intense controls for a specific period;
- Systematic and intensive exchange of risk information between Customs;
- The contribution of Authorised Economic Operators in a Customs–Trade partnership to securing and facilitating legitimate trade; and
- Pre-arrival/pre-departure security risk analysis based on cargo information submitted electronically by traders prior to arrival or departure of goods in/from the EU specifically to cater primarily for security and safety risks.

(A) The Common Risk Criteria and Standards

The Commission has adopted a set of criteria to be applied in the Member States' risk analysis systems in order to continuously screen electronic advance cargo information for security and safety purposes. The criteria are set out in an implementing act based on the empowerment of Article 50(1) UCC, which was not made public for several reasons. The CRC are aimed primarily towards identifying high-risk consignments/goods that could have serious implications for the security and safety of the EU and its citizens and providing equivalent protection throughout the external frontier based on common risk analysis.

While in all other types of movements, the Customs office where goods and declarations are presented is responsible for the processing of the declarations and for the risk analysis, Customs at the first point of EU entry has a legal obligation to carry out the security and safety risk analysis on all the cargo regardless of the country of EU destination. Consignments crossing the EU border are thus screened on the basis of those criteria 365 days a year.

(B) Priority Control Areas

Priority Control Areas (PCAs) are the key mechanism in the CRMF allowing the Union to designate specific areas to be treated as a priority for Customs control. The identified areas are subjected to reinforced Customs controls carried out in a co-ordinated manner based on common risk assessment criteria and real-time exchange of risk information.

Characteristics of Priority Control Areas

Priority areas may relate to any Customs procedure, types of goods, traffic routes, modes of transport or economic operators;

The chosen areas are to be subject to increased levels of risk analysis and Customs controls for a pre-determined limited period with a start and end date and possibility for interim review.

PCAs will have built-in assessment procedures and flexibility for Member States in order to ensure that the control action to be taken is not disproportionate or unduly disruptive in terms of the effect on trade flows within a Member State or a particular port or frontier point.

The Commission together with the Member States have organised PCAs on counterfeit medicine, drug precursors and the issues of valuation of textiles, smuggling of cigarettes and control of dual-use goods.

(C) The Exchange of Risk Information

The Common Customs Risk Management System is designed to provide a fast and easy-to-use mechanism to distribute and exchange Customs control and risk-related information directly amongst operational officials and risk analysis centres in the 28 Member States.

It facilitates EU-wide Customs intervention for the highest risks at the external frontier and inland and is thus an integral element in the development of a Union risk-management framework. It consists of a form (Risk Information Form, RIF) to be filled in on-line and instantly made available to all Customs offices connected.

The RIF is an effective means of ensuring that a consistent level of Customs control is applied at the external frontier of the Union in relation to identified risks thereby offering the necessary level of protection to citizens and to the financial interests of the EU and MS while ensuring equivalent treatment of traders throughout the Union.

In summary, the system is a practical way to ensure that information about identified risks is distributed as quickly as possible to operational Customs offices in all Member States; this ensures that immediate measures can be taken across the whole EU to tackle such risks, establishes a level playing field for traders and combats diversion of dangerous, irregular or fraudulent trade.

Union Customs Code EU Regulation 952/2013

Article 46

Risk Management and Customs Controls

1. The customs authorities may carry out any customs controls they deem necessary.

   Customscontrols may in particular consist of examining goods, taking samples, verifying the accuracy and completeness of the information given in a declaration or notification and the existence, authenticity, accuracy and validity of documents, examining the accounts of economic operators and other records, inspecting means of transport, inspecting luggage and other goods carried by or on persons and carrying out official enquiries and other similar acts.

2. Customs controls, other than random checks, shall primarily be based on risk analysis using electronic data-processing techniques, with the purpose of identifying and evaluating the risks and developing the necessary counter-measures, on the basis of criteria developed at national, Union and, where available, international level.
3. Customs controls shall be performed within a common risk-management framework, based upon the exchange of risk information and risk analysis results between customs administrations and establishing common risk criteria and standards, control measures and priority control areas.
   Controls based upon such information and criteria shall be carried out without prejudice to other controls carried out in accordance with paragraph 1 or with other provisions in force. EN L 269/26 Official Journal of the European Union 10.10.2013
4. Customs authorities shall undertake risk management to differentiate between the levels of risk associated with goods subject to customs control or supervision and to determine whether the goods will be subject to specific customs controls, and if so, where.
   The risk management shall include activities such as collecting data and information, analysing and assessing risk, prescribing and taking action and regularly monitoring and reviewing that process and its outcomes, based on international, Union and national sources and strategies.
5. Customs authorities shall exchange risk information and risk analysis results where:
   (a) the risks are assessed by a customs authority as being significant and requiring customs control and the results of the control establish that the event triggering the risks has occurred; or
   (b) the control results do not establish that the event triggering the risks has occurred, but the customs authority concerned considers the threat to present a high risk elsewhere in the Union.
6. For the establishment of the common risk criteria and standards, the control measures and the priority control areas referred to in paragraph 3, account shall be taken of all of the following:
   (a) the proportionality to the risk;
   (b) the urgency of the necessary application of the controls;

(c) the probable impact on trade flow, on individual Member States and on control resources.

7. The common risk criteria and standards referred to in paragraph 3 shall include all of the following:
   (a) a description of the risks;
   (b) the factors or indicators of risk to be used to select goods or economic operators for customs control;
   (c) the nature of customs controls to be undertaken by the customs authorities;
   (d) the duration of the application of the customs controls referred to in point (c).
8. Priority control areas shall cover particular customs procedures, types of goods, traffic routes, modes of transport or economic operators which are subject to increased levels of risk analysis and customs controls during a certain period, without prejudice to other controls usually carried out by the customs authorities.

The US/Canadian Perspective – The C-TPAT 5-Step Process

In the wake of the tragic events of 11 September 2001, the US Trade Act 2002 sought to tighten up border controls for the import of goods into the US. This was subsequently also enacted in Canadian legislation as part of the overall Customs-Trade Partnership Against Terrorism (C-TPAT) initiative, and imposed strict controls over imports into North America. As part of the C-TPAT initiative, a 5-step risk management process was also established, to assess any perceived or actual threat to Customs and Border security. A report published by the US Customs and Border Protection Agency on their website describes this process as follows.

The 5-step process described below can be used by partners of all entities to determine what threats exist to their business models, even if a partner does not physically handle cargo. Those partners that only handle data are also at risk, for if a terrorist or other criminal seeks access to a cargo shipment, the first thing they require is knowledge of a shipment and the identifying information of the companies involved in the cargo movement.

An example of how the C-TPAT minimum security criteria addresses these issues is under Broker Procedural Security, "Security measures must be in place to ensure the integrity of any data or documents relevant to security of processes, transportation, handling, and storage of cargo in the supply chain".

While many partners use a numerical rating system to assess risk, an alternative method can be used. It is up to each partner to determine how risk will be assessed. The threat and vulnerability factors described in this document should be used to determine the level of risk, which should be described appropriately (e.g. high, medium, or low; acceptable or unacceptable; pass or fail, etc.). A complex rating system may be used, but is not appropriate for all business models.

Partners should be aware that INCOTERMS have little to do with security assessments for terrorism and criminal activity. INCOTERMS are primarily directed towards cost, ownership, and insurance purposes. A terrorist willing to explode a device within a US harbour, or a human trafficker impersonating a legitimate shipment through identity theft, cares not for legitimate ownership and insurance claims. The C-TPAT Partners responsible for the importation and exportation of goods across US borders, no matter where the actual transfer of ownership occurs, are ultimately responsible for the security of that shipment, regardless of the INCOTERMS. The acknowledgement of this fact, and the willingness to be proactive and energetic in addressing Supply Chain security, is what separates C-TPAT Partners from those who are not partners. Companies that feel the requirements of the C-TPAT minimum security criteria are too burdensome are not suited for the C-TPAT Programme. For exporters particularly, it is critical shipments are protected from threats to US allies to whom shipments are destined. The reputation of the entire US business community rests on exporters being proactive and conscientious of their responsibilities concerning Supply Chain security. It is thus critical for the survival of all C-TPAT Partners to be aware, and selective of, its business partners.

The 5-step risk-assessment process includes:

1. Mapping cargo/data flow and control and identifying business partners (whether directly or indirectly contracted) and how cargo moves throughout the Supply Chain to include modes of transportation (air, sea, rail or truck) and nodes (country of origin, transit points);
2. Conducting a threat assessment focusing on terrorism, contraband smuggling, human smuggling, agricultural and public safety threats, organised crime, and conditions in a country/region which may foster such threats, and ranking those threats;
3. Conducting a vulnerability assessment in accordance with the C-TPAT minimum security criteria. A vulnerability assessment includes identifying what the Partner has that a terrorist or criminal might desire. For brokers this might be data; for importers, manufacturers, and exporters, this might be access to cargo and company information. Then, identifying weaknesses in company procedures that would allow a terrorist or criminal to gain access to these processes, data or cargo;
4. Preparing a written action plan to address vulnerabilities. This includes mechanisms to record identified weaknesses, who is

responsible for addressing the issues, and due dates. Reporting results to appropriate company officials and employees on completed follow-up and changes is also essential;
5. Documenting the procedure for how risk assessments are conducted, to include reviewing and revising the procedure periodically. The process itself should be reviewed and updated as needed at least annually, and a risk assessment should be conducted – and documented – at least annually, more frequently for highway carriers and high-risk Supply Chains.

This can be summarised as:

1. Cargo Mapping;
2. Threat;
3. Vulnerability;
4. Action Plan;
5. Documented Procedures.

This essential 5-step plan has effectively been used as part of the new WCO SAFE Framework of Standards that should be adopted by all global Customs Authorities.

It is understood that some C-TPAT Partners have numerous Supply Chains, which may present a major task when conducting a comprehensive security risk assessment of their International Supply Chains. Therefore, it is recommended that C-TPAT Partners first identify their "High-Risk" Supply Chains by conducting a threat assessment at the point of origin/region and where the cargo is routed/trans-shipped, and then conducting a comprehensive security vulnerability assessment of those Supply Chains. Subsequently the partner should address the Supply Chains identified as medium and then low risk. This is to ensure the assumptions made in identifying risk levels as medium or low are in fact accurate. Companies that seek to elevate their security procedures to a Tier III status would be expected to complete threat, vulnerability, and risk assessments on all partners and Supply Chains.

Documenting the Risk Assessment Process

The 5-step process above is generic in nature to allow its application to all business entities and models. A sample risk assessment procedure, as described in Step 5 above, is displayed here. A company's documented risk assessment process (e.g. policies and procedures) should contain, at minimum, the following information:

1. Date the risk assessment process was established by the partner, and latest revision date;

2. Identify company personnel responsible for keeping the process up to date, including "back-up" personnel;
3. When or how often a risk assessment must be conducted (e.g. annually, quarterly (recommended especially for highway carriers); a new business partner in a Supply Chain; threat conditions change in a country or region);
4. Required frequency of review and update to the actual risk assessment procedure (e.g. annually, quarterly, etc.);
5. How threat assessments of International Supply Chains are to be conducted;
6. How vulnerability assessments on the International Supply Chain are to be conducted (e.g. verification of C-TPAT/PIP/AEO Status, site visits by Quality Assurance Managers, analysis of completed security questionnaires);
7. How follow-up is conducted on "action items" (e.g. site visits to address vulnerabilities, termination of contracts);
8. Procedure for training key individuals who are responsible for the risk assessment process, to include regional employees who frequently visit foreign sites for other purposes (e.g. quality assurance managers, sales representatives);
9. Internal management oversight and accountability for ensuring the process is carried out consistently and effectively.

This framework is now used by the major global Customs Authorities (including the EU) to ensure that traders applying for Customs facilities must be able to adhere to the above procedures as part of their overall compliance programmes.

US CBP Account Management

The Account Management programme, which is part of the US Customs and Border Protection Initiative, began in 1997 as a method to increase compliance while reducing costs and inefficiencies for CBP and the trade. The mission of account management is to use account-based (rather than transaction-based) methods consistent with risk-management principles to develop and maintain the highest levels of trade compliance, and to enforce, regulate, and administer US trade laws, while fostering the flow of lawful international trade.

By viewing a company and its trade performance in the aggregate, account management is intended to raise compliance, facilitate the flow of legitimate trade, and increase efficiencies. It does so, in part, by providing a National Account Manager to significant importers and broker accounts.

An account is an importer or a customhouse broker. The account may be defined by a single Importer of Record number or by a group of Importer of Record numbers or by 1 or more filer codes. All participants in the Importer Self-Assessment (ISA) programme are assigned to an Account Manager. This is a significant incentive to join the ISA programme. The Account Manager performs oversight of these accounts for the ISA programme.

The Account Manager serves as a primary point of contact to the account for trade related issues and also serves as a primary point of contact for the account within CBP, to establish and support smooth-working relationships among the many CBP disciplines that interact with the account. The Account Manager also provides guidance and assistance to the account and collaborates with other CBP disciplines to create and implement comprehensive strategies to manage and segment risk, solve problems, and increase efficiencies.

As part of CBP's trade transformation efforts, each Account Manager is now a core member of 1 of the 10 Centres of Excellence and Expertise. The 10 Centres are:

- Agriculture and Prepared Products;
- Apparel, Footwear and Textiles;
- Automotive and Aerospace;
- Base Metals;
- Consumer Products and Mass Merchandising;
- Electronics;
- Industrial and Manufacturing Materials;
- Machinery;
- Petroleum, Natural Gas and Minerals;
- Pharmaceuticals, Health and Chemicals.

Essentially, these sectors adhere to the Harmonised System (HS) Tariff structure, each covering several Tariff Chapters, with each Account Manager specialising on specific sections of the Tariff which, in turn, refer to specific industrial and commercial sectors of US business.

Canadian Border Intelligence and Risk Management

The Canada Border Services Agency (CBSA) continually works on new ways to protect the safety of all Canadians and help the flow of legitimate travellers crossing the border into Canada. It also screens visitors from overseas through electronic passport verifications, as well as using the C-TPAT system for the control of the import of goods from elsewhere, including the US where appropriate.

Targeting

The Targeting Program identifies people and goods bound for Canada that may pose a threat to the security and safety of the country. The CBSA uses a number of automated advance information sources from carriers and importers to identify people, goods and conveyances that may pose a threat to Canada.

Advance Passenger Information and Advance Commercial Information provide the CBSA with electronic pre-arrival information on people and goods that can be used to perform risk assessments in advance of their arrival in Canada. People and goods that are identified as posing a threat to Canada are referred for verification and examination upon their arrival at a port of entry.

Intelligence

The CBSA's Intelligence Program plays a key role in the identification of border-related risks and in protecting the safety and security of Canadians. Intelligence activities are conducted to identify, investigate and prosecute individuals and entities that are of interest to the CBSA in connection to organised crime, human smuggling, immigration fraud, terrorism and other violations of the Customs Act and the Immigration and Refugee Protection Act.

Through the collection and analysis of traveller and cargo information, the CBSA produces actionable tactical, operational and strategic intelligence to support the agency's operations and border enforcement mandate.

In addition, the CBSA collaborates with other domestic and international law enforcement agencies to enhance the Intelligence Program and Canada's border security.

Advance Commercial Information (ACI)

The Advance Commercial Information programme introduces more effective risk-management processes and tools to identify threats to our health, safety, and security prior to the arrival of cargo and conveyances in Canada.

The purpose of this web page is to provide general information on the ACI programme.

Programme Overview

The ACI programme is about providing CBSA officers with electronic pre-arrival information so that they are equipped with the right information at the right time to identify health, safety and security threats related to commercial goods before the goods arrive in Canada.

Phase 1: Marine Mode

Phase 1 of the Advance Commercial Information programme was implemented on 19 April 2004, requiring marine carriers to electronically transmit marine cargo data to the CBSA 24 hours prior to loading cargo at a foreign port. This requirement allows the CBSA to effectively identify threats to Canada's health, safety and security prior to the arrival of cargo and conveyances in Canada.

Phase 2: Air Mode and Marine Shipments Loaded in the United States

Implementation of Phase 2 of the ACI programme was completed on 26 July 2006, requiring air carriers and freight forwarders, where applicable, to electronically transmit conveyance, cargo and supplementary cargo data to the CBSA 4 hours prior to arrival in Canada or, if the duration of the flight to Canada is less than 4 hours, before the aircraft's time of departure.

As well, ACI Phase 2 also expanded marine requirements to include shipments loaded in the United States.

Phase 3: eManifest

eManifest will require the electronic transmission of advance cargo and conveyance information from carriers for all highway and rail shipments. In addition, the electronic transmission of advance secondary data will be required from freight forwarders and the electronic transmission of advance importer data will be required from importers or their brokers.

CHAPTER 13

The Union Customs Code (UCC)

This section has been largely derived from the http://www.gov.uk website. It can be referred to accordingly.

At the time of writing (July 2022), the Community Customs Code (CCC) was 30 years old, having been implemented under the provisions of EC Regulation 2913/92 in 1992 and EC Regulation 2454/93 in 1993, and was very much a product of its time. Quite naturally, since its adoption in 1992, the world of international commerce has changed significantly. The use of Information Technology (IT) by both Customs and international traders, otherwise known in Customs parlance as Economic Operators, and the complexity of Supply Chains have developed to previously unimagined levels, which have effectively rendered the previous legislation obsolete. A new set of legislation therefore became necessary to reflect these changes, especially in the light of the Revised Kyoto Convention and the subsequent SAFE Framework of Standards.

The Union Customs Code (UCC), introduced in 2016, is therefore a revision of the Modernised Customs Code (MCC) to take account of the Lisbon Treaty which became law on 1 December 2009. The Lisbon Treaty introduced new powers for the European Union (EU) Commission, and these had to be taken into account in all post-Lisbon legislation. The opportunity was also taken to make a few necessary amendments to the MCC to take further account of IT developments. However, since the withdrawal of the UK form the European Union at the end of 2020, some elements of the UCC have been adopted as applicable to UK Customs requirements, as these requirements are still in line with the SAFE Framework of Standards, which also embraces the UCC. It is therefore prudent to refer to the UCC, as it applies in full to the EU and in part to the UK.

The main changes embodied in the UCC are:

1. The introduction of self-assessment and centralised clearance;
2. Mandatory guarantees for special procedures' and temporary storage;
3. The ability to move goods under temporary storage rather than national transit or New Computerised Transit System (NCTS);

DOI: 10.4324/9781003341345-14

4. The removal of the earlier sales provisions relating to valuation;
5. All communications between Customs Authorities and Economic Operators must be electronic.

Because of these substantial changes, some changes to internet systems would be required. However, much depends on what authorisations are held by traders and what procedures or processes the business utilises.

One of the main provisions of the UCC is that manual declarations to Customs are no longer allowed. The UCC requires that all exchanges of information, for example, declarations between Customs Authorities and Economic Operators, must be electronic.

The Union Customs Code was finalised by 2013 by way of EC Directive 952/2013 and issued accordingly, but the supporting legislation in the form of the implementing and delegated acts were still the subject of negotiation right up to the date of implementation of the Code. The only confirmed date for UCC changes to start, especially those involving AEO status and the use of Customs Procedures with Economic Impact (CPEI), such as Inward Processing Relief, was 1 May 2016. However, it was stated by the EU that there would be a staggered introduction of some of the changes.

Legislation

The legislation can be found on the EU's main website (http://ec.europa.eu), as well as EU national Customs/Revenue websites, including the UK's website at http://www.gov.uk. It is then possible to follow the link to the UCC.

Internet Changes

It is very likely that some changes have been required to the trader's systems to conform to the new UCC. To this extent, much will depend on what authorisations held by the trader and what procedures/processes the trader's business uses. However, a plan for the major IT changes is already in place.

The Multi-Annual Strategic Plan (MASP) and its supporting legislation contained in the work programme lays down dates by which functional specifications must be provided together with proposed implementation dates between 2016 and 2020. The MASP can be read on the EU website, namely:

http://ec.europa.eu/taxation_customs/customs/policy_issues/electronic_customs_initiative/electronic_customs_legislation/index_en.htm.

Manual Declarations Are Not Allowed Under UCC

The UCC requires that all exchanges of information for example declarations between Customs Authorities and Economic Operators must be electronic.

This will be a significant change to many traders and all EU Customs Authorities have had to scope the impact.

Economic Operator Registrations Identification (EORI)

EORI rules have not changed in the current draft text. The trader needs an EORI number if they intend to be involved in the movement of goods into or out of the EU, even if they have an agent that handles everything. The EORI number comprises the trader's VAT Number plus 3 zeros, e.g. 123456789000, where the trader's VAT Number (in the case of the UK) is GB 123 4567 89.

Authorised Economic Operator (AEO)

In the EU, it is not mandatory to become an AEO unless the trader wishes to obtain a duty deferment guarantee reduction or they wish to be authorised for:

- Moving goods in temporary storage between different Member States;
- Centralised clearance;
- Waiver of the presentation of goods requirement when making declarations in your records;
- Self-assessment;
- Single transport contract.

In the UK, as long as the importer does not incur Import Duty liabilities of £10,000 per month, it is possible to obtain a guarantee waiver on the deferment account, as Import VAT is taken care of through the Postponed VAT Accounting (PVA) facility, and is accounted for through a combination of an online monthly Import VAT Statement and the consequent VAT Return.

Many authorisations and simplifications within the UCC require the trader to meet some or all of the AEO (c) criteria. Unless the trader wishes to obtain an authorisation for any of the above (and therefore an AEO (c) certificate is required), they will need to make a commercial decision about AEO status based on the information available, their business activities and their role in the Supply Chain.

AEO Criteria Have Changed

A new condition has been introduced concerning professional competence. The European Commission is working with Member States to determine the details behind the new criterion: "Practical standards of competence or professional qualifications related to the activity carried out". In addition, the current test on compliance with Customs rules has been expanded to cover all the taxation elements of the trader's business activities (VAT, Corporation Tax and National Insurance, for example).

In real terms there is little difference between meeting AEO criteria and being an authorised AEO apart from those areas where authorisation is a specific requirement. The main difference is that in most instances only some of the AEO criteria have to be met (perhaps only 2 or 3 of the basic conditions) and therefore you might not wish to go through the whole authorisation process.

AEO authorisation does not automatically qualify the trader for an authorisation within the UCC, but in most cases it will make the authorisation process easier. For example, if the trader is an authorised AEO who wishes to expand your business to include Customs Warehousing, your AEO status would not automatically qualify you for a Customs warehouse authorisation. Some additional checks would have to be carried out concerning your new venture but we would not repeat tests previously carried out.

Existing AEO Traders

If the trader already holds AEO status, they do not need to reapply but their authorisation will need to be re-assessed to take into account the new conditions. Those who cannot meet the new criteria may lose their status, but they will be given time to make the necessary changes. HMRC will work with the trader wherever possible to ensure the new criteria can be met. The EU Commission indicated that for EU traders there would be a transitional period to allow current AEO businesses time to meet the new criteria.

Valuation

There are a number of changes embodied within the UCC. The main ones are to Earlier Sales, the First Sale and Last Sale principle, Royalties and License Fees.

Earlier Sales Rules

It is proposed that the current earlier sale facility (First Sale) be withdrawn and will be replaced by a last sale only rule.

Royalties and License Fees

Currently, the very basic requirements as to whether or not a royalty fee is dutiable are that:

- It relates to the imported goods;
- It is paid as a condition of sale of those imported goods.

Under the UCC, Royalties/License Fees will generally be considered to be paid as a condition of sale of the goods and should therefore be included in the Customs value.

Guarantees

Under the current legislation, a Member State has the discretion to decide when a guarantee is or is not required. Under the UCC there will be circumstances where the provision of a guarantee is compulsory. The UK now asks for guarantees under the UCC.

Calculation of the Guarantee

Guarantee reference amounts will be calculated on the basis of:

- The volume of goods placed under the procedure (using data from the previous 12 months or commercial records that indicate the intended volumes);
- The length of time the goods will remain in the procedure;
- The revenue that would be due on them at the time they entered the procedure.

How to Waive or Reduce a Guarantee

A reduction/waiver will depend on the type of guarantee held or required and the circumstances in which the guarantee can be used. For example, a single guarantee (transaction by transaction) cannot be waived. A comprehensive guarantee for a special procedure can be reduced or waived while a guarantee for a deferment account can only be reduced, not waived.

The trader will need to hold an AEO (c) authorisation in order to reduce the guarantee to cover the payment of actual debts (for example, reduce the level of deferment guarantee). The trader will not need to hold an AEO (c) authorisation to benefit from a waiver or reduction in the level of the guarantee for potential debts (for example, goods held in duty suspension) but certain AEO criteria will have to be met.

Multiple Authorisations Requiring a Guarantee

The total volume of goods entered to each procedure will need to be covered by a guarantee, but you do not need to hold separate guarantees for each. The trader may choose to apply for a comprehensive guarantee for all your potential liabilities under a single guarantee.

Using Guarantees (and Any Relevant Waivers/ Reductions) Across the EU

There may be certain circumstances in which guarantees may be used in more than 1 Member State.

Imports That Attract 0% Duty Under Preference

If the goods are to be placed under an authorised procedure (resulting in revenue not being paid at the time of import) then a guarantee would be required to cover the potential duty liability. This would be calculated at the highest applicable duty rate. However, where the imported goods attract a duty rate of 0% according to the tariff (e.g. computers), then a guarantee would not be required, as only Import VAT would be payable.

How to Obtain a Guarantee

Although the provisions of the UCC concerning guaranteed have been announced, operational procedures for guarantees under the UCC are not yet known.

Apply for a Guarantee if the Trader Qualifies for a Waiver

The trader needs to apply for a comprehensive guarantee and provide evidence to support any waiver of the amount secured.

Imports

Manual import entries under the UCC will no longer be allowed. The UCC requires that all exchanges of information for example declarations, between Customs Authorities and Economic Operators must be electronic. HMRC is currently scoping the impact of this and will consult through the established JCCC route when HMRC has further details. The same will be true of all other EU national Customs Authorities.

Temporary Storage (TS)

TS will fundamentally remain unchanged except in 2 important areas guarantees and movement of goods. In addition, new data items may be required.

Guarantees

In order to operate a TS facility after 1 May 2016, the trader needs to provide a financial guarantee. If the trader can meet certain criteria, they may be able to obtain a guarantee waiver or reduction. However, the trader will not require a guarantee to simply place goods under TS.

Additional Terms and Conditions

If the trader wishes to continue to operate a TS facility after 1 May 2016, they will need to sign up to additional terms and conditions that will added to their existing TS approval.

Customs Declaration

As TS is not a Customs procedure, no Customs Declaration is required. However, certain data will need to be provided in the form of a TS declaration by way of a manifest or transport documentation. The range of data has still to be agreed but indications are that it will be similar to that currently provided.

External Temporary Storage Facility (ETSF)

TS situated outside of the traditional air/port environment will be treated in a similar manner to those TS facilities within an (air)port. Therefore Item 1.3 will equally apply to ETSF.

Movements Between TS Sites in the UK

Goods are able to move, subject to certain conditions, between TS facilities under cover of the TS authorisation. This method will be available for movements between different authorisation holders or within the same authorisation. Alternatively, NCTS can be used.

Movements Between Member States Involving 1 Authorisation

If the trader has a TS authorisation covering facilities in more than 1 Member State, movements can be carried out under cover of the authorisation provided that the trader holds an AEO authorisation. Alternatively, NCTS can be used.

Movements Between Member States Involving More Than 1 Authorisation

In the EU, if the trader wishes to move TS goods to another authorisation holder in another Member State, the movement can be carried out under cover of the TS authorisation provided both parties are AEO (c) authorisation holders. Alternatively, NCTS can be used.

Simplified Customs Declarations

Customs Freight Simplified Procedures will stay the same under the Union Customs Code, but there are increased requirements regarding notification of arrival under Local Clearance Procedures (LCP), which has been renamed "Entry in the Declarants Records" (EIDR). However, EIDR remains subject to discussion, as it applies to both Simplified Import Procedures, Export procedures to the Continental Shelf and simplified procedures into the UK as a result of the UK's withdrawal from the EU.

National Transit/Temporary Storage/LCP for Imported Goods

All movement of goods from TS at the (air)port will be permitted under the terms and conditions of the TS approval. As an alternative, NCTS will be available.

Centralised Clearance

In the EU, the scope of centralised Customs clearance and exactly how it will work is still the subject of negotiations and a degree of uncertainty. However, the basic theory is that a declaration will be lodged at an office in the EU Member State which granted that authorisation while the goods will be presented and imported in another Member State.

The current single authorisation for simplified procedures which can be seen as a form of centralised clearance will continue in its current form until centralised clearance is finalised.

One or more of 4 possible models for centralised clearance may eventually be adopted:

- Full declaration;
- Entry in the declarant's records with notification;
- Entry in the declarant's records with notification waiver;
- Simplified declaration.

Anyone who is an authorised AEO (c) and that meets any additional conditions that may be in place will be able to use centralised clearance.

Self-Assessment

The scope of self-assessment has not been established and is still the subject of negotiations. However, the principle of self-assessment is that an authorised person will take responsibility for and perform certain formalities/controls normally undertaken by Customs.

HMRC envisage the basic principle of self-assessment to be:

1. Economic Operators will manage and monitor their Customs activities through their own business account and financial administration and its supporting IT systems;
2. Economic Operators will determine the amount of Import/Export Duty payable and notify Customs periodically of the amount of duty payable for the defined period for example monthly.

Customs activities to be covered by self-assessment have yet to be defined, it may be limited to declarations to free circulation or include all Customs Declarations. It may include exports as well as imports, include prohibitions and restrictions, trade policy measures, Supply Chain security, trade statistics, Import VAT and Excise Duty, or not.

Anyone use it provided that they are an (AEO) authorised AEO (c) and meet any additional conditions that may be in place.

Returned Goods Relief (RGR)

The current draft text does not suggest any changes to RGR.

Customs Procedures with Economic Impact (CPEI)

All authorisations issued under the current Customs Code and used from 1 May 2016 must be in line with the UCC. This also applies to the use by the UK of such authorisations. However, the use of CPEI in the UK is no longer subject to mandatory financial guarantees, as this depends largely on the financial liquidity of the company applying for any of the CPEI authorisations.

CPEI have become:

- "Special Procedures" composed of processing (Inward Processing and Outward Processing);
- Specific use (temporary admission and end use), transit (external and internal transit);
- Storage (Customs Warehousing and free zones).

Previous authorisations expired on 30 April 2016. For traders wanting to continue to use special procedures, a new application (including any new requirements) is required.

The following CPEI are no longer available:

- Free zone Type II;
- Customs warehouse Type D;
- Processing under Customs control (but see Inward Processing (IP) below);
- Inward processing drawback system;
- Addition, the following changes will be introduced;
- A financial guarantee will be a mandatory requirement of authorisation;
- The requirement to re-export IP goods will be removed;
- Compensatory interest will be abolished.

In the EU, in order to operate IP after 1 May 2016, the trader needs to provide a financial guarantee. In the UK, this requirement is no longer mandatory and depends upon the financial status of the applicant. If the trader can meet certain criteria, they may be able to obtain a guarantee waiver, or reduction, a policy continued by HMRC following the exit of the UK from the EU at the end of 2020.

With the removal of the re-export requirement and compensatory interest, the trader will normally be able to choose how the amount of duty payable on release to free circulation can be calculated – either on the basis of the imported goods or on the basis of the processed products. Goods cannot be entered to IP drawback on or after 1 May 2016. However, goods entered to IP drawback prior to that date can be kept under that procedure until the expiry of the through put period. Provided that the goods are correctly disposed of (for example, by export) drawback claims can be submitted and paid.

In order to operate a Customs warehouse after 1 May 2016, the trader will need to provide a financial guarantee. If the trader can meet certain criteria, they may be able to obtain a guarantee waiver or reduction.

Goods cannot be entered to a Type D Customs warehouse on or after 1 May 2016. However, goods entered prior to that date can be kept under Type D arrangements until they are correctly disposed of (for example, by release to free circulation) and the charging rules appropriate at the time of entry can be maintained.

From 1 May 2016 and in addition to those sales currently permitted, the trader is able to make retail sales from the premises of a Customs warehouse provided that it is by means of the internet, catalogue or any other distance selling method. However, the trader will not be able to invite customers into the premises to make face to face retails sales.

In order to operate end use after 1 May 2016, the trader needs to provide a financial guarantee, subject to the guarantee waiver status mentioned above. If they can meet certain criteria, they may be able to obtain a guarantee waiver or reduction.

A periodic return has been introduced, and is similar to the Bill of Discharge originally currently used under IP.

Where a comprehensive guarantee is used, a waiver or reduction may be available.

There is no provision for UK national transit simplifications using the port/airport inventory systems within the UCC. However, the UCC will allow for goods in temporary storage to be moved between different facilities as an alternative to placing them under the external transit procedure.

As the level 1 procedure is based on the use of a paper manifest, this simplification will no longer be available. The UCC provides for operators to apply for authorisation to use an electronic transport document as a Customs Declaration to the transit procedure. It is expected that this will allow the use of an electronic manifest similar to the current air/sea level 2 simplifications. This simplification will also be available to other modes of transport (road/rail).

The current simplifications for authorised consignor, authorised consignee and the use of seals of a special type will continue to be available. There will also be a new simplification allowing the use of a Customs Declaration (on the NCTS) with reduced data requirements.

The trader will not need to hold an AEO authorisation to apply for transit simplifications. However, they will need to demonstrate that they can meet certain AEO (c) criteria.

The T2F transit procedure for movements between the UK and the Channel Islands or other special fiscal territories of the EU is no longer required for direct movements of Union goods between 1 of the EU special fiscal territories and a single Member State. Therefore, direct movements between the Channel Islands and the UK will no longer require the T2F transit procedure and the current simplification for these movements will no longer be applicable. Following the exit of the UK form the EU at the end of 2020, the T2F procedure no longer applies for such movements.

However, the T2F procedure will still be required for Union goods moved from 1 of the special fiscal territories where the movement ends in a Member State other than the Member State of first entry into the EU.

A new electronic system will replace paper T2L. Traders will communicate with Customs electronically to request endorsement of a Proof of Union Status (POUS). The proof will be "presented" to Customs by communicating the Master Reference Number (MRN) of the proof. Traders who are approved as "authorised issuers" will not need to request endorsement of the POUS.

The Single Transport Contract (STC) remains under the UCC. Anyone who holds an STC authorisation and an AEO (c) authorisation can operate an STC.

A hard copy EAD no longer needs to be presented at the office of exit with the goods. Instead, the Master Reference Number of the Export Declaration needs only to be communicated to the office of exit when presenting the goods for exit from the Union.

Further UCC criteria were announced in October 2015, and these include the following issues:

- The UCC introduces a new criterion of practical competence *or* a professional qualification (UCC Article 39(d)) directly related to the Customs activities. In the UK it is understood that it is unlikely that businesses will have a professional qualification, so focus will be on the demonstration and evidence of practical competence over the previous 3 years;
- This new criterion only applies to AEO Customs Simplifications (AEO-c);
- The European Commission has produced an EU Customs Competency Framework (EU Customs CFW) which is now available for use by national Customs services and businesses having to deal with Customs. (www.ec.europa.eu/taxation customs /common/ eu training/competency/indexen.htm)

Dependent on the size and type of business, competence will relate to:

1. The applicant; or
2. The person in charge of the Customs matters, for example if the Customs work is outsourced to 1 or more business partner(s) then they must be competent to carry out that role or hold an AEO (c) authorisation. The AEO business will need to determine the roles being outsourced and evidence how this is controlled and assured.

Further detailed information on this new criterion were made available in December 2015, upon the finalisation of EU discussions. However, there was no provision made for mandatory training in Customs procedures in most EU countries, although Customs have stated that they will accept international trade training courses which include major elements of Customs practices and procedures.

For all types of AEO authorisation the business will need to demonstrate that they are compliant with all taxes related to their business activities over the past 3 years (UCC Article 39 (a)), and have undergone training in Customs procedures. In practice for UK businesses, this assessment, in respect of tax compliance, along with the other validation checks will be carried out when the trader's application is received using data available to HMRC.

The changes will affect any new AEO application from 2 January 2016. Although HMRC has 120 calendar days to issue a decision, either the applicant or HMRC can also arrange extensions to the time period in justifiable circumstances to address any issues identified. A decision issued on or after the 1 May 2016 will be under the UCC rules, though the processing and any queries will fall under the current Customs Code legislation until that date.

There will be a transition period until 1 May 2019 for current AEOs by which time the AEO must have met all the new UCC requirements. However, HMRC will need to manage the re-assessment work over this period and each AEO will be contacted with more information on how this work will be undertaken in 2016.

It has been suggested that businesses consider the impact of the new requirements on their authorisations and commence any activities necessary to enable a successful outcome of the re-assessment.

The AEO (s) (Security and Safety) type of authorisation will not give the trader access to the new fiscal benefits being introduced under the UCC. However, the trader may wish to consider, if appropriate, applying for AEO (c) as well.

Guarantees – if the trader holds an AEO (c) authorisation, they are entitled to request a reduction in their duty deferment guarantee for Customs Duties (actual debt). The reduction available is 70%. There is no reduction available to businesses without an AEO (c) authorisation.

The trader is also entitled to request a waiver of the potential debt guarantees (covering Customs Duty and Import VAT and applicable if they hold Customs Authorisations/Approvals, for example Customs warehouse, inward processing, temporary storage), when/if that is appropriate to their business activities. These benefits are effective from 1 May 2016.

Reductions and waivers for potential debts are also available to businesses who do not hold an AEO authorisation but who would then need to meet some or all of the AEO (c) criteria.

Under the UCC, AEO becomes a Customs decision and there is no legislative requirement to issue a certificate. However, the EU Commission understands that the certificate is important to business to demonstrate their membership of the AEO programme and Member States will still issue a certificate.

Electronic communication – under the UCC all communication must be by an electronic method. All EU Customs Authorities will therefore not be able to accept paper applications from 1 May 2016 and all communications are intended to be via email unless there are exceptional circumstances. New digital services will be available over the next few years.

CHAPTER 14

Authorised Economic Operator (AEO)

An Authorised Economic Operator (AEO) is defined by the WCO SAFE Framework of Standards as a party involved in the international movement of goods, in whatever function, that has been approved by, or on behalf of, a national Customs administration as complying with WCO or equivalent Supply Chain security standards. AEOs include *inter alia* manufacturers, importers, exporters, brokers, carriers, consolidators, intermediaries, ports, airports, terminal operators, integrated operators, warehouses and distributors.

Since many years, in some cases even since the 1970s, Customs administrations have been increasingly involved in the security of the international trade Supply Chain, and have more recently developed security programmes in a global context. The AEO is part of these programmes and the WCO adopted an international AEO standard, the SAFE Framework of Standards, in 2005. Since then, traders have to make, in a number of cases, substantial investments in order to obtain AEO status and must continue to invest to maintain such a status. However, in return, Customs often do not offer substantial benefits in the form of trade facilitation, which increases the cost of trading. Consequently, the uptake of AEO programmes worldwide is slow.

Customs must work on a substantial benefits package as part of their AEO programme in close consultation with their trading community. Standard 6 of Pillar II of the WCO SAFE Framework of Standards encourages cooperation between Customs and trade for maximising security and facilitation. However, this standard puts security before facilitation, which is part of the dilemma. To overcome this, the WCO developed specific AEO Guidance (contained as Chapter 5 in the SAFE Framework of Standards) and an AEO Benefits Paper, which was a private sector contribution. These benefits include fewer inspections and priority treatment for inspections, mutual recognition with foreign AEO programmes, reduced security and guarantee requirements, expedited release and pre-clearance, simplified procedures, priority treatment in emergency situations, etc.

 DOI: 10.4324/9781003341345-15

Under the Union Customs Code (UCC), it is not mandatory to become an AEO unless the trader wishes to obtain a duty deferment guarantee reduction or wishes to be authorised for 1 of the following:

1. Moving goods in temporary storage between different member states;
2. Centralised clearance;
3. Waiver of the presentation of goods requirement when making declarations in your records;
4. Self-assessment;
5. Single Transport Contract (STC).

There are 2 types of AEO certification available under the UCC, namely AEO Simplified status (AEO (c)), which accounts for all measures used with regard to Customs Procedures with Economic Impact (CPEI), and Safety and Security AEO (AEO (s)) status, which is more related to security and safety measures as defined under the provisions of ISO 28000. It is possible for a trader to hold both types of AEO status, but for economic measures where Customs Duty is an issue, only AEO (c) status is required.

However, many authorisations and simplifications within the UCC require the trader to meet some or all of the AEO Simplified Procedures (AEO (c)) criteria. Unless the trader wishes to obtain an authorisation for any of the above (and therefore an AEO (c) certificate is required), they will need to make a commercial decision based on the information available, their business activities, and their role in the Supply Chain on whether AEO certification is for the trader or it is sufficient for the trader to prove that they meet the AEO standards.

The AEO criteria have also changed. A new condition has been introduced concerning professional competence, in that personnel in AEO applicant companies are required to have either a qualification in Customs knowledge or competence or at least 3 years' experience in dealing with Customs import and/or export practices, activities, and requirements. In reality, only certain countries have regimes that offer courses in Customs competence and knowledge, e.g. the US and Germany. In addition, the current test on compliance with Customs rules has been expanded to cover all the taxation elements of the trader's business activities (e.g. VAT, Corporation Tax and National Insurance). Under the UCC, traders will need to be reassessed to take into account the new conditions.

There is very little difference between meeting AEO criteria and being an authorised AEO, apart from those areas where authorisation is a specific requirement. The main difference is that in most instances only some of the AEO criteria have to be met (perhaps only 2 or 3 of the basic conditions) and therefore you might not wish to go through the whole authorisation process.

In most cases, holding an AEO authorisation will make the authorisation process easier. For example, if the trader is an authorised AEO who wishes to expand their business to include, for example, Customs Warehousing, their AEO status would not automatically qualify them for a Customs warehouse authorisation. Some additional checks would have to be carried out concerning their new venture, but Customs would not repeat tests previously carried out.

As part of the ongoing relationship between AEOs and Customs, HMRC will work with the trader whenever possible to ensure the new criteria can be met. The EU Commission has indicated that there is likely to be a transitional period to allow current AEO businesses time to meet the new criteria, but that has yet to be agreed.

Authorised Traders

Definition/Scope

Authorised traders are defined, according to Transitional Standard 3.32 of the Revised Kyoto Convention (RKC), as persons (natural and legal) who meet criteria specified by Customs, including having an appropriate record of compliance with Customs requirements and a satisfactory system for managing their commercial records. The status of "authorised trader" provides access to simplified procedures, where Customs reduces the level of controls and relies more on internal controls applied by the trader to ensure compliance with all relevant laws and regulations.

It is important to differentiate between Authorised Traders as defined in the Revised Kyoto Convention and the Authorised Economic Operator as defined by the WCO SAFE Framework of Standards. The focus with Authorised Traders is on trade compliance, while AEOs also have to comply with a range of (mostly physical) security standards as laid out in the WCO SAFE Framework of Standards to ensure Supply Chain security. AEOs receive additional benefits from their voluntary participation in an AEO programme, such as reduced physical inspections, lower risk-scoring and participation in mutual recognition programmes. However, in order to obtain access to simplified procedures, traders do not have to become an AEO; it is sufficient to comply with the requirements laid down for Authorised Traders. Customs can combine both programmes to ensure consistency and clarity. For example, the AEO programme of the European Union consists of distinct AEO statuses: "AEO – Simplification" (corresponding to an "authorised trader" and providing access to simplified procedures) and "AEO – Simplification and Security" (in addition to simplified procedures, providing better risk-scoring, lower inspection rates and participation, for example, in the mutual recognition programme of the EU with the US).

If traders who regularly import or export cargo and who have a good compliance record and bookkeeping system in place are treated in the same manner as traders who do not comply, they are penalised rather than rewarded for their compliance and corporate citizenship behaviour. This has a negative impact on the cost of trading as well as on the cost of administration, as Customs allocates too many resources to low-risk traders. Instead, such low-risk traders should be offered special and simplified treatment as incentives for compliance.

Authorised trader programmes require a supporting environment that defines the conditions under which a company can qualify for authorised trader status and the privileges that are granted by the Customs administration. One such pre-condition is the existence and proper application of accounting standards (e.g. based on the International Financial Reporting Standards (IFRS) as adopted by the International Accounting Standards Board) based on which companies keep their records. In following such accounting standards, Customs will be in a position to introduce audit-based controls that are essential for any authorised trader programme. Customs will also require a risk management programme to be in place based on which the trustworthiness of traders can be weighted and a specific risk-scoring assigned. This risk-scoring will assist in selectivity, for example, at import and for audit-based controls. Depending on the degree and maturity of implementation of accounting standards and audit-based controls, authorised trader regimes as defined in Transitional Standard (TS) 3.32 of the Revised Kyoto Convention can relate to:

- The release of goods with the provision of minimum information;
- Clearance of goods at the declarant's premises;
- Periodic declarations;
- Trader self-assessment;
- Local clearance.

These simplified procedures are explained in greater detail in the Guidelines to TS 3.32 of the Revised Kyoto Convention.

ISO 28000/28001

Part of the AEO process includes the ability of the trader to satisfy the requirements of the ISO 28000/28001 set of benchmarks covering the Supply Chain and the audit trail within it. The International Standards Organisation (ISO) published the ISO 28000 Specifications for Security Management Systems for the Supply Chain standard in 2007. This standard specifies the requirements for a Supply Chain security management system, linking security management to many other aspects of business management. These include all activities controlled or influenced by organisations that impact on Supply Chain security, including the transportation of goods along the Supply Chain. It uses a PDCA model and risk assessment to determine the corresponding control measures, resource provisions and training needs of the organisation concerned.

PDCA (plan–do–check–act or plan–do–check–adjust) is an iterative 4-step management method used in business for the control and continuous improvement of processes and products. It is also known as the Deming circle/cycle/wheel.

The cyclical structure is:

Plan

Establish the objectives and processes necessary to deliver results in accordance with the expected output (the target or goals). By establishing output expectations, the completeness and accuracy of the specification is also a part of the targeted improvement. When possible start on a small scale to test possible effects.

Do

Implement the plan, execute the process, make the product. Collect data for charting and analysis in the following "Check" and "Act" steps.

Check

Study the actual results (measured and collected in "Do" above) and compare against the expected results (targets or goals from the "Plan") to ascertain any differences. Look for deviation in implementation from the plan and also look for the appropriateness and completeness of the plan to enable the execution, i.e. "Do". Charting data can make this much easier to see trends over several PDCA cycles and in order to convert the collected data into information. Information is what you need for the next step "Act".

Act

If the Check shows that the Plan that was implemented in Do is an improvement to the prior standard (baseline), then that becomes the new standard (baseline) for how the organisation should Act going forward (new standards are en*act*ed). If the Check shows that the Plan that was implemented in Do is not an improvement, then the existing standard (baseline) will remain in place. In either case, if the Check showed something different than expected (whether better or worse), then there is some more learning to be done … and that will suggest potential future PDCA cycles. Note that some who teach PDCA assert that the ACT involves making adjustments or corrective actions … but generally it would be counter to PDCA thinking to propose and decide upon alternative changes without using a proper Plan phase, or to make them the new standard (baseline) without going through Do and Check steps.

In this respect, the PDCA structure functions in a similar manner to the DMAIC principle of Six Sigma or the Continuous Improvement cycle.

ISO 28000 brings big benefits to companies of all sizes. By allowing the trader to respond to the increasing customer demands for proof of systematic security management, an ISO 28000-compliant management system can improve the trader's business confidence, reputation and future growth. It also helps the trader:

- Facilitate trade and expedite the transport of goods across borders;
- Monitor and manage security risks throughout your business and Supply Chain;
- Gain a competitive advantage and win new business;
- Encourage companies to secure their own processes within Supply Chains;
- Reassure stakeholders of the organisation's commitment to the safety of individuals and the security of goods and services;
- Allows management to focus finite resources in areas of greatest concern;
- Benchmarks the organisation's security management practices with international best practice;
- Achieve cost savings through a reduction in security incidents and a potential reduction in corporate insurance premiums;
- Gain opportunities to improve efficiency across working practices.

Adopting the ISO 28000 has broad strategic, organisational and operational benefits that are realised throughout Supply Chains and business practices.

Benefits include but are not limited to:

- Integrated enterprise resilience;
- Systematised management practices;
- Enhanced credibility and brand recognition;
- Aligned terminology and conceptual usage;
- Improved Supply Chain performance;
- Benchmarking against internationally recognisable criteria;
- Greater compliance processes.

Organisations that choose third-party certification can further demonstrate that they are contributing significantly to Supply Chain security.

ISO 28000:2007 was developed to codify operations of security within the broader Supply Chain management system, such that organisations of varying scale could apply the standard to Supply Chains of various degrees of complexity.

The general rationale for organisations to adopt ISO 28000:2007 pertains to:

- Developing a security management system;
- Internal compliance with the objectives of a security management policy;
- External compliance with best-practice benchmarks;
- ISO accreditation.

ISO 28000:2007, which is a certifiable standard as part of the ISO regime, specifies the requirements for a security management system, including those aspects critical to the security assurance of the Supply Chain. Security management is linked to many other aspects of business management. Aspects include all activities controlled or influenced by organisations that impact on Supply Chain security. These other aspects should be considered directly, where and when they have an impact on security management, including transporting these goods along the Supply Chain.

ISO 28000:2007 is applicable to all sizes of organisations, from small to multinational, in manufacturing, service, storage or transportation at any stage of the production or Supply Chain that wishes to:

a) Establish, implement, maintain and improve a security management system;
b) Assure conformance with the stated security management policy;
c) Demonstrate such conformance to others;
d) Seek certification/registration of its security management system by an Accredited Third Party Certification Body; or
e) Make a self-determination and self-declaration of conformance with ISO 28000:2007.

There are legislative and regulatory codes that address some of the requirements in ISO 28000:2007.

It is not the intention of ISO 28000:2007 to require duplicative demonstration of conformance. The following is the basic text of ISO 28001:2007 derived from the ISO website at www.iso.org.

ISO 28001:2007 – Security Management Systems for the Supply Chain

Best practices for implementing Supply Chain security, assessments and plans. Requirements and guidance

BS ISO 28001 is the standard that provides requirements and guidance for organisations in international Supply Chains to:

- Develop and implement Supply Chain security processes;
- Establish and document a minimum level of security within a Supply Chain(s) or segment of a Supply Chain;
- Assist in meeting the applicable Authorised Economic Operator criteria set forth in the World Customs Organization Framework of Standards and conforming national Supply Chain security programmes.

Only a participating National Customs Agency can designate organisations as AEOs in accordance with its Supply Chain security programme and its attendant certification and validation requirements.

In addition, BS ISO28001 establishes certain documentation requirements that would permit verification. BS ISO28001 can be used to:

- Define the portion of an international Supply Chain within which they have established security;
- Conduct security assessments on that portion of the Supply Chain and develop adequate countermeasures;
- Develop and implement a Supply Chain security plan;
- Train security personnel in their security-related duties.

Security incidents against international Supply Chains are threats to international trade and the economic growth of trading nations. People, goods, infrastructure and equipment, including means of transport, need to be protected against security incidents and their potentially devastating effects. Such protection benefits the economy and society as a whole.

International Supply Chains are highly dynamic and consist of many entities and business partners. ISO 28001 has been designed to recognise this complexity. It has therefore been developed to allow an individual organisation in the Supply Chain to apply its requirements in conformance with the organisation's particular business model and its role and function in the international Supply Chain.

ISO 28001 provides an option for organisations to establish and document reasonable levels of security within international Supply Chains and their components. It will enable such organisations to make better risk-based decisions concerning security in those international Supply Chains.

ISO 28001 is multimodal and is intended to be in concert with and to complement the World Customs Organisation's Framework of Standards to secure and facilitate global trade (Framework). It does not attempt to cover, replace or supersede individual Customs agencies' Supply Chain security programmes and their certification and validation requirements.

Organisations can implement BS ISO 28001 in order to establish adequate levels of security within the parts of the international Supply Chain that it controls. It is also a basis for determining or validating the level of existing security within an organisation's Supply Chain by internal or external auditors or by those government agencies that choose to use compliance with BS ISO 28001 as the baseline for acceptance into their Supply Chain security programmes.

Customers, business partners, government agencies and others might request organisations that claim compliance with BS ISO 28001 to undergo an audit or validation to confirm such compliance. Government agencies might find it mutually agreeable to accept validations conducted by other government agencies. If a third-party organisation audit is to be conducted, then the organisation needs to consider employing a third-party certification body accredited by a competent body, which is a member of the International Accreditation Forum.

ISO 28001 is not intended to duplicate governmental requirements and standards regarding Supply Chain security in compliance with the WCO SAFE Framework. Organisations that have already been certified or validated by mutually recognising governments are compliant with ISO 28001.

Outputs Resulting from ISO 28001

- A statement of coverage defines the boundaries of the Supply Chain that are covered by the security plan;
- A security assessment that documents the vulnerabilities of the Supply Chain to defined security threat scenarios. It also describes the impacts that can reasonably be expected from each of the potential security threat scenarios;
- A security plan that describes security measures in place to manage the security threat scenarios identified by the Security assessment;
- A training programme setting out how security personnel will be trained to meet their assigned security-related duties.

To undertake the security assessment needed to produce the security plan, an organisation using ISO 28001 will be able to:

- Identify the threats posed (security threat scenarios);
- Determine how likely persons could progress each of the security threat scenarios identified by the security assessment into a security incident.

This determination is made by reviewing the current state of security in the Supply Chain. Based on the findings of that review, professional judgement is used to identify how vulnerable the Supply Chain is to each security threat scenario.

If the Supply Chain is considered unacceptably vulnerable to a security threat scenario, the organisation will develop additional procedures or operational changes to lower the likelihood, consequence or both. These are called countermeasures. Based on a system of priorities, countermeasures need to be incorporated into the security plan to reduce the threat to an acceptable level.

ISO 28001 contains illustrative examples of risk management-based security processes for protecting people, assets and international Supply Chain missions. They facilitate both a macro approach for complex Supply Chains and/or more discrete approaches for some aspects:

These examples are also intended to:

- Facilitate the understanding, adoption and implementation of methodologies, which can be customised by organizations;
- Provide guidance for baseline security management for continual improvement;
- Assist organisations in managing resources to address existing and emerging security risks;
- Describe possible means for assessment of risk and mitigation of security threats in the Supply Chain from raw material allocation through storage, manufacturing and transportation of finished goods to the marketplace.

ISO 28001 also contains guidance for obtaining advice and certification for BS ISO 28001 if an organisation using it chooses to exercise this option.

ISO 28001:2007 provides requirements and guidance for organisations in international Supply Chains to carry out the following measures:

- Develop and implement Supply Chain security processes;
- Establish and document a minimum level of security within a Supply Chain(s) or segment of a Supply Chain;
- Assist in meeting the applicable Authorised Economic Operator (AEO) criteria set forth in the World Customs Organization Framework of Standards and conforming national Supply Chain security programmes.

In addition, ISO 28001:2007 establishes certain documentation requirements that would permit verification.

Users of ISO 28001:2007 will be able to:

- Define the portion of an international Supply Chain within which they have established security;
- Conduct security assessments on that portion of the Supply Chain and develop adequate countermeasures;
- Develop and implement a Supply Chain security plan;
- Train security personnel in their security-related duties.

Because of the above measures and the fact that ISO 28001 includes the condition of AEO status, any AEO authorisation holder is automatically eligible for ISO 28001 status under the provisions of ISO 28001:2007.

CHAPTER 15

Cargo Pre-Clearance

In an age of increased risk awareness and management, especially concerning Customs issues and an increasing reliance on trader awareness and self-assessment, the principle of cargo pre-clearance has become somewhat of a necessity. The idea of simply submitting an Export Declaration and shipping the cargo is no longer an option. In an era of increased security and vigilance, where it has become far easier for terrorists or political extremists to dispatch potential weapons by various means of transport, including unmanned drones, as seen in the Middle East, there is a far greater need to control movements of goods by sea, air or land. The aviation sector has had a cargo screening system in place for some years, implemented and controlled by way of the various aviation Conventions and UNCTAD, but maritime freight has been for some time been left behind; until recently, that is. The tragedies of 9/11 concentrated the minds of many in the areas of international Customs, and part of the SAFE Framework of Standards was to create a regime where sea cargo could not simply be declared at the point of export and shipped, but would need to be screened by the Customs computer of destination and pre-cleared prior to being loaded aboard vessel. The C-TPAT (Customs–Trade Partnership Against Terrorism) initiatives of the US and Canada post-9/11 initiated the process, and these were soon followed by a series of pre-shipment Customs clearance initiatives, commonly referred to as Advance Cargo Information (ACI) or Advance Manifest System (AMS) reporting systems, based on prior submission of cargo manifests scheduled to be loaded aboard a vessel to the Customs computer of destination at least 24 hours prior to loading the vessel, otherwise known as the 24-hour rule. This would enable the Customs computer at destination to examine the manifest and make 1 of 2 decisions: either clear the cargo for loading by way of a Movement Reference Number (MRN) or refuse loading permission in the form of a DNL (Do Not Load) message, based on perceived risks, including trader risk, country risk or cargo risk, especially where the cargo was not properly described. Presently, several countries use this system as a means of international cargo security, including the following:

DOI: 10.4324/9781003341345-16

- US;
- Canada;
- Mexico;
- EU;
- Turkey;
- Israel;
- Ivory Coast;
- Madagascar;
- South Korea;
- Philippines;
- China;
- Japan.

Others, including the UAE, are soon to follow.

The whole purpose of this initiative is to prevent high-risk cargoes from being loaded aboard the vessel for shipment to the target country. Part of the structure as provided by Customs law in the country concerned forbids the use of phrases such as "Freight of All Kinds" (FAK) or "Said to Contain" and requires an exact description of the cargo in question and its Harmonised System (HS) Commodity Code to be entered on the cargo manifest at the point of generation of the manifest. Failure to do so by the shipping agent will automatically result in the rejection of the cargo manifest by the Customs computer and the message DNL being issued.

The following is an example of a typical ACI system in operation, namely that of the EU.

Advance Cargo Reporting: ENS and EXS

In order to improve the safety and security of its Member States, the European Union (EU) introduced in 2010 a mandatory advance notification requirement regarding the import, export and transit of goods, in addition to existing EU Customs regulations. The new requirements, which entered into force on 1 January 2011, have been laid down in various EU Commission Regulations known as "*The Security Amendment to the Community Customs Code*", in particular EU Regulation No. **1875/2006**. They apply to all sectors of the shipping industry, and are in principle similar to the AMS reporting system required by the US and Canada as a result of the C-TPAT (Customs and Trade Partnership Against Terrorism) initiative launched in the wake of the 9/11 tragedy.

For goods which are being imported, cargo information in the form of an Entry Summary Declaration (ENS) must be submitted in advance to the Customs office at the first port of entry into the EU. For goods which are being exported, cargo information is also to be submitted in advance either in the form of a Customs Declaration for Export, Re-export or Outward Processing, or if such a declaration does not apply, then in the form of an Exit Summary Declaration (EXS). The time limits for submission of the required information differ depending on the cargo being carried and the nature of the trade. For deep sea containerised shipments, e.g. from the Americas or Asia to the EU, the ENS must be lodged at least 24 hours prior to commencement of loading in each non-EU load port.

As long as traders can show they have followed certain criteria, including their ability to demonstrate a transparent Supply Chain audit trail in terms of documentation and procedures, the individual Customs administrations may waive the need for an ENS, provided that:

- They have access to all the necessary electronic information in the trader's records;
- They are able to carry out full risk analysis for safety and security purposes.

Operators which are based in the EU or have regional offices in the EU can apply for Authorised Economic Operator (AEO) status. Traders are encouraged to apply for AEO-c (Customs Procedures) status, whilst Freight Forwarders and Customs Brokers are encouraged to apply for AEO-s (Safety and Security) status. The benefit to the operator of being awarded AEO status is a reduction in the amount of cargo information that needs to be submitted to Customs at the initial stage of reporting, although more details are generally submitted later to Customs in the form of monthly reports. This status is essentially governed by the ability of the trader to satisfy Supply Chain security and transparency requirements, especially with regard to Customs and logistics compliance issues. Given that the AEO facility is a global initiative, it is becoming essential for streamlined trade facilitation in line with the initiatives of the SAFE Framework of Standards, and indeed will eventually become the key element in ensuring global cargo security and simplified Customs procedures, especially where Advance Cargo Reporting is concerned.

In each non-EU load port, the transmission must be carried out no later than 24 hours prior to start of loading to the vessel bound for an EU port. To comply with this regulation, the shipping line will require complete and correct shipping instructions. The documentation closing times will follow the same timelines as other "advance manifest" 24-Hour Rule locations such as the US, Canada or Mexico, and they are stipulated in the marine carrier's booking confirmation.

Transmission of ENS is obligatory for all cargo discharged in an EU port (including trans-shipment cargo) as well as FROB cargo (Foreign Cargo Remaining on Board), i.e. cargo which is discharged in a port outside the EU after the vessel has called an EU port.

In many cases, the advance notification which is issued at the Port of Loading needs to be given by the ship operator, carrier or his representative, such as the ship's agent. At present there is no distinction within the regulations as to whether, in the case of a chartered vessel, the charterer or the owner is considered to be the operator/carrier for the purposes of submission of the required declarations. However, it is expected that the charterer will be defined as the operator/carrier under a time charter, and the owner will be the operator/carrier under a voyage charter party. In containerised shipping, a freight forwarder, or Non Vessel Operating Common Carrier (NVOCC), will normally issue the advance notice, although this can also be carried out by the shipping agency at the Port of Loading. However, in the case of submission by a freight forwarder or NVOCC, this submission can only be carried out with the ship operator's full knowledge and consent. In the case of combined transport operations where trucks are driven on to a RO/RO ferry, it is the duty of the haulage company, its representative or the truck driver, to submit the advance notification prior to arrival at the Port of Loading. With regard to vessel-sharing arrangements such as slot carrier agreements in the container trade, the declaration is to be issued by the carrier issuing the Bill of Lading rather than the ship operator.

If the information is submitted by a nominated third party, such as an Agent or Freight Forwarder, the ship operator will still be held responsible if notice is not delivered in advance or on time, and this delay may result in a penalty being imposed. However, the third party will still be liable for the accuracy of the information provided. Regardless of who provides the advance cargo declaration, the responsible party must also provide their **Economic Operator Registration and Identification Number** (EORI), which is essentially the trader's VAT Number plus an additional set of digits, in the case of the UK "000". For example, if a UK-based trader's VAT Number is 123 4567 89, their EORI will be 123456789000. The use of an EORI has been mandatory within the EU since 1 July 2009. Once advance notice had been submitted, a confirmation will be issued containing a unique 18-digit number called a **Movement Reference Number** (MRN), used hitherto for Community Transit movements. The entire system is electronic, and therefore the person giving notice to Customs requires a computer system which can interface with the national Customs system. However, at the present time there is no system that is common throughout the EU capable of handling the new declarations, and for the present each Member State retains its own national system.

An exemption from the requirement to submit declarations for cargo being imported or exported may be granted for vessels trading purely between ports of EU Member States if certain specific criteria are met. Further exemptions exist for goods that remain on board a vessel whilst in the EU which are destined for a port outside the EU, and these do not need to be declared for export, even when loaded at a previous EU port. In addition, a vessel departing the EU and then calling at a foreign port before returning to the EU is not required to submit export documentation prior to departing from the first EU port. However, the cargo must be declared in an ENS before the vessel returns to the EU.

The information submitted in the various declarations is used by Customs to conduct a risk assessment of the cargo from a viewpoint of security and safety. As a result of this assessment, the cargo will then be classed as either risk type A, B or C, which in turn determines how the Customs Authority will respond. For example, if the Customs office identifies a serious safety and security risk in relation to cargo to be loaded onto a deep sea container ship and classifies it as risk type A, it will issue a "Do Not Load" or "Customs Hold" message preventing the carrier from shipping the cargo. DNL is the message returned by the EU Customs office of first entry in receipt of the ENS in the place of an MRN. It means that analysis has been carried out on the declaration and that an unacceptable risk exists concerning the goods covered by the ENS declaration. This risk level may be further compounded by a lack of information entered on the cargo manifest with relation to details of the cargo. In the same way that the US and Canada outlawed the terms FAK (Freight of All Kinds) and "Said to Contain …", the ENS system allows for a similar level of controls applied to scrutiny of the Entry Declaration, hence the risk assessment carried out by the relevant EU Customs Authority on each declaration.

The shipper is therefore required to submit an accurate and detailed set of shipping instructions to the carrier or their agent in order to facilitate an Entry Summary Declaration. The required data elements for the Entry Summary Declaration are:

- Full name and address of shipper and consignee;
- Full name and address of notify party where goods are carried under a negotiable "to order" B/L;
- Container number;
- Acceptable goods description (general terms for example "consolidated cargo", "general cargo", "Freight All Kinds", "Said to Contain", cannot be accepted);
- Minimally, the first 4 digits of the HS Commodity Code, although the 6-digit HS Code is recommended;
- Marks and Numbers of packages;
- Cargo gross weight (in kilograms);

- Seal number;
- UN Dangerous Goods Code and IMDG Classification Code, where applicable;
- Method of payment for transport charges in case of "Freight Prepaid" (CFR, CIF, CPT, CIP), for example payment in cash, payment by cheque, electronic credit transfer, etc.

The ENS will be sent to the Customs office of the first port of entry (first port of call) in the EU, and this Customs office will carry out a security risk assessment.

In the event that a risk is identified, subsequent ports of arrival and ports of loading will be informed:

- Risk Type A = Do Not Load;
- Risk Type B = Interception of a suspicious shipment at the first port of entry;
- Risk Type C = Interception of a suspicious shipment at the port of discharge.

For **short sea** container traffic, e.g. Russia to the EU, apart from the following variations, the same information and procedures apply as above.

For short sea movements, in each non-EU load port, the transmission of the ENS Declaration must be carried out no later than 2 hours before arrival at the first port of entry in the EU.

Under such circumstances, there are only the following 2 risk types:

- Risk Type B = Interception of a suspicious shipment at the first port of entry;
- Risk Type C = Interception of a suspicious shipment at the port of discharge.

In this case, information about the ultimate shipper/consignee is not required in an ENS. If, however, an independent freight forwarder wants to file the ENS himself, i.e. instead of the ocean carrier, he will still require the consent of the ocean carrier to do so. Only in cases where the appointed agent of the ocean carrier, or the agency division of the ocean carrier, files the ENS will prior consent from the ocean carrier not be required.

In addition to submitting an ENS, an operator must also advise the national Customs Authority of a vessel's arrival by the submission of an Arrival Notification (AN) by a means acceptable to the Customs office in that particular Member State. The AN may comprise of a list of MRNs relating to the vessel, or what is termed an "Entry Key", which consists of information about the vessel and the cargo (e.g. mode of transport, the vessel's IMO number, expected date of arrival).

There are certain drawbacks with the new Entry Declaration system. First, each national Customs Authority in the EU still retains its own national control system, which, as explained earlier, may not be compatible with those of other national Customs Authorities within the EU. This implies that information submitted in the form of an ENS to 1 Customs Authority cannot necessarily be transmitted to other Customs Authorities, especially in the case of the diversion of a vessel from 1 EU port to another port in another EU Member State, owing to a perceived lack of compatibility in systems used by each authority.

Second, the information provided for each cargo as contained within the ENS is only transmitted to the Customs Authority and not to any other national organisation. This means that any information deemed as being sensitive or prejudicial to national security may not necessarily be passed to other security authorities, such as other government departments, e.g. Defence or Interior. In this sense, the effectiveness of such information may be reduced, as it cannot be disseminated amongst the parties which ultimately may still have an interest in it, and thus leading to the risk of prejudicing national security interests.

Other examples are as follows, namely Israel, Turkey and China.

Israel 24-Hour Advanced Manifest Regulation

CRI (Cargo Report Import) is a regulation within the scope of the Israeli **SAFE via conex** system and concerns the Israeli advance security declaration. **SAFE via conex** also enables the management of advance security declarations for Japan (AFR Advanced Filing Rule) and ICS (Import Control System)-related messages for a large number of the 28 EU Member States.

The CRI (Cargo Report Import) is the electronic security declaration management system for the arrival of goods into the Israeli Customs territory. CRI follows on from the SAFE Framework of Standards for international trade advocated by the World Customs Organisation and ensures the protection of the movement of goods arriving in Israel.

This new regulation requires that a certain number of data elements be sent to Israeli Customs before the goods are introduced into the Israeli Customs territory. Based on this data, a risk analysis will be performed and Japan Customs will respond either with an approval or a refusal to load, eventually requesting further details.

SAFE via conex CRI enables operators to communicate with the Israeli administration and respects the World Customs Organisation's "WCO Data Model" along with other international standards such as UN/CEFACT and ISO.

For **maritime** transport, it is necessary to send a "sea" version of the electronic CRI message, regardless of whether the goods are unloaded in Israel or not.

For **air** transport, there are 2 messages:

The first is systematically a "MASTER" accompanied by either:

- A "DIRECT" message for a House Air Waybill drawn up by an air carrier;
- A "HOUSE" message for a House Air Waybill drawn up by an NVACC;
- A "FROB" message if the declaration concerns goods not unloaded in Israel.

There are 3 kinds of electronic messages returned by Customs:

- Accepted;
- Accepted but with errors (it is then necessary to correct the errors);
- Errors and rejected.

The time-frame for submitting CRI Cargo Report Import advance security declarations depends on the mode of transport:

- Air Cargo – Long Haul: At least 4 hours prior to arrival;
- Air Cargo – Short Haul: At least by the time of the actual take off of the aircraft;
- Maritime: 24 hours prior to loading.

How to Make a Declaration with SAFE via Conex CRI

The agent transmits their XML files containing all the required data to our communication platform.

SAFE via conex CRI then takes care of the **secure transmission** of the data to Israeli Customs **in compliance with the regulation** and the technical specifications in force.

SAFE via conex CRI covers **all the CRI electronic messages** between operators and the Israeli Customs administration.

Israel Customs has announced a new rule in the 24-hour Advanced Manifest Regulation. The new rule requires all ocean carriers to submit a list of Customs-defined manifest data to the Israel Customs at least 24 hours prior to cargo loading at Port of Loading and will affect the ABX service (with direct calls to Israel) and EUM service (with Public Feeders to various ports which may include calls to Israel). The rule ONLY applies to all FROB

(Freight Remain On Board) Cargo (cargo that will remain onboard the vessel when calling an Israel port).

Note: Israel import and trans-shipments through Israel ports are NOT within the scope of this new regulation.

Based on the information provided, the following details are also highlighted:

- The new rule came into effect on 9 September 2013. There was a pilot run period from 1 July to 8 September;
- Submission is on the Master B/L level only. There is no Self Filer process involved;
- To Order B/L is Acceptable;
- Split B/L is acceptable, but penalties may be applied to any amendments made to the B/L after Customs submission. The details on the penalties have yet to be published by the Israel Customs.

To comply with this regulation, customers must provide complete and accurate shipping instructions before the closing time found posted on the shipping line's website and in their Booking Acknowledgements/Confirmations document.

The charges for advance manifest filing and amendment came into effective on 17 November 2013:

Description	*Charge Amount*
Advance Manifest Filing Charge	US$25 per B/L
Advance Manifest Amendment Charge	US$40 per B/L

Turkey Customs 24-hour Advanced Manifest Regulation

Turkish Customs announced a new 24-hour Advanced Manifest Regulation to take effect on 1 January 2012. The rule requires all ocean carriers to submit a list of Customs-defined manifest data to Turkey Customs at least 24 hours prior to cargo loading at Port of Load. The regulation is applicable to all import and transshipped cargo to/via Turkey.

With the information provided for maritime shipments, we would like to highlight the following details regarding the implementation of the summary declaration submissions:

- New applications will be effective from 1 January 2012. All Entry Summary Declaration and summary declarations shall be lodged electronically with the Turkish Customs;
- Mediterranean and Black Sea ports will be evaluated as Short Sea, and the deadline for summary declaration submission is at least 2 hours before arrival at the first port in Turkish Customs territory;
- Other ports other than the Mediterranean and Black Sea ones, will be evaluated as Deep Sea, and the deadline for Entry Summary Declaration is at least 24 hours before commencement of loading in each foreign load port(s);
- Empty containers must be placed in Entry Summary Declaration and summary declarations;
- Description of goods must be submitted with 6-digit harmonised codes;
- Trans-shipments via Turkey are subject to summary declarations;
- Consignee tax number is required.

To comply with this regulation, shipping lines shipping goods to Turkey request their customers to provide complete and accurate shipping instructions before the closing time, which is similar to what is currently in place for other advance manifest procedures required for EU countries. This information is published on the shipping line's website and also available in the line's Booking Acknowledgements/Confirmations document.

China 24-Hour Advance Manifest Regulation Update – Shanghai

Further to our previous customer advisories issued on China's 24-hour advance manifest regulation, we would like to update the latest announcement from Shanghai Customs who advised the advance manifest submission will be mandatory for all China import cargoes that are discharged or transshipped at Shanghai port with effect from 3 June 2014, thereafter Do Not Load and Do Not Unload messages may be issued at the discretion of Customs.

To comply with the regulation, OOCL will submit the advance manifest for all applicable shipments at least 24 hours before loading onto the vessel bound for Shanghai from 3 June 2014 onwards.

Hence, OOCL respectfully request our customers to provide complete and accurate shipping instructions before the documentation cutoff time in each loading region. This information will be published on our website and also available in our Booking Acknowledgements/Confirmations document.

1. Voyage Number;
2. Vessel Name;

3. Bill of Lading Number;
4. Port of Loading;
5. Payment Method For Ocean Freight (Prepaid or Collect);
6. Total Number of Packages;
7. Type of Packages;
8. Total Gross Weight of Cargo Including Packaging But Excluding Container Tare Weight;
9. Name of Consignee;
10. Complete Street Address Or P.O. Box Number Of Consignee;
11. Name Of Shipper;
12. Complete Street Address Or P.O. Box Number Of Shipper;
13. Name of Notify Party (This is mandatory if consignee is "To Order".);
14. Complete Street Address or P.O. Box Number of Notify Party (This is mandatory if consignee is "To Order".);
15. Name of Contact Person for Dangerous Cargo (This is mandatory when such a commodity is being shipped.);
16. Contact Number of Contact Person for Dangerous Cargo (This is mandatory when such a commodity is being shipped.);
17. Container Number;
18. Container Size and Type;
19. Seal Numbers For All Seals Affixed to Containers;
20. Type of Packages Per Commodity Item;
21. Number of Packages Per Commodity Item;
22. Cargo Description;
23. Gross Weight Per Commodity Item;
24. UNDG Number for Dangerous Cargo (This is mandatory when such a commodity is being shipped.);
25. Marks and Numbers.

CHAPTER 16

Trader Awareness

In an era of heightened Supply Chain security, it is inevitable that Customs and VAT rules and procedures require a greater degree of stringency and control. This has been reinforced in many ways by an inability of many traders to correctly use several of the Duty Relief mechanisms, owing to a combination of lack of knowledge and a failure to use the correct INCOTERMS, couples with a breakdown in the Supply Chain audit trail.

The concept and principle of multimodalism has in many ways contributed to this challenge. The principle of multimodalism enables a container to be loaded at the premises of the shipper, transported to the port of loading and loaded aboard vessel, shipped across the ocean to the port of destination, unloaded from the vessel and transported directly to the importer with hardly any controls along the way. The concept can also be used for the carriage of consignments by air, and using road transport to carry the consignment to the local or regional airport for loading aboard aircraft, and collecting the consignment from the aircraft at the airport of destination. The resulting movement is a direct door-to-door shipment, and the International Terms of Delivery (INCOTERMs) have been amended over the years to allow for and facilitate such movements. International controls, including Customs checks, have been kept to a minimum, and in reality the trader, be it the exporter or importer, has been given the task of self-regulation when it comes to monitoring and controlling such movements, with the reliance for accurate Export and Import Declarations placed on the shipper and the recipient by the Customs authorities. At one time, there was a significant presence of Customs Officers at all seaports, and their job was to monitor and control the movement of all import and export cargoes through the ports. Today, this presence has been removed, to the extent that in the UK, with the merger of HM Customs and Excise with HM Inland Revenue in 2004 to form HM Revenue and Customs (HMRC), the border element of the Customs function was removed from HM Revenue and Customs and was transferred to the Home Office as part of the new UK Border Agency. However, the overall remit of the UK Border Agency is to act on behalf of HMRC at the frontiers and, given the limited number of personnel involved owing to the emphasis on electronic controls

 DOI: 10.4324/9781003341345-17

and measures, there is rarely a presence by UK Border Agency personnel at ports with regard to the inward and outward movement of cargos. To this extent, any checks on port activities are generally conducted on an *ad hoc* basis based on random checks or intelligence reports, while HMRC concentrates on inland Customs issues directly concerning import/export traders.

Roles and Responsibilities of the Importer and Exporter

The importer or exporter is responsible for all transactions made in the course of its business, be they national or international. In an era of cost-cutting, downsizing and outsourcing, many corporate responsibilities have been devolved to outside contractors, especially in the logistics and transport sector, leaving only the absolute basic or essential responsibilities within the company itself. Such responsibilities include sales and accounts functions, as well as manufacturing functions wherever appropriate. Export functions are split between the sales function and the accounts function depending on whether the matter concerns obtaining an export order or securing payment. The import function, if it ever exists, is split between the purchasing section and the accounts payable section, which in reality often belong to the same overall accounts function. This is where such corporate responsibility ends. All other functions, including that of logistics, are devolved to outside contractors such as freight agents. It is also often the case that the company concerned has little or no idea whatsoever about the actual role of the freight agent and assumes that it can simply pass the whole logistics process over to the agent without any reason for communication other than to pay the bill from the agent when it arrives.

Such reliance on other parties is, to say the least, extremely short-sighted. The actual responsibility for importing or exporting placed on the importer or exporter is, in reality, very substantial, and cannot be taken lightly. For the purposes of Customs clearance in either importing or exporting, the freight agent acts on behalf of the importer or exporter and cannot be held directly responsible for the actions of either party. The freight agent acts on the express instructions of the importer or exporter and ships or clears the consignment accordingly. It is often the case that what appeared to be lucrative deals between buyer and seller have become nightmares because the seller did not properly negotiate the deal based on common internationally accepted terms of delivery, otherwise known as INCOTERMS. Freight and duty costs were not taken into account, and the resulting burden had to be borne by the seller, thus completely eliminating any profit that might have been gained. Thus an exporter cannot simply tell a freight agent to ship a consignment without ensuring that both parties, i.e. the exporter or importer, are aware of who takes responsibility for the shipment and who will pay the freight charges. As a result, the importer is liable for all Import Duty and Tax Payments whether or not they take responsibility for the shipment of the consignment. In this respect, the common opt-out for the exporter is to use the INCOTERM "EX WORKS", which implies that the importer will take complete control over the whole shipping process. If, however, the exporter is proficient in the exporting process, then a variety of terms become applicable, from FOB (Free on Board named port of shipment) through CIF (Cost Insurance Freight named port of unloading or arrival) to DPU (Delivered at Place Unloaded) direct to the importer's premises. Given the complexity of these terms and the different implications they hold, the exact term of delivery to be used must be included in the transaction at the time of negotiation. The term EXW implies the exporter does nothing more than make the consignment ready for shipment, whereas the term DPU implies that the exporter arranges everything related to the shipment of the consignment up to the point of delivery to the customer's premises, with the customer doing no more than paying Import Duty and any other associated taxes. All other terms fall between these 2 with respect to responsibility for shipment, payment of freight costs and acceptance of the risk of shipment.

However, the logistics element is only part of the international transaction equation. There remains the question of tax liability on the part of the importer and exporter alike. An exporter does not pay taxes to export goods from the UK but must prove to HM Customs and Excise that the consignment has indeed been exported. In the case of goods consumed in the UK, VAT is liable on such sales. In the case of goods exported to the rest of the European Union, VAT is zero-rated since the consignment will become liable for VAT upon importation into another member state at the VAT rate of that member state. In the case of goods exported to a non-EU country, VAT is exempt on the exported consignment, since the importing country may not have a VAT regime or equivalent. Whichever the export destination, the exporting company must obtain a Certificate of Shipment to prove that the consignment was exported. If this cannot be produced, HM Customs and Excise can take the view that there is no evidence that the consignment was indeed exported, and can thus charge the company VAT on that consignment. The Certificate of Shipment must be obtained from the freight agent, since the agent would clear the consignment through Customs controls and would therefore retain all documentation related to the shipment.

For the importer, the responsibility becomes greater still. All imports from non-EU countries into the UK are liable for the payment of Import Duty to HM Customs and Excise. Import Duty can only be waived on 3 basic conditions:

- Duty-free status as dictated by the Customs Tariff;
- Preferential duty-free status according to preference agreements between the EU and other countries (on production of a valid Certificate of Origin or Movement Certificate);

- Import Duty Relief Authorisation approved by the appropriate Customs Authority.

Unless any one of the above conditions can be satisfied, the import consignment concerned is liable to Import Duty being paid to HM Customs at the time of importation. Although the clearing agent may pay the Import Duty plus VAT at the time the consignment is imported, this will only be done on behalf of the importer and will be charged ultimately to the importer's account. The agent is thus not responsible for the payment of Import Duty and VAT on their own account. Ultimate responsibility for Import Duty and VAT liability lies with the importer. Thus, the importer holds the responsibility for instructing the clearing agent on how to clear the import consignment through Customs controls, and what information is necessary to ensure a declaration fully compliant with Customs procedures. It is often the case, unfortunately, that many importers have little or no idea as to what information is required for the purposes of Customs clearance. Many importers have never seen a Customs Tariff, let alone used 1. They assume that the clearing agent is fully conversant with such information, and that all they need to do is to tell the agent that an import consignment is expected imminently. End of story? Not so. The agent is employed to act on the importer's behalf, and thus requires a considerable amount of information concerning the exact details of the consignment, including its description, value and quantity. It is also preferable that the importer has some basic idea of the Tariff Commodity Code concerned in order to ascertain the exact Import Duty rate to be applied. In many cases, however, the ignorance of the importer in such matters means that the agent has to resort to their own copy of the Customs Tariff to supply such information.

Even assuming that the agent has been furnished with all appropriate information to clear the consignment properly, the importer is still required to obtain copies of all relevant associated import documentation from the clearing agent for their own filing system. If a national Customs Authority sees the need to challenge an import at any stage following the clearance of the consignment in question, they will approach the importer for any appropriate information, not the agent. If the importer cannot produce such information, then the importer is liable for any penalties associated with such matters as determined by the national Customs Authority under any national Customs legislation pertinent to the country concerned. If the importer has total access to such documentation relating to the import in question, then at least there is a better chance that the importer can successfully argue a case with HM Customs should a problem arise. As far as the European Union is concerned, the other main reason for the importer to retain all records relating to an import consignment is that for VAT purposes it is necessary for the importer to maintain adequate records of all import transactions. VAT is paid on all imports other than foodstuffs and other zero-rated or exempt items, and thus it is essential for every importer to maintain copies of all import documentation to prove the validity of each transaction for the purposes of VAT records.

Assumptions, Perceptions and Communications

Each party has its own defined responsibility, and such responsibilities are sanctioned by the legislative process as detailed in the 1979 C&E Management Act. But it is also evident that the act is only known to members of HM Revenue and Customs and is not widely appreciated in the commercial sector, which would undoubtedly explain the multiplicity of problems encountered by the commercial sector when dealing with HM Revenue and Customs. There is an inherent fear on the part of the commercial sector when faced with a problem concerning Revenue and Customs matters, which appears to stem from 5 main sources:

- A lack of knowledge or ignorance of Customs regulations;
- A refusal by the importer or exporter to admit to the existence of a problem;
- A fear that if a problem is admitted to the Customs Authority, then more problems will emerge as a result;
- An incapacity or lack of understanding on the part of the importer or exporter to solve the problem;
- An inherent lack of willingness on the part of the importer or exporter to seek help, especially when it is most needed.

These issues are, regrettably, endemic throughout the importing or exporting community, and many of the issues concerned have arisen as a direct result of corporate downsizing or outsourcing of importing or exporting technicalities to outside contractors without retaining any expertise relating to such issues within the company itself.

Such ignorance of basic procedures allows for a large number of assumptions when relating to the international process. Such assumptions are often mutual between importers or exporters and freight agents. The importer or exporter assumes that the freight agent is responsible for many activities and has all the appropriate information available, whereas the agent may equally assume that the importer or exporter has all the relevant information to ensure speedy and efficient Customs clearance of all consignments. Equally, in the process of international shipping transactions, the importer or exporter perceives that the freight agent can do everything and that the importer or exporter needs to do little or nothing, expecting that the whole operation will perform like clockwork.

This is not so. The respective roles and responsibilities of each party dictate that each performs its own part of the bargain to ensure that the right information is conveyed in order to undertake the transaction of clearing imports or exports through Customs control. A vital part of this exercise lies in clear and understandable communication between 1 party and the other. The importer or exporter conveys the necessary information to the agent concerning the means by which they require clearing a consignment through Customs. The agent completes the appropriate documentation according to the information provided, and duly undertakes the clearance. If, subsequent to the import or export clearance, Customs discovers that some of the information provided on the declaration was incorrect, they will challenge the importer or exporter, not the agent, since the agent carried out the instructions of the importer or exporter.

There is thus no room for assumptions or perceptions in the process of Import or Export Declarations. Accurate communication is vital in the process, and such communication cannot depend or rely on assumptions of any kind. Every piece of information essential for correct declarations to be made must be conveyed prior to the declaration being carried out, since after the event such information is useless. It is futile to explain to Customs when they are knocking on the door seeking unpaid revenue that the company did not have the information at the time, or did not know that such information was required at the time of submitting the Customs Declaration. Customs will not accept such arguments or excuses under any circumstances whatsoever, and the importer or exporter must pay as a result.

If, however, the importer or exporter accepts all necessary responsibilities and ensures that they are fully conversant with all necessary Customs procedures, such mistakes are less likely to arise. Companies that are in full control of their logistics and Customs requirements stand a better chance of being able to address problems should they arise or will at least be able to seek the appropriate advice where and when necessary. Not every company may be able to solve all problems related to importing or exporting activities, especially where Customs are concerned, but they will at least know where to seek assistance in resolving such issues. Customs is not in a position to help every company all the time, but they can and are willing to give basic information to the public when required and when asked the right questions. If the problem is of a more complex nature, extra help may be required from other sources in the form of business advice or staff training. The advice given by business consultants is not free of charge as opposed to that given by Customs. Given that the role of Customs Officers has become more limited over time, a certain level of investment in business or consultancy advice can, over the long term, be far more valuable than having to spend money on penalties or liabilities to Customs as a result of not taking advice earlier.

Customs Documentation

As well as logistics and shipping documentation, Customs documentation is a vital part of the shipping and transport/logistics process and must be accurate in every way. The Customs Declaration, whether for export or import purposes, must be totally accurate, as UK Customs law (Customs and Excise Management Act 1979, s. 167 (1)) states that if a declaration is not accurate or even made at all, this is an offence, and the declarant is deemed to have submitted a false declaration, thus making the declarant liable to summary prosecution. Equivalent legislation exists in all other countries.

In the above cases, although a formal declaration is not required for intra-EU shipments, the supplier is required to hold sufficient dispatch records to show that the consignment has been exported in the form of some kind of shipping documentation or a Certificate of Shipment issued by the carrier. Where shipments are carried on short-sea container vessels between 2 EU ports, such as on a feeder service, a T2L Document is required for the consignment in question to show that it is of EU origin and is thus in EU Free Circulation. In the case of fully international shipments to non-EU destinations, there is a need for a Customs Declaration for both exported and imported consignments. In this way, the issue of consolidations has no bearing whatsoever on whether there should be an Export Declaration for either the consolidated load or each individual consignment within the consolidation. The law states that there is a need for an individual Export and Import Declaration for each consignment, whether consolidated or not, and this means that for every export consolidation, there is a need for an individual Export Declaration for each individual load in the form of a Declaration Unique Consignment Reference (DUCR), as well as an overall declaration for the overall consignment on the basis of a Master Consignment Reference (MUCR). These details must appear on the declaration itself when it is being submitted to the Customs computer at the point of lodgement. In the case of trans-shipments from the UK via another EU port such as Antwerp or Rotterdam, then the UK NES Export Declaration is submitted at the port of exit from the UK, and trans-shipment formalities are carried out in the EU port of trans-shipment. This EU procedure is required as the consignment is under Community Transit Customs-controlled conditions from the moment it is exported from the UK until it is loaded on board the deep-sea vessel at the port of trans-shipment and is shipped out of the European Union.

The Export Declaration

The declaration must reflect and represent all aspects of the consignment, and, in the case of UK Export Declarations, must include the following details:

- Consignor;
- Consignee;
- Declarant (where different from the exporter, as in the case of the clearing agent);
- EORI (Economic Operator Registration Identifier);
- Description of the Consignment;
- Tariff Commodity Code (TTCN);
- Customs Procedure Code (CPC);
- Unique Consignment Reference (UCR);
- Details of Licenses (where appropriate);
- Port of Loading;
- Destination.

Although there may be slight differences from country to country concerning the exact details required on a typical Export Declaration, the essential information required remains the same. In the case of the European Union, the systems by which both export and Import Declarations are submitted electronically to Customs have been harmonised as part of the SAD-H Declaration Harmonisation Initiative, with the same information required for submission in each of the EU member countries.

Once the declaration has been submitted to the Customs computer and has been acknowledged by the computer, the consignment may be transported to the port of loading. The shipping agent or representative of the shipping line at the port then inputs the basic information regarding the consignment into the computer, including the UCR, and the computer decides what action must be taken. This is usually automatic electronic clearance to load, although a documentary check may be required. Using the US-based AMS system, this also means submitting the information at the same time into the AMS prior to loading the container aboard the vessel. Assuming clearance of the consignment, the container may then be loaded aboard the vessel, and a further message to this effect is submitted to the Customs computer, also using the UCR. Once this procedure has been carried out for all containers being loaded aboard the vessel, the vessel is cleared for departure, and the computer issues a further message notifying the agents of this clearance. This final message is seen as the absolute proof of clearance and can be used for compliance purposes to show proof of dispatch and export.

The overall procedural summary is thus:

- Submission of Export Declaration to the Customs computer in the form of a Pre-Shipment Advice using the creation of a Unique Consignment Reference;
- Acknowledgement and Acceptance by the Customs computer;
- Movement of the consignment to the Port of Loading;
- Submission of Arrival Message (Goods arrived at Port) by the Agent in the form of the UCR;
- Electronic Clearance to Load authorised by Customs computer (Route 6);
- Consignment loaded aboard the vessel;
- Departure Message issued by the computer;
- Vessel Clearance Message issued by the computer;
- Vessel sails.

This procedure ensures that all necessary steps have been taken to ensure export compliance and that all Customs regulations and requirements have been satisfied. It should be noted, however, that the clearance process allows for the examination of the cargo by an officer should it be deemed necessary to verify the details of the consignment. Although this can be carried out at the trader's premises, it can also be effected at the port of dispatch, which often means opening the container at the port for an examination to be carried out. The same is true of the AMS systems, where a US Customs Officer could carry out similar checks if required. If a documentary check is required, this entails presenting the full set of export documentation (minus the Bill of Lading but including a copy of the manifest referring to the individual consignment in question) to the examining officer, who then checks the information for accuracy and identifies any discrepancies in the documentation, should they exist. The officer then makes the decision whether to delay the consignment pending clarification of information or whether to release the load for shipment. Once the consignment has been released, a further message is submitted to the Customs computer acknowledging clearance following examination, and the consignment may then be loaded aboard the vessel. It is thus important for all information pertinent to the declaration and clearance to be submitted in advance of the vessel arriving at port, as there is always a deadline time for containers to be received at the port of loading prior to the vessel being loaded, in order to allow for delays in clearance as well as the receipt and full acknowledgement on the port computer of all consignments to be loaded aboard the vessel. Because of the deadlines imposed on the receipt of cargoes at the port, the Customs Declarations must be submitted well in advance in order to allow sufficient time for full clearance by the Customs computer. There are often delays to loading caused by failure to clear, usually because the Customs computer requires more information concerning the consignment itself. These delays are often caused by the lack of information submitted by the shipper concerning the consignment, leading to incomplete declarations being submitted to the Customs computer. It is therefore vital that the shipper ensures that at the time of submission of the Export Declaration, all information pertaining to that declaration is correct at the point of entry.

The Import Declaration

The Import Declaration (in the case of the UK, the C88/E2 Entry Acceptance Advice; in the EU, the IM1) works in the same way as the Export Declaration, except in reverse, in that it is used to declare an imported consignment to Customs for the purposes of Import Duty and tax, as well as other controls such as licensing and quotas. The transport documentation plus the commercial invoice give details of the consignment itself, namely the following information:

- The Importer;
- The Declarant (The Clearing Agent);
- The Description of the Consignment;
- The Origin of the Consignment;
- The Value of the Consignment;
- The correct Tariff Commodity Code;
- The Freight Cost;
- The Insurance Cost.

Other details, such as Import Licenses or Preferential Certificate details, must also be included on the declaration where required. The accuracy of the declaration depends upon the above information provided, since Import Duty and national tax will be calculated and levied against that consignment at the point of import, for payment by the importer. Thus, it is vital that all information used for input into the declaration is correct, including details of the container used to import the goods, as well as all freight and insurance costs, which, when added to the purchase invoice cost, give rise to the CIF import landed cost value for Import Duty purposes. The declaration also acts as proof of import for the purposes of auditing, and must be made available should an audit be carried out on either an internal or external basis. All freight and insurance details must be itemised separately from the purchase cost details, as these are required as evidence under the CIF principle.

It is appreciated that in an era of increasing use of information technology, there is increasing reliance on the international trader to regulate and control their own affairs. Indeed, the recent initiatives of Authorised Economic

Operator (AEO) and its equivalents elsewhere in the world have done much to implement international Supply Chain controls and audit trails. Customs authorities in all major countries subscribing to such initiatives place increasing levels of reliance on traders to ensure that they can comply with these Customs initiatives. The purpose of the AEO initiative is to ensure that only traders with a history of Customs compliance and adherence to international Supply Chain audit trails through other initiatives such as ISO 28000/28001 can be authorised to use the AEO facility, thus enabling these traders to use fast-track abbreviated Customs clearance regimes for import and export control procedures.

However, neither AEO nor ISO 28000/28001 can substitute the need for physical checks and examinations of cargoes in transit. It has been admitted that 100% scanning of containers in many ports, including those in the US and at Rotterdam, is nearly impossible, as it could lead to severe congestion of the port systems, which are designed for the rapid transit of containerised cargoes through the ports for the purposes of loading aboard vessels or unloading from the vessel and transfer inland to the importer. It is also recognised that in the process of scanning a container by X-Ray machine, should any prohibited cargoes be discovered, that container will have to be isolated and fully examined to determine the nature of such cargoes. This procedure takes time and risks delaying other container movements, although in general containers found to contain prohibited cargoes will be moved aside and isolated for further scrutiny and examination.

The result is a series of prior requirements and authorisations for all traders involved in international trade who use any form of Customs authorisation to operate a specific facility, based on the basis of perceived or inherent risk calculation. This means that such traders must demonstrate a history of absolute compliance with Customs regulations and control requirements to continue using such facilities, and they must be able to prove such compliance to Customs through the AEO application before being authorised for such activities.

The Rationale Behind Customs Compliance

The Customs Authority is responsible for Customs debts and collections, as well as revenue protection. It always treats import and export traders with a degree of mistrust and therefore needs to protect its revenue interests, given that the revenue goes straight into the Government Treasury. For this reason, any Customs Authority has its own risk assessment structure, and HM Revenue and Customs is no exception to this. HMRC has a specific risk assessment structure on its website with regard to imports and exports, concerned primarily with the National Import Clearance Hub, and the following text is derived from this source.

Principles and Definitions of Risk Analysis

The objective of the national Customs administrations of the Member States and DG XXI of the European Commission in the risk programme is to achieve equivalent levels of control at the Community's external frontiers. Risk analysis aims to concentrate controls on areas of highest risk while at the same time allowing the majority of trade to flow relatively freely through Customs. Principles concerning risk analysis and profiling need to be established on a Community-wide basis. Guidelines for implementation and improvement in the use of risk analysis can now be defined at the Community level.

Customs regulations are designed to ensure payment of Customs Duties, observance of prohibitions and restrictions, and the application of special rules on quotas, preferences and other trade measures. Every regulation has a corresponding risk. Traders may breach it, deliberately or unintentionally. Risk analysis techniques try to identify and quantify these risks in order to develop control procedures, for example, selection for documentary checks or physical examinations, and to concentrate control efforts by Customs Officers on risk areas where breaches of the regulations are most likely to occur – whether deliberate or not.

Review of Customs Risk

Risk can be defined as what is at stake in terms of the likelihood of a loss of revenue combined with the impact of national revenue loss. In the context of Customs freight control, risk is the possibility that the collection of revenue or the enforcement of controls may be adversely affected.

Risk Analysis

Risk analysis in the context of Customs control is a working method that aims to maximise the use of Customs resources while minimising the risk. This is achieved by:

- Identifying risks;
- Assessing the level or degree of risk;
- Expressing the risk;
- Allocating resources to target the risks.

Risk Assessment

Risk assessment can be identified as the estimated degree of risk inherent in any Customs activity. Depending on the agreed parameters, a risk can be determined as:

HIGH = (H)
MEDIUM = (M)
LOW = (L)

In most cases, these risk levels will be calculated on the basis of the Composite Risk Index (CRI), taking into account both Likelihood and Impact, and the results formulated on the basis of:

1–8 (Low);
9–16 (Medium);
17–25 (High).

Another method to estimate the degree of risk may consist of allocating a numerical value to each identified risk.

By the use of risk assessment, Customs resources can be more effectively allocated and should result in goods or traders with the same quantified risk receiving similar resources and priorities.

Risk Areas

Risk areas in Customs freight control are those Customs or Customs-related regimes and procedures that involve revenue collection or enforcement functions (for example VAT, Customs and/or Excise Duties, CAP, common commercial policy measures, environment and public health). Risk areas can extend to Customs regimes with economic impact and also traders who fail to comply with the conditions of Customs regimes.

For an effective risk analysis programme to be followed, the following criteria need to be met:

- Policy and operational objectives are clearly set out;
- Accountability to both to management and auditors is clearly identified;
- There is a satisfactory management information system in place to enable performance to be measured;
- Local Customs managers have the right information to enable risk analysis to be effective.

Risk Indicators

Risk indicators are those factors that can increase or decrease the level or degree of risk to the revenue or enforcement function within each risk area. Depending on the risk area, several risk indicators can be used for risk assessment. For Customs freight, risk indicators include:

- Commodity Code;

- Country of origin;
- Country consigned from;
- Licensing indicator;
- Value;
- Trader compliance;
- Financial consequences;
- Means of transport;
- Financial situation of the trader.

Risk Profile

A risk profile is the means by which a Customs office puts risk analysis into practice. It is a practical means of replacing the random examination of documents and consignments with a planned and targeted working method, making maximum use of Customs resources. A risk profile is a document that can be set out in any number of ways but should be comprehensive and relevant to the Customs locations. The risk profile should:

- Be a source of information which Customs managers can use as a basis for allocating resources;
- Identify the risk areas in freight for the Customs location;
- Express the risk areas in agreed terms, for example, high (h), medium (m) or low (l) (or numerically where this approach is chosen);
- Test the effectiveness of the counter-measures taken.

To remain effective the risk profile must be flexible so that new risks are identified and tested. Where risks have been tested and found to be satisfactory, record as low risk.

A risk profile can be kept in a binder or on a local computer and should be as accessible as possible to all Customs Officers. A risk profile can have a number of sections dealing with different types of freight – general cargo, CAP goods and goods liable to Excise Duties. Different risk profiles will apply to imports and exports. However, under the ACI cargo reporting systems, the import risk for a specific cargo may be seen as the same as the export risk for a cargo prior to loading, especially if essential information concerning the nature of the cargo is not included on the cargo manifest prior to loading and submission of the manifest to the Customs computer in the country of destination.

The risk profile should contain a description of the risk area, an assessment of the risk, the counter-measures to be taken, an action date, the results, and an evaluation of the effectiveness of the action taken.

Additional Risk Indicators

Additional risk indicators could be issues such as:

- The basis for tax;
- The time (for tariff quotas);
- Any particular conditions, such as:
  - Licenses;
  - Reliefs;
  - Origin certificates;
  - Diversions (lost in transit).

In some cases, the extent to which simplified procedures are used could be an indicator of risk in a certain area. Most of the above risk indicators are product- or transaction-related.

The trader or economic operator is an important factor that will influence the overall risk assessment and risk profiling at several stages. Unusual behaviour in trade, any change of habits relating to the import or export of goods such as new types of goods, new places of operating or new commercial partners may be risk indicators according to the particular case. Generally, the fact that they have or have not already been guilty of infringements or irregularities against Customs or fiscal law has to be taken into consideration. Solvency will also be an important factor.

Freight Declarations

Risk assessment and targeting strategy build on and refines the processing of freight declarations. All freight declarations are processed in some way, either manually or electronically, to calculate and collect duties/levies, collect trade statistics, ensure that appropriate control documents are attached, endorsed, removed, returned or scrutinised to decide whether the goods should be checked.

Freight declarations can be divided into 2 categories:

1. Where Customs must intervene on every occasion because EU legislation requires it or because without such intervention the control regime would not function;
2. Where Customs intervention is not necessarily systematic but may vary according to the assessment of risk.

Depending on the level of sophistication of risk assessment techniques, this second category may be subject to a minimum mandatory low interception rate to ensure and check general levels of compliance. Beyond this, Customs intervention can be based on risk assessment.

Authorised Economic Operators who have met the required criteria are entitled under Regulation 1875/06 to fewer physical and document-based controls. Goods may still be selected for examination, but AEOs should be given priority treatment.

The existence of interactive computerisation processing of declarations greatly assists by automatically selecting consignments for either documentary or physical checks if required.

Risk Analysis Sheet

Every piece of EU legislation involving the international trade of goods may have with it a **Risk Analysis Sheet**. For modifications of existing acts and new pieces of legislation, this sheet could be prepared before their final adoption in order to allow the assessment of the impact of the proposed legislation on Customs controls.

The following Risk Analysis Sheet can be constructed and used as a starting point for the assessment of risk in the area concerned.

EC Council Regulation No. 3651/88 of 24/11/88
Anti-dumping duty of 47% on matrix printers originating in Japan from 25/11/88
CN Code: 84 71 92 90

Comments:

Risk area: Common Commercial Policy (ADD Anti-Dumping Duties).

Risk indicators: The 5 main risk indicators are identified as:

- Origin: False declaration of origin;
- Value: False declaration of the value in order to reduce the amount of duty;
- CN Code: False declaration of the product to another code where no duty is applied (84 71 99 10 "other peripheral units");
- Quantity is the same as value;
- Place of consignment: False declaration to facilitate falsification of origin.

Risk assessment (to determine the level or degree of risk to each one of them): a comparative analysis of the flow of imports of goods under the above-mentioned CN codes for the period before and after the application of the anti-dumping duty is carried out, based on statistical data on enterprises including: number of declarations, declared values, Customs offices. The analysis is both product and trader based, as it focuses on the study of trends in business strategies for the activity concerned (import of a specific product). Results of this risk analysis can show:

- A possible misdeclaration of goods liable to 8471 9290 being declared under 8471 9910;
- An unexpected change in the Customs Officers' office or Member State where the goods are imported;
- An unusual change in the unit price of the commodity;
- An unusual declaration of origin for goods under code 8471 9290.

According to the results of the analysis, a high, medium or low degree of risk will be applied to each of the risk indicators for selection operators; different "profiles" will be constructed, which will determine the framework of control at each specific Customs office according to its particular situation (resources, volume of trade, etc.). When all 4 indicators prove to be of low risk, no control might be necessary. Results of the controls could be used to update the Risk Analysis Sheet.

In general terms, once the risk assessment is completed in each case, the (x) in the checklist will appear as (h) = high risk, (m) = medium risk, (l) = low risk; they can also be numbers, for example x = 1, n, to show ranged priorities for control according to risk. They can also be assigned a letter in addition to show the type of control that is needed, for example: (d) = control of documents accompanying the goods, (p) = a later control in the business premises, or (h) = physical control of goods.

More risk areas can be identified in the above case of anti-dumping measures; in fact, the economic procedures (temporary admission, warehouses or free-zones, IP and OP) and transit procedures may be involved in the operators' trade activities for the goods in question. Risk analysis of these areas as well would result in different levels of the same indicators, whereas additional ones can be identified (e.g. destination).

(Source: www.hmrc.gov.uk)

CHAPTER 17

Export Licenses and Controls

One of the critical areas of Customs control is that of export controls and licensing. HR Revenue and Customs does not *per se* issue licenses, but frontier controls (carried out in the UK by the UK Border Agency) are nevertheless an area of compliance which the exporter needs to be aware of, as there are significant ramifications for exporters who are not aware of export restrictions and controls as imposed by the Export Control Organisation (ECO) subject to the Export Control Act 2002 and the subsequent Export Control Order 2008. Both pieces of legislation impose strict rules and regulations covering the export of restricted and controlled goods, and must be complied with at all times. Although the ECO governs the area of export licenses, HM Revenue and Customs and the UK Border Agency retain the ability to scrutinise export licenses upon use, and undertake all action deemed necessary in the event of contravention of the UK's export regulations.

There are several reasons why governments aim to control the export of goods, depending on the nature and destinations of the proposed export. The export of strategic goods and technology is the specific remit of the Export Control Organisation. Exports of such goods are controlled for various reasons, including:

- Concerns about internal repression, regional instability or other human rights violations;
- Concerns about the development of weapons of mass destruction;
- Foreign policy and international treaty commitments including as a result of the imposition of EU or United Nations trade sanctions or arms embargoes;
- National and collective security of the UK and its allies.

Export controls are not unique to the UK. All countries should have some form of export control policy, legislation and enforcement mechanisms. The UK has a well-developed and coherent export control system based on EU and national legislation.

DOI: 10.4324/9781003341345-18

The following text is a summary of the information provided on the ECO website, but it is still necessary for exporters to consult the website for more specific details about the licenses required.

End-User Undertakings

When applying for an export license from the Export Control Organisation, now known as the Export Controls Joint Unit (ECJU), 1 of the most important elements is to ensure that the trader has attached an accurate and correct undertaking form, completed by the end-user customer, along with all their submitted export details.

One of the most common errors in applications received by the Export Control Organisation is an incorrect or missing undertaking, which can cause substantial delays with the application for an export license, as it is the undertaking that effectively determines the validity of the intention to purchase controlled goods from the exporter. This does not mean that a license application will be automatically refused under such circumstances, but the ECO will require absolute information concerning the proposed export prior to authorising it. Correct completion of the undertakings needs to be taken seriously by any exporting company. It is also vital that the exporter has a good understanding of how these undertakings affect their business operations and license application.

The purpose of a completed undertaking for export control purposes is to guard against the risk of UK exports being diverted or re-exported to end-users deemed by the UK government to be "undesirable". This diversionary risk is among those identified in the Consolidated EU and National Arms Export Licensing Criteria, which sets out the factors to be considered in all case-by-case assessments for applications of strategic (military or dual-use) items. It should be pointed out at this stage that many items can be used by both commercial and military organisations, hence their description as "dual-use" items. Such items can be used in, for example, the automotive or aviation sectors, either in either commercial or military vehicles, or in helicopters, which could be either commercial or military.

The government believes the best way of minimising the risk of diversion is a thorough risk assessment at the licensing stage. This process includes a careful examination by the ECO of information about the proposed end-use and end-user of the proposed export. A low-risk assessment would yield little reason to prohibit the issuing of a license, whereas medium-risk or high-risk shipments would, by definition be more carefully and thoroughly considered.

As an export license applicant, the exporter has an important part to play in ensuring that their end-user customer completes the relevant undertaking as required by the ECO and that they take the utmost care in attaching the relevant undertaking to any license application.

An undertaking is required when an application is being made for a Standard Individual Export Licence (SIEL) or standard individual trade control license (SITCL), both of which are issued by the UK's Export Control Organisation, part of the Department for Business, Innovation and Skills (BIS). The organisation was originally part of the Department for Trade and Industry (DTI) but was re-organised upon the change to the BIS. The undertaking is part of the supporting documentation for end-use control purposes, which needs to be provided when an exporter submits an export license application via SPIRE to the ECO.

There are 2 types of undertaking forms available; however, which one the exporter chooses to obtain in support of an application depends on how the intended exported goods will be used.

If goods are being exported (whether or not via a consignee):

- For their end-use or if an end-user is incorporating the goods (i.e. installing them into another product or higher-level system) – then the exporter should obtain an end-user undertaking (EUU) form;
- To be held in stock for future delivery or resale – then the exporter should obtain a Stockist Undertaking (SU) Form.

The end-user or stockist end-user must be advised to complete the relevant version of these forms together with a covering letter (on original official headed paper of the overseas company).

It is the exporter's responsibility to ensure that all sections of the correct undertaking and covering letter are completed legibly, in English and signed by an appropriate responsible official. They should also attach an electronic or scanned copy of the undertaking to the license application on the electronic SPIRE application system and retain the original hard copy in their records. The ECO reserves the right to require an exporter to produce the original document, if necessary, but they would expect to make such requests on rare occasions only.

However, if the exporter is specifically asked to provide the original undertaking during the course of the export license application process, then they should be aware that ECO will not issue a license if the exporter fails to provide the original document.

Export Licenses

The main element of the approval or authorisation for the export of controlled goods is the export license itself. There are several types of license, and each one is issued depending upon the circumstances relating to the application for an export license.

OGL

Open General Licences (OGLs) are pre-published export licenses in the public domain. There are various types of OGLs, including the following:

- Open General Export Licences (OGELs);
- Open General Trade Control Licences (OGTCLs); and
- Open General Trans-Shipment Licences (OGTLs).

All of these licenses are issued by the Export Control Organisation.

OGLs are designed to license controlled military or dual-use goods that are of a less restricted nature or are being exported to non-sensitive destinations. The use of OGLs can potentially benefit an exporter's business by saving time in the application for either a Standard Individual Export Licence or an Open Individual Export Licence (OIEL). If the exporter can meet all the terms and conditions of an appropriate OGL, then they can register to use the license by way of the electronic SPIRE export licensing database.

By registering to use an OGL on SPIRE, the exporter is legally bound to comply with all the specified conditions and keep appropriate records. Otherwise, they risk being in breach of the license. It is, therefore, the responsibility of the exporter to check and comply with the license requirements before use and to stay updated with any changes through the ECO's Notices to Exporters update service.

There are a wide variety of OGLs available, which are categorised as follows:

- Dual-Use Open General Export Licences – dual-use items are goods and technology with both military and civilian applications;
- European Union General Export Authorisations – EU GEAs are the EU equivalent of an OGEL and are designed to provide licensing coverage for certain specified dual-use items to specified non-EU destinations;
- Military Goods Open General Export Licences – permit for the export of less restricted controlled military goods;
- Trans-Shipment OGLs – this category, known as OGTLs, allows, subject to certain conditions, controlled goods to be exported from 1 country to another via the UK;
- Open General Trade Control Licences – these are known as OGTCLs. They control the trafficking and brokering activity between a third country and another where the transaction or deal is brokered in the UK or by a UK person;
- Other types of Open General Export Licences – these include various OGLs that do not fit neatly into other categories, including the

Radioactive Sources OGEL, the Sporting Goods OGEL, the OGEL (Iraq) and the OGEL (Government of Sierra Leone).

The exporter needs to decide in advance which OGL is applicable to their export activity depending on the type of goods and destination of exports and the conditions contained in the license, and therefore needs to study carefully the nature and use of each type of license. In reality, the title of each license usually gives an indication as to its purpose, but the exporter must never rely on this alone, as they must read the license thoroughly before using it to make sure that they can comply with all its terms and conditions. This includes:

- Checking the list of permitted or non-permitted destinations specifically listed on each OGL;
- Double-checking the control entry heading or "rating" codes permitted on each individual OGL. A "control entry" or "rating" code is referenced on the UK Strategic Export Control Lists.

If the exporter uses an OGL without checking that they can comply with the description or type of goods, destination or other specified conditions, then they will be in breach of the license conditions.

Each OGL is written in a certain legal format comprising several key parts, including:

- Terms and conditions of the license;
- Schedules – containing a list of items permitted for export with a specific license and a list of destinations eligible or ineligible for export;
- Explanatory notes.

In all cases, the exporter must read, understand and adhere to all the specific schedules, terms and conditions, and other details of the license.

It is a condition of the license that the exporter must register with the ECO before using most OGLs or an EU General Export Authorisation (EU GEA), as their details need to be processed by the ECO in order to properly authorise any application for an export license.

Shipments exported under the authority of an OGL do not require the physical presentation of the license document to HM Revenue and Customs, although the reference number of the license must be submitted to the agent completing the Export Declaration and inserted in Box 44 of the electronic NES Export Declaration. The exporter must therefore state the exact license name or unique SPIRE reference number on any accompanying commercial documentation, including in Box 44 of the Single Applicant Declaration (SAD) submitted via CDS Customs computer to HMRC.

OGELs

Open General Export Licences (OGELs) are pre-published export licenses issued by the Export Control Organisation. They are the most flexible type of strategic export license available for use by exporters, as long as all pre-set conditions can be met. In each case they allow the export of specified controlled items, identified by a "control list entry" heading, to specific destinations permitted by the license.

The ECO issues a wide range of OGELs, including for dual-use items (i.e. controlled goods and technology with both civil and military applications). Dual-use items are controlled under EU legislation – the EU Dual-Use Regulation. A summary list of when OGELs came into force is provided in the table below.

Title of OGEL	*Date license entered into force*
OGEL (Chemicals)	27 August 2009
OGEL (Cryptographic development)	19 December 2011
OGEL (Export after exhibition: dual-use items)	15 June 2012
OGEL (Export after repair/replacement under warranty: dual-use items)	15 June 2012
OGEL (Export for repair/replacement under warranty: dual-use items)	15 June 2012
OGEL (Dual-use items: Hong Kong Special Administrative Region)	15 June 2012
OGEL (International non-proliferation regime de-controls: dual-use items)	15 June 2012
OGEL (Low value shipments)	15 June 2012
OGEL (Oil and gas exploration: dual-use items)	15 June 2012
OGEL (Technology for dual-use items)	15 June 2012
OGEL (Turkey)	15 June 2012
OGEL (X)	15 June 2012
OGEL (Military and dual-use goods: UK forces deployed in embargoed destinations)	26 March 2010
OGEL (Military and dual-use goods: UK forces deployed in non-embargoed destinations)	6 July 2011
OGEL (Exports of non-lethal military and dual-use goods: to UK diplomatic missions or consular posts)	10 August 2012

EU GEAs

European Union General Export Authorisations are the European equivalent of the national system of Open General Licences issued under UK export control law and are designed to license dual-use exports. Dual-use items are defined as goods, software or technology that can be used for either civil/ commercial or military purposes. The EU is responsible for issuing legislation in this area, which is applicable on an EU-wide basis.

EU GEAs are only 1 of several licensing categories that are issued by the UK's Export Control Organisation, the UK's national export licensing authority. They specifically permit the export of certain specified dual-use Items to certain specified non-EU destinations.

As with OGLs, EU GEAs are legal documents. In order to legally use the authorisations, UK exporters need to ensure that they meet all the licensing terms and conditions, including registering before use with the ECO.

EU GEAs are published as Annex II of the Council Regulation (EC) No 428/2009 (the re-cast European Union Dual-Use Regulation). They are also published as part of Council Regulation (EC) No 1232/2011.

Council Regulation (EC) No. 428/2009 (otherwise known as the European Union Dual-Use Regulation) established an EU-wide regime for the control of exports of dual-use items, software and technology. This originally included 1 EU-issued license, known as the Community General Export Authorisation listed in Annex 2 of this book.

On 8 December 2011, the EU published an amending regulation that introduced an amendment to the existing CGEA and an additional set of EU GEAs designed to license certain specified dual-use items for export to named non-EU destinations. This amendment was published as Council Regulation (EU) No. 1232/2011.

There are 6 EU GEAs, all of which came into force on 7 January 2012, and these are:

- **EU001** – exports to Australia, Canada, Japan, New Zealand, Norway, Switzerland (including Liechtenstein) and the United States – Note: this was previously known as the Community General Export Authorisation or CGEA;
- **EU002** – export of certain dual-use items to certain destinations;
- **EU003** – export after repair/replacement;
- **EU004** – temporary export for exhibition or fair;
- **EU005** – telecommunications;
- **EU006** – chemicals.

Each of the EU GEAs contains:

- A precise list of destinations to which exports are permitted;
- A specific list of items that may be exported to those destinations;
- A specific set of conditions of use, which must be adhered to when exporting under the particular general authorisation.

These GEAs are being revised by the UK for its own requirements following the UK's exit from the EU at the end of 2020.

The items listed on each license refer to a control entry heading (or 'rating') which should be cross-referenced to goods described on the EU Dual-Use List (as published in the EU legislation). This listing is published in the UK as a part of the UK Strategic Export Control Lists.

Each EU GEA also comprises a number of general legally binding conditions to which you must adhere. This includes specific conditions outlining when an EU GEA may not be used to authorise an export in the following circumstances:

- If an exporter has been informed by the competent authorities of the member state (i.e. the ECO in the UK) in which they are established that the items in question are or may be intended (either in their entirety or in part) for use in connection with the development, production, handling, operation, maintenance, storage, detection, identification or dissemination of chemical, biological or nuclear weapons or other nuclear explosive devices or the development, production, maintenance or storage of missiles capable of delivering such weapons, or if the exporter is aware that the items in question are intended for such use;
- If an exporter has been informed that the items in question are or may be intended for a military end-use as defined in Article 4(2) of the Regulation in a country subject to an arms embargo, or if the exporter is aware that the items in question are intended for such use;
- When the relevant items are to be exported to a destination within a Customs free zone or free warehouse.

It is also a standard condition that where a goods declaration is required, the exporter must quote code X002 and the specific license code (except in the case of dual-use intangible electronic transfers).

In the UK, record-keeping and registration requirements for EU GEAs are contained in Articles 28–31 of the Export Control Order 2008 (SI 2008/3231). A summary of the requirements for exporting under an EU GEA from the United Kingdom is given below:

- Any person established in the UK who exports any item under the authority of an EU GEA shall keep records relating to each export, which shall be maintained for at least 3 years from the end of the calendar year in which the export takes place;
- Any person authorised by the Secretary of State shall be permitted to inspect and copy such records;
- Any person (including a person established in another member state) who exports cryptographic items from the UK under the authority of the EU GEA shall, in addition to normal record-keeping requirements, provide details (see the next section) in writing to the Secretary of State no later than 30 days after the first export, to the extent that the information is available or can reasonably be expected to be obtained within that time;
- Before or within 30 days after the first occasion of use, any person established in the United Kingdom shall register to use an EU GEA on SPIRE, giving of the name of the exporter and the address at which copies of records may be inspected. Notice of any change to these details must be provided via SPIRE no later than 30 days after any such change.

OIELs

An **Open Individual Export Licence** (OIEL) is a type of license issued by the ECO that is more flexible and tailored to the specific needs of an exporter. OIELs allow a named exporter to export multiple shipments of specific goods to specific destinations, subject to meeting detailed terms and conditions. An OIEL can potentially save the exporter time and money, which means that if the exporter meets the eligibility criteria, they should give serious consideration to making an application.

OIELs cover multiple shipments of specific controlled goods to named destinations. They may also name the consignees or end-users of the goods concerned, unlike Standard Individual Export Licences, which always name these parties.

There are no open individual trans-shipment licenses, meaning that controlled goods cannot be imported into the UK for export elsewhere under an OIEL.

Controlled goods are items of strategic importance, including:

- Dual-use goods (military and civilian);
- Torture goods (including drugs used for execution by lethal injection);
- Radioactive sources;

- Military goods;
- Electronic technology.

There are various categories of OIELs which the exporter can apply for, depending on:

- The nature of the exporting business;
- The exporter's track record in applying for export licenses;
- The conditions of the license.

OIELs are issued by ECO on a concessionary basis. To justify an application for an OIEL, the exporter must have:

- A record of at least 20 relevant SIEL applications in the previous year for exports that the exporter now wishes to cover on an OIEL;
- Where this is not possible (for example, because the license application relates to new business), the exporter needs a good business case to support their application.

The exporter's business case needs to set out how many exports they anticipate making in the next year, of what nature and to which destinations. The exporter must provide evidence (such as contract excerpts) to back up their case, and they should ensure that it is carefully considered and not simply an extensive wish list of countries.

If the exporter already holds an OIEL and wishes to renew their coverage, the ECO will expect them to have used it at least 20 times during the previous year. For dealer-to-dealer OIELs, usage of at least 6 times a year is acceptable. The exporter will also be expected to meet the original criteria for use as detailed in their business case application.

It should, however, be noted that applications can, on some occasions, be rejected. Typical reasons why OIEL applications might be rejected include:

- Failure to include adequate goods descriptions;
- Inclusion of unrealistic country lists;
- Failure to provide an adequate business case.

The exporter should be aware that there is no formal appeal procedure if their OIEL application is rejected. If this happens, they will need to apply for a SIEL.

Although an OIEL is a more flexible export license, it is not an authorisation to apply for a wide range of countries or goods. Therefore, the exporter should:

- Be careful and realistic in identifying which goods are to be exported to destinations;
- Be careful in applying for sensitive destinations. As a guide, if a SIEL is denied to a specific destination, it is likely that this export destination, if requested on an OIEL, will also be denied;
- Try to avoid making 1 application for a wide range of goods to multiple destinations – you should make separate applications for fewer countries, for example, groups of countries in different regions.

The OIEL application must:

- Include detailed technical information about the goods being exported;
- Be supported by the provision of consignee undertakings from the exporter's end-user.

The exporter is usually not required to provide consignee or end-user details up front at the time of application. However, they are required to obtain the undertaking before the goods are shipped and ensure the undertaking is valid when the shipment is made. To this extent, the exporter must retain and produce original versions of consignee undertakings for compliance audits.

In a consignee undertaking, the consignee is asked to confirm the nature of the goods ordered, what they will be used for, and that they will not be re-exported or incorporated into goods which will subsequently be exported to a destination outside that permitted by the license. They are also asked to declare that the goods will not be used for activities associated with weapons of mass destruction (WMD).

There are 6 main types of OIEL, and these are:

- Military;
- Dual-use;
- Dealer;
- UK Continental Shelf;
- Media;
- Cryptographic.

These categories broadly cover exports of goods listed on the government's UK Strategic Export Control Lists, including firearms and ammunition dealers, exporters to UK continental shelf installations such as oil platforms, media and similar companies exporting protection equipment, and suppliers of cryptographic technology. It should be pointed out that not all dispatches to the continental shelf require an export license, but goods such as electronic hardware, software and other control equipment and devices will be subject to an export license.

Military and Dual-Use OIELs

These OIELs allow the exporter to export items and technology on the government's strategic export control lists. They are usually valid for 5 years.

UK Continental Shelf OIELs

This OIEL authorises the export of controlled items for use exclusively in offshore installations and associated vessels within the UK sector of the continental shelf. Continental shelf OIELs are valid for 5 years.

If the exporter holds an OIEL, they must obtain a written consignee undertaking that the goods are not intended for re-export to a destination not listed as permitted on the license. The undertakings must be received from each consignee before the first export. The exporter must also remember to:

- Retain the original undertaking (which must be signed and dated);
- Obtain an undertaking (in advance) if the contract or project is ongoing.

In the case of transfers to governments, a purchase order or contract can be accepted in place of an undertaking.

The exporter must also keep records of all shipments of their goods for the period of the license, and these records must be made available for inspection by the Department for Business, Innovation and Skills officials at an ECO compliance audit.

It should also be noted that the exporter cannot export controlled goods under an OIEL if they are aware, or have been informed by the authorities, that the goods will be used in connection with:

- Chemical, biological or nuclear weapons;
- Other nuclear explosive devices;
- Missiles capable of delivering such weapons.

During the license period, the exporter may request small changes to their OIEL without having to submit a new application. These include the:

- Name or address of the existing consignee and/or end-user already on the license (documentary evidence required);
- New consignee for a destination which is already on the license;

- Colour of the equipment listed in the license;
- Part number of the exact same material or product;
- Increase in the value of the goods.

The ECO will not amend a license if:

- There is a new destination;
- There is a new end-user;
- The goods have changed;
- There is an increased quantity of goods.

If the exporter holds an OIEL, they must satisfy the ECO that they are complying with all the procedures needed for using the license, including familiarity with current export legislation. To check this, the ECO will undertake a compliance audit of the exporter's business, usually within 3 months of their first OIEL being granted. The ECO also conducts audits to check whether businesses are exporting goods or technology with an appropriate license.

Compliance audits take place within a few months of the exporting company being granted its first open license (OIEL or OGEL) and thereafter at intervals of between 3 and 36 months. Most exporters are visited every 12 to 18 months, but the exact timing depends on the ECO's risk assessment of the exporter's business. This audit takes into account factors such as:

- Volume of exports;
- Variety of licenses used;
- Compliance record;
- Procedures in place;
- Goods exported and destinations on the licenses;
- Any special conditions.

It is also essential that the exporter holds all relevant records and documentation on file, either electronically or in hard copy, or even both, in order to facilitate a trouble-free audit to ensure compliance. Failure to do so can result in additional investigations taking place, with the possible result of punitive action.

Export Control Order 2008Export regulations in the UK are implemented under the Export Control Order 2008. This secondary legislation is based on the Export Control Act 2002, the UK's main legislation on export controls.

Areas covered by the order include:

- Strategic goods export controls;
- Transfer of technology and technical assistance provision;

- Controls on trade in military equipment between overseas countries where part of the process takes place in the UK;
- controls on trade with embargoed destinations, e.g. embargoes imposed by the UK following EU or Organisation for Security and Co-operation in Europe embargoes.

Dual-Use Regulation

The main European legislation is Council Regulation (EC) No. 428/2009 (the re-cast Dual-Use Regulation), which set up an EU system to control exports of dual-use items and technology. Under the regulations, OIELs and similar permits issued in 1 Member State can normally be used to export from other Member States.

The exporter does not need a license to export most dual-use items to other Member States, unless the goods are intended to be forwarded to a third country, in which case more detailed information is required concerning the identity of the third country, the nature and description of the goods and any other essential information.

Dual-use items include:

- Software and technology with civil and military applications;
- Goods that can be used for non-explosive purposes or in the manufacture of nuclear explosive devices.

SIELs

A **Standard Individual Export Licence** is the most common of several different types of strategic export control licenses. In particular, it gives permission to the exporter to export specific items to specific destinations. The goods must be addressed to a stated person or company, and the exporter may also have to identify the end-user. The goods must be of the same quantity and value as described on the license.

The exporter is required to apply for a SIEL if they need an export license and cannot meet all the stated terms and conditions of an Open General Export Licence.

A SIEL is a form of export license for controlled goods, specific to 1 exporter and 1 consignee.

Controlled goods are items of strategic importance, including:

- Dual-use goods (military and civilian);
- Torture goods (including drugs used in execution by lethal injection);
- Radioactive sources;
- Military goods;

- Electronic technology.

SIELs are normally valid for 2 years and allow the export of:

- Specific items as listed on the license;
- Specific quantities and values of each item;
- Specific consignees and end-users for your exports.

The ECO also issues a form of SIEL that covers long-term contracts, projects and repeat business. Items covered by this type of license do not have to be sent in a single shipment.

The exporter should apply for a SIEL to the ECO, and each application must include supporting documentation, such as end-user undertakings. Original end-user documentation, completed by the end-user company overseas, must be included with the exporter's application, as this helps prevent UK exports from being diverted or re-exported to undesirable end-users.

Holders of SIELs must follow standard conditions, and the license can be revoked if the exporter does not comply with these conditions.

Standard SIEL conditions require that the exporter must:

- Produce the license to HM Revenue and Customs (HMRC) officers with shipping documents when goods are presented for exportation;
- For exports to European Community (EC) Member States, the exporter must produce the license to HMRC officials and specify a place for the goods to be inspected at least 3 days before exportation;
- Ensure a copy of the license accompanies the goods to an EC destination;
- For exports by post, include the license in a separate envelope attached to the package; photocopies are acceptable for sequential postings of technology;
- for electronic transfer, keep detailed records of the type of technology, dates and end-users.

Temporary SIELs

The exporter may need a temporary SIEL if they are exporting goods for demonstration, exhibition, or repair and maintenance purposes, along with any associated minimum electronic transfer required to undertake such tasks.

In the case of incidental electronic transfers, temporary SIELs are intended for cases where a UK exporter might, for example, be exhibiting overseas and need to email the minimum technology required to maintain, repair, install or operate the goods listed on the license. A temporary SIEL is not intended for cases where a UK exporter passes technology to an overseas customer by email and subsequent download. Such transfers require a permanent SIEL.

In the case of temporary SIELs, the exporter must return the goods to the UK before their license expires and send any expired licenses to the Licence Reception Unit within the ECO. If the exporter does not use their license at all, they should return it to the unit with a covering letter explaining why the license was not used.

Goods exported on a temporary license must not be disposed of abroad unless the ECO has given specific permission for this to happen. Nor should the exporter allow the goods to remain abroad beyond the expiry date without first contacting the ECO. The exporter should not assume that such permission is necessarily granted, as such cases are considered on a case-by-case basis against the Consolidated EU and National Arms Export Licensing Criteria. On many occasions, such cases need to be referred to advisory government departments before a decision is reached.

It should be noted that failure to comply with any condition attached to a temporary license may lead to forfeiture of the goods or to prosecution by HMRC.

If the exporter holds a SIEL, they must satisfy the ECO that they are complying with all the terms and conditions of the license, including familiarity with current export legislation, and should be able to demonstrate that they have direct access, in either electronic or hard copy format, to all such legislation. Such legislation can be found electronically on the internet, and can be downloaded directly onto a computer file, or printed off as a hard copy.

Companies are liable to receive compliance visits from the ECO if they hold SIELs for electronic transfers of software or technology. To check this, the ECO will undertake a compliance audit of the exporting company, usually within 3 months of a license being granted. The ECO also uses audits to check whether companies are exporting goods or technology without an appropriate license.

While ECO Compliance Officers do not specifically audit all SIELs, relevant records may be checked in relation to an associated compliance audit.

Timing of Compliance Audits

Compliance audits can take place between 3 and 12 months to 36 months. Most exporters are visited every 12–18 months. The exact timing depends on the ECJU/ECO's risk assessment of the exporting company and takes into account factors such as:

- License usage;
- Number of licenses used;

- Compliance record;
- Procedures in place, volume of exports, goods;
- Destinations on the licenses;
- Any special conditions;
- Exports involving electronic transfers of software or technology.

Most non-compliance issues found by the ECO relate to documentation and records. The emphasis is on helping companies take action to comply with the license requirements. Remedial measures are usually set out in a warning letter, with a timescale for implementation.

Exporters should be aware that there are legal penalties for exporting controlled goods without a license. This includes the potential seizure of goods by Customs, financial penalties or even prosecution in the form of a prison term. Such penalties are maintained in accordance with Section 167(1) of the Customs and Excise Management Act 1979 as well as the Export Control Act 2002.

For exporters subject to compliance audits who have failed to demonstrate a sufficient level of compliance, the ECO will revisit exporters previously issued a warning letter to check whether the necessary action has been taken to ensure compliance. If there has been little or no progress, the ECO may consider suspending the relevant license. In serious cases, HMRC officials may decide to prosecute.

Mandatory Changes to SPIRE Applications

Applications made through the UK Export Control Organisation's SPIRE online electronic system have recently been changed to take into account various issues previously seen as being more vague. These include:

- The 'Return Date' question on temporary applications is now mandatory;
- SPIRE users will no longer have the ability to choose 'Named Individual for this application' with regard to 'relationship to the licensee' if the proposed licensee is an 'Organisation'. This will ensure that applications are submitted by the correct signatory;
- 'United Kingdom' and 'Vessel or Platform in International Waters' as a permitted destination have been restricted to specific application types.

CHAPTER 18

Trading with Northern Ireland

UK to Northern Ireland: One Customs Territory

Although Great Britain left the European Union at the end of 2020, the province of Northern Ireland remained within the EU Single Market, retaining a regime of open borders between the province and the Republic of Ireland. To this end, a separate protocol was devised to allow for this status, with a separate set of Customs measures for controlling trade across the North Channel between Great Britain and Northern Ireland. According to the UK–Northern Ireland Protocol, the UK government stated at the beginning of 2021 that there would be some changes for the movement of goods from Great Britain into Northern Ireland. Whereas the UK as a whole left the EU and its Customs Union, the province of Northern Ireland technically remained part of the UK's Customs territory, but also remained within the EU Single Market, with no cross-border controls between Northern Ireland and the Republic of Ireland.

That meant:

- No new Customs infrastructure would be required to be built in Northern Ireland (or in Great Britain ports facing Northern Ireland);
- There would be no Exit or Export Declarations for goods leaving Great Britain for Northern Ireland, although this was changed with the introduction of safety and security declarations and cargo pre-clearance required for all shipments from GB to Northern Ireland. It also resulted in the Trader Support System (TSS), where declarations would have to be submitted by traders for all shipments being sent from Great Britain to Northern Ireland;
- Processes would be fully digital and eligible to be facilitated by the Trader Support Service;
- The regime would be administered by UK authorities – meaning a minimal proportion of checks only as required by the levels of risk;

 DOI: 10.4324/9781003341345-19

- There should be no tariffs payable on all internal UK trade, and in any case, full use would be made of waivers and reimbursements to minimise the impact on business in any scenario;
- An end-to-end Trader Support Service is available at no cost to all businesses who wish to or required to use it.

UK to Northern Ireland: Digital Declarations

The protocol entailed some new administrative processes for traders, notably new digital Import Declaration requirements, and digital safety and security information, for goods entering Northern Ireland from the rest of the UK. These processes, which would be administered by UK authorities in the form of HMRC and Border Force, were supposedly needed to make sure that tariffs were not paid on trade within the UK, that Northern Ireland could benefit from UK FTAs, and that goods destined for Ireland and the EU (i.e. at a genuine and substantial risk of doing so) should be subject to tariffs when they were subject to Irish cross-border movements (i.e. goods deemed "At Risk" as far as movements between the GB mainland and Northern Ireland were concerned). In reality, much of the traffic between GB and Northern Ireland is deemed to be at risk (of crossing into the Irish Republic) by the Trader Support System, and in reality, has made the TSS declaration process fraught with difficulties concerning documentary and procedural requirements.

The UK government stated that there should be no tariffs on internal UK trade, and that in any case full use would be made of waivers and reimbursements to minimise the impact on business in any scenario. The stark reality is that many businesses have been severely impacted and compromised by the TSS requirements on trade with Northern Ireland. The protocol required a UK–EU Joint Committee decision on the application of tariffs on "At Risk" goods moving into Northern Ireland, and for these purposes it is important to note that the ultimate destination of goods and whether, for example, traders will be selling them in Northern Ireland or moving them on to Ireland/the EU, has become relevant as 2021 has progressed, with a significant impact on trade with Northern Ireland.

In the event, the TSS process has resulted in the imposition of simplified Export Declarations for goods leaving Great Britain for Northern Ireland, along with Exit Declarations, and a degree of regulatory clearance for goods as they leave the rest of the UK for Northern Ireland. Furthermore, the new **Trader Support Service** did not ensure that the process of shipments to Northern Ireland was straightforward, even for businesses who had not previously engaged with Customs, and that fines would be imposed on traders who did not fulfil the requirements of the TSS system. However, it has become clear that the process for the completion of the TSS declarations is far from simple, and in reality is a significant challenge for all traders required to complete them.

UK to Northern Ireland: Trader Support Service

The UK government established a new, free service, the Trader Support Service, which records electronic information on the movement of goods. Although the declaration system has meant that traders do have to engage with new digital Customs systems or processes, especially on "At Risk" shipments, i.e. those shipments deemed at risk of crossing from Northern Ireland into the Irish Republic by way of the road links. This service deals with formalities such as summary Export Declarations from the UK mainland, Import Declarations into Northern Ireland, and safety and security information on behalf of traders, providing support for Northern Ireland businesses.

Initially, traders have been able to register with the service and receive support and guidance on what the protocol means for them. This includes the steps they need to take to comply with the new regulations (including obtaining an XI Economic Operators Registration and Identification (EORI) number), based on the trader's VAT Registration Number. Traders are also being supported to understand the information they need to collect about their goods, including their description, value and any supporting documentation required. However, such support has been inconsistent, especially concerning the efficiency and complexity of the TSS system, and at best conflicting, and has done little to bolster confidence on the part of many UK traders.

The service uses this information to complete import and safety and security declarations on behalf of traders. Where a trader uses the TSS to complete these declarations, they do not need to access HMRC systems, such as CDS or ICS, themselves. In theory, the system is up and running, whereas in practice, it has yielded many challenges and operational errors and anomalies which have yet to be resolved.

VAT and Excise

The protocol means that Northern Ireland maintains alignment on some administrative processes included within the EU VAT and Excise rules for goods, in that excise and VAT rates remain different between Northern Ireland and the Irish Republic. Northern Ireland is, and will remain, part of the UK's VAT and Excise system, reflecting the fact that each jurisdiction across Europe already operates separate VAT and Excise regimes. HMRC will continue to be responsible for the operation and collection of the Excise and VAT revenues in Northern Ireland, which will not be passed on to the EU. The protocol notes that implementation of these measures will take into account Northern Ireland's integral place in the UK's internal market. The

UK government has stated that traders can use the flexibilities available, in the context of the wider commitments to Northern Ireland's place in the UK internal market, to implement these aspects of the protocol in a way that minimises new costs and burdens on businesses in Northern Ireland. As this is subject to ongoing consultation and discussion, further guidance will be set out and clarified on the application of VAT and Excise rules for goods in Northern Ireland in due course.

Records

EIDR (Entry in Declarants Records) Import and Export Transaction records in Excel format are required to be maintained and kept by all traders. For all cross-border shipments between Northern Ireland and the Republic of Ireland, INTRASTAT records and monthly supplementary declarations will continue to be used, as will conventional VAT Numbers in invoices for all cross-border transactions.

There is no need for any new procedures for the movement of goods between Northern Ireland and the UK mainland, other than for goods moving in transit across the UK bound for the European continent. There are therefore no Customs checks or documentation required for these movements to the UK. However, Customs Declarations are required at the point of UK import for movements from the Republic of Ireland to the UK via Northern Ireland. These can be submitted either in Northern Ireland or on the UK mainland.

Declaring Goods Brought into Northern Ireland "Not At Risk" of Moving to the EU

There are some goods which cannot be declared "Not At Risk". These goods will be automatically deemed "At Risk" [of crossing the border from Northern Ireland to the Republic of Ireland], and the appropriate EU Import Duty, which is higher than UK Import Duty, will be payable.

Goods which are subject to commercial processing, where the additional requirements to declare these goods "Not At Risk" are not met, cannot be declared "Not At Risk", and are therefore automatically "At Risk".

Goods which enter Northern Ireland from countries outside of both the EU and UK, where the applicable EU duty is greater than the applicable UK duty by 3 percentage points or more, cannot be declared "Not At Risk" and are therefore automatically "At Risk". In reality, this increased duty rate concerning the difference between levels of UK Import Duty and EU Import Duty applies in most cases regardless of the 3 percentage point ruling.

When Goods Can Be Declared As "Not At Risk"

If goods brought into Northern Ireland are not automatically "At Risk", they can be declared "Not At Risk" when they are either:

- "Not At Risk" due to the applicable duties;
- "Not At Risk" under the UK Trader Scheme.

When Goods Brought into Northern Ireland from Great Britain are "Not At Risk" Due to the Applicable Duties

Goods brought into Northern Ireland from Great Britain are "Not At Risk" if the applicable EU duty is zero. This is unless the goods are subject to processing and the trader does not meet the additional criteria to declare goods for processing "Not At Risk".

Goods brought into Northern Ireland from countries outside of both the EU and the UK, i.e. which are non-originating, are "Not At Risk" where the applicable UK duty is equal to or higher than the applicable EU duty, which in reality is not the case, as the UK Import Duty rates are now lower than those of the EU. This is unless the goods are subject to processing and the trader does not meet the additional criteria to declare goods for processing "Not At Risk".

To work out what the applicable UK duty and EU duty would be, the trader needs to take account of the Customs (Import) Duty and any other applicable measures that apply to their goods. This includes preferential rates where goods meet rules of origin requirements under relevant Free Trade Agreements.

You do not need to be authorised under the UK Trader Scheme to declare goods "Not At Risk" based on the applicable duties. Find out how to make a "Not At Risk" declaration.

When Goods Brought into Northern Ireland Can Be Declared "Not At Risk" Under the UK Trader Scheme

Where the applicable EU duties are higher than the applicable UK duties (which are zero in the case of movements from Great Britain to Northern Ireland), goods brought into Northern Ireland can still be declared "Not At Risk" when they are all of the following:

- For sale to, or final use by, end consumers located in Northern Ireland (and England, Scotland and Wales in the case of movements from Great Britain);
- Declared by a trader authorised under the UK Trader Scheme;
- Not subject to an EU trade remedy.

Goods brought into Northern Ireland from countries outside of both the EU and UK cannot be declared "Not At Risk" if the applicable EU duty is greater than the applicable EU duty by 3 percentage points or more.

If the goods you bring into Northern Ireland will be subject to processing, you must meet additional criteria when applying for UK Trader Scheme authorisation before you can declare these goods "Not At Risk".

In declaring goods "Not At Risk" under the UK Trader Scheme, you must be satisfied that these goods entered Northern Ireland for the purpose of being sold or used by end consumers located in Northern Ireland (and England, Scotland and Wales in the case of movements from Great Britain). You'll need to keep evidence to demonstrate this.

Some examples include:

- Selling goods in a shop in Northern Ireland;
- Buying stationery for use in Northern Ireland;
- A farmer buying a tractor for their own use in Northern Ireland;
- Selling furniture from a wholesale outlet to shops, or to businesses for their own use, in Northern Ireland;
- Bringing goods into Northern Ireland from Great Britain, storing them in a warehouse in Northern Ireland before selling to other parts of the UK.

If the trader is a wholesaler, their customer must sell or use the materials in the appropriate territory according to the declaration that they have made – for example, they could sell a chair which was declared "Not At Risk" if it will be used at an office location in Northern Ireland.

If the trader did not declare your goods "Not At Risk", and this was a mistake, they may be able to apply for a repayment. If the trader applies for a repayment, they must provide proof that they are authorised under the UK Trader Scheme. This proof should be the letter or the email they received confirming their authorisation.

"At Risk" goods will be charged the applicable EU duty. "Not At Risk" goods will be charged:

- No duty if entering Northern Ireland from free circulation in Great Britain;
- UK duty if entering Northern Ireland from outside of both the EU and the UK;
- UK duty if entering Northern Ireland from Great Britain and the good was not in free circulation in Great Britain.

Whether goods are "At Risk" or "Not At Risk" is determined by the applicable duties and the trader's certainty of the final destination of the goods.

When Goods Cannot be Declared as "Not At Risk"

There are some goods which cannot be declared "Not At Risk". These goods will be automatically "At Risk" and the EU duty will be payable.

Goods which are subject to commercial processing, where the additional requirements to declare these goods "Not At Risk" are not met, cannot be declared "Not At Risk", and are therefore automatically "At Risk".

Goods which enter Northern Ireland from countries outside of both the EU and UK, where the applicable EU duty is greater than the applicable UK duty by 3 percentage points or more, cannot be declared "Not At Risk" and are therefore automatically "At Risk".

When You Can Declare Goods as "Not At Risk"

If goods brought into Northern Ireland are not automatically "At Risk", they can be declared "Not At Risk" when they are either:

- "Not At Risk" due to the applicable duties;
- "Not At Risk" under the UK Trader Scheme.

When Goods You Bring into Northern Ireland Are "Not At Risk" Due to the Applicable Duties

Goods brought into Northern Ireland from Great Britain are "Not At Risk" if the applicable EU duty is zero. This is unless the goods are subject to processing and you do not meet the additional criteria to declare goods for processing "Not At Risk".

Goods brought into Northern Ireland from countries outside of both the EU and the UK are "Not At Risk" where the applicable UK duty is equal to or higher than the applicable EU duty. This is unless the goods are subject to processing and you do not meet the additional criteria to declare goods for processing "Not At Risk".

To work out what the applicable UK duty and EU duty would be, the UK trader needs to take account of the Customs Duty and any other applicable measures that apply to their goods. This includes preferential rates where goods meet rules of origin requirements under relevant Free Trade Agreements.

The trader does not need to be authorised under the UK Trader Scheme to declare goods "Not At Risk" based on the applicable duties. Find out how to make a "Not At Risk" declaration.

When Goods Brought into Northern Ireland Can Be Declared "Not At Risk" Under the UK Trader Scheme

Where the applicable EU duties are higher than the applicable UK duties (which are zero in the case of movements from Great Britain to Northern Ireland), goods brought into Northern Ireland can still be declared "Not At Risk" when they are all of the following:

- For sale to, or final use by, end consumers located in Northern Ireland (and England, Wales and Scotland in the case of movements from Great Britain);
- Declared by a trader authorised under the UK Trader Scheme;
- Not subject to an EU trade remedy.

Goods brought into Northern Ireland from countries outside of both the EU and UK cannot be declared "Not At Risk" if the applicable EU duty is greater than the applicable UK duty by 3 percentage points or more.

If the goods brought into Northern Ireland will be subject to processing, it is necessary to meet additional criteria when applying for UK Trader Scheme authorisation before these goods can be declared as "Not At Risk".

In declaring goods "Not At Risk" under the UK Trader Scheme, the trader must be satisfied that these goods entered Northern Ireland for the purpose of being sold or used by end consumers located in Northern Ireland (and England, Wales and Scotland in the case of movements from Great Britain).

The trader will need to keep evidence to demonstrate this.

Some examples include:

- Selling goods in a shop in Northern Ireland;
- Buying stationery for use in Northern Ireland;
- A farmer buying a tractor for their own use in Northern Ireland;
- Selling furniture from a wholesale outlet to shops, or to businesses for their own use, in Northern Ireland;
- Bringing goods into Northern Ireland from Great Britain, storing them in a warehouse in Northern Ireland before selling to other parts of the UK.

If you are a wholesaler, your customer must sell or use the good in the appropriate territory according to the declaration you've made – for example, you could sell a chair which was declared "Not At Risk" if it will be used at an office location in Northern Ireland.

If you did not declare your goods "Not At Risk", and this was a mistake, you may be able to apply for a repayment. If you apply for a repayment, you must provide proof that you are authorised under the UK Trader Scheme. This proof should be the letter or the email you received confirming your authorisation. If you declared your goods "Not At Risk" by mistake, you should apply for a voluntary clearance amendment (under-payment).

Check the Additional Requirements for Goods Subject to Processing

If you bring goods into Northern Ireland which will be subject to processing, and wish to declare these goods "Not At Risk", you will need to meet additional criteria. When applying for UK Trader Scheme authorisation, you will need to tell us that either your:

- Annual turnover is less than £500,000;
- Goods are for 1 of the approved purposes.

The approved purposes are:

- Food for sale to end consumers in the UK;
- Construction – where the processed goods form a permanent part of a structure that is constructed and located in Northern Ireland by the importer;
- Directly providing health or care services by the importer in Northern Ireland;
- Non-profit activities in Northern Ireland, where there is no subsequent sale of the processed goods by the importer;
- The final use of animal feed on premises located in Northern Ireland by the importer.

Once authorised, the trader will then be able to declare their goods for processing as "Not At Risk" in line with the treatment of other goods.

These additional requirements for declaring goods "Not At Risk" apply only to goods that will be processed in Northern Ireland.

If the trader also moves goods that are not to be processed, they can still apply for authorisation under the UK Trader Scheme and declare those goods "Not At Risk" under the usual process, regardless of whether their business meets the processing criteria.

How to Declare Goods "Not At Risk"

The trader does not need to complete these declarations themselves, as they can:

- Sign up for the free Trader Support Service if they are moving goods into Northern Ireland from Great Britain;
- Get a specialist to complete declarations for them by using a Customs Intermediary (Clearing Agent) or a Customs Declaration service-enabled software provider;
- Move goods in parcels via a courier.

How to Declare Goods "Not At Risk" in the Customs Declaration Service

If the trader is submitting declarations in the Customs Declaration Service, they will need to use the Additional Information Code "NIREM" in Data Element 2/2 of their Import Declaration to declare their goods "Not At Risk".

If the trader wishes to declare a proportion of a single line item "Not At Risk", they must submit those goods as a separate line item using this Additional Information Code. The remaining proportion, which is "At Risk", must be a separate line item for which no code is necessary.

If the trader is using a specialist to complete declarations, then they will need to make the specialist aware that the goods to be brought into Northern Ireland are "Not At Risk". The trader will also need to confirm whether they are authorised for the UK Trader Scheme.

Find Out What Supporting Evidence Is Needed to Make a "Not At Risk" Declaration

If the trader is declaring their goods "Not At Risk" under the UK Trader Scheme, they need to keep supporting evidence for each consignment that they move into Northern Ireland, and this evidence will need to be accessible in Northern Ireland for 5 years.

The types of evidence to support a "Not At Risk" declaration include:

- Commercial receipts and invoices;
- VAT invoices;
- Commercial contracts and purchase orders;
- Delivery receipts;
- Consignment notes;
- Proof of installation;
- Electronic records;

- Proof that goods comply with rules of origin (if you have claimed a preferential rate of duty, you can check what proof you should hold).

The trader does not need to provide this evidence to HMRC on a routine basis, only when asked to do so.

UK Trader Scheme

If the trader wants to declare their goods "Not At Risk" and the EU tariff rate on these goods is above zero, they must apply for authorisation under the UK Trader Scheme.

"At Risk" goods will be charged the applicable EU duty. "Not At Risk" goods will be charged either:

- No duty if entering Northern Ireland from free circulation in Great Britain;
- UK duty if entering Northern Ireland from outside of both the EU and the UK;
- UK duty if entering Northern Ireland from Great Britain and the good was not in free circulation in Great Britain.

If the trader does not have experience in Customs or would like to find out more information, they can register with the Trader Support Service to receive support them with this process.

Who Can Apply to the UK Trader Scheme

To apply, the trader must meet 1 of the 2 establishment criteria. They must either:

- Be established in Northern Ireland;
- Have a fixed place of business in Northern Ireland and meet the additional requirements outlined.

The trader must also meet all of the:

- Customs compliance requirements;
- Records, systems, controls and evidence requirements and meet the additional requirements.

The trader can continue to use the current arrangements. This means that they can be authorised to declare goods "Not At Risk" without having their own fixed address in Northern Ireland.

If the trader moves goods into Northern Ireland to be processed, and wishes to declare these goods "Not At Risk", the trader will need to meet additional requirements.

Applying If the Trader Is Established in Northern Ireland

The trader is established in Northern Ireland if they have their central headquarters or a registered office there, where human and technical resources are present and all or part of their Customs operations are carried out.

Applying If the Trader Has a Fixed Place of Business in Northern Ireland

If the trader is not established in Northern Ireland, they can still meet the UK Trader Scheme establishment criteria, provided that they meet all of the following conditions:

- Their Customs operations are carried out in the UK;
- They have an indirect Customs representative in Northern Ireland, such as the Trader Support Service;
- They have a fixed place of business in Northern Ireland, which is all of the following:
  - Where part or all of their business takes place;
  - A physical location they rent or own, which they must staff;
  - Where they sell or provide goods for final use by end consumers (including use by their own business or sale to retail outlets in Northern Ireland);
  - Where relevant Customs, transport and commercial documentation is available.

For example, a fixed place of business could be:

- A retail outlet or warehouse from which goods brought into Northern Ireland are sold or sent directly to consumers;
- Your own business site where the goods you bring into Northern Ireland are used.

If the Trader Supplies Goods to a Business in Northern Ireland But Does Not Have a Fixed Address in Northern Ireland

The trader can be authorised to declare goods "Not At Risk" without having their own fixed address in Northern Ireland, if all of the following apply:

- the trader does not have a fixed address in Northern Ireland, but their Customs operations are carried out in the UK, and they have an indirect Customs representative in Northern Ireland (such as the Trader Support Service);
- The trader supplies goods to a business in Northern Ireland that has a fixed place of business from where those goods are provided or sold to end consumers, and that business is either:
  - authorised under the UK Trader Scheme;
  - could be authorised if they were the importer of those goods.

To be authorised to declare goods "Not At Risk" in these circumstances, the trader must:

- Meet all of the other UK Trader Scheme criteria;
- Be able to declare goods as "Not At Risk" because they are for sale to, or final use by, end consumers located in the UK.

In their application, the trader will need to:

- list the addresses of the businesses in Northern Ireland that they supply who are authorised or meet the criteria to be authorised;
- tell HMRC that they are supplying goods to a business in Northern Ireland who is authorised or meets the criteria to be authorised, but you do not currently have a fixed premise in Northern Ireland – you should state this in your covering email when submitting their application for authorisation.

The Customs Compliance Requirements

The trader must have:

- A good Customs and Tax Compliance record;
- No record of serious criminal offences related to your economic activity.

Their record is based on the 3 years prior to application or on all available information, including your involvement in any previous businesses. They must have no record of any serious or repeated infringements of Customs rules.

Records, Systems, Controls and Evidence Requirements

The trader needs to give details of the records, systems and controls that they have in place that allow them to accurately declare that goods are "Not At Risk".

When the trader applies for authorisation, they should give details of:

- The systems and processes to track goods from import to end-use – such as logistics systems or stock control processes;
- Documented procedures and administrative systems to determine whether goods are "Not At Risk";
- Internal controls and processes that ensure goods are correctly declared "Not At Risk";
- Commercial or transport records – such as delivery records or inventory systems that confirm end-use of the goods.

The records that the trader tells HMRC about will be specific and appropriate to their business, and they will need to show:

- Where the trader sources goods;
- How and where they will be used or sold.

If the trader is a small or medium-sized business, they do not need complex systems, but these systems must be appropriate to the size, nature and complexity of the business.

For example, if the trader is:

- A large business – they may tell HMRC about the logistical software that they have which tracks goods from import to end-use;
- A small or medium-sized business – the trader may instead tell HMRC about the internal processes or procedures they have in place which allow them to document the goods that the trader imports and evidence that these goods are "Not At Risk", like purchase and sales records.

The trader must keep evidence that their goods are not "At Risk" (for example, sales receipts) for 5 years. HMRC reserves the right to visit the trader to check the trader's records. The trader must be able to provide access to a Customs officer to check the records, systems and controls about which the trader has informed HMRC, and evidence to confirm each declaration.

Additional Requirements for Processing

When the trader applies for authorisation under the UK Trader Scheme, they will be asked if they move goods that are subject to processing and if they meet the additional processing requirements.

If the trader does not meet these processing requirements, they will not be able to declare goods which will be subject to processing in Northern Ireland, as "Not At Risk", even if they are granted authorisation under the UK Trader Scheme.

The trader can still declare goods which are not subject to processing as "Not At Risk" where the "Not At Risk" requirements are met.

If the trader wants to declare goods which will be processed as "Not At Risk", as part of their application for authorisation, they will need to either:

- State that their turnover for the most recent financial year is below £500,000. If they are a newly established business, they will need to provide records approved by the directors, partners or sole proprietor, to enable an assessment of anticipated turnover. Examples include:
  - Latest cash flow;
  - Balance sheet;
  - Profit and loss forecasts.
- State that they intend to bring goods for processing into Northern Ireland, where the goods are to be processed for 1 or more of the following sole purposes:
  - Food for sale to end consumers in the UK;
  - Construction – where the processed goods form a permanent part of a structure that is constructed and located in Northern Ireland by the importer;
  - Direct provision to the recipient of health or care services by the importer in Northern Ireland;
  - Not-for-profit activities in Northern Ireland, where there is no subsequent sale of the processed good by the importer;
  - The final use of animal feed on premises located in Northern Ireland by the importer.

When to Apply

If the trader wants to declare their goods "Not At Risk" and the EU duty rate on these goods is above zero, they must apply for authorisation under the UK Trader Scheme.

If the trader applied before the end of February 2021, they would have received a provisional authorisation for up to 4 months while HMRC processed their application. While provisionally authorised, it was possible for the trader to declare goods as "Not At Risk" if they met the appropriate criteria.

Applications After February 2021

The trader will have to have received their UK Trader Scheme authorisation before declaring their goods "Not At Risk".

How to Apply

The trader needs to:

1. Fill in the form on screen by selecting "Start now";
2. Save the form onto your computer;
3. Email the completed form to: uktraderscheme@hmrc.gov.uk with any supporting documentation. The trader must type their EORI Number in the subject of the email.

The trader should complete the application form and submit it to HMRC with proof of permanent business establishment or document of establishment.

The trader also needs to provide evidence of their record-keeping to supplement the information provided in your application, but this is not mandatory.

If the trader is applying for authorisation and does not have a fixed place of business in Northern Ireland, then they must provide the necessary additional information when submitting their application.

For support throughout this process, the trader can register with the Trader Support Service.

To apply for authorisation, the trader needs:

- Details of any other Customs authorisations you hold, such as Authorised Economic Operator, Customs Freight Simplified Procedures or Customs special procedures – this means the trader does not need to provide as much information when they apply;
- The trader's GB or XI EORI Number;
- Details of the trader's business and its directors;
- The trader's company registration number or Unique Taxpayer Reference if they are a sole trader or partnership;
- The trader's VAT Registration Number if they have 1;
- The estimated number of "Not At Risk" declarations that the trader will make annually;
- Details of the trader's business premises in Northern Ireland, such as where they undertake processing or sell goods to consumers – the trader must provide details of all the premises that they have in Northern Ireland.

CHAPTER 19

The Implications of the Decision by the UK to Leave the European Union (Brexit)

On 23 June 2016, the British public voted in a national plebiscite to leave the European Union. After much confusion, it was realised that this meant a complete withdrawal from the European Single Market, as it was determined that it would not be possible to remain part of the Single Market and adhere to all of its pillars, namely the Free Movement of goods, services, capital and labour, which are the 4 main elements of a Common Market. Failing the negotiation of a separate Free Trade Agreement between the UK and the EU, normal WTO rules would apply following the exit from the EU, namely the imposition of full Customs controls on all imports and exports between the UK and the EU, as well as the imposition of Customs Import Duty and VAT on all imports between the countries. As 1 of the primary reasons for the withdrawal from the EU was based on the issue of immigration and the perceived lack of immigration controls concerning the UK, as well as the imposition of laws by the EU on the UK which were seen as unjust and repressive, then the principles of the continued membership of the EU could no longer be satisfied. The UK formally left the EU at the beginning of 2021 (officially at 11 pm on 31 December 2020).

At the time of completion of this text (2022), the exit of the UK from the EU has resulted in the complete withdrawal from the Single Market without any preconditions of a Customs Union, and there was a complete renegotiation of terms concerning trade with the EU. However, this also meant that Customs controls were re-imposed on all movements of goods between the UK and the EU, in a manner similar to the UK's trade with non-EU countries. This has also meant that the full nature of the SAFE Framework of Standards, as well as the WTO's Trade Facilitation Agreement, applies to the UK as a fully sovereign separate nation-state. UK Customs now applies its own set of rules and regulations separately from the EU, but in accordance with the rules of the World Customs Organisation (WCO) and hence the SAFE Framework of Standards and the Revised Kyoto Convention. To this extent, there is little difference in an independent UK Customs policy away from the EU insofar as overall practices and procedures, as these are still governed by the SAFE Framework of Standards. Indeed, at the time of the withdrawal of the UK

 DOI: 10.4324/9781003341345-20

from the EU, it was stated by HMRC that some of the Union Customs Code would continue to apply to the UK because of its foundation in the SAFE Framework of Standards, given the latter's global implications.

Procedural Summary

As of the night of 31 December 2020, the UK was no longer part of the EU Single Market, and therefore implemented full Customs controls over imported and exported goods.

Customs Controls and Declarations

There was also the implementation of full import and export Customs controls at UK frontiers, as well as the implementation of full Import and Export Customs Declarations for the movement of goods into and out of the UK. The implementation of Transitional Simplified Procedures (TSP) is designed to streamline and simplify all Import and Export Declarations concerning traffic between the UK and the EU, but eventually this will be replaced by the CFSP (Customs Freight Simplified Procedures) system.

Tariffs

Although the World Trade Organisation implemented a significant change in Tariff Commodity Codes on 1 January 2017, it was still necessary for HM government to review Import Duty rates in line with national economic requirements. In the main, UK Import Duty rates were significantly reduced from those of the EU, and as of 2022, these reductions still apply.

Origin and Preferences

In leaving the EU, the UK forfeited the ability to use existing trade preferences and Free Trade Agreements agreed with overseas countries. The UK entered into negotiation as quickly as possible with many nations, including the EU, to create a new regime of international Free Trade Agreements. In doing so, a new set of UK Certificates of Origin and Movement Certificates was required, in order to provide evidence of origin status, especially where trade preferences apply. However, concerning trade with the EU, this was circumvented by the use of Invoice Declarations stating the origin of the goods concerned along with the EU exporter's REX (Registered Exporter) Number or the UK exporter's EORI Number. As part of any Free Trade Agreements negotiated by the UK, a full set of Rules of Origin has been negotiated in order to satisfy origin requirements for trade preference purposes.

Typically, for preferential origin, around 50%+ of the value has to be added to claim origin. Post-Brexit, what was once European value-added will have to be separated into UK and EU value-added. That will make it harder to reach the threshold to export to the EU without tariffs.

One of the ways this problem is avoided by other countries is to allow "cumulation" of value-added. There are different kinds of cumulation, but the main purpose is to allow the value of components contributed by different countries to be combined to meet the threshold when a product is re-exported, in a facility known as Diagonal Cumulation. In this arrangement, each country involved in the cumulation chain has a Free Trade Agreement with the other countries in the chain. Therefore, in order to maintain existing Supply Chains, the UK needs to be able to count EU components toward UK content so that it can reach the threshold to re-export to the EU.

The Union Customs Code

HMRC is continuing with parts of the UCC, but has decided upon certain applications of the Code on a case-by-case basis. AEO status is continuing to exist in the UK given its global importance, albeit with the possibility of some amendments and relaxations of some requirements to encompass a rather less stringent Trusted Trader status.

Excise

Excise management is now entirely controlled by the UK government, with all imports and exports of Excise goods covered by full Import and Export Declarations.

VAT

Although UK Import VAT and VAT zero-rating are already covered by UK Import and Export Customs Declarations, the INTRASTAT regime for the Customs control over intra-EU transactions has ceased to apply to the UK. Furthermore, the UK has introduced the Postponed VAT Accounting (PVA) facility, where Import VAT is accounted for on the VAT return, rather than being paid outright against the Import Declaration.

Postponed VAT Accounting

Prior to the withdrawal of the UK from the EU, Import VAT was due at the same time as Customs Import Duty on goods imported from a non-EU country. This was usually on or soon after the goods arrived at the UK border, upon the release of the goods into free circulation. Although payment of Customs Duty and Import VAT was due immediately, it could usually be deferred to the 15th day of the following month by using a duty deferment account, if available. The Import VAT could then usually be reclaimed as input tax on the next VAT return (subject to the normal VAT rules on input tax deduction).

From 11 pm on 31 December 2020, VAT-registered importers were able (or in some instances required) to account for VAT on goods imported for use in their business on their VAT returns. This facility is called Postponed VAT Accounting.

This facility does not cover matters specified in the Northern Ireland Protocol, as these matters are detailed in other texts issued by HM government in the UK. The government continues to work through the implications of the Northern Ireland Protocol, including issues in relation to VAT and Excise. The government is providing guidance on how the Northern Ireland Protocol will work ahead of the end of the transition period, which includes the use of the new XI EORI Numbers for trade with Northern Ireland.

VAT collection on imported goods in consignments not exceeding £135 has also changed from 1 January 2021, and Postponed VAT Accounting is not available for those consignments. These changes do not apply to consignments containing Excise goods or non-commercial consignments. It should also be noted that these changes are not subject to the staged approach to import controls. Further information in respect of these changes can be found at GOV.UK.

Changes to Import VAT for Importers

UK VAT-registered importers can use PVA on their Customs Declaration. PVA is not ordinarily mandatory, and it is possible for importers to continue to use the current process to pay, defer or, if appropriate, secure the VAT on importation if they so wish. However, in most cases, PVA has been applied by default, meaning that importers not wishing to use the PVA facility must instruct their freight agents or clearance brokers accordingly. They can choose to start using PVA at any time. It is also possible for importers to use PVA for some imports and existing means of payment for others.

The introduction of PVA has enabled importers to account for and recover Import VAT as input tax on the same periodic (usually quarterly) VAT return, rather than having to pay it up-front and recover it on a subsequent return using the C79 VAT certificate as evidence of entitlement. Indeed, the PVA system allows for the use of online Import VAT Statements rather than a hard copy of the C79 Import VAT certificate.

These changes do not affect non-VAT-registered importers and individuals, who must continue to pay (or defer) Import VAT on imported goods at the same time as Customs Import Duty, as they have previously done.

How PVA works

All UK VAT-registered importers are eligible to use PVA, and no prior authorisation is required. They simply make the appropriate import entry and provide their EORI and/or VAT registration number (VRN) on their Customs Import Declaration, but need to put the letters "PVA" on the entry or instruct their Clearing Agents to do so. This process, which is subject to Customs clearance, allows the goods to enter into free circulation without up-front outright payment of the Import VAT. The Customs Declaration generates an online Monthly Postponed Import VAT Statement (MPIVS) that is the evidence required to account for and recover the Import VAT as input tax on their next VAT return. (Note: The C79 continues to be produced for those entries where any VAT is physically paid on importation.)

PVA is only available on declarations where Import VAT would ordinarily be due and where goods are being declared to free circulation. Where goods are placed into a Customs special procedure, e.g. Customs Warehousing, PVA is available on the declaration that removes them from that special procedure and places the goods into free circulation.

UK VAT-registered importers who import standard, i.e. non-controlled, goods into GB from the EU and who make an Entry in Declarants Records (EIDR) under the staged approach to import controls are required to use PVA to account for the Import VAT on those goods.

Making the EIDR allows the VAT-registered importer to defer submission of their supplementary declaration by up to 6 months from the point of import, and they will be required to use PVA irrespective of when they submit their supplementary declaration.

Where the importer does defer their supplementary declaration, they will not have an MPIVS when they complete their VAT return. They will therefore need to use the information on their EIDR or other commercial import records to estimate the amount of Import VAT due and account for that tax on the VAT return relating to the month of import. For example, the Import VAT on goods imported in January 2021 will be accounted for on the VAT return that covers January 2021.

When the deferred declaration is subsequently submitted, the actual amount of Import VAT will be calculated, and tax due to be accounted for will be recorded on the MPIVS for the month the declaration is submitted. This should be compared to the estimated amount, and any adjustments required should be made on the next VAT return.

How to Complete the Customs Declaration

If the trader or Clearing Agent uses software or the CDS Customs computer system to declare your Customs Duties, they need to:

- Enter either the EORI Number (which includes the importer's VAT Registration Number) into Box 8 (Header Consignee) or, if applicable, the VRN in Box 44h (Registered Consignee) of the declaration;
- Enter "G" as the method of payment in box 47e.

If they use the Customs Declaration Service to declare their Customs Duties they need to enter their VAT Registration Number at the header level in data element 3/40.

VAT is recorded against the importer's EORI and will be at the declaration level only.

PVA will not be available in CDS Customs computer where:

- The individual lines on the declarations show more than 1 importer;
- On any item that CDS Customs computer requires the input of a separate Secured VAT Tax Line.

Importers using CDS Customs computer and opting to use PVA will also need to subscribe to CDS (Customs Declaration System) in order to receive their online MPIVS (Import VAT Statement). Practical details of how to subscribe to this service will be released as soon as they are available. Although this subscription is connected to CDS, it will only provide the importer with access to their MPIVS and should not be used for any other purposes.

Changes for Customs intermediaries acting on behalf of an importer
For intermediaries submitting on behalf of an importer, i.e. Clearing Agents, the EORI (for CDS Customs computer users) or VRN (for CDS users) must be that of the importer. VAT cannot be postponed against the intermediary's account on behalf of an importer. Where an agent is acting for an importer, they must ensure that they have the importer's permission to use PVA.

Changes to Import Customs Controls and Procedures 1 January 2022

The UK government reminded companies importing goods into the UK from the EU that new documentation and Customs checks are being introduced from 1 October 2021, and there are concerns that many companies importing goods from the EU are still not prepared, thus heightening the risk of both non-compliance and possible delays to import clearance.

The government postponed the start of import controls in March 2021 for 6 months to give businesses more time to prepare and for border control infrastructure to be set up and implemented. These controls apply as of 1 January 2022 without any further delay.

New Rules

Importers have been required to keep internal records of imports since the start of the year, but may have to start providing documentation from 1 October 2021 – initially for goods subject to sanitary and phytosanitary (SPS) controls, such as meat, cheese and eggs.

However, full Customs checks on all imports began on 1 January 2022, with tariffs, and VAT deferrable until the end of 2022. Full Customs Declarations have been required from 1 January 2022.

New Responsibilities

HMRC has made every effort to inform businesses, reminding them of their responsibilities, either by email bulletins or letters. Those who deferred Customs Declarations in January 2021 now have to file supplementary declarations for their goods movements. These declarations must be completed 175 days after the date that the goods were imported into the UK.

Non-compliant businesses could lose the right to delay future declarations and could face financial penalties.

End of Easements

Some EU importers have mistaken the ongoing easements from the government as a permanent "light touch" approach to Customs checks. Businesses should check that their partners are ready to comply.

2022: Full Customs Procedures

According to Lloyd's Loading List in an article published in mid-2021, freight companies view 1 January 2022, i.e. the date when full Customs procedures will come into effect for all imports, as an even bigger challenge than January 2021 because there are more new processes to master.

Traders should consider appointing an intermediary, i.e. a Customs Clearing Agent, to deal with their Customs documentation, whilst they concentrate on their core business.

Upcoming changes include:

The End of Delayed Declarations

From 1 January 2021, importers were allowed 175 days before the full (supplementary) Import Declaration needed to be submitted, and VAT and duty (if any) to be paid. This is facilitated as long as the correct authorisations, such as CFSP and EIDR, are in place. If the Customs Broker (Clearing Agent) has a CFSP facility in place, then the importer of record can use their facility.

The delayed declaration facility ends on 1 January 2022, and confirmation of this has been given by HMRC.

Pre-Lodgement or Temporary Storage

Pre-lodgement works by ensuring that the export and import documentation are *both* completed before the vehicle checks in at the port of departure (unless it is a transit movement). If this is not carried out, the trailer cannot be loaded aboard the ferry at the point of EU departure.

This is very different from the Temporary Storage model, where containers can be shipped and even landed before they are Customs cleared. The reason that Roll-on/Roll-off (Ro-Ro) ports have opted for pre-lodgement is because of the volumes of traffic they ship, the lack of space in ferry terminals, and the need to turn vessels around quickly.

Rules of Origin

From 1 January 2021, the EU and UK Customs Authorities agreed that they would not request proof of origin for goods. This will change on 1 January 2022. All exporters and importers must be able to prove the original manufacturing country for the goods they are shipping. Furthermore, they will be able to retrospectively request proof for goods that were shipped during 2021.

REX – Invoice Statements – Declaration of Origin

If you are importing goods into the UK from a country or bloc with whom the UK has a Free Trade Agreement (FTA), your overseas supplier will need to declare that the goods originated in their country. Each FTA will have an official notification in the documentation. It could be a statement on the invoice, a Certificate of Origin, a preferential trade certificate, a supplier's declaration, a Trusted Trader status (REX, Approved Exporter (AE) or AEO) (or the goods originate in a GSP country). Whatever it is, you, as the importer of record, must show HMRC that you have done sufficient due diligence to prove the goods you are importing meet FTA preference rules.

As this is a new chapter in our relationship with the EU, from 1 January 2022 all suppliers from Europe must have a REX (Registered Exporter) authorisation. The REX registered number must be shown on their Commercial Invoice for the goods to enter the UK duty-free. Any goods arriving at the UK Customs border point without the REX authorisation number will incur an Import Duty charge if the product's commodity code carries duty.

It is important that all businesses bring this to the attention of all their EU suppliers. It is very easy to get REX authorisation and it is free. For UK companies exporting to the EU, they will continue to put officially worded origin declarations on their commercial invoices. For the rest of the world, UK-EUR1 preferential trade certificates, Certificates of Origin, invoice statement declarations, long term supplier's declarations, or a Trusted Trader status (REX, AE, AEO) etc. will be used to prove origin.

Products of Animal Origin (POAO), Sanitary and Phytosanitary Products

Sanitary products relate to animal health, and certification is required to determine the health of the animals. Phytosanitary relates to plants and fauna certification. These are referred to as SPS checks. POAO relates mainly to the food chain; however, it does include other industry sectors, such as products from leather, gelatine, etc.

From 1 January 2022, UK importers of Products of Animal Origin (POAO), animal by-products and high-risk food and feed not of animal origin, must pre-notify UK Import Authorities of incoming consignments. Shipments coming from the EU or European Economic Area must be pre-notified before the consignment is due to arrive in Great Britain.

Exporting POAO from the EU to UK

From 1 January 2022, an Export Health Certificate (EHC) will be required for exports of POAO from the EU into the UK. EU exporters must be registered on TRACES NT to apply for an EHC. TRACES NT (TNT) is the European Commission's digital certification and management platform for all sanitary and phytosanitary requirements, supporting the importation of animals, animal products, food and feed of non-animal origin, and plants in the European Union.

Importing POAO into the UK

As of 1 January 2022, UK importers must be registered with IPAFFS (Import of Products, Animals, Food, and Feed System) and are responsible for the import. They must have a UK address and are responsible for submitting the pre-notification of incoming consignments with the attached EHC via IPAFFS before the consignment is due to arrive. IPAFFS is a web-based service used to notify UK authorities of imports of live animals, their products, and germplasm.

The Goods Vehicle Movement (GVMS) System

This new system will be in place by 1 January 2022, and primarily affects hauliers, Customs Brokers and Clearing Agents.

CHIEF versus CDS

The old and outdated Customs control system known as CHIEF (Customs Handling of Import and Export Freight) will be replaced for imports from 30 September 2022. The new digital system will take over this important function. Known as CDS (Customs Declaration Service), it is being developed to accommodate all procedures and process changes to the EU legislation brought by the Union Customs Code in 2016.

It is planned that all Export Declarations will be introduced on CDS by 31 March 2023, after which the old CHIEF system will be discontinued. This means more detailed information will be required for Import and Export Declarations.

Whilst this is important for the Customs Brokers rather than the importer or exporter of record, it does mean that digital records are more traceable; thus, compliance is essential. This is just part of the bigger picture of the way we will move goods around the world.

UK and EU Customs will be stepping up their scrutiny of goods moving across borders from 1 January 2022. If the trader is a UK Importer or Exporter of Record, they are responsible for ensuring that all their documentation, proof of due diligence, origin, VAT and duty payments are in order and filed ready for HMRC inspection. HMRC has stated that failure to comply with these requirements will result in penalties and could affect the ability of the trader to apply for Customs authorisations in the future.

Safety and Security Declarations

From 1 July 2022, safety and security declarations will become due on goods being imported from the EU and other territories that did not require these before 1 January 2021 to Great Britain. This will reflect the existing model already in place for trade between Great Britain and countries outside the EU.

From 1 October 2021, safety and security declarations will become due on goods leaving Great Britain in vehicles and for empty containers, pallets and vehicles moving to the EU under a transport contract. This will reflect the existing model already in place for Great Britain's trade with countries outside the EU.

Safety and security requirements for goods moving from Great Britain to Northern Ireland have been in place since 1 January 2021 and are covered in the Northern Ireland section.

Safety and security declarations continue to be required for goods entering and leaving the UK from countries outside the EU.

The UK is committed to upholding the principles of the World Customs Organisation SAFE framework.

Any references to Great Britain within this document include the 3 island territories off the coast of Great Britain, which are Crown Dependencies. These are:

- The Isle of Man;
- The Bailiwick of Jersey – Channel Islands;
- The Bailiwick of Guernsey (which includes Alderney and Sark) – Channel Islands.

The safety and security regulations mandate pre-arrival information for all consignments entering Great Britain, with exceptions for qualifying Northern Ireland goods moving from either:

- Northern Ireland to Great Britain;
- Northern Ireland to Ireland, and then to Great Britain;

The government has legislated to guarantee unfettered access for Northern Ireland businesses to the whole of the UK internal market.

For safety and security, that means:

- No entry summary (ENS) declaration is required as qualifying Northern Ireland goods enter the rest of the UK from Northern Ireland;
- No requirement to submit export or exit summary (EXS) declarations for qualifying Northern Ireland goods leaving Northern Ireland for the rest of the UK.

The only exceptions to these arrangements will be goods falling within the very limited number of procedures relating to specific international obligations binding on the UK and the EU – for example, obligations on the movement of endangered species and where traders want to use special procedures like duty suspension where we would continue to provide facilitation.

On 9 September 2021, the government legislated to ensure that no ENS declaration will be required for qualifying Northern Ireland goods which arrive in Great Britain having moved through Ireland. Further guidance will be provided closer to this change coming into effect.

All information submitted will be assessed against a set of risk rules, allowing the UK to continue to secure its borders effectively.

Imports into Great Britain and Northern Ireland

Safety and security data for imports is submitted by the lodgement of an ENS declaration.

Responsibility

The legal requirement to submit an ENS declaration lies with the operator of the active means of transport – for example, the vessel, aircraft, train or road vehicle – on or in which the goods are brought into the Customs territory (either Great Britain or Northern Ireland). We will refer to this party as the carrier.

For rail, this means the Rail Freight Operator who is authorised to traction the train through the Channel Tunnel into Great Britain.

For maritime and air, the legal requirement is with the party that has contracted and issued the Bill of Lading or an air waybill for the carriage of the goods into Great Britain or Northern Ireland. For sea, this means the shipping company is responsible, and for air, the airline.

For Ro-Ro, this means the haulage company is responsible for lodging the declaration for "accompanied" goods and the ferry operator for "unaccompanied" goods.

In the case of "combined transport" – such as a truck carried on a ferry – the obligation to file an ENS lies with the operator of the active means of transport on arrival in the UK. Where a truck is carried on a ferry and will drive off the ferry on arrival in the UK, the obligation lies with the trucking company.

Where a ferry is transporting an unaccompanied trailer or container, the active means of transport is the ferry, even when the trailer or container could be attached to a truck when it arrives at its destination.

Accuracy and Completeness

Customs authorities and economic operators must be able to identify who is responsible for compliance with these requirements.

The declarant must provide the information known to them at the time of lodgement of the ENS. They are entitled to base their ENS filing on data provided by the trading or contracting parties.

All the data elements prescribed in the table in Appendix 1 for safety and security and Appendix 2 for ICS NI must be contained in the ENS filing. If the declarant learns later that 1 or more particulars contained in the ENS filing have been incorrectly declared, the provisions on amendments will apply.

Safety and security declarations are an important part of Border Force's frontier risk assessment processes. The timely provision of complete and accurate data will help your goods flow through the border more smoothly.

The government will continue to engage with carriers, hauliers and traders to make sure that their obligations to meet safety and security requirements are fully understood. HMRC will seek to support those who make genuine errors to get it right, including education and intervention. Enforcement action in respect of non-compliance will be evidence-based and proportionate. This action could involve goods being delayed at the border for further checks and risking fines.

Who Can Submit the ENS

Someone other than the carrier may lodge an ENS. However, as it is the carrier's responsibility to make sure that it is submitted within the legal time limits, it must only be done by a representative or third party with the carrier's knowledge and consent.

Arranging for an alternative third-party ENS filing may be done through the use of commercial terms and conditions and may involve the third-party declarant and the carrier making amendments to an existing, or creating a new, contractual agreement that the third party is to file the ENS instead of the carrier.

How the carrier's consent to the third-party ENS filing is to be evidenced and under which conditions and terms are subject to contractual agreement between the commercial parties. For example, the time for submission of the ENS, the shipments involved, and the duration of the filing arrangement.

Except where there is evidence to the contrary, the Customs Authorities may assume that the carrier has given its consent under contractual arrangements and that the third party's lodging of the ENS is made with the carrier's knowledge and consent.

If responsibility is passed on to a third party, the legal liability to make sure that an ENS declaration is submitted remains with the carrier. However, the responsibility for ensuring that the information provided is accurate lies with the declarant – in this case, the third party.

When to Submit

Legislation requires that an electronic ENS must be lodged before arrival in Great Britain or Northern Ireland or, in the case of maritime deep-sea containerised shipments, before loading onto the vessel that will carry the goods into Great Britain or Northern Ireland.

Time Limits for Submitting an ENS to
Great Britain or Northern Ireland
Check the time limits for submitting an ENS for:

- Maritime containerised cargo (except short sea containerised shipping) – at least 24 hours before loading onto the vessel that will carry the goods into Great Britain or Northern Ireland;
- Maritime bulk or break bulk (except short sea bulk or break bulk shipping) – at least 4 hours before arrival at the Office of First Entry in Great Britain or Northern Ireland;
- Short sea voyages – at least 2 hours before arrival at the Office of First Entry in Great Britain or Northern Ireland;
- Short-haul flights less than 4 hours in duration – at least by the time of the actual take-off;
- Long-haul flights more than 4 hours in duration – at least 4 hours before arrival at the Office of First Entry in Great Britain or Northern Ireland;
- Rail – at least 2 hours before arrival at the UK Customs Office of Entry (Dollands Moor for rail) or at least 1 hour if the journey is less than 2 hours.

Short sea journeys into Great Britain refer to journeys from:

- The English Channel – or the Atlantic coast of Europe from the point where it meets the English Channel to and including the port of Algeciras;
- Norway;
- Ireland;
- The Faroe Islands and Iceland;
- Ports on the Baltic Sea and the North Sea.

Short sea journeys into Northern Ireland refer to journeys from:

- Great Britain and the Channel Islands;
- Greenland;
- The Faroe Islands;
- Iceland;
- Ports on the Baltic Sea, the North Sea, the Black Sea and the Mediterranean Sea;
- All ports of Morocco.

Time Limits for Ro-Ro Accompanied and Unaccompanied

For Ro-Ro accompanied, this must be lodged at least 2 hours before the goods are due to arrive in Great Britain or Northern Ireland. For the Channel Tunnel, due to juxtaposed controls, this must be lodged at least 1 hour before arrival at the Eurotunnel EU terminal by the haulage company if goods are accompanied.

For Ro-Ro unaccompanied, this must be lodged at least 2 hours before the goods are due to arrive in Great Britain or Northern Ireland by the ferry operator if goods are unaccompanied.

If the Trader Is Using the Goods Vehicle Movement Service (GVMS)

The entry summary declaration will need to be submitted at the earliest of either:

- The minimum timing requirement;
- Before check-in closes.

This is to allow for the Movement Reference Number (MRN) from the entry summary declaration to be recorded in the Goods Movement Reference, which will be validated by the carrier at check-in.

CHAPTER 20

SAF-T – The Standard Audit File for Tax

The Standard Audit File for Tax Purposes (SAF-T) is a standardised XML file used for exporting the accounting information of a company to the tax authorities. The file contains accounting data that can be exported from an original accounting system for a specific time period.

The SAF-T file is based on a directive by the Organisation for Economic Co-operation and Development.

The Standard Audit File for Tax was developed by the Organisation for Economic Co-operation and Development in 2005 with the aim of producing a global standardised format for the electronic exchange of accounting data from organisations to their national tax authority and external auditors' reports. It was therefore designed to ensure consistency from country to country to facilitate exchange of data between tax authorities. The file requirements are expressed using XML, although the EU does not specify the exact file format.

The 2 key principles behind SAF-T are that:

1. Organisations should be able to export information from their accounting systems (invoices, payments, general ledger journals and master files) into a standardised format; *and*
2. Tax authorities and external auditors should be able to make their tax inspections and audits more efficient and effective as a result of data being made available to them in that standardised format.

There are generally 5 reporting requirements:

1. General ledger and supporting journals;
2. Accounts payable, including supplier master data and invoices;
3. Accounts receivable, with customer master data and invoices;
4. Warehouse inventories, and master data;
5. Fixed assets ledger, including amortisation.

In 2005 the OECD released the first version of the SAF-T schema which provides details of what should be included in a SAF-T XML reporting file and

DOI: 10.4324/9781003341345-21

how that data should be formatted and structured. The original schema was based on the general ledger and details of invoices and payments, together with customer and supplier master files. A second version of the SAF-T schema was released in 2010 to incorporate information about Inventory and Fixed Assets.

What the OECD has not defined, and what remains the responsibility of the tax administration in each country to decide, is the exact format in which the data is to be captured and when and how it is required to be sent to the tax administration.

Different Approaches

What has emerged from those countries which have adopted SAF-T are 3 broad approaches:

- Data to be provided at the request of the tax authority (usually prior to a tax inspection or audit);
- Submission of data periodically in addition to the periodic VAT return;
- Submission of transactional data as a replacement to the periodic VAT return.

In some cases, the mandate starts with a requirement to produce data on request and evolves through to periodic submissions.

Where Are We Now?

There are currently 7 countries that have introduced legislation enforcing SAF-T requirements.

Portugal
Portugal was 1 of the first adopters, and Portuguese entities have been required to extract data into the SAF-T file format (based on version 1 of the OECD SAF-T schema) since 2008 on an annual basis. Further extensions to collect sales invoice data and other documents on a monthly basis followed in 2013.

Luxembourg
Luxembourg introduced the requirement to extract data in the relevant format in 2011. It only applies to Luxembourg resident companies subject to the local chart of accounts and is only required to be submitted when requested by the tax authority.

France

France introduced a SAF-T requirement in 2014, using a proprietary format rather than the OECD standard SAF-T schema, requiring files to be submitted in .txt format. France's version of SAF-T, *Fichier des Écritures Comptables* (FEC), is aligned to the national chart of accounts, the *Plan Comptable General.* It is therefore at variance with the global OECD standard. At present, French SAF-T is only required on demand by the tax authorities, usually prior to a VAT audit by the French tax authorities. The required format is .txt.

Austria

Austria introduced SAF-T in 2009 and is currently only required on demand when requested by the tax authority.

Poland

Possibly the most significant implementer of SAF-T to date, with large companies having had to file monthly JPK (*Jednolity Plik Kontrolny*) returns since 2016. However, the new SAF-T has been postponed until October 2020.

SAF-T has brought significant benefits to governments and taxpayers. Reduced costs and audit durations, and increased effectiveness are some of them. SAF-T is easily readable thanks to its standardised layout and format, and extensible according to need.

Poland introduced its own SAF-T version JPK on 1 July 2016, first for large taxpayers. Currently it is compulsory for all taxpayers.

Components of the monthly/quarterly submissions are as follows:

JPK_KR	(Accounting books)
JPK_WB	(Bank statements)
JPK_MAG	(Warehouse/Storage)
JPK_VAT	(VAT evidence)*
JPK_FA	(VAT invoices)
JPK_PKPIR	(Revenue and expense tax books)
JPK_EWP	(Revenues registry)

** JPK_VAT submission is compulsory for every period. The other JPK files must be submitted on demand.*

New JPK_VAT with Declaration (Used to Be Known as JPK_VDEK)

An update was scheduled for July 2020 which will replace the old JPK_VAT and will be mandatory for all companies, independent from the annual revenue.

The taxpayer will prepare and send only 1 file that contains:

- VAT records, a set of information about purchases and sales for a given period;
- VAT declaration (current VAT-7 and VAT-7K declaration).

New JPK_VAT will be submitted monthly only in the electronic version, up to the 25th of the month for the previous month.

Lithuania

Lithuania introduced the requirement to file the SAF-T based i.MAS on a phased basis, starting with the largest organisations in 2016 and working towards mandating SAF-T for all businesses by 2020. The i.MAS comprises 3 parts, i.SAF reporting of sales and purchase invoices on a monthly basis, i.VAZ reporting of transport/consignment documents and the i.SAF-T accounting transaction report, which is only required when requested by the tax authority.

Norway

SAF-T has been in place on a voluntary basis since 2017, but was introduced on a mandatory basis as from 1 January 2020. However, it is only required on an "on demand" basis by the tax authorities, typically immediately before a tax audit. Businesses with a turnover of less than NOK5 million, and not storing their data electronically, are exempted from using the system.

Norwegian SAF-T is standard file format for exporting various types of accounting transactional data using the XML format.

The first version of SAF-T Financial is limited to the general ledger level including customer and supplier transactions. Necessary master data is also included. Future versions of SAF-T Financial will include source documents such as detailed invoice data and movements of goods and asset transactions. Furthermore, other data elements will be added to support SAF-T Financial as a format for migration of data between different accounting software.

The SAF-T Cash Register containing journal data from electronic cash register systems was finalised in 2016.

The primary purpose of the SAF-T Financial data format is to:

- Serve as an export format for accounting data after request from the Norwegian Tax Administration, public accountants and other parties;
- Serve as archiving format for the necessary accounting data for those who are obliged to keep accounts as stated in the Norwegian bookkeeping legislation;

- Serve as a format for moving data when changing accounting software;
- Serve as a format for moving data from accounting software to other financial systems such as year-end closing systems, tax computation systems, business intelligence software, advisory systems, etc.

What Lies Ahead for the Future of SAF-T?
Countries which are receiving regular, transactional level details under SAF-T may look to reduce the periodic VAT return requirements. This is because the need to prepare a VAT return summarising the details which the tax authority already receives on a transactional basis can be seen as unnecessary duplication.

Poland is proposing that SAF-T data submissions will displace the need for filing a VAT return from January 2020.

Romania is proposing a phased transition to filing of transactional data from 2020, starting with large organisations, with a reduction in the VAT returns which are required to be filed.

System Setup

The ERP/Bespoke software system (in this case Oracle) generates the SAF-T XML report in a version 2.0 format for XML documents using the following steps:

1. The OECD SAF-T Generic Extractor Report (R705001) gathers the required information and produces the intermediate XML file;
2. The Business Intelligence Publisher (BIP) XSL transformation and report definition converts the intermediate XML file to the legal SAF-T XML file.

You set up UDC values when you process OECD SAF-T XML.

Address Type (70/TA)
Select a value from the (70/TA) table to set up the address type required for SAF-T reporting.

Values are:

Codes	*Description*
0	StreetAddress
1	PostalAddress
2	BillingAddress
3	ShipToAddress
4	ShipFromAddress

Accounting System (70/AS)

Select a value from the (70/AS) table to set up the accounting system required for SAF-T reporting.

Values are:

Codes	*Description*
C	Accounting
E	Billing, shipping and working
F	Invoicing
I	Integrated Invoices and Accounts
P	Partial Data
S	Self-Billing

Tax Exemption Reason (70/ER)

Select a value from the (70/ER) table to specify the tax exemption reason required for SAF-T reporting. You specify a value in the Additional Information section from the Work with Tax Area Additional Information program (P704008A).

Values are:

Codes	*Description*
1	Healthcare
2	Social welfare
3	Education and training
	Blank

Tax Type (70/TT)

Select a value from the (70/TT) table to specify the tax type required for SAF-T reporting. You specify a value in the Additional Information section from the Work with Tax Area Additional Information program (P704008A).

Values are:

Codes	*Description*
	Blank
IS	Stamp Duty
IVA	Value-Added Tax

Tax Code (70/TC)

Select a value from the (70/TC) table to specify the Tax Code required for SAF-T reporting. You specify a value in the Additional Information section from the Work with Tax Area Additional Information program (P704008A).

Values are:

Codes	*Description*
	Blank
INT	Intermediate tax rate
ISE	Exempted
NOR	Normal tax rate
OUT	Others
RED	Reduced tax rate

Account Type (70/AT)

Select a value from the (70/AT) table to specify the account type required for SAF-T reporting. You specify a value in the Additional Information section from the Work with Account Master Additional Information program (P700901A).

Values are:

Codes	*Description*
1	Asset
2	Liability
3	Sale
4	Expense

Country Code (70/CN)
Set up this UDC to specify the ISO Country Code in the Description 02 column required for SAF-T reporting. You need to specify this if the ISO Country Code is different from the Country Code available in the Country Codes (00/CN) UDC table.

Tax Country Region (70/TR)
Set up this UDC to specify the tax country region in the Description 02 column required for SAF-T reporting.

Invoice Type (70/IV)
Set up this UDC to specify the invoice type in the Special Handling column to relate it with the document type of the purchase and sales transactions.

Line Type (70/LT)
Set up this UDC to specify the line type for the movement sub-type.

Setting Up Additional Information

Localisations Additional Information is a tag-table methodology that captures and stores country-specific information. The system uses this information for different purposes.

Before you can start working with Localisations Additional Information, you must run the Additional Info Setup program (R7000100) to generate the required tables that store the additional data.

This setup also generates the forms where you enter predefined information that is saved to the Localisations Additional Fields tables.

The system launches the Localisations Additional Information forms from the Regional Info row menu option from the specific programs that require additional data.

When you run the Additional Information Setup program, the system also generates all the additional fields required in the appropriate Regional Info forms. The forms for Localisations Additional Information group the predefined data fields into the following tabs, according to the type of data that you enter:

String Data: You enter a set of alphanumeric characters.
Numeric Data: You enter a set of numeric characters.
Date: You enter a date.
Character: You enter single characters.

Every time you run the Additional Information Setup program, the system regenerates the tables required to work with the solution. You do not need to run this program multiple times but if you do, the existing data that you entered and that is saved in the Additional Information tables is not affected.

Prerequisites

Before you complete the tasks in this section:

Verify that the Localisation Country Code field in your user profile is set up. For example, NO for Norway or AT for Austria.

Set up the following processing option for the Additional Info Setup program (R7000100):

Code – Localisation Country: Select a value from the Localisation Country Code UDC table (00/LC) to specify the country for which the system generates the Additional Information tables and forms.

Running the Additional Info Setup Program (R7000100)

Select System Administration Tools (GH9011), Batch Versions.

Alternatively, enter BV in the Fast Path field.

In the Work With Batch Versions – Available Versions form, enter R7000100 in the Batch Application field to work with the Additional Info Setup program.

Working with the OECD SAF-T Generic Extractor Report

You generate the OECD SAF-T Generic Extractor Report to get an intermediate XML file.

Prerequisites

Before you generate the OECD SAF-T Generic Extractor Report:

Verify that the localisation country code is set up for the country for which you want to generate the SAF-T report.

See "Country Code (70/CN)".

Run the Additional Info Setup program (R7000100) to generate the required tables that store the additional data.

See "Setting Up Additional Information".

Verify that the invoice number is available for the purchase transactions.

Verify that the original document information of credit note and debit note is available in the reference column of the Customer Ledger table (F03B11) and the Accounts Payable Ledger table (F0411).

Verify that the transaction is posted. The report does not consider void transactions.

Run the As of Regeneration program (R41542) to ensure that the item stock quantity balance forwards are restored for each fiscal year.

Set up processing options for the R705001 report. For more information.

See "Setting Processing Options for the OECD SAF-T Generic Extractor Report (R705001)".

Set up the Additional Information for the Address Book (P01012), Tax Rate/Areas (P4008), and Account Masters (P0901) program. For more information.

See "Setting Up Additional Information for the OECD SAF-T Generic Extractor Report (R705001)".

Setting Processing Options for the OECD SAF-T Generic Extractor Report (R705001)

Before you generate the SAF-T report, set the processing options for the OECD SAF-T Generic Extractor Report (R705001):

DEFAULT

Company

Use this option to specify the code that identifies a specific organisation, fund, or other reporting entity. The company code must exist in the Company Constants table (F0010). This processing option must not be blank.

From

Use this option to specify the start of the fiscal year and the accounting period for which the system generates the SAF-T report.

To

Use this option to specify the end of the fiscal year and the accounting period for which the system generates the SAF-T report.

The start of the fiscal year value in the From processing option should be earlier than the end of the fiscal year value in the To processing option.

Enter the Item Number to be used for the A/R invoices without sales information.

Enter the Item Number to be used for the A/P vouchers without purchase information.

General

Audit File Version

Specify the audit file version of the XML schema that is used for SAF-T reporting.

Audit File Country

Specify the code that identifies the country for which the system generates the SAF-T report. The value that you enter must exist in the Country Codes (00/CN) UDC table.

Contact Line ID

Company's International Bank Account Number

Company Bank Account Number

Either company bank account or IBAN should be available to generate the report.

Company's Account ID

Address Type

Ledger Types

The value that you enter must exist in the Ledger Types (09/LT) UDC.

Cost Method

The value that you enter must exist in the Cost Method (40/CM) UDC.

Process

Accounting System

The value that you enter must exist in the Accounting System (70/AS) UDC table. This processing option must not be blank.

Setting Up Additional Information for the OECD
SAF-T Generic Extractor Report (R705001)

Before you generate the SAF-T report, you must set up the Additional Information for following programs:

- Address Book (P01012);
- Tax Rate/Areas (P4008);
- Accounts Master (P0901).

Address Book (P01012)

Set the following Additional Information of the Address Book Additional Information program (P700101A):

Characters

Self Billing Indicator: Specify the self-billing indicator to identify the existence of a self-billing agreement between the customer and the supplier.

Tax Rate/Areas (P4008)

Set the following Additional Information of the Work with Tax Area Additional Information program (P704008A):

String Data

Tax Exemption Reason: Specify the tax exemption reason associated with the tax rate or tax area. The value that you enter must exist in the Tax Exemption Reasons (70/ER) UDC table.

Tax Type: Specify the tax type for the record. The value that you enter must exist in the Tax Type (70/TT) UDC table.

Tax Country Region: Specify the classified tax region of the country. The value that you enter must exist in the State and Province Codes (00/S) UDC table.

Tax Code: Specify the Tax Code for the record required by the tax authorities. The value that you enter must exist in the Tax Code (70/TC) UDC table.

Country: Specify the Country Code to apply the Tax Rate/Area. The value that you enter must exist in the Country Code (00/CN) UDC table.

Characters

Tax Exempt: Specify the code indicating whether the tax rate or tax area is tax exempt or taxable. If it is tax exempt, provide the reason for the exemption. The value that you enter must exist in the Tax Exempt (70/TE) UDC table.

Accounts Master (P0901)

Set the following Additional Information of the Work with Account Master Additional Information program (P700901A):

String Data

Standard Account ID: Specify the account ID based on the standard prescribed by the authorities.

Account Type: Specify the account type – that is, asset, liability, sale, or expense. The value that you enter must exist in the Account Type (70/AT) UDC table.Generating the OECD SAF-T Generic Extractor Report

To generate the OECD SAF-T Generic Extractor Report, from the OECD SAF-T Generic Reporting (G7006) menu, select OECD SAF-T Generic Extractor Report (R705001). When you run the OECD SAF-T Generic Extractor Report, the system validates and generates the SAF-T XML file.

The software system populates various sections of the OECD SAF-T report:

Header Section

The header section of the OECD SAF-T report includes company information, audit file information, information about the software company producing the file, and the selection criteria.

Master Files Section

The master files section includes:

Master File Sections	*Description*
General Ledger Accounts	This section prints the general ledger account details. The R705001 report identifies the transactions from the General Ledger Entries section to print the required details.
Customers	This section prints the required details related to the customer. The R705001 report identifies customer-related information from the Source Documents section and the General Ledger Entries section.
Supplier	This section prints the required details related to the supplier. The R705001 report identifies supplier-related information from the Source Documents section and the General Ledger Entries section.
Tax Table	The R705001 identifies the tax area or tax rate from the Source Documents section and the General Ledger Entries section, and retrieves information from the Work with Tax Area Additional Information program (P704008A) to print the details.
UOM Table	This section prints the UOM details. The R705001 report identifies item-related information from the Source Documents section.
Movement Type Table	This section prints the movement type details. The R705001 report identifies the transactions from the Movement of Goods section.
Products	This section prints the product details. The R705001 report identifies item-related information from the Source Documents section.
Owners	The R705001 report identifies company-related information from the processing option to print the details.

Master File Sections	*Description*
Physical Stock	This section prints the physical stock details. The R705001 report identifies item-related information from the Source Documents section to print the physical stock details. You must set up the unit price in the primary Unit of Measure (UOM) in the Cost Revisions program (P4105).

General Ledger Entries

The general ledger entries section lists the journal entries for the selected period. The R075001 report identifies the posted transactions from the Account Ledger table (F0911) to print the journal entry details.

The system prints the tax information of the transaction if the transaction is created using the Journal Entries with VAT program (P09106).

Source Documents Section

The Source Documents section includes:

Source Documents Section	*Description*
Sales Invoices	This section prints the Sales and A/R transactions. The report retrieves the posted and non-void transactions from the Customer Ledger table (F03B11). The system considers a transaction line in the F03B11 table for printing sales order details if the Document Company (PKCO), Document No (DOCO), Document type (DCTO), and Line ID (LNID) fields are populated.
Purchase Invoices	This section prints the purchase and A/P transactions. The report retrieves the posted and non-void transactions from the Accounts Payable Ledger table (F0411). The system considers a transaction line in the F0411 table for printing purchase invoice details if the Document Company (KCOO), Document No (DOCO), Document type (DCTO), and Line ID (LNID) fields are populated.
Payments	This section prints the payment details of the posted and non-void transactions. The R075001 report retrieves the posted and non-void transactions from the Accounts Payable Matching Document Detail table (F0414) and the Receipts Header table (F03B13).

Source Documents Section	*Description*
Movement of Goods	This section prints the movement of goods details of the transactions. The R075001 report retrieves the transactions from the Sales Order Detail table (F4211) or the Sales History table (F42119), and the Purchase Order Receiver table (F43121) to print the movement of goods details. You must confirm shipment and complete the sales update process to include the sales transactions in the report. You must complete the voucher match process and purchase order receipt to include the purchase transactions in the report. See “Shipment Planning” in the JD Edwards EnterpriseOne Applications Transportation Management Implementation Guide to know the process of generating a shipment number.

Notes

The system prints the details of only sales or purchase transactions for UOM Table, Products and Physical Stock sections.

If the Tax Rate/Area is available for the transaction, the system prints the Tax Information Block. The Tax Information Block is applicable to Sales Invoices, Purchase Invoices, General Ledger Entries and Movement of Goods sections.

The Tax Information Block is not applicable to the Payments section.

CHAPTER 21

Conclusions

In a world of economic and fiscal uncertainty, there is significantly greater emphasis on the part of government fiscal and regulatory authorities to ensure revenue collection and protection, as well as significantly increased levels of risk assessment, analysis, management and assurance. In turn, this implies and requires a far more rigorous regime of trader compliance, which then means far greater degrees of due diligence on the part of the trader. There are different means and techniques involved in achieving this, but overall the trader is required to acquire far higher levels of knowledge concerning Customs and Tax Compliance than ever before. This text goes part way in highlighting and detailing such levels of compliance through illustration of government fiscal risk management policy, but it cannot physically do the job required on the part of the trader. That is the responsibility of the trader themselves. Trader compliance is an absolute necessity and should be regarded as such by all import and/or export traders.

The Revised Kyoto Convention and the SAFE Framework of Standards placed far more emphasis on trader compliance and risk management than ever before, and have, as a result, imposed far higher standards on the process of international trade. However, although it is expected that major international industries will have the resources to ensure such compliance, smaller companies simply do not have the internal resources to devote to dedicated import/export compliance teams, and indeed may not have the knowledge required to achieve the standards set by Customs. To this extent, this text serves as a means of acquiring that knowledge to a degree and applying some basic principles of risk management to the international trade process, as defined by import and export strategy.

To this end, there are 7 specific principles of Customs and Tax Planning that every company involved in international trade should adhere to. These are as follows:

 DOI: 10.4324/9781003341345-22

Tax Planning Principles

1. Businesses should only engage in reasonable Customs and Tax planning that is aligned with commercial and economic activity and does not lead to an abusive result;
2. Businesses may respond to Customs incentives and exemptions;
3. Businesses should interpret the relevant Customs laws in a reasonable way consistent with a relationship of "co-operative compliance" with the national Customs Authority;
4. In international matters, businesses should follow the terms of the various Double Taxation Treaties and relevant OECD guidelines in dealing with such issues as transfer pricing and establishing taxable presence, and should engage constructively in international dialogue on the review of global tax rules and the need for any changes.

Transparency and Reporting Principles

Relationships between businesses and the national Customs Authority should be transparent, constructive and based on mutual trust, resulting in the national Customs Authority treating businesses fairly and with respect, and with an appropriate focus on areas of risk.

5. Businesses should be open and transparent with the national Customs Authority about their Customs and Tax affairs and provide all relevant information that is necessary for the Revenue Authority to review possible Customs and Tax risks;
6. They should work collaboratively with the national Customs Authority to achieve early agreement on disputed issues and certainty on a real-time basis, wherever possible;
7. Companies should seek to increase public understanding in the Customs and Tax system in order to build public trust in that system, and, to that end:
   - They should consider how best to explain more fully to the public their economic contribution and taxes paid in their country;
   - This could include an explanation of their policy for tax management, the governance process that applies to tax decisions, and some details of the amount and type of duties and taxes paid.

The Aim of These Principles

- To enhance co-operation, trust and confidence between HMRC, UK business taxpayers and the public regarding the operation of the UK tax system;

- To promote the efficient working of the tax system to fund public services and promote sustainable growth.

It is also the duty and obligation of the national Customs Authority to ensure that there is complete transparency in the way that duties are calculated and collected, and that all issues are dealt with in a completely fair and just manner, with no one more liable than is absolutely necessary. This is essentially part of the Revised Kyoto Convention and SAFE Framework of Standards, to ensure that all Customs matters are dealt with in accordance with international rules and standards.

However, Customs and Tax Administrations need to ensure that the needs of the trader are fully taken into account. Although Customs Duties and VAT are part of any national fiscal landscape, there is a need to ensure that government resources are put into the following areas:

- Efficient Customs clearance and administration;
- Efficient risk analysis;
- Trader awareness and education;
- Fully trained Customs and Tax staff;
- Better use of Customs and Tax personnel;
- Better use of electronic facilities;
- Efficient use of government website portals;
- Full collaboration between Customs and traders;
- Easier use of and access to Customs facilities.

There is a global need for the maximisation of Customs and Tax efficiency, which means that resources are used more efficiently and wisely in ensuring efficient revenue collection and protection. According to the Revised Kyoto Convention and the SAFE Framework of Standards, although much more emphasis is placed on the reduction of personnel resources in terms of Customs and Tax administration, there comes a point where human resources cannot be reduced any further without compromising the essential elements of Customs, namely efficient revenue collection and protection. There is therefore a great need for the use of properly trained and competent Customs personnel at both border/frontier controls and internal national administration, and that means a keener awareness of potential risks and the need to mitigate these risks wherever possible, in order to protect the national revenue and achieve revenue targets set by the government. To this extent, efficient risk analysis and management are required on the part of all government revenue authorities, especially in the area of Customs and International Trade, to ensure that while government revenue is collected efficiently, it does not cost a fortune to do so.

On the flip side of the coin, the responsibilities of the trader are no less serious and complex. There is a need on the part of any company involved in international trade to seriously address many issues concerning international trade management in order to avoid becoming a high-risk target by the national Customs Authority. Raw risk areas include the following:

- Import and Export Documentation;
- Import and Export Documented Procedures, including Customs Procedures;
- Import and Export Compliance;
- Import/Export Training and Awareness.

Within this framework, the need also arises for specific attention to:

- Import and Export Valuations;
- Logistics Costs;
- Tariff Commodity Codes;
- Customs Procedure Codes;
- Import Duty Reliefs;
- Origin and Preferences.

Because these areas are considered by any Customs Authority as being subject to high risk and therefore increased scrutiny and investigation, the trader should spend time ensuring that their procedures are sufficiently robust to account for these issues and give the trader enough confidence to know that they have the correct documented procedures in their organisation to manage such issues. After all, such issues account for a significant amount of Customs Import Duties, and because of the primary areas of revenue collection and protection, any national Customs Authority will concentrate on ensuring that all traders involved in importing pay the correct amounts of Import Duty and, in most cases, VAT. Compliant traders have no need to worry about this, whereas non-compliant traders have much to lose, as they will be penalised far more because of their non-compliance, and will as a result be monitored more frequently and intensively by the national Customs Authority.

Any remedial action to address import and export practices will enable international traders to avoid frequent audits by Customs, and thus ensure that they are on a much lower risk level as far as the Customs Authority is concerned. The net result is that with a degree of due diligence and risk mitigation, by way of investment in serious review of its systems, through the creation of documented import and export procedures and International Trade and Customs Training, a company involved in international trade can successfully reduce its risk status from high (raw risk) to low (residual risk). In doing so, it could save itself some serious time and effort in its import and export trade practices, as well as saving some serious money.

In short, what is required for all traders involved in international business is a combination of due diligence, vigilance and competence. Nothing less will suffice.

As it is written, "*Render unto Caesar that which is Caesar's*". Not a penny more, not a penny less.

REFERENCES

Australian Taxation Office.

Ayres, I. & Braithwaite J.; *Responsive Regulation* (Oxford Socio-Legal Studies, 1992).

EU Commission Directorate General Taxation & Customs Union.

HMRC Manual EDDC 01010; 1030.

HMRC Risk Analysis Internal Manual 08000/08050.

HMRC Notice 252: Valuation of Imported Goods.

HMRC Notice 3001: Special Procedures.

International Chambers of Commerce (ICC): INCOTERMS 2020.

ISO 28000/28001.

Keenan D.; *Advanced Business Law* (Pitman, 1997).

The Union Customs Code.

WCO – Agreement on Implementation of Article VII of the General Agreement on Tariffs and Trade 1994.

WCO Risk Management Compendium 2007, Volume 1.

ANNEX 1

Agreement on Implementation of Article VII of the General Agreement on Tariffs and Trade 1994

PART 1 – RULES ON CUSTOMS VALUATION

Article 1

1. The customs value of imported goods shall be the transaction value, that is the price actually paid or payable for the goods when sold for export to the country of importation adjusted in accordance with the provisions of Article 8, provided:

(a) that there are no restrictions as to the disposition or use of the goods by the buyer other than restrictions which:
   (i) are imposed or required by law or by the public authorities in the country of importation;
   (ii) limit the geographical area in which the goods may be resold; or
   (iii) do not substantially affect the value of the goods;

(b) that the sale or price is not subject to some condition or consideration for which a value cannot be determined with respect to the goods being valued;

(c) that no part of the proceeds of any subsequent resale, disposal or use of the goods by the buyer will accrue directly or indirectly to the seller, unless an appropriate adjustment can be made in accordance with the provisions of Article 8; and

(d) that the buyer and seller are not related, or where the buyer and seller are related, that the transaction value is acceptable for customs purposes under the provisions of paragraph 2.

2. (a) In determining whether the transaction value is acceptable for the purposes of paragraph 1, the fact that the buyer and the seller are related within the meaning of Article 15 shall not in itself be grounds for regarding the transaction value as unacceptable. In such case the circumstances surrounding the sale shall be examined and the transaction value shall be accepted provided that the relationship did not influence the price. If, in the light of information provided by the importer

or otherwise, the customs administration has grounds for considering that the relationship influenced the price, it shall communicate its grounds to the importer and the importer shall be given a reasonable opportunity to respond. If the importer so requests, the communication of the grounds shall be in writing.

(b) In a sale between related persons, the transaction value shall be accepted and the goods valued in accordance with the provisions of paragraph 1 whenever the importer demonstrates that such value closely approximates to one of the following occurring at or about the same time:

(i) the transaction value in sales to unrelated buyers of identical or similar goods for export to the same country of importation;
(ii) the customs value of identical or similar goods as determined under the provisions of Article 5;
(iii) the customs value of identical or similar goods as determined under the provisions of Article 6;
In applying the foregoing tests, due account shall be taken of demonstrated differences in commercial levels, quantity levels, the elements enumerated in Article 8 and costs incurred by the seller in sales in which the seller and the buyer are not related that are not incurred by the seller in sales in which the seller and the buyer are related.

(c) The tests set forth in paragraph 2 (b) are to be used at the initiative of the importer and only for comparison purposes. Substitute values may not be established under the provisions of paragraph 2 (b).

Article 2

1. (a) If the customs value of the imported goods cannot be determined under the provisions of Article 1, the customs value shall be the transaction value of identical goods sold for export to the same country of importation and exported at or about the same time as the goods being valued.
(b) In applying this Article, the transaction value of identical goods in a sale at the same commercial level and in substantially the same quantity as the goods being valued shall be used to determine the customs value. Where no such sale is found, the transaction value of identical goods sold at a different commercial level and/or in different quantities, adjusted to take account of differences attributable to commercial level and/or to quantity, shall be used, provided that such adjustments can be made on the basis of demonstrated evidence which clearly establishes the reasonableness and accuracy of the adjustment, whether the adjustment leads to an increase or a decrease in the value.

2. Where the costs and charges referred to in paragraph 2 of Article 8 are included in the transaction value, an adjustment shall be made to take account of significant differences in such costs and charges between the imported goods and the identical goods in question arising from differences in distances and modes of transport.
3. If, in applying this Article, more than one transaction value of identical goods is found, the lowest such value shall be used to determine the customs value of the imported goods.

Article 3

1. (a) If the customs value of the imported goods cannot be determined under the provisions of Articles 1 and 2, the customs value shall be the transaction value of similar goods sold for export to the same country of importation and exported at or about the same time as the goods being valued.
   (b) In applying this Article, the transaction value of similar goods in a sale at the same commercial level and in substantially the same quantity as the goods being valued shall be used to determine the customs value. Where no such sale is found, the transaction value of similar goods sold at a different commercial level and/or in different quantities, adjusted to take account of differences attributable to commercial level and/or to quantity, shall be used, provided that such adjustments can be made on the basis of demonstrated evidence which clearly establishes the reasonableness and accuracy of the adjustment, whether the adjustment leads to an increase or a decrease in the value.
2. Where the costs and charges referred to in paragraph 2 of Article 8 are included in the transaction value, an adjustment shall be made to take account of significant differences in such costs and charges between the imported goods and the similar goods in question arising from differences in distances and modes of transport.
3. If, in applying this Article, more than one transaction value of similar goods is found, the lowest such value shall be used to determine the customs value of the imported goods.

Article 4

If the customs value of the imported goods cannot be determined under the provisions of Articles 1, 2 and 3, the customs value shall be determined under the provisions of Article 5 or, when the customs value cannot be determined under that Article, under the provisions of Article 6 except that, at the request of the importer, the order of application of Articles 5 and 6 shall be reversed.

Article 5

1. (a) If the imported goods or identical or similar imported goods are sold in the country of importation in the condition as imported, the customs value of the imported goods under the provisions of this Article shall be based on the unit price at which the imported goods or identical or similar imported goods are so sold in the greatest aggregate quantity, at or about the time of the importation of the goods being valued, to persons who are not related to the persons from whom they buy such goods, subject to deductions for the following:

(i) either the commissions usually paid or agreed to be paid or the additions usually made for profit and general expenses in connection with sales in such country of imported goods of the same class or kind;
(ii) the usual costs of transport and insurance and associated costs incurred within the country of importation;
(iii) where appropriate, the costs and charges referred to in paragraph 2 of Article 8; and
(iv) the customs duties and other national taxes payable in the country of importation by reason of the importation or sale of the goods.

(b) If neither the imported goods nor identical nor similar imported goods are sold at or about the time of importation of the goods being valued, the customs value shall, subject otherwise to the provisions of paragraph 1 (a), be based on the unit price at which the imported goods or identical or similar imported goods are sold in the country of importation in the condition as imported at the earliest date after the importation of the goods being valued but before the expiration of 90 days after such importation.

2. If neither the imported goods nor identical nor similar imported goods are sold in the country of importation in the condition as imported, then, if the importer so requests, the customs value shall be based on the unit price at which the imported goods, after further processing, are sold in the greatest aggregate quantity to persons in the country of importation who are not related to the persons from whom they buy such goods, due allowance being made for the value added by such processing and the deductions provided for in paragraph 1 (a).

Article 6

1. The customs value of imported goods under the provisions of this Article shall be based on a computed value. Computed value shall consist of the sum of:

(a) the cost or value of materials and fabrication or other processing employed in producing the imported goods;
(b) an amount for profit and general expenses equal to that usually reflected in sales of goods of the same class or kind as the goods being valued which are made by producers in the country of exportation for export to the country of importation;
(c) the cost or value of all other expenses necessary to reflect the valuation option chosen by the Member under paragraph 2 of Article 8.

2. No Member may require or compel any person not resident in its own territory to produce for examination, or to allow access to, any account or other record for the purposes of determining a computed value. However, information supplied by the producer of the goods for the purposes of determining the customs value under the provisions of this Article may be verified in another country by the authorities of the country of importation with the agreement of the producer and provided they give sufficient advance notice to the government of the country in question and the latter does not object to the investigation.

Article 7

1. If the customs value of the imported goods cannot be determined under the provisions of Articles 1 through 6, inclusive, the customs value shall be determined using reasonable means consistent with the principles and general provisions of this Agreement and of Article VII of GATT 1994 and on the basis of data available in the country of importation.
2. No customs value shall be determined under the provisions of this Article on the basis of :

(a) the selling price in the country of importation of goods produced in such country;
(b) a system which provides for the acceptance for customs purposes of the higher of two alternative values;
(c) the price of goods on the domestic market of the country of exportation;
(d) the cost of production other than computed values which have been determined for identical or similar goods in accordance with the provisions of Article 6;
(e) the price of the goods for export to a country other than the country of importation;
(f) minimum customs values; or
(g) arbitrary or fictitious values.

3. If the importer so requests, the importer shall be informed in writing of the customs value determined under the provisions of this Article and the method used to determine such value.

Article 8

1. In determining the customs value under the provisions of Article 1, there shall be added to the price actually paid or payable for the imported goods :

   (a) the following, to the extent that they are incurred by the buyer but are not included in the price actually paid or payable for the goods:
      (i) commissions and brokerage, except buying commissions;
      (ii) the cost of containers which are treated as being one for customs purposes with the goods in question;
      (iv) the cost of packing whether for labour or materials;

   (b) the value, apportioned as appropriate, of the following goods and services where supplied directly or indirectly by the buyer free of charge or at reduced cost for use in connection with the production and sale for export of the imported goods, to the extent that such value has not been included in the price actually paid or payable :
      (i) materials, components, parts and similar items incorporated in the imported goods;
      (ii) tools, dies, moulds and similar items used in the production of the imported goods;
      (iii) materials consumed in the production of the imported goods;
      (iv) engineering, development, artwork, design work, plans and sketches, undertaken elsewhere than in the country of importation and necessary for the production of the imported goods;

   (c) royalties and licence fees related to the goods being valued that the buyer must pay, either directly or indirectly, as a condition of sale of the goods being valued, to the extent that such royalties and fees are not included in the price actually paid or payable;

   (d) the value of any part of the proceeds of any subsequent resale, disposal or use of the imported goods that accrues directly or indirectly to the seller.

2. In framing its legislation, each Member shall provide for the inclusion in or the exclusion from the customs value, in whole or in part, of the following:

   (a) the cost of transport of the imported goods to the port or place of importation;

(b) loading, unloading and handling charges associated with the transport of the imported goods to the port or place of importation; and
(c) the cost of insurance.

3. Additions to the price actually paid or payable shall be made under this Article only on the basis of objective and quantifiable data.
4. No additions shall be made to the price actually paid or payable in determining the customs value except as provided in this Article.

Article 9

1. Where the conversion of currency is necessary for the determination of the customs value, the rate of exchange to be used shall be that duly published by the competent authorities of the country of importation concerned and shall reflect as effectively as possible, in respect of the period covered by each such document of publication, the current value of such currency in commercial transactions in terms of the currency of the country of importation.
2. The conversion rate to be used shall be that in effect at the time of exportation or the time of importation, as provided by each Member.

Article 10

All information which is by nature confidential or which is provided on a confidential basis for the purposes of customs valuation shall be treated as strictly confidential by the authorities concerned who shall not disclose it without the specific permission of the person or government providing such information, except to the extent that it may be required to be disclosed in the context of judicial proceedings.

Article 11

1. The legislation of each Member shall provide in regard to a determination of customs value for the right of appeal, without penalty, by the importer or any other person liable for the payment of the duty.
2. An initial right of appeal without penalty may be to an authority within the customs administration or to an independent body, but the legislation of each Member shall provide for the right of appeal without penalty to a judicial authority.
3. Notice of the decision on appeal shall be given to the appellant and the reasons for such decision shall be provided in writing. The appellant shall also be informed of any rights of further appeal.

Article 12

Laws, regulations, judicial decisions and administrative rulings of general application giving effect to this Agreement shall be published in conformity with Article X of GATT 1994 by the country of importation concerned.

Article 13

If, in the course of determining the customs value of imported goods, it becomes necessary to delay the final determination of such customs value, the importer of the goods shall nevertheless be able to withdraw them from customs if, where so required, the importer provides sufficient guarantee in the form of a surety, a deposit or some other appropriate instrument, covering the ultimate payment of customs duties for which the goods may be liable. The legislation of each Member shall make provisions for such circumstances.

Article 14

The notes at Annex I to this Agreement form an integral part of this Agreement and the Articles of this Agreement are to be read and applied in conjunction with their respective notes. Annexes II and III also form an integral part of this Agreement.

Article 15

1. In this Agreement :

   (a) "Customs value of imported goods" means the value of goods for the purposes of levying ad valorem duties of customs on imported goods;
   (b) "country of importation" means country or customs territory of importation; and
   (c) "produced" includes grown, manufactured and mined.

2. In this Agreement :

   (a) "identical goods" means goods which are the same in all respects, including physical characteristics, quality and reputation. Minor differences in appearance would not preclude goods otherwise conforming to the definition from being regarded as identical;
   (b) "similar goods" means goods which, although not alike in all respects, have like characteristics and like component materials which enable them to perform the same functions and to be commercially interchangeable. The quality of the goods, their reputation

and the existence of a trademark are among the factors to be considered in determining whether goods are similar;

(c) the terms "identical goods" and "similar goods" do not include, as the case may be, goods which incorporate or reflect engineering, development, artwork, design work, and plans and sketches for which no adjustment has been made under paragraph 1 (b) (iv) of Article 8 because such elements were undertaken in the country of importation;

(d) goods shall not be regarded as "identical goods" or "similar goods" unless they were produced in the same country as the goods being valued;

(e) goods produced by a different person shall be taken into account only when there are no identical goods or similar goods, as the case may be, produced by the same person as the goods being valued.

3. In this Agreement "goods of the same class or kind" means goods which fall within a group or range of goods produced by a particular industry or industry sector, and includes identical or similar goods.

4. For the purposes of this Agreement, persons shall be deemed to be related only if:

(a) they are officers or directors of one another's businesses;
(b) they are legally recognized partners in business;
(c) they are employer and employee;
(d) any person directly or indirectly owns, controls or holds 5 per cent or more of the outstanding voting stock or shares of both of them;
(e) one of them directly or indirectly controls the other;
(f) both of them are directly or indirectly controlled by a third person;
(g) together they directly or indirectly control a third person; or
(h) they are members of the same family.

5. Persons who are associated in business with one another in that one is the sole agent, sole distributor or sole concessionaire, however described, of the other shall be deemed to be related for the purposes of this Agreement if they fall within the criteria of paragraph 4.

Article 16

Upon written request, the importer shall have the right to an explanation in writing from the customs administration of the country of importation as to how the customs value of the importer's goods was determined.

Article 17

Nothing in this Agreement shall be construed as restricting or calling into question the rights of customs administrations to satisfy themselves as to the truth or accuracy of any statement, document or declaration presented for customs valuation purposes.

ANNEX 2

UK End-User Undertaking Form

END USER UNDERTAKING (EUU) Form

(for SIEL/SITCL applications required by Export Control Organisation)

Guidance for UK Licensees

An undertaking is required when applying for a Standard Individual Export Licence (SIEL) or Standard Individual Trade Control Licence (SITCL) issued by the UK's Export Control Organisation, part of the Department for Business, Innovation and Skills. This undertaking forms part of the required supporting documentation for End-Use Control purposes which is provided when making a licence application to the ECO.

Please note that we will only normally accept undertakings as valid within 6 months of the date of the application.

There are two types of undertaking forms available. Which one you – the licensee – obtain in support of your application depends on how the items will be used.

If goods are being shipped (whether via a consignee or not):

- for their **end-use** or if an end-user is **incorporating** the goods (ie installing them into another product or higher level system) – then you should obtain an End-User Undertaking (EUU) Form.
- to be **held in stock** for future delivery or re-sale – then you should obtain a Stockist Undertaking (SU) Form.

If the overseas company chooses not to use the relevant template, then you should advise them that the UK Authorities (i.e. ECO) require an original (not 'digital') signed and dated undertaking in English on their headed paper providing the same information and assurances.

IT IS THE UK LICENSEE'S RESPONSIBILITY TO ENSURE THAT:

- The **correct** undertaking type – i.e. EUU or SU – is supplied with your licence application to cover the relevant scenario. An **incorrect** undertaking type will not be accepted by ECO and will therefore need to be resubmitted, which is likely to result in your application being delayed or withdrawn.
- All sections of the undertaking are completed **legibly and in English** (or accompanied by an authorised translation, **including header details,** if written in a foreign language) by the End User or Stockist End User on their **original official headed paper** (where the End User is a company or a legal entity). The English translation should be verified by the licensee - that is the owner of the business applying for a licence, or a partner, director or company secretary of the firm, or anyone authorised to sign the licence application on behalf of the company. Alternatively, if you prefer, translations may be verified by a member of the Institute of Translators or a Notary Public.
- The undertaking form needs to be **signed and dated by a person properly authorised by the End User** organisation **or Stockist End User** organisation to sign on their behalf (the responsible official). 'Digital' signatures are not acceptable.
- The same responsible official of the End User organisation or Stockist End User organisation should also complete, sign, date and attach a **covering letter** (i.e. see Annex A to either EUU or SU Form). This letter must be on their **original** official headed paper. It should also be accompanied by an authorised translation if written in a foreign language (please see above regarding verification of authorised translations). If the End User or Stockist End user is an individual then the documents do not have to be on letter headed paper
- Copies of the relevant form and covering letter should be attached to the completed licence application on ECO's SPIRE database – https://www.spire.bis.gov.uk
- The **original** EUU or SU together with the Covering Letter must be obtained and kept by you at your premises. These **original** documents may be requested by ECO at any time.
- To help reduce further 'requests for information' from ECO during licence processing you should establish as part of your standard procedures whether the items are being shipped to an end user or a stockist and forward the relevant guidance to them about which form to complete and how to complete it correctly.

- If we request a revised EUU during processing of your application, it should include **all** of the EUU pages and be newly dated.
- Be mindful of references to any unfamiliar abbreviations or acronyms particularly those referring to consignees or end-users. To avoid requests for information (RFIs) from ECO which might delay your application, acronyms should be spelt out in full.

Guidance for end-users to complete template and covering letter

This End User Undertaking (EUU) Form and Annex A must be provided when you order goods which are to be used by you (whether via a Consignee or not). Both documents must be completed on your company's letter headed paper. Please note that if you are an individual these documents do not have to be on letter headed paper.

Please read the following 'Explanation of Terminology' carefully for guidance on completing the EUU form.

1 The UK Licensee is the person or body who is either exporting the goods abroad, or brokering the movement of the goods concerned, each of which may be direct to you or via a separate consignee.
2 If not known, the Licensee's Reference can be left blank for completion by the Licensee.
3 The Consignee is the person or body, who is the first recipient of the goods .This can be yourselves or it can be another person or body within your country or in another country. If you are both the Consignee and the End User, then you must enter your own details in boxes (c) and (d).
4 As the End User you will be receiving the goods for **end-use** so boxes (e) and (f) must be completed. If you incorporate the goods into another product or higher level system, then you are still the End User for the purposes of the movement of the items.
5 The End User in this section refers to the entity at the time of shipment.
6 The goods in this section refer to those at the time of shipment. **NB**: If goods are being incorporated into another product or higher level system then this information should be included in Section 3.
7 The UK Authorities need to understand what the goods are and so a detailed description of the main item or items is required. If, for example, the main item or items are accompanied by a long list of spares, components or accessories, you should also indicate this in section 2.
8 If the goods are to be 'incorporated' by you (ie: installed into another product or higher level system) then that product/higher

level system, its use and ultimate end user (which may be within or outside your destination) should be described where known in Section 3.

9 Section 4 must be signed and dated by you as the End User since you are using the goods mentioned in Section 2. This includes where you incorporate the goods into another product or higher level system. This section should be signed and dated by a person within your organisation with authority to sign on behalf of the company/organisation. 'Digital' signatures are **not** acceptable

10 For an up-to-date list of applicable destinations subject to arms embargoes, please go to the export control pages of the Businesslink website and access the link to "Current Export Restrictions"

EUU FORM

SECTION 1 – PARTIES

(a) Name of UK Licensee *1*	**(b) Licensee's Reference** *2*
(c) Name of Consignee 3	**(d) Consignee's Address**
(e) Name of End-User 4	**(f) End-User's Address**
(g) Is the End user the armed forces or internal security forces of the country ? [5] Please DELETE an option: Yes / No	**(h) Specific location where goods will be used or based (if known) and if different from (f)** 6

SECTION 2 – GOODS

(a) Quantity of Goods	**(b) Description of the Goods** *7* *(for consumable goods, include length of time supplies are expected to last)*
(If you need to use continuation sheets, each must carry the licensee's reference, and must be signed and dated by the same person who signs this form.)	

SECTION 3 – END-USE OF THE GOODS

Please set out the specific purposes for which the goods are to be <u>used</u> by the end-user *(including, if applicable, where the goods are being incorporated) 8*

SECTION 4 – END-USER UNDERTAKING[9] (to be completed by the person or body named in 1(e) and 1(f))

We – the person or body named at 1(e) and 1(f) – certify that we are the end-user of the goods described in Section 2, which are to be supplied by the licensee named in 1(a). We further certify that we shall use the goods for the purposes described in Section 3; that the goods will not be used for any purpose connected with chemical, biological or nuclear weapons, or missiles capable of delivering such weapons; that they will not be re-exported or otherwise re-sold or transferred if it is known or suspected that they are intended or likely to be used for such purposes; that the goods will not be re-exported or otherwise re-sold or transferred to a destination subject to UN, EU or OSCE embargo where that act would be in breach of the terms of that embargo [10]; and that the goods, or any replica of them, will not be used in any nuclear explosive activity [i] or unsafeguarded nuclear fuel cycle [ii].

Sign Here ______________________ **Date** ____________
(Signature of official of End User)

Print Name __________________________
(Add Name of Signatory in Capitals)

Role __________________________
(Add Job Title of Signatory in Capitals)

Note

i includes research on or development, design, manufacture, construction, testing or maintenance of any nuclear explosive device or components of subsystems of such a device.

ii includes research on or development, design, manufacture, construction, operation or maintenance of any reactor, critical facility, conversion plant, fabrication plant, reprocessing plant, plant for the separation of isotopes of source or special fissionable material, or separate storage installation, where there is no obligation to accept IAEA safeguards at the relevant facility or installation, existing or future, when it contains any source or special fissionable material; or of any heavy water production plant where there is no obligation to accept IAEA safeguards on any nuclear material produced by or used in connection with any heavy water produced therefrom; or where any such obligation is not met.

ANNEX A TO EUU FORM

Model covering letter for End User Undertaking *[to be amended where indicated]*

[***NAME AND ADDRESS OF END USER ON THEIR ORIGINAL HEADED PAPER***]

[***DATE***]

End User Undertaking relating to the UK licence application made by [**STATE** ***NAME OF LICENSEE***]

I attach a completed End User Undertaking made on the EUU Form

Yours sincerely

[**TO BE SIGNED** ***BY THE SAME SIGNATORY WHO COMPLETED AND SIGNED THE END USER UNDERTAKING (EUU) FORM TOGETHER WITH THEIR ROLE***]

INDEX

Note: Page numbers in *italics* indicate figures, and page numbers in **bold** indicate tables in the text

For Product Safety Concerns and Information please contact our EU
representative GPSR@taylorandfrancis.com
Taylor & Francis Verlag GmbH, Kaufingerstraße 24, 80331 München, Germany

www.ingramcontent.com/pod-product-compliance
Ingram Content Group UK Ltd.
Pitfield, Milton Keynes, MK11 3LW, UK
UKHW022018230926
475702UK00029B/2041

* 9 7 8 1 0 3 2 3 7 6 7 2 1 *